DATE DUE

Psychological Aspects
of Depression

THE WILEY SERIES IN
CLINICAL PSYCHOLOGY

Series Editors:

Fraser N. Watts

MRC Applied Psychology Unit
Cambridge, UK

J. Mark G. Williams

Department of Psychology
University College of North Wales, Bangor, UK

Severe Learning Disability and Psychological Handicap
John Clements

Cognitive Psychology and Emotional Disorders
J. Mark G. Williams, Fraser N. Watts,
Colin MacLeod and Andrew Mathews

Community Care in Practice
Services for the Continuing Care Client
Edited by Anthony Lavender and Frank Holloway

Attribution Theory in Clinical Psychology
Freidrich Försterling

Panic Disorder:
Theory, Research and Therapy
Edited by Roger Baker

Measuring Human Problems
A Practical Guide
Edited by David Peck and C. M. Shapiro

Clinical Child Psychology
Social Learning, Development and Behaviour
Martin Herbert

The Psychological Treatment of Insomnia
Colin A. Espie

The Challenge of Severe Mental Handicap
A Behaviour Analytic Approach
Edited by Bob Remington

Microcomputers and Clinical Psychology
Issues, Applications and Future Developments
Edited by Alastair Ager

Anxiety
Theory, Research and Intervention
in Clinical and Health Psychology
Robert J. Edelmann

Innovations in the Psychological
Management of Schizophrenia
Assessment, Treatment and Services
Edited by Max Birchwood and Nicholas Tarrier

Psychological Aspects of Depression
Toward a Cognitive–Interpersonal Integration
Ian H. Gotlib and Constance L. Hammen

Psychological Aspects of Depression

Toward a Cognitive–Interpersonal Integration

Ian H. Gotlib

The University of Western Ontario,
Canada

and

Constance L. Hammen

University of California, Los Angeles,
USA

JOHN WILEY & SONS

Chichester · New York · Brisbane · Toronto · Singapore

Other Wiley Editorial Offices

John Wiley & Sons, Inc., 605 Third Avenue,
New York, NY 10158-0012, USA

Jacaranda Wiley Ltd, G.P.O. Box 859, Brisbane,
Queensland 4001, Australia

John Wiley & Sons (Canada) Ltd, 22 Worcester Road,
Rexdale, Ontario M9W 1L1, Canada

John Wiley & Sons (SEA) Pte Ltd, 37 Jalan Pemimpin #05-04,
Block B, Union Industrial Building, Singapore 2057

Library of Congress Cataloging-in-Publication Data:

Gotlib, Ian, H.
    Psychological aspects of depression : toward a cognitive–interpersonal
integration / Ian H. Gotlib, Constance L. Hammen.
        p.   cm. — (The Wiley series in clinical psychology)
    Includes bibliographical references and index.
    ISBN 0-471-93486-0 (ppc)
    1. Depression, Mental.   2. Depression, Mental—Social aspects.
3. Depressed persons.   I. Hammen, Constance L.   II. Title.
III. Series.
    [DNLM: 1. Depressive Disorder—psychology.   2. Interpersonal
Relations.   WM 207 G684p]
RC537.G67   1992
616.85'27—dc20
DNLM/DLC
for Library of Congress   92–15774
                                                                                CIP

British Library Cataloguing in Publication Data:

A catalogue record for this book is available from the British Library

ISBN 0-471-93486-0

Typeset in 10/12pt Palatino from author's disks by Text Processing Department,
John Wiley & Sons Ltd, Chichester
Printed and bound in Great Britain by Biddles Ltd, Guildford and King's Lynn

Contents

Series Editor's Preface   vii

Preface   ix

1 Symptomatology, Diagnostic Criteria, and Epidemiology of Adult Depression   1

2 Child and Adolescent Depression: Features and Correlates   36

3 Psychological Theories of Depression   67

4 Assessment of Depression in Adults and Children   90

5 The Cognitive Functioning of Depressed Persons   113

6 The Social Functioning of Depressed Persons: I. Life Events, Social Support and Interpersonal Behaviour   141

7 The Social Functioning of Depressed Persons: II. Marital and Family Relationships   166

8 Treatment of Depression: I. Cognitive Approaches   193

9 Treatment of Depression: II. Behavioral and Interpersonal Approaches   215

10 Toward a Cognitive-Interpersonal Conceptualization of Depression   245

References   268

Index   315

Series Editor's Preface

The Wiley Series in Clinical Psychology aims to include authoritative surveys of core fields of clinical psychology. No series of books on clinical psychology would be complete without one on depression, which is one of the most prevalent and incapacitating of psychological problems. It is also one that has been the focus of a particularly rich body of research in recent years. Both cognitive and social psychological research have converged to give us a much improved understanding of the factors which cause and maintain depression. This has been accompanied by major clinical advances in the assessment and psychological treatment of depression.

The authors of this book, both well known for their own work in the field, have here met the need for a survey of recent psychological work on depression. They have given us a book which is readable, judicious and impressively comprehensive and up-to-date. It will be an invaluable resource, for practitioners, researchers and students, and one can predict with confidence that it will establish itself as a core text on the psychology of depression.

A wide range of professions are involved in the care of depressed patients, including nurses, psychiatrists, psychotherapists and many others. Equally, many disciplines are involved in the investigation of depression. I hope that this book in the Wiley Series in Clinical Psychology will be a resource to those concerned with depression, whatever their background. This text will be invaluable to both practitioners and researchers.

FRASER WATTS
Series Editor

Preface

Depression is by far the most common of psychiatric disorders, accounting for 75% of all psychiatric hospitalizations. Each year more than 100 million people worldwide develop clinically recognizable depression, an incidence ten times greater than that of schizophrenia. Furthermore, during the course of a lifetime, it is estimated that 25% of the general population will experience at least one debilitating episode of depression. In addition to the enormous costs of this disorder in terms of lowered productivity, job absenteeism, and permanent withdrawal from the work force, there is also inestimable social damage: grief and pain, marital and family conflict, physical illness, and death.

Over the past two decades, increasing attention has been given to the study of psychological aspects of depression. Indeed, the number of experimentally-based investigations of the etiology, course, and treatment appearing in psychological journals in recent years has increased dramatically. In particular, researchers have focused on examinations of the cognitive functioning of depressed persons, and on studies of the social context of depression. Unfortunately, these two lines of research have developed and continue to progress virtually independently. Cognitive investigators and theorists take little notice of advances made in the study of social processes in depression; similarly, interpersonally-focused researchers essentially ignore the results of studies examining the cognitive functioning of depressed persons. Moreover, the study of adult depression and childhood depression have remained fairly separate. Two major goals of this book, therefore, are to provide the reader with a critical review and evaluation of theory and research examining both the cognitive and the interpersonal functioning of depressed persons, and to integrate these literatures concerning both adults and children into a more comprehensive conceptualization of depression.

This book consists of ten chapters. In the first chapter we present an overview of the nature of depression. We examine the signs and symptoms that comprise a diagnosis of depression. In this context, we present the criteria necessary for an individual to be diagnosed as depressed, and we discuss various subtypes and dimensions of depression. In addition, we examine the incidence, prevalence, and course of depression and comorbid disorders in the general population, and we discuss findings from research involving those sociodemographic factors that are most strongly associated with depression, including marital status, age, and gender. In Chapter 2 we focus more specifically on depression in children. We discuss criteria for diagnosing depression in children, and present data concerning the symptoms and epidemiology of childhood depression. We examine cognitive and interpersonal aspects of depression in children, and we explore the issue concerning continuity of depression from childhood to adulthood.

In Chapter 3 we survey the major psychological theories of depression. We pay particular attention to psychoanalytic, behavioral, and cognitive formulations of depression, and highlight common and critical aspects of these theories. In Chapter 4 we examine the assessment of depression in adults and children. We present information concerning both structured diagnostic interviews for depression and frequently used self-report measures of depressive symptomatology. In this context, we discuss important differences between interview and self-report methodologies, particularly with respect to the assessment of depression in children. In the subsequent three chapters we examine the cognitive and social functioning of depressed persons. Chapter 5 offers a discussion of cognitive theories of depression, and we critically review the empirical literature testing these formulations. In Chapters 6 and 7 we examine the social functioning of depressed persons. In these chapters we discuss investigations focusing on stressful life events and depression, and particularly on the increased vulnerability of depressed persons to interpersonal stressors. We also review data indicating that depressed individuals differ from nondepressed persons with respect to size and quality of social networks, and the quality of their interactions with strangers, friends, and family members. In this context we discuss the results of studies examining the psychological functioning and adjustment of offspring of depressed parents.

The next two chapters are devoted to an examination of the psychological treatment of depressive disorders. In Chapter 8 we explore cognitive therapies for depression. We discuss the efficacy of these therapies, present possible mechanisms by which cognitive therapy might lead to change in depressed patients, and explore recent developments in cognitive therapy for depression. In Chapter 9 we focus on behavioral and interpersonal interventions for depression. We discuss methods of behavioral assessment for depression and then review a number of behavioral approaches to the treatment of depressive disorders. In particular, we present in considerable detail marital and family therapies for depression. Finally, in Chapter 10, we present a conceptualization of depression that draws on, and integrates, theory and research that we have reviewed throughout the book concerning the cognitive and interpersonal functioning of depressed persons. We describe how the childhood experiences of depressed persons may alter their vulnerability to depression, and we discuss cognitive and interpersonal factors that are likely to affect the onset and maintenance of, and recovery from, this disorder. We conclude by discussing research directions that might be taken by investigators examining psychological aspects of depression in order that the field might make significant and integrative advances.

We gratefully acknowledge the support provided to us by the Medical Research Council of Canada, the National Health and Research Development Program, and a Senior Research Fellowship from the Ontario Mental Health Foundation (IHG), and by the William T. Grant Foundation (CLH). We are also indebted to the depressed individuals and families who participated in our investigations and helped us to appreciate the complexity of this disorder. Finally, we are both fortunate to have enjoyed the stimulation and challenge of talented students over the part few years, and we are grateful for their efforts and enthusiasm in our research activities.

Chapter 1

Symptomatology, Diagnostic Criteria, and Epidemiology of Adult Depression

Nearly everyone experiences some aspects of depression; it is a normal part of living that attends the losses, frustrations, failures, and disappointments that all of us face. While for some the depression may be brief, a temporary reaction that has little impact on functioning, others may find themselves impaired over weeks or even months with an array of symptoms of the full syndrome of depression. At any given time, it has been estimated that between 9 and 20% of the US population has significant symptoms of depression, and a substantial minority of men and women will have a clinically definable depressive episode in their lifetimes.

While depression, at least in the form of a sad mood, is almost a universal experience, depression is almost universally *misunderstood* as well, in a culture that prides itself on controlling excessive emotions. Few people are sympathetic or understanding about prolonged depression, believing it to be largely under personal control. And few understand the impact that depression has on lives, making it as impairing if not more so, than most major chronic medical illnesses. Only recently have we come to understand that for many sufferers of major depression the disorder is recurrent, if not chronic.

Added to the sheer numbers of people affected by depression, and its detrimental impact on their lives, is yet another grim feature: depression often runs in families, and the significant distress of one family member is highly likely to have a negative impact on others, especially children. Moreover, intriguing and disturbing demographic trends suggest that rates of depression are increasing and that young people are at particular risk.

Whether we focus on the molecular level of understanding neurotransmitter defects, on the family level to understand depression in the family context, or on the cultural level to understand demographic patterns and shifts in the incidence of depression, there are challenges for all psychopathologists to participate in the study of this most pervasive of psychological maladies.

In this chapter we describe depression and identify the features of this disorder that a useful theory must take into account. This is a critical matter, since as we shall see, not all the perspectives that we will review deal with the same construct of depression. Moreover, some of the different features of depression are given extra emphasis in some models, while other features may be relatively ignored. Finally, it is important to bear in mind that what we know today about depressive disorders has changed over time, so that earlier theories of depression may have arisen from a different knowledge base than what is available today. Thus, the definitions and features of depression are central to evaluating the utility of any theoretical perspective, and what we identify here informs the integrated model that will be developed in a later chapter.

DESCRIPTION OF DEPRESSION

Depression is the same word that is applied to a brief negative mood, an interrelated set of symptoms and experiences, and a medically-defined syndrome. As a mood state, depression is a normal and usually transitory reaction to life's hassles—minor failures, disappointments, disruptions. Such negative states may last a few moments, hours, or sometimes a few days, but cause little impairment. Sometimes there are additional experiences besides depressed mood; these can include negative thoughts and feelings about oneself and pessimism about the future, physical experiences of low energy, as well as reduced feelings of pleasure and motivation. Such symptoms can last for hours, or even days, and even though unpleasant, are in the normal range of typical reactions to the stresses and losses that are present in most lives. Most people find that such depressive periods pass quickly, and they expect themselves and others to "tough it out" and not let the experiences bother them too much. People in this culture expect to have significant control over their moods, and it is considered unseemly to remain depressed or dysfunctional for very long. One is expected to overcome such experiences through activity, effort, or will.

In contrast to the normal and transitory experiences of mood depression and its attendant symptoms, the *syndrome* of depression is defined as depressed mood along with a set of additional symptoms, persisting over time, and causing disruption and impairment of functioning. This is what we mean by clinically significant depression—whether it is treated or not. Certain diagnostic criteria, which will be discussed below, are used to define the presence of the clinical syndrome. First, however, consider the phenomenology of a major depressive episode.

Phenomenology of depression

Clinically significant depression consists of far more than just an emotional experience of being sad or low. The *mood* symptoms influence, and interact with, sets of other symptoms in the domains of cognition, behavior, and bodily functioning. Each of these areas of symptoms in turn affect each other. For some people the predominant mood is not one of feeling blue, as much as it is the experience of loss of enjoyment of formerly pleasurable experiences. Since depression is also a disorder of the way people think about themselves and construe the world and the future, a depressed person also "interprets" her symptoms negatively. Loss of pleasure or lack of motivation, for instance, might be seen as further evidence of one's worthlessness. A depressed person may be critical of herself and others, believe that she is useless, defective, and unattractive—and that such experiences will never change. Depression also alters intellectual functioning and impairs concentration, memory, and decision-making. There are also characteristic physical and behavioral changes: a depressed person may feel listless, lacking in energy, and withdrawn from usual activities. There are likely to be changes in sleep and appetite, and sometimes attendant aches and pains. Because of negative expectations and loss of energy, the person may feel unmotivated, and unable to plan or initiate new activities. Negative thoughts about one's worthlessness may cause the person to want to avoid contact with others, and each negative interpretation of the world and the future is likely to deepen the dysphoria. Failure to engage in activities that are capable of generating enjoyment or a sense of mastery may further enhance one's sense of futility and inertia. In many ways, depressive experiences seem to perpetuate each other.

A depressed man may have paralyzing doubts about his ability to perform a new job and find that his work is indeed impaired by his difficulty in concentrating and the slowness of his activities. At home, he finds that he cannot enjoy the support and encouragement of his family, and finds that he feels enormously guilty because he interprets his lack of enjoyment to mean that he must not love them any more or is unappreciative of their efforts. A depressed woman who has prided herself in the past for managing a career while raising children can barely get up in the morning, and feels great resentment at her family for the demands she feels incapable of meeting. She reacts to her children with great irritation that only serves to deepen her negative views of herself.

Depressive symptoms often appear irrational to outsiders: the individual who views himself as incompetent and a failure may actually appear to others as the same competent, capable worker as before the depression. An attractive and effective woman who is seen by her family as an able and loving parent may experience herself as ugly, hateful, and incompetent in her family roles. Even when others notice the changes in the depressed person's behaviors, they do not imagine the changes are permanent, as does the depressed person himself. To the extent that friends and family members cannot comprehend the negative outlook that is so pervasive in clinical depression, the symptoms are baffling and the thoughts of the depressed person appear to be unreasonable and irrational. To the degree that others expect the depressed person to "pull out of it" and "stop feeling sorry for yourself," considerable tension and conflict may develop with a cycle of misunderstanding and increased guilt and hopelessness.

Diagnostic criteria for DSM-III-R Syndromes

It is not an overstatement to say that the development of reliable diagnostic systems for the affective disorders over the past two decades has stimulated and enabled pursuit of the enormous interest in these disorders, and the outpouring of research that has typified the area in recent times. The DSM-III-R criteria provide the essential ingredients for defining depressive disorders in reliable ways that serve as the basis for common treatments and for comparing and interpreting research findings. Nevertheless, the criteria are not necessarily *valid* for all uses, and are definitely somewhat arbitrary and incomplete, changing as new information becomes available. Also, despite reliability of diagnoses, unipolar depressions are notoriously heterogeneous both in their clinical presentation and in their likely etiologies. The key diagnostic categories, Major Depression and Dysthymia, may therefore include diverse populations. Some of the key subtypes will be discussed below.

Major depression

The criteria for Major Depressive Episode are presented in Table 1.1. The key ingredients besides mood (or loss of interest or pleasure) are the presence of additional bodily or behavioral changes. Only one of the nine symptoms might be construed as a subjective experience: feelings of worthlessness or guilt. Although clinical diagnosable depression is marked by negative thinking, physiological and biological changes must be present beyond just the negative views of the self, world, and the future. The other major ingredient of the diagnostic picture is *duration* of symptomatology, requiring at least two weeks during which the symptoms occur nearly every day. While it is essential to distinguish enduring symptoms from the transitory features of mood depression, it is important to recognize that the duration criterion introduces considerable variation, in that some individuals' depressive episodes might last several months while others

Table 1.1 DSM III-R criteria for Major Depressive Episode

A. At least five of the following symptoms have been present during the same two-week period and represent a change from previous functioning; at least one of the symptoms is either 1. depressed mood, or 2. loss of interest or pleasure. (Do not include symptoms that are clearly due to a physical condition, mood-incongruent delusions or hallucinations, incoherence, or marked loosening of associations.)
   1. Depressed mood (or can be irritable mood in children and adolescents) most of the day, nearly every day, as indicated either by subjective account or observation by others.
   2. Markedly diminished interest or pleasure in all, or almost all, activities most of the day, nearly every day (as indicated either by subjective account or observation by others of apathy most of the time).
   3. Significant weight loss or weight gain when not dieting (e.g. more than 5% of body weight in a month), or decrease or increase in appetite nearly every day (in children, consider failure to make expected weight gains).
   4. Insomnia or hypersomnia nearly every day.
   5. Psychomotor agitation or retardation nearly every day (observable by others, not merely subjective feelings of restlessness or being slowed down).
   6. Fatigue or loss of energy nearly every day.
   7. Feelings of worthlessness or excessive or inappropriate guilt (which may be delusional) nearly every day (not merely self-reproach or guilt about being sick).
   8. Diminished ability to think or concentrate, or indecisiveness, nearly every day (either by subjective account or as observed by others.)
   9. Recurrent thoughts of death (not just fear of dying), recurrent suicidal ideation without a specific plan, or a suicide attempt or a specific plan for committing suicide.
B. 1. It cannot be established that an organic factor initiated and maintained the disturbance.
   2. The disturbance is not a normal reaction to the death of a loved one (Uncomplicated Bereavement).
      Note: Morbid preoccupation with worthlessness, suicidal ideation, marked functional impairment of psychomotor retardation, or prolonged duration suggest bereavement complicated by Major Depression.
C. At no time during the disturbance have there been delusions or hallucinations for as long as two weeks in the absence of prominent mood symptoms (i.e. before the mood symptoms developed or after they have remitted).
D. Not superimposed on Schizophrenia, Schizophreniform Disorder, Delusional Disorder, or Psychotic Disorder NOS.

are only the two weeks or slightly more. Major Depressive Episode can be further characterized as single episode, recurrent, or chronic, as psychotic or nonpsychotic, and by level of severity. Additionally, a qualitative distinction in types of symptoms, termed Melancholia, will be discussed below among subtypes.

Dysthymia

Dysthymia, previously termed depressive neurosis, refers to chronic depressive symptoms lasting most of the time for at least two years, during which at least two of six symptoms of the depression syndrome occur. This category was formerly termed "neurotic depression" in older versions of the DSM. Dysthymia can vary widely in its severity and pervasiveness, age of onset, and by whether it may be a baseline level of mood occasionally punctuated by more severe major depressive episodes (termed "double depression"). As with major depression, this is a heterogeneous category with several proposed subtypes that will be discussed later.

Continuity: are symptoms and syndromes on the same dimension?

Is depression a continuous, quantitative dimension? Or, are there qualitative differences between mild depression and more severe clinical syndromes? Continuity between mild and severe depression differing only in degree is often implicitly assumed when research subjects are selected on the basis of scores on measures of symptom level. Our psychometric achievements have made it possible to assess symptoms of depression on self-report or interviewer-administered scales. Scores on the scales then indicate severity of current symptomatology, but they do not necessarily translate into diagnoses of depression in the DSM-III-R usage. As we shall see in Chapter 3, in which we review assessment methods, most depression scales are highly sensitive but not very specific for depression. Thus, high levels of symptoms *may* indicate clinical depression, but likely also include diffuse, non-specific negative symptomatology (e.g. Gotlib, 1984). Thus, *continuity* between mild and severe levels of depressive symptomatology differing only in degree may occur, but high and low scorers on depression measures may differ on various other characteristics as well. For instance, Lewinsohn Hoberman, & Rosenbaum (1988) have speculated that elevated self-report scores such as the CES-D may indicate nonspecific negative affect (per Watson & Tellegen, 1985) that underlies emotional distress. According to this view, clinical depression includes a core of nonspecific negative affectivity, but also includes other characteristics of the person that may be specific risk factors for an episode of depression. Data from the Lewinsohn Hoberman & Rosenbaum (1988) study of risk factors for depression indicate that there are different correlates of elevated CES-D scores and clinical diagnoses, thus calling into question the assumption of continuity.

Along similar lines of argument, there may be a discontinuity between mild and clinical forms of depression in the sense that most people do not get clinically depressed, even though they may show mild and transient symptoms following stressful conditions. Considerable research evidence suggests that most depressive episodes are actually recurrences in people who have been depressed before, while new onsets in never-before depressed people are relatively rare. This issue will be discussed more fully in later sections and chapters.

There is yet another reason to suspect that use of college students or mildly symptomatic community residents in research to test hypotheses about depression is based on a questionable continuity assumption. Clinical depression involves disruption of functioning and impairment in role enactments. While college student depression might truly represent clinical conditions (e.g. Hammen, 1980; Hammen, Mayol, deMayo, & Marks, 1986), information is rarely provided about functioning. If the depressive experience is very brief, no matter how elevated the current symptoms, it is likely not to resemble the depression of a diagnosed individual that involves more prolonged symptoms affecting the person's life. Even in diagnosed college students, the duration of the episode often may be closer to the two-week minimum for major depressive episode, rather than of longer duration. Our conclusion about continuity, therefore, is that while depression can certainly be scaled on a single dimension of severity, qualitative differences exist that distinguish more severe, persisting, diagnosable depression.

Subtypes of unipolar depression

As noted, major depression and dysthymia are diagnostic categories that cast wide nets encompassing a diverse group that is likely composed of different subtypes of depression. Although research in the etiology and treatment of depression will undoubtedly be enhanced by refinements in subtyping, the complexity of this challenge has limited the gains of such research so far. As Keller (1988) noted, there is little evidence to support the utility of current unipolar subtype distinctions in terms of their contributions to treatment, or to understanding course or etiology.

One of the traditional strategies adopted by investigators in this area has been to try to find a biological "disease" subtype that can be distinguished from psychosocial "disorder" subtypes. For instance, reactive-endogenous, neurotic-psychotic, and endogenous-nonendogenous were some of the distinctions drawn in earlier work on depression. The implicit corollary of this biological-psychological distinction is that the biological types will respond best to medication, while the psychological types will respond to nonsomatic treatments. Empirical evidence fails to support either the etiologic or treatment notion, however.

Melancholic depression

The reactive-endogenous distinction of some years ago hypothesized that some depressions were responses to stressors or psychological events, while the endogenous kinds emerged from biological processes. There has been little support for this distinction. Depressions that seem to arise from stressors do not necessarily differ in symptoms from those that do not, while depressions with "endogenous" symptoms have often been found to follow stressful circumstances (e.g. Hirschfeld, 1981; Keller, 1988; Leber, Beckham, & Danker-Brown, 1985).

Abandoning the notion of different etiologies, a more recent strategy has been to make a distinction between depressions on the basis of *qualitative* aspects of the symptom profiles. There does appear to be some validity to a descriptive subtype of depression with certain predominantly biological features. Thus, according to the DSM-III-R, major depressive episodes may be classified as *melancholia*, avoiding the term "endogenous" with its etiological presumption. The melancholic subtype of depression may be diagnosed if at least five of the following are present in a major depressive episode: loss of interest or pleasure in activities, lack of reactivity to usually pleasurable stimuli such that the person doesn't feel better even temporarily when pleasant things happen, diurnal variation of mood (worse in the morning), early morning awakening, observable psychomotor changes (slowed or agitated), significant weight loss. Also, to be diagnosed, the criteria require lack of significant personality disturbance prior to major depression, one or more previous major depressions followed by complete or nearly complete recovery, and previous good response to antidepressant medication. The rationale for these criteria and the evolution of the present definition of melancholia differing from the DSM-III version are reported in Zimmerman and Spitzer (1989).

Although there is evidence that the melancholia symptom cluster appears with enough frequency and consistency to warrant a diagnostic distinction, its meaning and implications are far less clear. Studies using earlier RDC or DSM-III criteria for melancholia failed to find evidence for a hypothesized greater presumed genetic loading or family aggregation (Andreasen, Scheftner, Reich, Hirschfeld, Endicott, & Keller, 1986; Zimmerman & Spitzer, 1989; Zimmerman, Black, & Coryell, 1989), and found only mixed evidence of differential time to recovery or relapse (Keller, 1988; Zimmerman, Black, & Coryell 1989). The assumption that melancholia marks a type of severe depression that is especially responsive to biological treatment such as medication or ECT has not been supported (Zimmerman & Spitzer, 1989).

While symptom severity is a known correlate of melancholia, there is some evidence suggesting that it may merely be a severe variant of depression rather than a qualitatively different subtype (reviewed in Zimmerman & Spitzer, 1989). Using the new criteria in DSM-III-R that require previous good response to somatic treatment and complete recovery, Zimmerman, Black, & Coryell (1989) examined the question of whether melancholia is merely severe depression. They found that such patients had more severe symptoms only for the melancholic signs of depression, but not for nonmelancholic symptoms. Zimmerman et al. (1989) also found support for their hypothesis that the melancholic subtype is characterized by less stress, less personality disorder, less likelihood of blaming others, and less family history of drug abuse and antisocial personality. Thus, there is some support for the idea that DSM-III-R melancholia is not merely severe depression, and may mark a subtype whose attributes need further investigation.

Neurotic depression

In contrast to the melancholic subtype is the *neurotic* subtype. The neurotic versus psychotic distinction had a long history prior to the DSM-III. Confusingly, it variously referred to presumed biological (psychotic) versus nonbiological (neurotic) categories, as well as to a severe (psychotic) versus mild (neurotic) distinction. In the DSM-III-R, psychotic depression refers specifically to the presence of hallucinations, delusions, or thought disorder that occur along with affective symptoms. It is a much less frequently occurring form of major depression, and the course of psychotic depression appears to be different from that of nonpsychotic depression (Keller, 1988).

Neurotic depression no longer exists in the official diagnostic nomenclature, having been replaced in large part by the concept of Dysthymia, referring to chronic mild depression. However, there has been somewhat renewed interest lately in the concept of a neurotic subtype of depression representing a possible psychosocial origin and distinguishing features of the course of the disorder. Zimmerman, Coryell, Stangl, and Pfohl (1987) developed operational criteria for neurotic depression and applied them to a series of hospitalized depressed patients in Iowa. The system included six criteria: personality disorder, psychosocial stressors, age of onset before 40, blames others for the depression, nonserious suicide attempts, and marital separation or divorce. The authors found that neurotic depression so defined had low rates of abnormal dexamethasone suppression test (DST) responses, higher family history of alcoholism, less improvement in the hospital, and more frequent relapses in the six-month follow-up. Although neurotic subtyping was negatively associated with DSM-III melancholic features, Zimmerman et al. (1987) viewed the two as orthogonal dimensions and proposed a four-fold classification system.

Iowa classification system

Winokur's Iowa classification system presents a concept of depressive spectrum disease that overlaps with the idea of a neurotic subtype of depression. In Winokur's model of neurotic depression, the defining features are presence of personality disturbances and evidence of a stormy lifestyle, as well as familial alcoholism. His criteria essentially exclude individuals with significant melancholic symptoms, and he views the reactive neurotic subtype as more homogeneous than the melancholic subtype.

The Winokur system proposes subgroups of unipolar depression based on familial patterns of disorder rather than on clinical presentation. There are three proposed subtypes: familial pure depressive disease, depression spectrum disease, and sporadic depressive disease (Winokur, 1979). The pure disease type is thought to be comprised of late-onset males with both male and female first-degree relatives with depression, and is considered to be a relatively severe disorder that often becomes chronic. The second type, depressive spectrum disease (now largely synonymous with the neurotic reactive type noted above), is typically female with onset before age 40, with depression in female relatives but alcoholism and sociopathy in male relatives. This disorder is seen as less severe, and more likely to arise from chaotic lifestyles. The third type, sporadic depressive disease, has no history of family psychiatric disorder.

Support for the proposed subtypes has been inconsistent (Keller, 1988; Leber, Beckham, & Danker-Brown, 1985). Zimmerman, Coryell, and Pfohl (1986) found evidence that the depressive spectrum disease type overlaps with neurotic depression, and familial pure depressive disease overlaps with melancholic depression. Differences between these groups of patients on psychosocial factors were especially pronounced when stringent criteria were used to define family history of depression or alcoholism. The sporadic depression type as distinct from familial pure depression has received little support.

The meaning and utility of the neurotic and melancholic subtypes remain to be established, but strongly suggest the importance of defining homogeneous groups in research efforts. The "neurotic" subgroup is especially intriguing for a cognitive-interpersonal perspective on depression. Consistent with Hammen (1991a; 1991b), there may be a type of depression that arises in the context of a history of dysfunctional parenting (as with parents who have depressive or other diagnosable disorders) with early onset of symptoms that impair mastery of important developmental skills for academic and social problem-solving. Such skill and cognitive vulnerabilities in turn may contribute to the occurrence of stressful situations that cause depression (or to the failure to resolve the stressors). Depression in turn is disruptive and contributes to further stressful situations, and the depression-stress cycle may be perpetuated. Evidence for such a model has been presented in the form of outcomes for children of depressed women (Hammen, 1991a), and the tendency of depressed persons to generate stressful events, especially interpersonal stressors (Hammen, 1991b). Recently, Hammen, Davila, Brown, Ellicott, and Gitlin (1992) demonstrated the utility of the model in a sample of unipolar depressed outpatients. Severity of depression during the follow-up was predicted by stressful events and chronic stressors, which in turn were predicted by family history of psychopathology and early age of onset of disorder. Thus, it is possible that a distinction such as the *neurotic* classification serves as an indicator of an ongoing transaction between persons and environments, linking the backgrounds and course features in a certain psychologically pernicious process. Other subtypes of depression may have entirely different etiologies and features.

Other possible subtypes and diagnostic distinctions

In addition to the neurotic-psychotic, reactive-endogenous, or melancholic-nonmelancholic distinctions of past or current usage, the primary-secondary dimension (Robins & Guze, 1982) was formerly used to distinguish whether the depression occurred in the absence of any other nonaffective or medical condition. Secondary depressions referred to those arising subsequent to the onset of, or superimposed on, any other psychiatric or medical condition. Although the distinction seemed to be a practical solution to the recognition that depressive syndromes frequently accompany or follow certain psychiatric or physical disorders such as alcoholism, anxiety disorders, or organic conditions, in reality it is often very difficult to clarify the timing of symptoms in relation to each other. Also, the clinical and theoretical utility of the primary-secondary distinction has not proven to be strong, and the diagnosis of secondary depression identifies an enormously heterogeneous group (Leber, Beckham, & Danker-Brown, 1985).

Another proposed biological subtype of episodic depression has recently gained prominence: seasonal affective disorder (SAD). At a recent workshop sponsored by the National Institute of Mental Health (NIMH), the validity of this subtype was said to be even stronger than melancholia (Blehar & Rosenthal, 1989). Typified by (although not limited to) a pattern of winter depression, the syndrome includes atypical depressive features such as overeating, carbohydrate craving, weight gain, fatigue, and hypersomnia. It appears to occur within both unipolar and bipolar disorders, and has been treated successfully with phototherapy involving exposure to full-spectrum light. It may have a unique pathophysiology related to disruption of circadian rhythms, although the exact mechanism is currently unknown but actively studied (see review by Blehar & Rosenthal, 1989).

Recent work by Klein (1990) has suggested a further method of reducing variability in major depression. He found that patients who had six or more groups of symptoms of major depressive episode were significantly more likely to have depression in family members. He argues that stricter symptom criteria, therefore, may define a more homogeneous subgroup—at least one with more familial affective disorder.

Subtypes of chronic depression (dysthymia)

Not only does major depressive disorder appear to be enormously heterogeneous, but such is also the case with chronic, low-grade depressions (Akiskal, Bitar, Puzantian, Rosenthal, & Walker, 1978). Akiskal (1983) has proposed a variety of subtypes that are differentiated by presumed etiological and clinical features. Depue and Monroe (1986) subsequently expanded the list to include five subgroups of dysthymic depressives, themselves a subset of chronic depressions. Studies establishing the validity of such groups remain to be done. Recently, Klein, Taylor, Dickstein, and Harding (1988) attempted to investigate the validity of the new DSM-III-R category of primary early-onset dysthymia. Klein et al. (1988) found that such patients show high levels of melancholic symptoms, elevated rates of affective disorders in relatives, and poorer social and role functioning, suggesting a comparatively severe form of disorder compared with nonchronic major depressives.

Summary

It is essential for psychologists to join in the efforts to characterize homogeneous subgroups of episodic and chronic depressed individuals. It has become increasingly clear that wide-band, sweeping theories of the etiology of depression do not fit the clinical reality of diverse types that differ in origin and course of disorder. Recurring themes in the research suggest some validity to the idea of an early-onset type with psychogenic patterns related to dysfunctional lifestyle, compared to a later-onset type that has better premorbid functioning and is possibly less reactive to life circumstances. These types may cut across episodic and chronic groups, but it is unclear whether they reflect a biological versus psychogenic vulnerability. It is also unclear whether other methods of characterizing the course of disorder or differential etiology will prove to be useful. At the very least, researchers are well-advised to avoid unitary models of presumed homogeneous depressions.

Depression and co-occurring disorders

Because of its frequency of occurrence, depression can be seen to coexist with a variety of psychiatric and medical conditions. Due to different implications for treatment and understanding course of disorder, it is important, therefore, to be able to distinguish whether unipolar depression is the primary disorder, whether depression is a complication or coeffect of another disorder, or whether both conditions have arisen from similar or different causes. Additionally, the presence of comorbid disorders appears to worsen the course of disorder. Keitner, Ryan, Miller, Kohn, & Epstein (1991) identified a subset of inpatients with major depressive disorder who also had Axis I, II, or III (medical) conditions—termed "compound depression." In a 12-month follow-up, compound depression patients compared to those with pure depression functioned significantly more poorly and had lower recovery rates.

Differential diagnosis of bipolar disorder

The unipolar-bipolar dichotomy, one of the most widely accepted sub-divisions of depressive disorders, rests on the proposition that depressions with and without manic periods should be viewed as distinct disorders (although this distinction is not without controversy). Good differential diagnosis is especially necessary, therefore, to distinguish unipolar major depression from bipolar disorder because of presumed differences in the likely causes, course, and treatment of the disorders. Such a diagnostic distinction is not always easy to make, however, in that the features of the depressive episode may be very similar for some individuals with unipolar or bipolar disorder. Distinguishing unipolar depression from "bipolar II" (atypical bipolar) disorder is especially difficult at times, if the hypomanic experiences that define the bipolar component are infrequent or brief. Thus, it is not surprising that the NIMH Consensus Development Conference on Pharmacologic Prevention of Recurrences estimated that the rate of individuals initially diagnosed as unipolar who are rediagnosed on follow-up as bipolar is about 15% (NIMH Conference Statement, 1985).

Medical conditions

Numerous medical conditions exist that are known to cause depressive symptoms, including a variety of endocrinological, neurological, and viral diseases (reviewed in Cassem, 1988). Good medical evaluation is essential to identify and properly treat such conditions (see Schulberg, McClelland,

& Burns, 1987, for a review of physical symptoms of depression, depressive symptoms of medical illnesses, and depressive reactions to medical illnesses).

Psychiatric comorbidity

Various psychiatric conditions are frequently accompanied by depressive symptoms or syndromes. For instance, depression co-occurs commonly with eating disorders, alcohol and drug abuse, and anxiety disorders; it may arise prior to such conditions, or as a consequence. For example, recently Sanderson, Beck, and Beck (1990) assessed 260 clinic patients with principal diagnoses of depressive disorders, and found that two-thirds of them had an additional concurrent diagnosis on Axis I (primarily anxiety disorders or substance use disorders). Data from a community sample are even more informative about the true rates of comorbid conditions. Rohde, Lewinsohn, and Seeley (1991) reported that 42% of depressed adolescents and about 25% of depressed adults in a large-scale community survey were found to have another lifetime diagnosis (principally anxiety and substance use disorders). Interestingly, depression was more likely to follow the other disorder than to precede it. The findings also suggested that depression of early onset was more likely to be associated with a comorbid disorder, possibly indicating a more severe form of the depression. A full review of comorbidity is beyond the scope of this chapter, although a discussion of anxiety and depression is included below because of the frequent overlap of symptoms of the two conditions.

One common form of co-occurrence of disorders concerns dysthymia and major depression. Keller, Lavori, Endicott, Coryell, & Klerman (1983) found that the pattern of major depression superimposed on dysthymia (double depression) occurred in 25% of patients. In community samples, such concurrence is also likely to occur more frequently than expected by chance alone, occurring in about 10% of the depressed sample (Lewinsohn, Rohde, Seeley, & Hops, 1991). These investigators also reported that dysthymia was more likely to precede than follow major depression. Sorenson, Rutter, and Aneshensel (1991) also reviewed epidemiological data for double depression, and while they did not report temporal ordering of onset, they did find that double depression had an earlier age of onset than major depression alone. In a later section we review the implications of comorbid dysthymia and major depression for course of disorder.

The so-called *personality disorders*, or Axis II, conditions, also commonly coexist with depression. Farmer and Nelson-Gray (1990) recently reviewed the research on personality disorders and depression, noting that there is a

30 to 70% comorbidity rate depending on the nature of the samples. Shea, Pilkonis, Beckham, Collins, Elkin et al., (1990) reported that 74% of the 239 patients with depressive disorders who were treated in the NIMH Treatment of Depression Collaborative Research Program received diagnoses of personality disorders. Disorders in the dramatic-erratic cluster such as the borderline personality disorder, or the anxious-fearful cluster, seem especially commonly linked with depression. As Farmer and Nelson-Gray (1990) note, this is an enormously difficult issue with numerous hypotheses about the nature of the co-occurrence, complicated by methodological problems such as reliability of the assessment of personality disorders, sample selection, and the effects of depressive symptoms on personality presentation. Although some investigators have argued that certain types of Axis II disorder such as the borderline personality disorder are actually a form of affective disorder (e.g. Akiskal, Hirschfeld, & Yerevanian, 1983), recent research disputes this argument and suggests more complex relationships between the conditions (e.g. Farmer & Nelson-Gray, 1990; Widiger & Frances, 1989). However, because of the high likelihood of personality disorders in unipolar depressed individuals, and the probability that such conditions may contribute uniquely to the course of depression and to more chronic or recurrent episodes, research samples should be carefully described or even selected to account for such comorbidity.

Depression and anxiety

As noted, while the DSM-III-R represents a great improvement in the reliability of diagnostic classification of affective disorders, its validity and completeness may be limited by our current knowledge. Thus, as greater information becomes available there will be alterations in the diagnostic system. A likely case in point concerns anxiety symptoms and depression. It is well-known that major depression and anxiety disorders frequently co-occur (e.g. Alloy, Kelly, Mineka, & Clements, 1990). For instance, Barlow (1988) reported that 39% of patients with agoraphobia, 35% of patients with panic disorder, and 17% of those with generalized anxiety disorder had concurrent major depression or dysthymia; past histories of episodes of major depression probably occur in the majority of anxiety disorder patients (Breier, Charney, & Heninger, 1985). Similarly, current symptoms of anxiety or even anxiety disorders are quite common in individuals with current depressive symptoms and diagnoses (see Clark, Beck, & Stewart, 1990; Gotlib, 1984; Gotlib & Cane, 1989).

By convention, representing a change from DSM-III, DSM-III-R permits dual diagnoses of anxiety and depressive disorders without trying to determine which is the "primary" disorder. In addition to distinct syndromes that can co-occur, recent research suggests that there may be naturally occurring conditions of mixtures of anxiety and depressive symptoms where the individual may fail to meet current criteria for one or the other. Barrett, Barrett, Oxman, and Gerber (1988) screened general medical patients on level of depressive symptoms, and then interviewed those scoring high on the self-report checklists. While a subset of the high-depression scorers met DSM-III criteria for depressive disorders, a significant subset (10.5%) had significant symptoms without meeting diagnostic criteria. One of these groups consisted of a mix of anxiety and depression symptoms (and the other group appeared to be depressed but denied depression). Blazer, Swartz, Woodbury, Manton, Hughes, and George (1988) found a similar mixed depression/anxiety pattern in community residents participating in an Epidemiological Catchment Area survey. The investigators used multivariate statistical methods to characterize the symptoms reported by respondents, and found several depression symptom profiles. Only one of the profiles, however, corresponded to DSM-III major depression. Another noteworthy pattern was a mixed anxiety/depression type. Blazer et al. (1988) suggest that because this picture does not meet current criteria for either depressive or anxiety disorders, it may go undetected and untreated. Based on extensive reviews of diagnostic and psychometric data, others have begun to call for a diagnostic system that includes a mixed anxiety-depression syndrome (Clark & Watson, 1991; Katon & Roy-Byrne, 1991). Recently, Clark, Beck, and Stewart (1990) identified a mixed anxious-depressed group of patients who showed more severe and pervasive pathology than did either the pure anxiety disorders or pure depressive disorders patients. They found that this mixed group showed more general maladjustment, and considered the group to represent a more severely disturbed group than the pure diagnosis groups. Katon and Roy-Byrne (1991) reach a similar conclusion in their review of community, primary care, and psychiatric populations.

In addition to the apparently naturally-occurring overlap of depression and anxiety, with the possibility that such individuals may differ from other groups, there also are more "pure" groups of anxiety and depression that apparently can be distinguished in various ways including the primary cognitive content of their disorders. For instance, Clark, Beck, and Stewart (1990; see also Beck, Brown, Steer, Eidelson, & Riskind, 1987) found that depressed patients reported significantly more negative thoughts involving loss and past failure, and more hopelessness and lower-self-worth, while anxiety patients had significantly more thoughts of anticipated harm and danger.

The Clark, Beck, and Stewart (1990) study of over 700 patients found a single major factor in analyses of self-reported and clinician-reported depression and anxiety symptoms, as well as the more specific depression and anxiety cognitive patterns noted above. The presence of a single general factor (see also Gotlib's 1984 analysis of college student self-reported symptoms) is consistent with a general component of distress termed Negative Affectivity (NA; Watson & Clark, 1984; Watson, Clark, & Carey, 1988). Research continues to pursue the question of how depression and anxiety might differ even when sharing a basic component of NA (e.g. Barlow, 1988; Clark, Beck, & Stewart 1990; Watson, Clark, & Carey 1988). One implication of the overlap, or shared component of NA, is that samples selected to represent depression might also include a mix of anxiety, or might be primarily characterized as nonspecific distress (Gotlib, 1984). Thus, theorists in the area of depression need to be mindful of the specificity of their models, and to develop research to test the differences in applications for samples of diverse composition.

WHO GETS DEPRESSED?

Epidemiology of depressive disorders and symptoms

Overall rates of disorder and symptoms

Using interview procedures and systematic diagnostic criteria, recent epidemiological studies suggest that across several major cities sampled, current rates of major depressive disorder ranged from 2.2 to 3.5%, and of dysthymia from 2.1 to 3.8% (Myers, Weissman, Tischler, Holzer, Leaf et al., 1984). When lifetime rates are determined from respondents' recollections of past symptoms, the rates of major depressive episode across cities ranged from 4.0% in Baltimore to 8.4% among non-Hispanic whites in Los Angeles, with rates of dysthymia ranging from 2.2 to 4.1% (Karno, Hough, Burnam, Escobar, Timbers et al., 1987). Earlier investigations that did not use such stringent methods as those employed in the Epidemiological Catchment Area studies, or that included milder forms of depression, estimated even higher lifetime rates—up to 18% in various US cities and Western countries (Boyd & Weissman, 1981).

Symptoms of the depression syndromes that do not meet full criteria for diagnoses are even more common. For example, Boyd and Weissman (1981) reviewed data suggesting that between 9 and 20% of the population will report significant symptomatology at any given time. As an example, Barrett, et al. (1988) studied the prevalence of psychiatric disorders in rural primary medical care practices, and found that 10% of people seeking medical care met Research Diagnostic Criteria for depressive disorders. Of particular note, an additional 11.2% of the medical help-seeking population had significant depressive symptoms that did not meet diagnostic criteria. Such findings suggest that depressive symptoms and disorders occur with substantial frequency in the population. As we shall see, the rates are even higher in some segments of the population than others, so that some groups have a high probability of significant depression, even including major depressive episodes, in their lifetimes.

Sex differences in depression

Considerable evidence across a wide array of methods of investigation suggests that women are about two times more likely to experience clinical depressions than men (Boyd & Weissman, 1981; Nolen-Hoeksema, 1987, 1990). For instance, current rates of major depression and dysthymia in an epidemiological study of three cities indicated rates ranging from 2.9 to 5.4 for women, and 1.2 to 2.6 for men (Myers et al., 1984). In a more recent ECA study in Los Angeles, lifetime rates of major depression across different age groups of non-Hispanic whites were 6.2% for men, and 10% for women. In younger adults (below age 40), rates were 8.7% for men and 15.3% for women.

Interestingly, sex differences seem to occur only in some demographic samples. For instance, in younger children of elementary school-age, there is little indication of higher rates of diagnosis or symptom scores for either sex. However, in adolescence, girls' levels of symptoms and diagnoses rise sharply, and are significantly higher than those of boys (e.g. Allgood-Merten, Lewinsohn, & Hops, 1990; Kashani, Carlson, Beck, Hoeper, Corcoran et al., 1987). On the other hand, college students generally do not show significant sex differences in depression scores, and elderly populations tend not to display sex differences in rates of depression (e.g. Hammen & Padesky, 1977; Nolen-Hoeksema, 1990). While a discussion of the theories invoked to explain sex differences is beyond the scope of this book, the differences do not seem to stem from reporting biases (e.g. Nolen- Hoeksema, 1990). Some investigators consider the gender differences to be "real" aspects of different psychological or biological susceptibility, while others argue that they are "artifacts" or indirect products of women's differences in employment, job status, education, income, and support (e.g. Golding, 1988). Also, as we shall see below, there is some evidence of a narrowing gap between men and women in experiences of depression, at least in younger age cohorts. At any rate, a valid theory of forms of depression needs to be able to account for such demographic differences.

Other demographic contributors to patterns of depression

In addition to the striking gender differences discussed above, and age effects to be considered in a later section, several other demographic correlates have been noted. In terms of race, most studies do not show significant differences between whites and nonwhites. Black samples in the ECA 3-site study were generally slightly but nonsignificantly lower in major depression and dysthymia (Robins, Helzer, Weissman, Orvaschel, Gruenberg et al., 1984). Hispanics included in the Los Angeles ECA study tended to have slightly lower rates of both depressive disorders than did non-Hispanic whites, with rates varying somewhat by age group (Karno et al., 1987). Ethnicity and cultural background may strongly influence the experience and expression of depression symptoms, however, with the possibility that instruments that are essentially standardized on white populations may give a somewhat misleading picture of depression in nonwhite samples.

Education is generally associated with psychopathology, in that the less educated are more likely to be diagnosed. However, this effect does not appear to hold for major depression and dysthymia, with generally similar rates for those who have college degrees and those who do not (Robins et al., 1984). Similarly, urban versus rural locations often show differences in rates of disorders, with higher levels of psychopathology in inner city or suburban sites compared to rural communities. Again, however, depression largely appears to ignore such distinctions. The ECA study comparison of St. Louis rural and urban rates failed to show significant differences in depression (Robins et al., 1984; see also Hirschfeld & Cross, 1982). Social class, which is a complex construct that seems to be an index of educational attainment, occupational status, and exposure to stressors and resources to cope with them, bears an ambiguous relationship to depressive symptoms and disorders. While the disadvantaged in general appear to report somewhat higher rates of depression (e.g. compare the Brown & Harris, 1978, working-class women vs. upper-class), lifetime reports rates of depression often have not been found to differ by socio-economic group (Hirschfeld & Cross, 1982). It is likely to be more instructive in pursuing sociological correlates of depression to examine the meaning of certain status groups. For instance Golding (1989) looked not only at roles such as employment or marital status, but their combinations, and whether there were stresses and resources associated with different roles. She found that role occupancy such as being unemployed or unmarried was associated with depressive symptoms, but that the amounts of strain and support within roles additionally modified the amount of depression.

Marital status has often been found to be associated with differential rates of disorder including depression. In general, currently married individuals report fewer symptoms and diagnosable conditions than do single and divorced individuals (reviewed in Hirschfeld & Cross, 1982). As will be discussed further in later chapters, marital discord and disruption are common correlates of depression (e.g. Gotlib & Hooley, 1988).

Increasing rates of depression

Several strands of investigation have recently converged to suggest an alarming trend: rates of depression seem to be on the rise, especially in younger people. For instance, Klerman, Lavori, Rice, Reich, Endicott et al. (1985) and Gershon, Hamovit, Guroff, and Nurnberger (1987) interviewed relatives of patients with affective disorders, and found that those relatives born more recently were significantly more likely to have had episodes of major depression than relatives born earlier, a "birth cohort" effect. Also, recent epidemiological studies have shown that in contrast to the conventional wisdom that depression was a disorder of middle age, rates of depression are highest in young adults (e.g. Karno et al., 1987; Myers et al., 1984). Add to such trends the findings of increased admissions to hospitals for affective disorders in the past two decades compared to earlier decades, and reported earlier ages of onset of clinical depression than in the past (see Klerman & Weissman, 1989). Also, new procedures for defining and assessing depression in children and adolescents have indicated that rates of childhood depression start to resemble those of adults (e.g. Anderson, Williams, McGee, & Silva, 1987) and in adolescence, rates of onsets are especially high (e.g. ref. Kandel & Davies, 1986). Moreover, not only are the rates of depression increasing for younger people, but also the sex differences seem to be narrowing as more young men display depression.

What might account for such temporal trends? Klerman and Weissman (1989) have reviewed evidence concerning possible artifacts, including changes in attitudes and psychological-mindedness, reporting and recall bias, and other confounding factors that might account for the effects. They concluded, however, that little evidence supports the operation of such variables in accounting for the significant changes in depression rates. For instance, rates of hospitalization and suicide have also increased, suggesting more than just subjective experiencing and reporting of depression. Instead, the authors speculate that alterations in environmental risk factors such as changes in family composition, mobility, social roles for women, and the like, may contribute to increased stress and reduced social supports and attachments that lead to depression. Klerman and Weissman (1989) argue that such factors may interact with genetic predisposition to determine who exhibits clinically significant depression. As with sex differences, it would seem that a useful theory of depressive disorders needs to be able to take into account apparent significant shifts in rates and ages of onset of depression.

THE COURSE AND CONSEQUENCES OF DEPRESSION

Impaired functioning of depressed persons

Clinical descriptions of depressed people are graphic in indicating considerable disruption in their functioning at work, in parental roles, as friends or at leisure, and in intimate relationships. Additionally, recent research has provided somewhat surprising evidence that the dysfunction is even more debilitating than that of many major chronic medical illnesses. For instance, the Medical Outcomes Study compared the physical, social, and role functioning, perceived health, and number of days in bed due to health in the last month of more than 11 000 patients seen in various health care facilities in three US sites (Wells, Stewart, Hays, Burnam, Rogers et al., 1989). Individuals in treatment for one of eight chronic medical conditions (hypertension, diabetes, advanced coronary artery disease, angina, arthritis, back problems, lung problems, and gastrointestinal diseases) were compared with depressed individuals and those without chronic conditions. Those with diagnosed depressive disorders and depressive symptoms not only differed significantly from those without chronic conditions, but also had significantly worse social functioning than patients with each of the eight chronic medical conditions. Their role functioning was significantly worse than for patients with any of the eight medical conditions, and they spent more time in bed than did those from six of the eight medical groups. Except for the patients with heart conditions, the depressed individuals perceived their health to be significantly worse than all other groups. Interestingly, when patients had subclinical depressive symptoms rather than meeting diagnostic criteria for major depression or dysthymia, they still tended to have worse functioning than most of the chronic medical patients. Thus, the impact of depressive symptoms on functioning and well-being in this population was very similar to that of diagnosed depressive disorder (Burnam, Wells, & Hays, 1990).

It could be argued that since depression is a condition marked by negativistic thinking, maybe the depressed subjects of the Medical Outcomes Study were exaggerating their plight, actually reporting worse functioning than was objectively true. While it would have been useful to have behavioral indicators of their functioning instead of reliance on self-reported impairment, results from Hammen's (1991a) study of families of depressed women suggest that actual functioning really is impaired. Women with recurrent unipolar depression were compared with women with bipolar disorder, chronic medical illness (insulin-dependent diabetes or severe arthritis) and normal women, all of whom had at least one child between the ages of 8 and 16, from comparable sociodemographic backgrounds. Functioning across several different realms was assessed with a chronic stress interview devised for the study. The interview inquired about conditions in each of several content areas, and scaled the results on an objectively-anchored 5-point scale for each topic.

Table 1.2 presents the means for each role area for each of the groups (a score of 5 is the best functioning, low-stress alternative, considered to be ideal, above-average conditions). As predicted, the unipolar women faced significantly more negative conditions in each area, compared to the medical and normal groups (except for physical health, although even in this area the unipolar women were substantially impaired). In many cases, the unipolar women were functioning less well than the bipolar women who also faced recurring or chronic symptoms. Thus, this analysis confirms that the actual role functioning of unipolar depressed women, in objective terms, indicates substantial debility and adverse conditions.

Table 1.2 Mean chronic stress scores by maternal group

| | Maternal Groups | | | |
	Unipolar	Bipolar	Medical	Normal
Marital/social	2.7	3.0	3.5	3.6
Job	2.7	3.1	3.5	3.7
Finances	2.9	3.2	3.5	3.6
Relations with extended family	3.4	3.7	3.9	3.8
Relations with children	2.5	3.1	3.3	3.6
Health: self	3.6	3.6	2.9	4.0
Health: others	3.4	3.9	3.7	3.7
Total chronic stress*	17.8	19.9	20.4	22.1

Higher scores represent *less* stress.
* Excludes relations with extended family due to extensive missing data.

An additional longitudinal study of depressed outpatients by Gotlib and Lee (1989) further illustrates functional impairment often observed in depressed persons. The authors studied women in treatment for unipolar depression, compared with women in treatment for nondepressive psychiatric disorders, and community women who did not have psychiatric problems. The women completed the Health and Daily Living Form B (Moos, Cronkite, Billings, & Finney, 1983) containing subscales that assess social functioning and resources, family activities and areas of conflict.

The women were reassessed 7–10 months later; at that time the depressed women showed significant reductions in their depression levels and were not significantly different from the nondepressed patients. Despite the reduction in their depression, however, the formerly depressed women reported significantly fewer social activities, had fewer close relationships, poorer quality of those relationships, and more areas of family conflict. Thus, women with unipolar depression appeared to show continuing social impairment, and such adversity was specific to the depressed group compared to the other psychiatric patients or normal women.

One of the important implications of the above studies is that impairment of functioning and stressful ongoing conditions go hand-in-hand. An individual who is impaired by depression is likely to experience disruption in work and social functioning, creating a variety of stressful conditions that affect both psychological morale and objective circumstances. Often, therefore, the disorder becomes confounded with the stressful conditions generated by the impairment; in turn, the stressful conditions may contribute to further depression, and so forth in a continuing cycle of debility and symptoms.

An extreme example is homelessness. An epidemiological study of mental illness among the homeless of Los Angeles found that the lifetime rates of major depressive disorder were three times higher in the homeless (18.3%) than in the general population, and the current rates were five times higher (Koegel, Burnam, & Farr, 1988). Interestingly, among the younger-age homeless (18–30) the rates of affective disorders were exceeded only by substance use disorders and were far higher than schizophrenia or antisocial personality disorder. Current rates of major depression in the young adult homeless included 21.3% experiencing a major depressive episode. While the causal relationship between significant depression and homelessness cannot be clarified in such studies, it is likely that major negative life events and depression go hand in hand in the sample, contributing to the ongoing cycle of symptoms and social debility. We will discuss further implications of such a "stress-generation" perspective in later chapters.

Course of disorder in unipolar depression

Studies of the natural history of depressive disorders in untreated populations are rare, and nowadays would be virtually impossible to conduct, given the wide array of effective treatments to which depressed people should be referred. Thus, most of what we believe to be true about the course of disorder is based on treated samples. Such samples may be unrepresentative of depressive disorders, in the sense that the vast number of people who become depressed do not seek treatment. Those that do seek treatment, and who then become part of research studies, may differ systematically in various ways from those who do not seek treatment. Moreover, it is unknown what characteristics might distinguish those likely to seek treatment in university-affiliated settings of the kinds commonly included in research projects from those who might seek treatment in community agencies or from private sources. An additional limitation in our knowledge of the true course of disorder is that most studies are retrospective, and not longitudinal, thus relying extensively on recollections that might be biased or incomplete.

What we currently consider to be a typical course probably differs considerably from what clinicians formerly believed to be typical, owing in large part to the important refinements in diagnostic criteria that have occurred in the past two decades. Except for conditions thought to be cyclic in nature and often mis-termed manic-depressive, most depressions were considered to be disorders of middle-age onset from which individuals recovered completely without further episodes, or went on to have a chronic course. Chronic or intermittent milder depressions were considered "neurotic" in nature, and thus of psychodynamic origins. Nowadays it would be difficult to define a "typical" course due to the enormous variability experienced by different individuals. Nevertheless, some of our old myths are clearly not true, and as we shall see, features of the course of depressive disorders may have enormous implications for theories of etiology, as well as for defining relatively homogeneous samples for study.

Age of onset

Once considered a disorder of middle age, and one that children did not experience and indeed were thought incapable of, we now know that actual age of onset of depression varies enormously with significant incidence in the younger years. For example, Lewinsohn, Duncan, Stanton, and Hautzinger (1986) interviewed community residents about previous depressions, variously categorized using the Research Diagnostic Criteria, and found that reported onsets were very low in childhood, increasing dramatically in adolescence, peaking sharply in middle age, and decreasingly sharply in the elderly years. Their sample was self-selected, however, rather than random, and was comprised of 74% women, as well as more educated and from higher socioeconomic backgrounds than the general population. Using stratified random samples in a community survey, the Epidemiological Catchment Area study of five communities found that the median age of onset of major depression is 25 years (Burke, Burke, Regier, & Rae, 1990). For both males and females the highest hazard rates for unipolar major depression occurred between the ages of 15–19, and 25–29. After the latter age, men's onset rates drop sharply, while for women the rates remain relatively high until age 49, after which they decline sharply. Similar results were obtained from the Los Angeles Epidemiological Catchment Area study. Sorenson, Rutter, and Aneshensel (1991) determined that 25% of those with a history of major depression reported onset during childhood or adolescence, and 50% had onset by age 25. Women were more likely than men to have earlier onsets. They did not find, however, that age of onset was a significant predictor of number, severity or relapse of episodes. Thus, as we shall discuss more fully later, depression appears to be a disorder of relatively younger onset than in the past, with particular risk in late adolescence and early adulthood.

There is some evidence suggesting that earlier age of onset of depression predicts a more pernicious course. Bland, Newman, and Orn (1986) found that early-onset major depressions predict a negative course and are also associated with higher family loading for depression in first-degree relatives. As noted previously, Klein et al. (1988) examined the correlates of early-onset dysthymia, a new DSM-III-R subtype, and found that such patients showed high levels of melancholic symptoms and high family rates of affective disorder. They concluded that this subtype represents a relatively severe form of depressive disorder. Lewinsohn, Fenn, Stanton, and Franklin (1986) did not find that earlier onset of depression was associated with longer episodes. Also, Lewinsohn, Zeiss, and Duncan (1989) did not find that earlier onset (defined as before age 40) was related to higher probability of a relapse; use of different age cutoffs might have altered the findings, however (see also Sorenson, Rutter, & Aneshensel, 1991, for negative findings). Recently, however, Hammen et al. (1992) found that earlier age of onset in unipolar depressed outpatients predicted more severe depression in a longitudinal follow-up, and that the effect of early onset was mediated by chronic stress. That is, early onset predicted chronic stress, which in turn, along with episodic stress, predicted symptom severity. It was speculated that early onset disrupts functioning and acquisition of skills and problem-solving capabilities. Such deficits may contribute to the causation of chronically stressful life conditions concerning jobs, finances, and social relationships, and may also impede the person's ability to cope with typical stressors. This interpretation is compatible with the Lewinsohn et al. (1991) study finding greater likelihood of early onset depression associated with comorbid conditions, which the authors hypothesize predicts a worse form of the disorder. Finally, early age of onset includes childhood depression; as we shall explore in a later chapter devoted to childhood and adolescent depression, such conditions predict high rates of recurrence, chronicity, and psychosocial impairment (Kovacs, Feinberg, Crouse-Novak, Paulauskas, & Finkelstein, 1984a).

Duration and typical course of depression

Major depressive episodes are generally considered to be time-limited, in the sense that the majority of individuals recover in a few months whether treated or not. Clayton (1984) reviewed research on typical duration of episodes with the conclusion that most depressions last 10–11 months. Keller, Shapiro, Lavori, and Wolfe (1982) found that 64% of help-seeking patients had recovered within 6 months of entry into their study. In their community sample, Lewinsohn, Fenn et al. (1986) found that 40% of major or minor depressions lasted less than three months. However, in contrast to somewhat widespread beliefs that depression is typically a somewhat benign disorder in the long run, recent research suggests that the typical course of disorder is often recurrent or chronic depression—as we discuss below.

Predictors of onset of depression

Lewinsohn, Hoberman and Rosenbaum (1988) have found that first onsets of clinically diagnosed depression in never-depressed persons are quite rare. Similar results were reported by Hammen, Mayol, de Mayo, and Marks (1986) in college students followed longitudinally with regular life stress and diagnostic assessments. While stressful life events were associated with increased self-reported symptoms in never-depressed students, it was quite rare for depressive episodes to develop unless the person had a previous history of depression. Thus, Hammen, Lewinsohn, and others (e.g., Brown & Harris, 1978; Thoits, 1983a) suggest that most people do not develop clinical depression even under potentially provoking conditions. Diagnosable depression may require some underlying vulnerability of a biological and psychological nature. In this respect, therefore, there may not be continuity between mild depression that is a brief, normal reaction to stressors, and more severe depression that may be a clinically significant response by someone who has previously been depressed. Or, as Gopelrud and Depue (1985) have argued, biologically vulnerable individuals may show similar levels of distress when provoked by negative life events as nonvulnerable subjects do, but the vulnerable individuals show more individual variability in symptoms and take longer to recover from symptoms. While a discussion of biological and genetic vulnerability to depression is beyond the scope of this chapter, it is particularly important to emphasize the need for integrated biological-psychological models of depression vulnerability (see review in Hammen, 1991c).

On the psychological front, there has been considerable emphasis on the role of stressors, marital and social status, and cognitive-self vulnerability in the onset of depression (e.g. Abramson, Alloy, & Metalsky, 1988;

Brown & Harris, 1978; Barnett & Gotlib, 1988b; Billings, Cronkite, & Moos 1983). These topics will be discussed fully in later chapters. It should be emphasized at this point, however, that the strongest predictor of depression is past depression (e.g. Lewinsohn, Hoberman and Rosenbaum, 1988; Hammen et al., 1986). Thus, in order to be clinically practical and valid, most of our models of psychological vulnerability to depression need to be models of relapse or recurrence, while onset models or predictors of other aspects of the course of disorder might include different ingredients. Barnett and Gotlib (1988b) and Belsher and Costello (1988) point out that initial onset of depression may significantly alter subsequent vulnerabilities that affect recovery from depression as well as recovery. Thus, different stages of the disorder—onset, maintenance, relapse, recovery—ought to be studied separately for their biopsychosocial predictors and correlates.

Recurrence and relapse

It is now apparent that for a substantial number of individuals with major depressive episodes, the disorder is recurrent (Zis & Goodwin, 1979). Keller (1985) reported that between 50 and 85% of patients with one major episode who seek treatment will have at least one additional episode. The mean number of lifetime episodes was estimated to be 5 or 6 (Angst et al., 1973). In his 20-year longitudinal study of 190 unipolar patients, Angst (1984) calculated that such individuals spend about 20% of their lives in episodes after onset of the disorder. Although as Clayton (1984) noted, many unipolar depressed persons experience symptom-free periods between episodes, there is a growing recognition that many individuals experience chronic or intermittent depressive symptoms (discussed more fully below).

With respect to the timing of relapses and recurrences, in a recent review, Belsher and Costello (1988) noted that around 20% of depressed patients relapse at 2 months postrecovery, increasing to 30% at 6 months, and stabilizing at about 50% relapse within two years. Much of the major work in this area was done by Keller and colleagues, who reported that by five years, 76% of patients in their NIMH sample had experienced a recurrence (Keller, 1988). Likelihood of relapse increases with number of prior episodes; Keller and colleagues (Keller et al., 1982, 1983) indicated that individuals with three or more previous episodes may have a relapse rate as high as 40% within only 11 to 15 weeks after recovery. Rapid relapse was also observed by Frank, Kupfer, and Perel (1989) in their sample of unipolar patients selected for recurrent episodes. Following withdrawal from medication, about 70% of the patients experienced a relapse of depression within about 6 months, and by the end of the 18 months of follow-up less than 20% remained well. Interestingly, in contrast, those recurrent-episode patients who were assigned to interpersonal psychotherapy administered once per month during the maintenance phase had significantly better outcomes with lower rates of recurrence. No clinical or demographic features of the patients significantly predicted outcome.

The patterns suggest that the period immediately after recovery is the highest risk period for relapse (Keller, 1988). Most studies indicate that the longer persons remain symptom-free, the less likely they are to relapse (Belsher & Costello, 1988; Keller, 1988). Also, those with more previous episodes have higher probabilities of recurrence (Belsher & Costello, 1988; Keller, 1988). This is a version of one of the strongest findings in research on depression: the best predictor of future depression is past depression. Research that explicates why this occurs will make an enormous practical and theoretical contribution.

Among the predictors of relapse besides past history of depression, investigators have studied demographic, psychosocial, and clinical factors. There are rather conflicting results on the effects of age and gender on relapse (reviewed in Belsher & Costello, 1988). For example, Lewinsohn, Hoberman, and Rosenbaum (1988; see also Lewinsohn, Zeiss, & Duncan, 1989) found higher relapse rates in young women in a community sample, while previous studies often based on clinical samples did not find gender effects. One of the largest studies to date has recently been reported by Coryell, Endicott, and Keller (1991) who did a 6-year follow-up on several hundred nonpatient adults who had been part of the NIMH Collaborative Program on the Psychobiology of Depression. Among those with a history of major depression who relapsed during the follow-up period, there were no significant differences between men and women. However, younger adults (under 40) were substantially more likely to have recurrences than were older adults. Research on psychosocial factors such as stressful life events has been suggestive (e.g. Hammen, Ellicott, Gitlin, & Jamison, 1989; Lewinsohn, Hoberman, & Rosenbaum, 1988) and will be discussed more fully in later chapters. Similarly, the influence of family members and lack of supportive relationships on relapse seems to be a significant determinant of course of disorder (e.g. Hooley, Orley, & Teasdale, 1986; see also Swindle, Cronkite, & Moos, 1989) and will be explored more fully in later chapters.

Finally, the clinical condition termed "double depression" appears to have a negative effect on the course of disorder. Defined as the superimposing of a major depressive episode on a preexisting dysthymic disorder, Keller et al. (1983) found that 25% of several hundred patients followed at NIMH displayed this pattern. Although such individuals were more likely to recover from their major depressive episode within two years compared to those with major depression alone, they had higher relapse rates, and relapsed faster. Also, nearly 60% remained chronically symptomatic even after recovery from the major depressive episode (Hirschfeld, 1984; Keller, 1988).

In addition to the higher rate of recurrence among double depressives, it appears that a history of nonaffective disorders such as anxiety and substance use disorders, along with depression, increases the risk for depression relapse. Coryell, Endicott, and Keller (1991) found that nearly one-half of nonpatients who had had previous depression and a history of nonaffective disorder, experienced a relapse in the 6-year follow-up.

Chronicity of symptoms

Depending on the level of severity of symptoms and whether they meet diagnostic criteria, it has been estimated that chronic depressive symptoms occur in at least 25% of cases (e.g. Depue & Monroe, 1986). As noted earlier in a discussion of subtypes of chronic depression, such cases may take various forms ranging from early onset dysthymia to failure to recover from an episode of major depression. In their longitudinal study of patients, Keller, Lavori, Rice, Coryell, and Hirschfeld (1986) found that about 20% of patients with major depressive episode failed to recover from a recurrent episode following initial recovery from the index episode. Over time, this led to a cumulative rate of 30% of chronicity in their sample. Sounding a somewhat more positive note in a recent study, however, Coryell, Endicott, and Keller (1990) reported that three-quarters of patients with chronic affective disorders (including both unipolar and bipolar conditions without remission for at least two years) eventually recovered during a 5-year follow-up. Nonchronic patients recovered much more quickly (3/4 recovered by 50 weeks), than did chronic patients (3/4 recovered by 190 weeks [4 years]). Predictors of eventual recovery, not surprisingly, included better previous impairment of functioning and less severe depression.

In the Medical Outcomes Study, a follow-up of individuals assessed for depression in general medical practices and mental health services found substantial rates of continuing (or at least intermittent) symptoms one year later (Burnam, Wells, & Hays, 1990), although the rates were not reported as diagnoses as such. Of particular interest was the observation that not only did the diagnosed individuals have a high likelihood of a period of depression in the follow-up year, but so did the subclinically depressed individuals. For instance, both those with prior major depression, as well as those with subclinical symptoms with a history of past depression, reported an average of around 8 weeks of symptoms during the follow-up year.

Investigators who have examined the correlates and predictors of chronicity of depression have generally studied treated samples. Clinical features of the course of disorder that have predicted increased likelihood of chronicity include *duration* of previous major depressive episode but not the *number* or the *severity* of episodes (Akiskal, 1982; Keller et al, 1986). Older age at relapse and low family income predicted chronicity (Keller et al., 1986). According to Akiskal (1982), chronicity is associated with family history of affective disorder, and his clinical studies suggested that a variety of adverse stressful conditions also predict continuing symptoms. On the other hand, Hirschfeld, Klerman, Andreasen, Clayton, and Keller (1986) did not find differences between matched chronic and recovered depressed patients on stressful life events and role functioning, although they did find greater dissatisfaction with major roles among the chronic patients. It is important to note, however, that their measures of stressful life events were not particularly thorough. Hirschfeld et al. (1986) did find personality correlates of chronicity, reflecting poorer ego resilience and higher neuroticism, but they note that such differences may reflect current symptoms rather than premorbid functioning.

Klein et al. (1988) found that early-onset dysthymics tended to have significantly more episodes of major depression, poorer global functioning, more personality disorder and negative traits, and higher levels of chronic strain and perceived stress than did patients with nonchronic major depression. The authors interpret the findings to suggest that the chronic depression overlaps with character pathology, and with social maladjustment and chronic strain, and urge further research to explore the direction of effects in these related processes.

Important follow-up studies of the functioning and social context of treated depressed patients have been reported by Moos and colleagues. For instance, Billings and Moos (1985b) obtained one-year follow-up data on 424 patients who had been in treatment with an RDC diagnosis of major or minor depression. Approximately one-third remitted, another one-third remitted partially, and one-third were nonremitted. Social functioning and stressors returned to levels comparable to those of normal controls in the remitted group, while the nonremitted continued to show high levels of stressors and reduced social resources. At the 4-year follow-up, Swindle, Cronkite, and Moos (1989) found continuing improvement, although noting that most improvement occurred during the first year, and that previous symptom levels continued to be a strong predictor of subsequent symptoms. Stressors, coping, and resources were associated with symptom levels, while stable stressful conditions such as medical problems and family conflict consistently predicted poor long-term outcome. In later chapters, we will present a fuller discussion of the contribution of stressful conditions to course of depression.

Interestingly, one of the predictors of chronicity is inadequate treatment. Both Berti Ceroni, Neri, and Pezzoli (1984) and Keller et al. (1986) found that a substantial subset of chronic major depressed patients were not treated earlier in their histories of disorder. They speculate that the course might have been different had early vigorous intervention been applied.

Because the above studies were based largely on clinical samples, their generalizability is unknown (since the great majority of diagnosable conditions of depressed people go untreated). Thus, it is useful to turn to the ECA study of a large probability sample of community residents. Sargeant, Bruce, Florio, and Weissman (1990) examined the one-year outcomes of 423 individuals who received a diagnosis of major depressive episode at the initial interviews. It was not possible using the methods of the epidemiological survey to separate those who had chronic unremitting symptoms from those whose current depression represented a relapse. However, 23.6% of the sample met criteria for major depression at the follow-up. Overall, women had higher rates of "persistent" depression (25.4%) than men did (17.1%) although the effect was not statistically significant. Women above the age of 30 were significantly more likely to have persistent depression than younger women, but for men age did not affect rates. The highest rates of persistence also varied by other demographic characteristics: women who were divorced, widowed, or separated, and women with lower levels of education, were most likely to have persistent depression. In terms of clinical predictors, indicators of more severe histories such as higher numbers of episodes and longer or more severe episodes, were associated with persistent depression. The authors note that the clinical factors tended to be stronger predictors than the socio-demographic factors, but that at best only moderate predictability was obtained. They urge further consideration of genetic loading, personality, and social environment factors.

Other outcomes in the course of disorder

There are two additional features of depression that ought to be noted. One concerns the association between health/mortality and depression, and the other concerns the question of whether depression causes psychological "scars". Apart from the debilitating consequences of the depression itself, it may also be a life-threatening disorder. Certainly in the sense of suicide, depression does claim lives, representing a considerable risk factor for suicide. Among psychiatric patients who commit suicide, depression is the most common diagnosis (Hirschfeld & Davidson, 1988). Brent, Kupfer, Bromet, and Dew (1988) indicated that psychological autopsy studies have reported that between 40 and 70% of suicide victims had an affective disorder (both bipolar and unipolar). Follow-up studies of patients with affective disorder found that 10–15% go on to commit suicide (Brent et al., 1988). Although there are a variety of predictors of suicidality (see Brent et al., 1988; Hirschfeld & Davidson, 1988), the psychological construct of *hopelessness*, itself often a symptom of the depression syndrome, is particularly associated with suicidal thinking and completed suicide (e.g., Beck, Steer, Kovacs, & Garrison, 1985).

Besides suicide, depression is also associated with increased mortality due to medical conditions and accidents (Tsuang & Simpson, 1985). A community study of individuals who were followed for 16 years indicated a ratio of 1.5 deaths in depressed compared to nondepressed individuals, especially for depressed men. These differences were observed even after the effects of age and baseline physical disorders were controlled, and appeared to be consequences of medical causes as well as "unnatural" deaths (Murphy, Monson, Olivier, Sobol, & Leighton, 1987). It might be speculated that depression interferes with medically ill individuals' ability or willingness to follow health regimens or to seek medical treatment. It is also possible that depression impairs immunological functioning directly, affecting depressed peoples' resistance to certain illnesses. Although psychoneuroimmunology is in its relative infancy and studies yield somewhat inconsistent results, recent research suggests a possible link between depressed and altered immunological functioning in at least some subtypes of depression (e.g. Schleifer, Keller, Bond, Cohen, & Stein, 1989).

Another possible consequence of depression is that major episodes leave "scars" that may impair subsequent functioning. There is little doubt, based on clinical observations, that individuals who have experienced a significant major episode of depression not only become depressed about their depression, but express fears of a recurrence. Such fears may sometimes lead to avoidant or cautious behaviors intended to forestall such outcomes, or at least cause worry and dread. Lewinsohn and colleagues have attempted to test a version of the "scar" hypothesis. Since past depression is a strong predictor of recurrence, Rohde, Lewinsohn, and Seeley (1990) pursued the question of whether formerly depressed people have distinguishing characteristics that contribute to increased vulnerability, and whether the marker is present after the first episode but not before. In a community sample of older residents aged 50 years or more, a group of 49 persons was identified who developed their first episode of depression between two assessment points in a longitudinal study. While numerous variables distinguished currently-depressed from nondepressed comparisons, few differences emerged between recovered depressed individuals and the nondepressed group. It seemed that the formerly depressed tended to view themselves as less socially skilled and as having poorer health, but the investigators suggest that these differences stemmed from negative self-appraisal rather than from objective indicators of functioning. Despite the overall lack of support for the "scar" hypothesis, Rohde, Lewinsohn, and Seeley (1990) caution that the results may not be generalizable to younger populations or to those whose onsets of depression are at younger ages. Also, the current sample of recovered depressives had experienced only a single episode. It will be important to pursue these questions in different samples. An important point to underscore is the idea that those factors that may contribute to recurrence of depression might be different from those that instigate a first episode.

IMPLICATIONS FOR THEORIES OF DEPRESSION

The brief review of the clinical features and distributions of depressive disorders presented in this chapter is intended to identify several realities about depression that any effective theory needs to be able to account for. The following is a summary and discussion of the central findings about unipolar depression.

1. *The continuity between mild and severe symptoms of depression, or between elevated symptoms and clinically diagnosable conditions, is questionable.* Duration of symptoms is an important factor in determining whether symptoms will have similar features compared to diagnosable conditions, but sheer elevation of scores is relatively uninformative in attempting to generalize to clinical conditions. Low-grade but persisting depressive symptoms may indeed cause impairment of functioning (e.g. Wells et al., 1989; Burnam, Wells, & Hays 1990). Nevertheless, low-grade symptoms may or may not be specific to depression, and may instead reflect negative affectivity or demoralization indicating emotional distress. Such conditions could have different correlates and predictors compared to clinical depression.

2. *Onset (first episodes) of depressive disorders may have different predictors and vulnerability factors than recurrent episodes.* What may precipitate a depression in a never-before depressed person may be very different from an episode of depression in someone with previous episodes (e.g. Lewinsohn, Hoberman, & Rosenbaum, 1988). There is some suggestion that new onsets are relatively rare, and that much observed depression results from recurrence of episodes or from chronic symptomatology (e.g. Depue & Monroe, 1986). It has often been argued that researchers need to particularize their theories to specific aspects of the course of disorder (e.g Depue & Monroe, 1986; Hammen et al., 1986).

3. *The best predictor of depression is past depression.* As Lewinsohn, Hoberman, and Rosenbaum (1988) and others have found, depression predicts depression. Therefore, further understanding of this phenomenon would serve practical and theoretical goals. Past depression may not only signal vulnerability that continues to operate under provoking conditions, but also may alter the person's life in negative ways. "Scars" that reflect subjective fears and defensive behaviors regarding relapses, continuing low-grade symptoms, recurrences that disrupt functioning, and stressors inadequately dealt with, may all contribute to further depression.

4. *For the majority of people with clinically diagnosable depression, it is*

a recurrent, and sometimes chronic, disorder. Not only does this reality differ somewhat from previous clinical lore, but also it has numerous implications—for treatment, for families of depressed persons, and for researchers. It definitely implies the need to understand depression as a dynamic process, occurring over time and in a context of mutually influential processes, and underscores the likelihood, as noted above, that what affects recurrences of depression may differ from what originally provoked an episode. It also suggests that samples including some with first onset or single episodes along with subjects with multiple episodes, are impossibly heterogeneous and may obstruct progress in research outcomes.

5. *Depression affects lives.* This most basic and obvious of principles is actually an indicator of major differences in viewpoints between a medical model perspective on depression and psychosocial formulations. If depression is a disease, then what goes on *within* the person is the major focus, and environmental factors are considered epiphenomena. In contrast, a psychological perspective sees depression as a disorder that affects the way people think about themselves, their worlds, and their futures, in turn affecting their behaviors. Thus, a depressed person who thinks about her depression and about her life, instigates (or fails to instigate) coping mechanisms including responses that elicit reactions from others. The depression-coping responses may set in motion events that reduce symptoms, or that create stressful conditions that may exacerbate or prolong symptoms. The work and social context of the depressed person are thus inextricably involved in the understanding of the disorder, its course, and outcome.

6. *Depression is a singular term for heterogeneous disorders.* A unitary approach positing a single theory for a single disorder is likely to be misleading. There are probably either different disorders with different causative and risk factors, or different expressions of underlying disorders that may be differentially affected by aspects of the person, the context, and the psychiatric history. Thus, even when samples are selected for similarity of symptom manifestations, outcomes may be modified by differences in prior course of disorder, or in current environmental context. Thus, differentiated theories with clear limits in generalizability ought to be the goal of researchers, and efforts to characterize meaningful subgroups would be most welcome.

7. *Complicating the understanding of depressive disorders is their high degree of overlap with other psychiatric conditions.* Theories about depression must take pains to demonstrate that they really are about depression, rather than about nonspecific emotional distress, or anxiety, or personality disorders with depressive symptoms. Similarly, research on other topics in psychopathology, such as the influence of parental disorder on children, needs to determine what role in the parent-child interactions is played by

depressive symptoms that occur in the presence of another disorder that might otherwise be erroneously attributed to the other disorder.

8. *There are important demographic trends in sex differences and age of onset, that need to be explained.* Why are women at greater risk for depression (or for recurrence)? Is the gender gap narrowing, and why? What is going on that appears to contribute to more depression in adolescents and young adults than ever before, and what are the implications of such trends? As we shall see, a particular implication of demographic findings about risk factors for depression is that women of child-bearing age are at particular risk, and that depression in women is likely to have very negative effects on their children. Children who are depressed may be especially likely to have a pernicious course of disorder that disrupts their acquisition of skills and problem-solving abilities—creating a new generation of young depressives.

9. *There are various high-risk populations with respect to depression.* These may include the young, women, those with prior episodes, families of depressed adults, and others. It is important to expand research protocols beyond treatment-seeking samples, to include such high-risk groups and other community samples. Considerable work is needed to clarify the processes that contribute to risk and resilience. Enormously important strides have been made in treating clinical depressions, and this work needs to be expanded to include the development of interventions that can help prevent recurrence of depression in vulnerable individuals.

Chapter 2

Child and Adolescent Depression: Features and Correlates

Until only a few years ago there were several prevailing myths about childhood depression: it is rare if it exists at all; it is transitory; it is a developmentally normal stage; if it exists it is "masked" instead of directly expressed. Psychoanalytic conceptions of depression assumed that since superego development is incomplete before adolescence, children lack the intrapsychic capability to experience depression. A variant of this approach suggested that children do not express depressive symptoms directly, but rather it is "masked" as the presentation of other "depression equivalents" such as conduct problems and behavior disorders, somatic complaints, and school problems.

Countering these earlier assumptions, however, clinical observations increasingly made it clear that children exhibited the essential features of the adult depression syndrome, that it could be diagnosed using adult criteria with age-specific modifications, and that even when a behavior disorder might be the more obvious presenting problem, the clinical syndrome of depression is commonly detectable through the application of adult criteria (e.g. Carlson & Cantwell, 1980; Cytryn, McKnew, & Bunney, 1980; Kashani, Husain, Shekim, Hodges, Cytryn, & McKnew, 1981). Moreover, although individual symptoms of the depression syndrome may be developmentally common, most current investigators disagree with the position of Lefkowitz and Burton (1978) that evidence for early childhood depression is "insufficient and insubstantial."

In the sections to follow, we first present information on the prevalence and characteristics of childhood and adolescent depression, including the well-known issues of comorbid conditions, and the emergence of increased rates of disorder and sex differences in adolescence. The relatively scant information on course of disorder and its continuity with adult depression is also reviewed. In the second half of the chapter the psychosocial correlates and predictors of childhood and adolescent depression are reviewed, including family and social, life stress, and cognitive factors.

FEATURES AND COURSE OF DEPRESSION IN CHILDREN AND ADOLESCENTS

Criteria for diagnosing depression

DSM-III-R criteria for adults are used to diagnose major depressive episode and dysthymic disorder in children. There are age-specific modifications to these criteria that are recommended, however, and we shall review these modifications in a later section on phenomenology related to age. Also, the duration criterion is one year, instead of two, for diagnosis of dysthymic disorder in children and adolescents.

Incidence and characteristics of depression in children

Studies have attempted to identify the frequency of occurrence of depressive symptoms and diagnostic syndromes in child samples in the community, and in treatment-referred children. While the former kinds of investigations would be particularly informative about the incidence and prevalence of depressive disorders in youngsters, such studies have been limited in size and scope. Unlike the adult counterpart Epidemiological Catchment Area studies that include only those above age 18, there are currently no comparable large-scale surveys of children, although such studies are underway. Nevertheless, limited community surveys, supplemented by samples in treatment, paint a fairly consistent picture: depression syndromes occur but are relatively rare in preschoolers, increase somewhat in preadolescents, and then rise sharply in adolescence.

Preschool children

Occasional clinical case studies, Spitz' (1946) observations of the despair and apathy (anaclitic depression) of institutionalized infants, and Bowlby's reports of a protest-despair-detachment pattern observed in toddlers admitted to hospitals or residential nurseries (Bowlby, 1969, 1978), would seem to suggest that depression occurs even in babies. However, Rutter (1986) points out that such infant reactions appear to be a "natural" response to severe separations and, in most cases, infants and children recover rapidly when returned to their families. It is unclear, therefore, that such patterns should be considered depressive disorders. It is also possible that the children's apparent apathy, difficulties in sleeping and eating, and other symptoms may reflect developmental retardation due to prolonged lack of stimulation in adverse settings. Thus, investigators generally prefer not to label such reactions occurring in infancy as depression.

For youngsters over the age of two or three, however, there is evidence of diagnosable depression using adult criteria. The condition is rare, however, occurring in less than 1% of the general population. Kashani, Holcomb, and Orvaschel (1986) gathered ratings of 109 children enrolled in two nursery schools from parents, teachers, and observers. They found that nine of the children met criteria for depressive disorders based on the DSM-III, and only one received a diagnosis of major depressive disorder from a child psychiatrist. Many of the children reported some sadness or other depressive symptoms, but not at sufficient levels to warrant clinical concern. A similar low rate of less than 1% of diagnosable depressive disorders in preschoolers was found in an extensive study of 1000 children referred to a child development unit for evaluation (Kashani & Carlson, 1987). In young children the common symptoms of depression include irritability, apathy, physical symptoms and somatic complaints, psychomotor agitation, and crying.

Middle childhood (6–12)

Surveys of community samples indicate that around 2% of school-age children meet criteria for diagnosable major depression or dysthymic disorder. Kashani and Simonds (1979) used DSM-III criteria to evaluate 103 children randomly selected from the community, and found only two children who were diagnosable (1.9%), although 17.4% of the sample displayed sad affect along with other symptoms of depression such as somatic complaints, overactivity and restlessness, low self-esteem, and school refusal. The authors note that this figure is similar to the 15% rate of the adult population that is estimated to experience significant symptoms of depression during any given year.

The most extensive community survey available to date is the New Zealand representative sample of 792 children assessed at age 11 (Anderson et al., 1987), based on the DISC-C structured interview. Major depression or dysthymic disorder were relatively infrequent, occurring in 1.8% of the children. The major US survey available on children's psychiatric disorders was based on 789 7–11-year-old children seen by their pediatricians in a Health Maintenance Organization (Costello, Costello, Edelbrock, Burns et al., 1988). Parents and doctors completed screening questionnaires and a subgroup of children and their parents were interviewed. Based on either parent or child report, the prevalence of major depression was 0.4%, and 1.3% for dysthymic disorder.

Preadolescent children in *treatment* settings have been reported to meet DSM-III criteria for depression at the rate of 15% (Kazdin, French, Unis, & Esveldt-Dawson, 1983) and 13% (Kashani, Cantwell, Shekim, & Reid, 1982). Some studies found that the rate of clinical depression in treated samples is even higher. In their classic "unmasking masked depression" study, Carlson and Cantwell (1980) found that 28% of inpatient children met criteria for a depressive disorder. Their sample included children between ages 7–17, however, and it is unclear what the rate would be for the preadolescent subgroup alone.

Adolescent depression

There are two major features of depression that are unique in the adolescent years. One is the substantial increase in rates of both depressive symptoms and diagnosable conditions, and the other is the emergence of distinct gender differences with girls having much higher rates of disorder than boys. For instance, it is estimated that the prevalence of depression in early to middle-adolescence is 2.6% in boys and 10.2% in girls (Kutcher & Marton, 1989).

Virtually all studies of rates of both symptoms and diagnosable depression in community samples have concluded that the rates are much higher for adolescents than children. For instance, the Kashani, Rosenberg, and Reid (1989) study of 8-, 12-, and 17-year-olds in the community found that the rate of depressive diagnoses was four times higher for the 17-year-olds than for the other two groups, and the older age group as a whole reported significantly more symptoms. Similar reports from the Isle of Wight study also indicated a three-fold increase in rates of diagnosable depression from age 10 to age 14–15 (Rutter, 1986).

In epidemiological surveys, the rates of major depression and dysthymia in teenagers resemble those of adults. Kashani et al. (1987) selected a stratified random sample of 14–16-year-olds in the community for systematic interviewing. They found that the prevalence of major depressive disorder was 4.7 and 3.3% for dysthymic disorder. Two larger scale surveys report similar rates. Lewinsohn and his colleagues have reported depression prevalence data for a community sample based on stratified sampling of youngsters in grades 9–12 in Oregon (Lewinsohn, Hops, Roberts, & Seeley, 1988). The point prevalence of major depression was 2.9% (with a lifetime prevalence reported of 20.3%), and 0.5% for dysthymia (3.3% lifetime). Whitaker, Johnson, Shaffer, Rapoport, Kalikow et al. (1990) screened 5596 students in grades 9–12 (ages 14–17), followed by diagnostic evaluations for high-scoring youngsters. They found lifetime rates of major depression of 4.5% for girls and 2.9% for boys, with 5.3% dysthymic disorder in girls and 2.3% for boys.

In addition to the large increase in rates of diagnosable depression in adolescence, there is an extraordinary level of self-reported depression and unhappiness in the teenage years. In his Isle of Wight study, Rutter (1986) found that depressed feelings were reported by 10–12% of the 10–11-year-old boys, but jumped to 40% among the same youngsters when they were 14–15. Kashani et al. (1987) found that 48% of their sample of teenagers reported appreciable misery. Similarly, using self-report questionnaires such as the Beck Depression Inventory, high rates of adolescents achieving a score of 16 or above (moderate depression) have been obtained. For instance, Albert and Beck (1975) reported a 33% prevalence, while more recently, Roberts, Lewinsohn, and Seeley (1991) reported that 27.7% scored in the mild-to-severe range. Using the CES-D scale, Roberts, Lewisohn, and Seeley (1991) found that 48% of the sample scored in the mild-to-moderate depression range. Roberts, Andrews, Lewinsohn, and Hops (1990) surveyed approximately 2000 students in grades 9–12 in Oregon and found that 46% of boys and 59% of girls scored 16 or above on the CES-D; such a cutpoint typically identifies 16–20% of adult populations.

Allgood-Merten, Lewinsohn, and Hops (1990) note that the rates of elevated self-reported depression scores and clinical diagnoses did not appear to increase significantly between ages 14–19 in their community sample. This suggests that the great jump in depression rates from childhood to adulthood may occur in the early adolescent years. Indeed, the authors speculate that grades 5–8 should be studied more intensively since experience during this transitional period may shed light on both the increased rates of depression and the gender differences that emerge.

Added to the high rates of reported distress and prevalence rates that are comparable to those of adults, is the apparent increase in depression in adolescents that has occurred in recent birth cohorts (reviewed in Klerman & Weissman, 1989). Rates of depression among persons born since 1950 have been much higher than in those born earlier, and it is unlikely that such cohort effects are due simply to methodological artifacts such as age differences in recollection or different psychological awareness in different cohorts.

The other major characteristic of adolescent depression is the clear emergence of the sex difference patterns that are typical of adult depression. While studies of *preadolescent* samples typically find either no sex differences or relative elevations in boys' rates of depression (e.g. Anderson et al., 1987), teenage girls are diagnosed and report symptoms of depression at two or three times the rate of boys. Rutter (1986, 1989) reported marked increases in girls' rates of depression compared to boys' rates in the Isle of Wight community study. Kandel and Davies (1982) reported higher rates of depressive symptoms in adolescent girls compared to boys—rates that persisted into early adulthood (Kandel & Davies, 1986). Kashani et al. (1987) found that among the community 14–16-year-olds they studied, 10 girls and only 2 boys met criteria for depressive disorders. Lewinsohn et al. (1988) found that girls had more than twice the rates of major depressive disorder, both currently and lifetime, than did boys. Girls also had significantly higher CES-D and BDI scores than did boys (see also Roberts et al., 1990). Petersen, Sarigiani, and Kennedy (1991) followed over 300 adolescents longitudinally, and found that the girls showed significantly more depressed affect than did boys by grade 12, and that the difference began to emerge about the eighth grade (age 13), increasing over time. They also found sharp increases in reported rates of past depressive periods lasting at least two weeks: 28% of the girls reported such periods in grades 6–8, compared to 59% by grades 9–12. The comparable rates for boys were 25 and 40%.

Several investigators have noted the high rates of self-reported symptoms in adolescents, and have wondered whether they represent "overreporting," suggesting that adolescent depression is an artifact possibly due to "adolescent turmoil." Data support the conclusion, however, that self-report is related to actual clinical condition. Shain, Naylor, and Alessi (1990) found high, significant correlations between self-reported depression scores on several instruments and clinician ratings of severity of symptoms, in an inpatient sample of adolescents. Correlations were especially high for girls' scores. Allgood-Merten, Lewinsohn, and Hops (1990) argue that adolescents do not show a generalized tendency to report more symptoms of all kinds and that symptoms of depression possibly truly reflect demoralization and negative cognitions. Moreover, rather than simply indicating momentary distress, elevated symptom reports appear to be a risk factor for depressive diagnoses (e.g. Lewinsohn, Hoberman, & Rosenbaum, 1988). High CES-D or BDI scores in adolescents are reasonably sensitive and specific for diagnoses (Roberts et al., 1990; Roberts, Lewinsohn, & Seeley, 1991), and may predict later hospitalization or treatment-seeking in adulthood (Kandel & Davies, 1986). Overall, therefore, the high rates of self-reported distress are reasonably accurate predictors of actual clinical status, and not merely transitory signs of teenage turmoil.

Age differences in the phenomenology of depression

The DSM-III-R criteria, as noted, can be applied to the diagnosis of depression in children. Nevertheless, there are aspects of the presentation of depression that appear to differ somewhat according to the child's developmental status, and it is important to consider normal developmental processes in the study of childhood depression (Digdon & Gotlib, 1985). For instance, preschool children are less equipped cognitively to report on the subjective experiences of depression. Instead, physical and somatic symptoms are relatively frequent and tend to decline with age. Indeed, Kashani and Carlson (1987) suggest that physically unjustified or exaggerated complaints may develop against a background of misery and distress that are not directly reported (and of which parents are likely to be unaware). Also, the Kashani, Holcomb, and Orvaschel (1986) study of children in nursery schools found that the depressed children showed high levels of irritability and anger—not depression—and they were apathetic, disinterested, and uncooperative.

Kashani, Rosenberg, and Reid (1989) specifically compared the symptoms in a community cohort of 8-, 12-, and 17-year-olds. On the semistructured Child Assessment Schedule for depression, children's overall levels of symptoms increased with age, while self-reported questionnaire scores did not. Several specific symptoms increased with age: being tired, not caring whether they hurt themselves, agitation when sad, and irritability. Only one item, crying, decreased in frequency with age. Regression analyses were computed to determine which self-report items on a depression scale and the Hopelessness Scale contributed to the interviewers' assessments of depression for the different age groups. Whereas depression in 8-year-olds was associated with withdrawal and pessimism, in 12-year-olds it was associated with pessimism and physical symptoms (not sleeping well, stomach aches, poor appetite). In the 17-year-old group, depressive symptoms were associated with having horrible dreams and suicidal ideation.

Carlson and Kashani (1988) presented a type of meta-analysis of depressive symptoms in clinic-referred individuals based on four different samples of different ages (preschool, preadolescent, adolescent, and adult). Although there are significant limitations of such comparisons, such as not using the same instruments or precisely the same criteria, the authors argued that the investigators obtained basically comparable RDC data. They found that several symptoms increased with age: anhedonia, diurnal variation, hopelessness, psychomotor retardation, and delusions. Several others decreased with age: depressed appearance, low self-esteem, somatic complaints, and hallucinations. Other symptoms tended to have a curvilinear (e.g. agitation) or nonspecific (e.g. suicidal ideation) relation to age. The authors conclude that although there are somewhat specific developmental modifications, in general severe depression presents the same picture regardless of age.

Ryan, Puig-Antich, Ambrosini, Rabinovich, Robinson et al. (1987) essentially agree with the conclusion of Carlson and Kashani (1988), based on their analyses of the symptoms of clinic-referred children (n = 95) and adolescents (n = 92). Although there were relatively few significant differences in the two age groups, the children did show greater depressed appearance, somatic complaints, psychomotor agitation, and separation anxiety, while the adolescents demonstrated greater anhedonia, hopelessness, hypersomnia and weight change, and drug/alcohol use. Ryan et al. (1987) concluded that the similarities outweighed the differences across this age range, but suggested several minor modifications of use of

DSM-III-R criteria to take into account developmental stage. For instance, irritability/anger might be considered equivalent to sad/depressive mood, and low self-esteem might be equivalent to excessive guilt. Also, somatic complaints, social withdrawal, and hopelessness are common in children and adolescents with major depressive disorder and ought to be included in the diagnostic criteria.

In their effort to explore sex differences in adolescent depression, Allgood-Merten, Lewinsohn, and Hops (1990) hypothesized that body image, an important part of self-esteem, may be a source of particular vulnerability for young women and an important aspect of adolescent female depression. They found significant sex differences in body image, and determined that negative body image is a particularly salient aspect of self-esteem for girls, and self-esteem is directly associated with depression. Further discussions of the possible causes of sex differences will be presented in the sections on psychosocial correlates of depression in children and adolescents.

Finally, comparison of adolescent and adult diagnosed depressed patients suggests few differences in symptom presentation. Carlson and Strober (1983) compared symptoms in adolescent inpatients to reported symptoms in other samples of adolescents and adults, and found very similar profiles. Friedman, Hurt, Clarkin, Corn, and Aronoff (1983) compared adolescent and young adult depressed inpatients, and found them to be very similar in the display of affective and cognitive symptoms. Also, these authors reported similar rates of mood-congruent psychotic features. Carlson and Strober also reported that depressed adolescent and adult inpatients showed similar rates of mood-congruent psychotic symptoms. In contrast, Chambers, Puig-Antich, Tabrizi, and Davies (1982) had found that preadolescent depressed children referred for treatment were far more likely to have auditory hallucinations than in adolescent or adult samples, while delusions were less prevalent than in adults (but comparable to adolescents).

Depressive subtypes that are common in adults are also found in children, including psychotic depression (e.g. Ryan et al., 1987) and melancholic depression (Strober, Green, & Carlson, 1981). It is also important to note that a percentage of children and adolescents initially diagnosed as unipolar depression sometimes go on to develop a bipolar course. For instance, Strober, Lampert, Schmidt, and Morrell (in press) found that 28% of depressed adolescent inpatients with psychotic symptoms displayed manic or hypomanic switches during a two-year follow-up.

Apart from formal diagnostic symptoms of depressive syndromes, numerous studies have examined cognitive and biological markers of depression in children, adolescents, and adults. It is apparent that cognitions such as negative self-concepts and self-schemas, depressive attribution styles, and other salient adult-based cognitive constructs appear to characterize the depression of children and adolescents, as they do adults (reviewed in Hammen, 1990). Nevertheless, it is important that such cognitions should not be assumed to operate in precisely the same ways or have the same meaning as those of adult depressives (Digdon & Gotlib, 1985). With respect to biological correlates of depression, certain biological markers thought to indicate depressive illnesses in adults have not consistently been found in younger samples (reviewed in Digdon & Gotlib, 1985). For instance, whereas Goetz, Puig-Antich, Ryan, Rabinovich, Ambrosini et al. (1987) failed to observe sleep patterns such as REM latencies that frequently characterize depressed adults in a sample of depressed adolescents, Emslie, Rush, Weinberg, Rintelmann, and Roffwarg (1990) did find REM latency differences between inpatient depressed children and age-matched controls. Emslie et al. noted, however, that the sleep patterns they observed were similar but not identical to those of depressed adults. Similarly, the typical elevated cortisol rates characteristic of hospitalized depressed adults have not been observed in depressed children (Puig-Antich, Dahl, Ryan, Novacenko, Goetz et al., 1989). Also, it is well known that antidepressant medications are not as effective in children and adolescents as in adults, and the side effects are of great concern in younger samples.

Comorbidity

One of the recurring findings in childhood and adolescent psychopathology in general is the high rate of co-occurrence of disorders. For instance, in a large community survey in New Zealand, 11-year-old children were systematically assessed, and of those with a diagnosable condition, 55% occurred as combinations of two or more disorders (Anderson et al., 1987).

With respect to *depressive disorders*, comorbidity is the rule rather than the exception. Depression in youngsters most frequently occurs with conduct or oppositional disorders, anxiety disorders, and somewhat less often, attention deficit disorder, and in older samples, with eating disorders, and drug or alcohol abuse. In clinical samples, as Carlson and Cantwell (1980) noted, such additional diagnoses may often appear to "mask" the depression in the sense that the behavioral disturbances are usually the ones that come to parental attention and result in treatment referral. One such disruptive coexisting diagnosis is conduct disorder, frequently found in clinical samples. In his clinical samples of preadolescent children, Puig-Antich (1982) reported that 33% also had conduct disorder. In a somewhat overlapping sample of both children and adolescents Ryan et al. (1987) reported that at least mild conduct disorder symptoms were present in 38% of the children and in 25% of the adolescents, with more severe levels in 16% of the children and 11% of the adolescents.

In the Kovacs et al. (1984a) clinical sample of depressed children, 79% of those with major depressive disorder had concurrent psychiatric disorders, including 7% with conduct disorder; the dysthymic disorder sample had a rate of 11% conduct disorder, and 14% attention deficit disorder. Recently Cole and Carpentieri (1990) found that even in a nonclinical community sample of children, symptoms of depression and conduct disorder overlap considerably. When method variance was controlled by using distinctly different assessment methods, 3.5% of the sample were dual problem children—a rate significantly higher than the probability of the two disorders occurring together by chance if independent. The authors speculate that such dual-diagnosis children appear to be at especially high risk for future academic, emotional, and behavioral problems.

Relatedly, depressed *adolescents* were found to have higher rates of illicit drug use (about 22%) and alcohol use or abuse (16%) than depressed children. In the Kashani et al. (1987) community survey of adolescent depression, all of the youth who met criteria for depression also had other diagnoses—50% oppositional and 33% conduct disorder, 25% alcohol abuse and 25% drug abuse. Keller, Beardslee, Lavori, Wunder, Dorer, & Samuelson (1988) found a 53% rate of coexisting disorders in their clinical sample of adolescents (conduct disorder, substance abuse, ADD, or anxiety). Based on their longitudinal follow-up of the sample, Keller et al. concluded that youngsters with nonaffective disorders concurrent with depression had a much more chronic course of depression. It should be noted that in most cases, the nonaffective disorder predated the onset of depression. These observations are also consistent with a large-scale community sample of adolescents, reported by Rohde, Lewinsohn, and Seeley (1991). These investigators found a rate of 42% comorbidity in their depressed youngsters, and typically the depression followed rather than preceded onset of the other disorder. Also, comorbidity was associated with greater frequency of suicidal behaviors and treatment-seeking, but did not affect the duration or severity of depression. In addition to studies of coexisting diagnoses in depressed children and adolescents, it is also apparent in studies of children of depressed parents that comorbidity of depression and additional diagnoses is common (e.g. see reviews in Hammen, 1991a; Weissman, 1988).

One of the most frequent types of coexisting illness in depressed children and adolescents is an anxiety disorder, commonly separation anxiety, overanxious disorder, severe phobia, or obsessive compulsive disorder— although the specific diagnosis is not always indicated. In their community sample of adolescents, Kashani et al. (1987) found that 75% of those diagnosed with depression had anxiety disorders, while Ryan et al. (1987) reported in a clinical sample that moderate to severe separation anxiety disorder occurred in 58% of the child and 37% of the adolescent depressed patients. There were also elevated rates of severe phobias, overanxious, and obsessive-compulsive disorder. The most extensive analysis of concurrent anxiety disorders has been reported by Kovacs et al. (1984a), who found anxiety disorder in 33% of the cases of major depressive disorder, and in 36% of the dysthymic disorder children. In a later report including additional children, Kovacs, Gatsonis, Paulauskas, and Richards (1989) found that 41% of the children had anxiety disorders during their index episode of depression. Notably, the investigators determined that most of the anxiety disorders had an onset between 9 and 11 years of age, and in two-thirds of the cases of major depression, the anxiety developed before the depression (the reverse was true for dysthymic disorder). Those who had comorbid anxiety disorders had an earlier age of onset of depression than those who did not; anxiety that antedated the major depressive episodes typically persisted beyond the episode of MDD. Kovacs and colleagues speculate about the possibility of depression and anxiety as a single disorder with anxiety temporally preceding, or whether they are distinct entities but the combination marks a particularly greater vulnerability and negative prognosis. Weissman, Leckman, Merikangas, Gammon, and Prusoff (1984) have suggested a possible relationship between depression and anxiety disorders, based on their findings of increased rates of anxiety disorders in children of parents with both depression and anxiety disorders (especially panic and agoraphobia).

Finally, it should be noted that only one study to date has systematically assessed and reported Axis II personality disorders in adolescents diagnosed with depression. Kutcher and Marton (1989) reported that depressed adolescents, compared with nondepressed diagnosed comparison youngsters, were more likely to meet criteria for an Axis II disorder, especially borderline and avoidant disorder. As we noted in Chapter 1, adult depression commonly coexists with Axis II disorders, so it is highly likely that depressed adolescent samples will also show such patterns.

Course of disorder in childhood and adolescent depression

Impairment of functioning in depressed youngsters

Depression clearly disrupts children's cognitive, interpersonal, and academic functioning. It is becoming increasingly apparent that depressed children and adolescents experience not only adult-like symptoms of depression, but also similar kinds of associations between interpersonal and role functioning difficulties and depressive symptoms. For example, academic difficulties or lower achievement are strongly correlated with depressive symptoms in community children (Cole, 1990; Nolen-Hoeksema,

Girgus, & Seligman, 1986); academically less competent children have more depressive symptoms (Blechman, McEnroe, Carella, & Audette, 1986). Forehand, Brody, Long, and Fauber (1988) similarly found that relatively more depressed adolescents had low grade point averages. Diagnosed depressed offspring of depressed mothers have more academic and school functioning difficulties compared with nondepressed children of normal mothers (e.g. Hammen, Adrian, Gordon, Burge, Jaenicke, & Hiroto, 1987; Anderson & Hammen, 1991a). Children with diagnoses of depression exhibited significant impairments in academic achievement and school behaviors (Puig-Antich, Lukens, Davies, Goetz, Brennan-Quattrock, & Todak, 1985a), although when recovered their performances improved significantly and did not differ from those of nonpsychiatric children (Puig-Antich et al., 1985b). Kandel and Davies (1986) found that adolescents who displayed higher rates of depressive symptoms were less likely to finish high school than nondepressed youngsters, and the depressed girls completed significantly fewer years of education than nondepressed girls. Moreover, work histories were relatively more impaired for the depressed adolescents in the nine-year period of follow-up study, especially with more unemployment for the males (Kandel & Davies, 1986).

The correlational nature of the designs and the relative paucity of longitudinal studies, especially of clinical samples, obscure the direction of effects in the link between school/work role functioning and depression. Nevertheless, it is likely true both that academic difficulties result in demoralization and dysphoria for children, and that depressive symptoms impair school and work achievement. Thus, a reciprocal relationship is highly likely, with the additional implication that early childhood academic difficulties may be especially pernicious, setting the stage for a downward spiral of poor performance and sustained dysphoria.

There are extensive data on the relation between children's depression and impairment of functioning in family, peer, and interpersonal spheres. We will review this information in a later section relevant to etiological models of children's depression. Finally, of course, suicidal thinking and behaviors are also common indicators of impairment in depressed children and adolescents (e.g. Kazdin et al., 1983).

Stability of depressive symptoms

Most of the sparse research on clinical course has come from longitudinal samples of children and adolescents in treatment, although certain studies of questionnaire-reported symptoms have also reported longitudinal course. However, before discussing such information it should be noted that a key characteristic of adult depression is also apparently true of children: past depression is a significant predictor of future depression.

With respect to symptoms reported on questionnaires, Garrison, Jackson, Marsteller, McKeown, and Addy (1990) administered the CES-D scale to 550 students three times in the seventh through ninth grades. The previous year's CES-D score accounted for between 12 and 20% of the total variance in current score. Repeated testings by Roberts et al. (1990, 1991) also confirm significant test-retest stability over one month (see also Seligman et al., 1984 and Tesiny & Lefkowitz, 1982). On the other hand, instability of elevated scores is also characteristic; while low scorers continue to be low scores over time, Garrison et al. (1990) found that only about 30% of those who scored at the highest level in one year had high scores the next. Roberts et al. (1990, 1991) also caution that self-report measures of symptoms yield volatile responses, reminding us that while they can serve a screening function adequately, they do not permit reliable identification of clinical cases.

Some information on depression stability comes from children of depressed parents who are thought to be at risk for depression. Three such studies have found that such children continue to report symptoms over time, even when parental depression improves (e.g., Billings & Moos, 1986; Lee & Gotlib, 1991a). Hammen, Burge, Burney, and Adrian (1990) observed that while there was considerable fluctuation in children's symptoms over a three-year follow-up, most who had symptoms initially continued to display them either intermittently or chronically.

Duration of episodes (time to recovery)

Only a handful of small-sample clinical studies are available to characterize course of disorder. Furthermore, as Keller et al. (1988) remind us, such studies by definition contain only the most seriously disturbed cases of unresolved symptoms for which treatment is sought. Kovacs et al. (1984a) followed 65 children (ages 8–13) who had been treated in outpatient facilities, and assessed their status five years after the index episode. They reported that many of the children experienced "double depression"—major depression superimposed on dysthymic disorder—and that the mean length of major depressive episodes was 32 weeks. The episodes were relatively persistent for many children, in that 41% were still depressed after one year, and 8% were still depressed at two years.

With respect to adolescent depression, Lewinsohn, Hoberman, and Rosenbaum's (1988) community survey (only 23% of those with diagnosable depression received treatment), found a somewhat shorter duration of major depressive episodes of 23 weeks. In contrast, Strober et al. (in press) reported that, in a clinical sample of inpatient adolescents, only 29% recovered by week 20, while two-thirds of the youngsters required more than 5 months to recover (mean of 27.5 weeks). Finally, Keller et al. (1988) reported duration data from a sample unique in composition, drawn from five different community or research samples including children of parents with affective disorders. The children were between the ages of 6 and 19. Of those who received a diagnosis of depression, 21% were still depressed at one year, and 10% at two years; while 24% of the youngsters were also diagnosed as dysthymic (all preceding the onset of major depression). Keller et al. observed that the course of disorder was more negative for youngsters whose depression was secondary to another nonaffective disorder, in that they took longer to recover than did those with primary depression.

Relapse and recurrence

Likelihood of relapse appears to be high for children with depression, as it is for adults. Kovacs et al. (1984a) reported that within one year of recovery, 26% of their child sample had a new episode, and 40% after two years. Kovacs et al. also reported a 72% risk of relapse within five years after the initial episode. Asarnow et al. (1988) followed child inpatients who had been diagnosed with major depression or dysthymic disorder for between one and six years. Fully 35% of the depressed children were rehospitalized within one year after discharge, and 45% within two years. The children with "double depression" had a greater probability of relapse. Garber, Kriss, Koch, and Lindholm (1988) followed up a sample of 20 formerly hospitalized youngsters approximately eight years after admission. Of the 11 who had originally been diagnosed as depressed, 7 of them subsequently had at least one episode of major depression, and 4 had several episodes. In the Ryan et al. (1987) sample of depressed children and adolescents, nearly half of both samples were found to have either chronic major depressive disorder or fluctuating MDD and dysthymia over the two-year period of observation. In the UCLA Family Stress Study of children of depressed mothers, Hammen et al. (1990a) found that ten offspring of unipolar depressed mothers had a major depressive episode, and of these, five had a recurrence during the follow-up period of up to three years. Finally, although additional data will be forthcoming from the Oregon adolescent study, at this point it has been reported that nearly 3% of the teenagers had had more than one episode of depression by the time of the study (Lewinsohn, Hops et al., 1988).

Age of onset

Obviously, sample selection determines the kinds of ages of onset reported for childhood depression. Nevertheless, many studies suggest that early adolescence or late childhood are characteristic times of development for first episodes of depression. For instance, Lewinsohn, Hoberman, and

Rosenbaum (1988) reported a mean age of 14.3 for major depressive disorder and 11.3 for dysthymic disorder in their community sample of adolescents. Kovacs et al. (1984a) indicated that their clinical samples had onsets of both disorders around age 11. These authors further indicated that age of onset is related to course of disorder, in that children with earlier onsets had a more protracted course of disorder.

It is interesting to note that studies of children of depressed parents appear to have earlier onset of depression than children not at similar risk. For instance, Weissman, Gammon, John, Merikangas, Warner et al (1987) found onset at 12 or 13 for children of depressed parents compared to 16 or 17 in the depressed children of normal parents. Hammen et al. (1990a) also found increasing probability of major depression onset after age 12, and the mean age of onset tended to be lower than for the comparison groups of bipolar and medically ill offspring (the normal group offspring had too few major depression onsets to compare). Weissman, Gammon, et al. (1987) suggest that among adult depressives, increased family loading for affective disorders was associated with earlier age of onset. Thus, the epidemiological studies that indicate relatively young ages of onset of depression in adult samples (e.g. Burke et al., 1990) might in fact obscure differences between those with family histories of depression and those without.

Clearly, the data available on course of disorder are sparse at best, and need to be supplemented with both community and clinical samples. Ironically, as Kovacs et al. (1984a) indicate, treatment does not seem to affect the outcome of childhood depression, so that even such samples may yield data representative of the natural course of disorder in severely ill populations. Despite the paucity of data, however, the conclusions are relatively consistent, suggesting that childhood onset of depression bodes ill for further symptoms and protracted course.

Continuity of depression from childhood to adulthood

Based on the above scant documentation, it appears that childhood depressions commonly recur—presumably from childhood into adolescence, or between early and later adolescence. What is now needed is further information on the continuity of such conditions into adulthood. There are two kinds of information to consider, one retrospectively evaluating age of onset of depression in adults, and the other presenting longitudinal studies of depressed children and adolescents into adulthood.

The most extensive retrospective analysis of age of onset of adult depression is based on the Epidemiological Catchment Area data (Burke et al., 1990). Nearly 1000 cases of unipolar depression were identified across various survey cites, and their ages of first onset were determined by interview. The median age of onset of major depressive disorder was 23 for women and 25 for men. However, for women there was an enormous peak onset in the 15–19-year-old interval, declining somewhat after that period; men's rates of onset also increased in the 15–19 period and in the 25–29-year range, then declined subsequently and never reached the same rates as those of women. The authors concluded that onset for major depression peaks at 15–19 years for women, and that the DSM-III-R should recognize a younger age of onset than it currently presents. These data do not address the specific issue of continuity of depression from adolescence to later episodes in adulthood. However, it is instructive to consider the community survey conducted by Lewinsohn, Hoberman, and Rosenbaum (1988), with the finding that most cases of major depression were actually relapses in persons with prior episodes—primarily young women. Thus, young women with prior episodes appear to be at high risk for recurrence, and it might be presumed that many had their first episodes as teenagers.

Actual longitudinal studies linking childhood or adolescent with adult depression are rare. Two studies have followed youngsters into adulthood. Kandel and Davies (1986) found that dysphoric feelings reported in adolescence were significant predictors of dysphoric feelings nine years later. Women who had reported such feelings earlier were more likely to be treated by mental health professionals and to have sought help at earlier ages than nondepressed adolescent women. Moreover, there were numerous indicators of impairment associated with early symptoms: school drop out, marital disruption and divorce (in females), and work disruption in men, and less close and satisfying relationships with parents.

In a second longitudinal study, Harrington, Fudge, Rutter, Pickles, and Hill (1990) followed children who had been treated clinically for depression. Recontacted an average of 18 years after treatment, the formerly depressed youth were found to have high rates of relapse, with 60% experiencing at least one recurrence of major depression during adulthood. They also had elevated rates of other diagnoses as well. Additionally, the small-scale follow-up study of adolescent depressed patients reported by Garber et al. (1988) also found that 7 of 11 had at least one recurrence of major depression during the eight-year period since discharge, and also had greater adjustment problems in various areas during the period.

Finally, Block, Gjerde, and Block (1991) have reported data from a longitudinal study of children retested at age 18. The 88 children studied in the Berkeley Growth Study since preschool ages were given the CES-D scale at age 18, and those with relatively elevated depression scores were compared on earlier personality testings with those who did not have elevated depression. There appeared to be several significant predictors from early childhood. Boys who later reported depression were seen as aggressive, self-aggrandizing, and undercontrolled since their early years.

On the other hand, girls who were depressive at age 18 were intropunitive, oversocialized, and overcontrolling. The gender differences in personality predictors were striking, and suggest that the forerunners of depressive symptoms may be different for the two sexes. It should be noted that the adolescents were not evaluated for clinical depression, so that the relationship of their elevated scores to diagnostic conditions is unknown.

Overall, despite the strong presumption that many adult depressions had early onset, and that depressed children are likely to have a pernicious course of disorder, the data on continuity of depression from childhood or adolescence into adulthood are very sparse, and longitudinal studies would be useful to pursue this issue.

PSYCHOSOCIAL CORRELATES OF DEPRESSION AND IMPLICATIONS FOR ETIOLOGY

As we noted in the previous discussion of children's impairment of functioning associated with depression, there is considerable evidence of a link between depressive symptoms and interpersonal difficulties. Since this work may be especially significant with respect to its implications for etiology and course of disorder, we review it in more detail here.

Peer relationships, interpersonal functioning, and depression

Community and experimental samples

Considerable research interest has recently been focused on the association between children's adjustment and quality of peer relationships, viewing the latter both as a consequence of psychiatric difficulties and as a contributor to further maladjustment (cf. Hartup, 1989). Many studies of community samples of children have indicated an association between depressive symptoms and lower social status (e.g. Blechman et al., 1986; Cole, 1991; Jacobsen, Lahey, & Strauss, 1983; Lefkowitz & Tesiny, 1985). However, social status is a heterogeneous construct such that low status may include both rejected and neglected children. Social rejection may be especially likely in children who display depression along with aggressive and conduct disorders suggesting that the latter, rather than depression as such, may be the source of rejection. Thus, children who are depressed-only may be less socially impaired than those depressed children with aggressive, conduct problems (e.g. Asarnow, 1988; Cole & Carpentieri, 1990), although such internalizing problems may nevertheless be associated with lower peer status (Kennedy, Spence, & Hensley, 1989; Strauss, Forehand, Smith, & Frame, 1986). Longitudinal data are sparse, but one study by Wierzbicki and McCabe (1988) found that parent- and self-reported lower levels of social skills were associated with both concurrent depression and depression one month later.

Other types of methodologies have also suggested a link between depression symptoms and relatively negative social functioning in community samples. For instance, Sacco and Graves (1984) found an association between impaired interpersonal problem-solving and depressive symptoms, although Mullins, Siegel, and Hodges (1985) did not find such a relation. In a laboratory study of children's responses to film depictions of depressed peers, Peterson, Mullins, and Ridley-Johnson (1985) found that children were more rejecting of such hypothetical peers, rating them as less likable and attractive. Interestingly, hypothetical peers whose depression could be attributed to highly stressful experiences were seen more positively than children whose depression was not attributable to external causes. Only one study was located that involved *observations* of relatively depressed community (nonpatient) children. Altmann and Gotlib (1988) found that while the relatively depressed children were likely to initiate activity and be approached by others, they were significantly more likely to spend time alone and to be more aggressive than were nondepressed children.

Wanting to spend time alone was also characteristic of both preadolescent and adolescent youngsters in a unique study that examined the ecology of depression by having nonclinically depressed and nondepressed fifth to eighth graders keep logs of their daily experiences—what they do, where they go, who they spend time with, and what they think about (Larson, Raffaelli, Richards, Ham, & Jewell, 1990). They were cued by electronic pagers to complete their logs when signalled, approximately seven times per day. Relatively depressed youngsters rated others as less friendly in all social contexts, and indicated wanting to be alone more often, especially in the family context. There were few differences overall in how the youngsters spent their time, except that depressed youth spent more time in their bedrooms and less time in public. Depressed boys in particular spent less time with friends, and both girls and boys who were depressed spent less time with sports activities. The authors suggest that social isolation for depressed boys and diminished interest and pleasure in family interactions are noteworthy patterns for further study. Data from the Larson et al. study are presented in Figure 2.1.

Studies of nonclinically depressed adolescents also indicate an association between social functioning difficulties and depressive symptoms. Buhrmester (1990) found that both self-rated and friend-rated lower social competence were significantly associated with scores on a

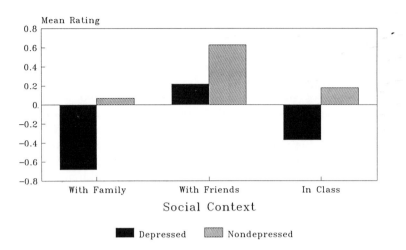

Figure 2.1 Perceived friendliness of others by social context. Source: adapted from Larson, Raffaelli, Richards, Ham, and Jewell (1990)

depression/anxiety factor. Hops, Lewinsohn, Andrews, and Roberts (1990) administered various self-report questionnaires regarding perceived social relations to high school students and found a significant association between depression and perceived social support (but not network size), and between depression and interpersonal sensitivity. In addition, the youngsters who were found to be stably depressed at two testings over a one-month period reported more interpersonal sensitivity.

Hodgens and McCoy (1989) found that junior-high school students who were rated as rejected-aggressive by peer nominations had higher CDI scores than did children in other groups. However, their depression scores did not differ from those of children in the other groups when items were removed that pertained to conduct problems and academic difficulties. Forehand et al. (1988) found that the relatively depressed adolescents in their study were rated lower on social competence by teachers, but only for those whose mothers were also relatively more depressed.

Patient samples of children and adolescents

There are relatively few studies of the social behaviors of clinically depressed youngsters. However, they do indicate some social difficulties. Armsden, McCauley, Greenberg, Burke, and Mitchell (1990) compared depressed adolescents with nonpsychiatric controls on perceived security of attachment with peers and parents. As predicted, the depressed youngsters reported less secure attachment to both peers and parents. Interestingly, depressed-resolved children had better perceived attachment than did children in the currently depressed group. Asarnow (1988) compared children hospitalized for externalizing disorders, for depression with externalizing disorders, and for depression only. She found that the depressed-only children were significantly higher on indices of social competence than were those with externalizing disorders. Asarnow noted that the depressed-only children may indeed have social problems compared with normal youngsters, but in comparison to those with externalizing disorders, they appear to fare much better. Preadolescent children with major depressive disorders were reported by interviewers and parents to have significant problems in social relations with parents, siblings, and friends, with less friend contact and more subject to teasing by peers (Puig-Antich et al., 1985a). Of particular importance, it was found that after recovery from the episode, although there was significant improvement compared to their previous social functioning, they continued to show deficits compared to normal children (Puig-Antich et al., 1985b). It should also be noted that on many of the initial indicators of social functioning, the children with major depression did not differ significantly from children with nondepressive emotional ("neurotic") disorders.

Commentary on social functioning

Although there is considerable information suggesting impairment of social functioning, there are far more questions than answers at this point. For instance, although it is likely that difficulties that impair peer relationships and social status are both symptoms of and contributors to dysphoria, little information exists to help identify the potentially etiological role of interpersonal difficulties. Longitudinal studies are needed to evaluate the temporal and possibly causal relationship between depression and social functioning. Another enormous gap is lack of specific information about what the social deficits consist of; few observational studies exist, and the questionnaire and interview data involve numerous constructs, from popularity to interpersonal problem-solving, to communication skills and friendship networks. What *are* the deficits, and importantly, how do they have an impact on the child's likelihood of displaying depression? Studies need to include not only overt behaviors, but also explorations of the social schemas of children that direct their expectations of social interactions and their scripts about appropriate behaviors, and their abilities to resolve problems in the social sphere. Finally, little information exists that clarifies what is *specific* to depression in youngsters, rather than characteristic of general difficulties that cut across boundaries of different behavioral and emotional disorders. There is certainly some evidence that aggressive and conduct disorders that coexist with depression may contribute to the peer difficulties experienced by these children, but the role of depression itself, or certain skill or attribute characteristics of depressed-only children, remains to be explored.

Family relationships and depression

Community samples of children and adolescents

Relatively little research has examined associations between depressive symptoms and family relationships in community samples, but the early such research found correlations between depressive symptoms and perceived rejection and negativity in the family environment (e.g. Lefkowitz & Tesiny, 1985; Kaslow, Rehm, & Siegel, 1984). One of the striking findings of the study by Larson et al. (1990) on the daily lives of relatively depressed children and adolescents was the extent of the youngsters' negative perceptions of their families. The relatively depressed children perceived their families as less friendly, and reported feelings of wanting to be alone when with their families. Garrison et al. (1990) found that young adolescent depressive symptoms were associated with reported lower family cohesion; however, ratings of family characteristics did not predict significant changes in depression level over a three-year follow-up. Burbach, Kashani, and Rosenberg (1989) diagnosed adolescent samples from a community population, and found that the youth who met DSM-III criteria for depressive disorders fell midway between normal and other psychiatric groups on their ratings of parents on the Parental Bonding Instrument. The authors note that a composite rating of mother and father was obtained, with the possibility that use of separate scales might have yielded the predicted results of perceived low care and high overprotection by the depressed group. Hops et al. (1990) found that adolescents who reported problems in their relationships with parents were more stably depressed at two testings a month apart, and extent of family relationship difficulties correlated with level of depressive symptoms.

The Kandel and Davies (1986) nine-year follow-up of adolescents with depressive symptoms indicated that the depressed women, but not men, reported more distance and dissatisfaction in their relationships with their mothers and fathers, compared to nondepressed women. Both depressed women and men reported more difficulties in their relationships with their spouses or romantic partners compared to the nondepressed groups.

Clinical samples of depressed children and adolescents

Several early small-sample studies of clinically depressed children in treatment reported significant problems in parent–child relationships, characterized by anger, detachment, punitiveness, or even abuse and neglect (reviewed in Burbach & Borduin, 1986). Kashani and Carlson (1987) noted that seriously depressed preschool children selected from a child evaluation service had all been abused or severely neglected, compared with only 22% of the nondepressed controls from the same unit. Kovacs et al. (1984a) also reported that outpatient depressed children had high rates of adverse parenting experiences such as absence of biological mother (22%), absence of biological father (35%), as well as highly stressful family conditions that would be likely to disrupt parenting practices (e.g. born out of wedlock: 32%; divorce or separation of parents: 45%). Notably, however, these rates were not significantly different from those reported by children with other psychiatric conditions.

The preadolescent children with major depressive episodes described by Puig-Antich and colleagues (1985a,b) also had significant impairment of their relationships with their parents. Mother-child relations were significantly more negative on additive scales across different dimensions, compared with both normal and psychiatric control groups, and were characterized by less communication and more hostility and rejection (Puig-Antich et al., 1985a). Moreover, despite improvement noted upon recovery from the clinical episode, mother-child relationships continued to be significantly impaired compared to the normal, nonpsychiatric group (Puig-Antich et al., 1985b). Armsden et al. (1990) compared clinically depressed adolescents and nondepressed controls on perceived security of attachment to parents, and found less secure attachment reported by the depressed youth. Asarnow, Carlson, and Guthrie (1987) did not find associations between children's perceptions of the family environment and extent of depressive symptoms in an inpatient sample. These authors did find, however, that degree of suicidal thinking was related to reports of lower cohesion, more conflict, and other indicators of family dysfunction.

There are few data based on observed parent-child interactions in clinical samples of depressed children. In one such study, Cole and Rehm (1986) found that mothers of depressed children rewarded their child less in an achievement interaction task (but did not differ from comparison groups on punishment). More recently, Cook, Asarnow, Goldstein, Marshall, and Weber (1990) found that inpatient depressed children were less positive and more negative in interactions with their mothers than were samples of schizophrenic children and their mothers. In contrast to these few studies, an extensive research literature is developing on observed interactions between symptomatic depressed or diagnosed depressed women and their children; uniformly such studies indicate negative interactions characterized by maternal negativism and unresponsiveness (cf. Downey & Coyne, 1990; Hammen, 1991a; Gotlib & Lee, 1990; we shall review these studies in greater detail in Chapter 7). Since many of the children of depressed mothers are themselves depressed, the findings are highly suggestive of a causal relationship between maternal quality of interaction and children's dysphoria and maladjustment.

Limited information exists on the long-term family functioning of depressed youngsters. A study by Garber et al. (1988) following up a small sample of adolescent psychiatric inpatients approximately eight years after discharge found that the depressed subgroup reported significantly worse current family relationships than did the nondepressed comparison group, and also indicated that they had had worse marital/relationship adjustment since the hospitalization.

Commentary

The somewhat sparse data on family functioning in depressed children and adolescents add to the consistent findings of negative parent–child relations in families with depressed parents. It appears that depression typically involves negative interpersonal relationships. However, as noted in the section on peer relationships and social functioning, it is unclear precisely what is the nature of the difficulties, and even more importantly, what might be the etiological contribution of such difficulties. There is evidence for continuing dysfunction in family relationships even when the depression has remitted, and therefore, such difficulties may contribute to vulnerability to subsequent depression. Further research is needed to explore the types of family relationship problems, their specificity to depressive disorders, and the mechanisms of their contribution to depression vulnerability. In Chapters 6 and 7 we further explore the role of interpersonal difficulties in the course of adult depression, and in Chapter 10 we present a theoretical analysis of the developmental psychopathology of depression involving childhood family relationships including attachment, and cognitive representations of interpersonal relationships and social behaviors.

Stressful life events

Community samples

Lagging behind the exploration of stress-depression linkages in adults, information is beginning to emerge on the association between stressors and children's depressive symptoms. In one of few studies of stressors in young children, Kashani, Holcomb, and Orvaschel (1986) found that preschoolers with depressive symptoms had significantly more recent life events (reported by parents) than did nondepressed children. Mullins, Siegel, and

Hodges (1985) found correlations between life stress questionnaires scores and depressive symptoms in fourth, fifth, and sixth grade children. Similar results were reported by Nolen-Hoeksema, Girgus, and Seligman (1986), who studied 8–11 year-olds at 5 testings over a one-year period. The impact of stressors on subsequent depression was mediated by negative attribution style in several of the prospective analyses.

In samples of community adolescents, Garrison et al. (1990) and Siegel and Brown (1988) found significant associations between recent stressors and self-reported depression. Additionally, both of these studies found that negative events predicted subsequent depression over a longitudinal follow-up, suggesting an etiological role of stressors. In the Siegel and Brown study, negative events, along with an absence of positive events, predicted subsequent depression. Similarly, Allgood-Merten, Lewinsohn, and Hops (1990), reporting on adolescent depression in the Oregon high school sample, found that current and future depression was related to stressful life events, and also that girls were especially likely to report stressful events. Additionally, the impact of stressful life events for girls was mediated by self-perceived body image, self-esteem, and self-efficacy as measured on a scale of masculine attributes. As the authors put it, "... if adolescent girls felt as physically attractive, effective, and generally good about themselves as their male peers did, they would not experience so much depression" (p. 61).

Compas and colleagues have found significant associations between child and adolescent stressors and general symptomatology (not depression specifically; e.g. Compas, Howell, Phares, Williams, & Giunta, 1989a; Compas, Wagner, Slavin, & Vanatta, 1986), but their work is particularly noteworthy for two additional contributions. First, they have shown that "daily hassles" are even more significant predictors of symptoms in children than are major events (e.g. Compas, Howell, Phares, Williams, & Ledoux, 1989b). Second, they have attempted to study the transactional process of stress-symptom occurrence in families, finding complex associations between parental stressors and symptoms and children's symptoms and stressors (Compas et al., 1989a,b).

Several studies have examined the influence of specific kinds of stressors on youngsters' levels of depression. For instance, Troutman and Cutrona (1990) examined the effect of teenage pregnancy on adolescent girls, and found elevated rates of postpartum depression, but not significantly greater than the depression in a nonchildbearing sample. The authors note, however, that rates of stressors are high in these relatively disadvantaged samples, possibly obscuring group differences. Cutrona (1989) reported that depressive symptoms in the pregnant teenagers were related to availability of social support. Petersen, Sarigiani, and Kennedy (1991) explored sex differences in depressive symptoms in young adolescents followed from sixth grade to twelfth grade, by examination of the extent and timing of stressors and challenges including onset of puberty, changes in school, and changes in the family. As predicted, the divergence in sex differences in depressive symptoms emerged in early adolescence and was associated with early maturing girls who experienced negative family and school events. Thus, the coinciding of pubertal onset (and possible negative body image) and stressful life events seemed to present challenges to the girls that resulted in demoralization, whereas for boys the occurrence of early stressors seemed to have a "steeling" effect in enhancing their adjustment. The authors also noted that closeness with parents moderated the negative effects of early adolescent changes on depressive symptoms.

Clinical samples

In their sample of clinically depressed children, Kovacs et al. (1984a) observed that many of the youngsters experienced highly traumatic circumstances, involving broken homes, socio-economic disadvantage, and unavailability of biological parents. The authors note, however, that such adverse conditions were also common in nondepressed children in treatment for other disorders, so that they were not specific to depression.

Little additional systematic information on stressors in clinical samples has been reported. However, Hammen and her colleagues developed extensive interview methods for evaluating children's exposure to stressful events in samples of youngsters at risk for depression due to maternal affective disorder or medical illness. Consistently, occurrence of children's stressful events predicted subsequent symptoms (e.g. Hammen, 1988; Hammen, Burge, & Adrian, 1991). Of particular note was the finding that children exposed to high stress levels were especially likely to become depressed under certain conditions: the stress matched their putative "vulnerability" to interpersonal or achievement negative events (Hammen & Goodman-Brown, 1990), or if their mothers were currently symptomatic. In the latter study, Hammen, Burge, and Adrian (1991) speculated that the availability of the mother to help buffer the ill effects of stress moderates the impact of stressors on children's likelihood of developing depression.

Finally, Hammen and colleagues also found that children of depressed women were especially likely to have high rates of events that they had partly contributed to, such as peer and family conflict (Adrian & Hammen, 1991). Table 2.1 shows the mean levels of stress (judged by independent rating teams) for offspring of depressed mothers, many of whom were themselves depressed, in comparison to offspring of bipolar, medically ill, or normal women.

Thus, event occurrence may be both a cause of subsequent symptoms but also a consequence of the vulnerable child's characteristics. This

Table 2.1 Children's mean adjusted 3-year objective stress totals for specific content

| Content category | Maternal groups | | | |
	Unipolar	Bipolar	Medical	Normal
Loss, bereavement	11.2	9.7	8.2	7.2
Family conflict	11.0	6.3	7.2	2.8
Peer conflict	4.9	3.5	1.4	1.6
Change, move	7.6	3.6	3.7	5.5
Failures	1.7	1.5	2.5	0.9
Other negative	14.3	12.9	19.8	7.0

Note: Other negative includes accidents, health and legal troubles; means are adjusted for the covariate of age.
Source: from "Children of depressed mothers: Stress exposure and responses to stressful life events" by C. Adrian & C. Hammen (in press).

contribution to the cause of negative interpersonal events has been called a "stress generation" effect and found to be characteristic of unipolar depressed women (Hammen, 1991a), as will be discussed further in Chapter 6. Thus, there is something about both depressed youngsters and their depressed mothers that suggests difficulties in interpersonal functioning, contributing to stressful conditions that likely cause or exacerbate further depression symptoms.

Commentary

The data on stressful life events are generally similar to that of adults: significant associations between depression and stressors occur cross-sectionally, and negative life events predict subsequent depression. This effect is undoubtedly mediated by certain aspects of the person's cognitive appraisals or preexisting attitudes, supports, and beliefs. Methodological limitations in the assessment of children's stressors such as overreliance on questionnaires and items not necessarily normed for children of different developmental stages (reviewed in Hammen, 1991a) suggest that further developments will help to improve the exploration of antecedents of depression in children and adolescents. Also, the specificity of depressive reactions to stressors has not been explored extensively in children. Several new directions for further research are indicated in considerations of the effect of the mother as a support to buffer the effects of children's stress, characteristics of the child that contribute to stress causation and coping with stressors, and specific vulnerability to particular types of stressors.

Cognitive correlates of depression and implications for etiology

Extensive research has been conducted on children's hypothesized depressogenic cognitions. Most of this work has been downward extensions of adult measures of depressive thinking and cognitive vulnerability, based on one of several adult models: the cognitive distortion model, the negative attribution style model, and miscellaneous cognitive approaches.

Studies of negative cognitive bias in children

Several early applications of Beck's theory to children found that depressive symptoms in community samples were linked with relatively negativistic thoughts or biased interpretations (Campbell-Goymer & Allgood, 1984; Leitenberg, Yost, & Carroll-Wilson, 1986; Robins & Hinkley, 1989). One study employed a clinical sample of youngsters in treatment, and also found the predicted association (Haley, Fine, Marriage, Moretti, & Freeman, 1985). Two additional constructs have also shown the predicted associations between negative interpretations and depressive symptoms. *Hopelessness* has frequently been studied in clinical samples (Asarnow, Goldstein, Carlson, Perdue, Bates, & Keller, 1988; Kazdin et al., 1983; Kazdin, Rodgers, & Colbus, 1986; McCauley, Mitchell, Burke, & Moss, 1988). Also, negative *self-concept* is associated with depression in various child and adolescent samples (e.g. Asarnow & Bates, 1988; Asarnow, Carlson, & Guthrie, 1987; Kazdin, Rodgers, & Colbus, 1986; Kaslow, Rehm, & Siegel, 1984; McCauley et al., 1988; Saylor, Finch, Baskin, Furey, & Kelley, 1984). A recent study of high school students also indicated that depressive symptoms were associated with various indicators of negative self-evaluation (Hops et al., 1990).

Extensions of Rehm's (1977) self-control model to children emphasized the role of negative cognitions about self-evaluation and self-reinforcement. Kaslow, Rehm, and Siegel (1984) found that relatively depressed children had more negative self-evaluation, lower expectations for performance, more stringent criteria for defining successes, and more likelihood of recommending punishment over reward. Kaslow, Rehm, Pollack, and Siegel (1988) observed that clinically depressed children had significantly more negative self-control cognitions than did normal and clinic comparison children. Cole and Rehm (1986), however, observed children and their parents playing an achievement game, and did not find that depressed children rewarded themselves less or punished themselves more than did nondepressed children.

Weisz and colleagues have examined control-related cognitions associated with depression in children, defining control as a joint function of perceived outcome contingency and perceived personal competence. Studies of clinic-referred and inpatient children and adolescents have consistently found associations between depressive symptoms and low levels of perceived personal competence, low control, and contingency uncertainty (Weisz, Weiss, Wasserman, & Rintoul, 1987; Weisz, Stevens, Curry, Cohen, Craighead et al., 1989).

Depressive attribution style in children

Early versions of this model emphasized the perceptions of helplessness and lack of control. Samples of normal children were tested, and correlations between external locus of control and depressive symptoms were observed (Lefkowitz & Tesiny, 1980; Tesiny & Lefkowitz, 1982). Assessments of children's causal attributions found that relatively more depressed children attributed positive events more to external causes, and negative events to internal causes (Leon, Kendall, & Garber, 1980). With the development of the Children's Attribution Style Questionnaire (Seligman, Peterson, Kaslow, Tenenbaum, Alloy, & Abramson, 1984), numerous studies demonstrated the predicted association of negative explanatory style and depressive symptoms (e.g. Blumberg & Izard, 1985; Hops et al., 1990; Kaslow, Rehm, & Siegel, 1984; Robins & Hinkley, 1989; Seligman et al., 1984). In clinical samples similar associations were reported (Kaslow et al., 1988; Saylor et al., 1984). A few studies attempted to test whether negative explanatory style is specific to depression or general to psychopathology. Whereas Benfield, Palmer, Pfefferbaum, and Stowe (1988) concluded that a negative explanatory style is general, several other investigators found that it was specific to depression (Asarnow & Bates, 1988; Kaslow et al., 1988; McCauley et al., 1988). Curry and Craighead (1990) attempted to address this issue more fully in an inpatient adolescent sample, characterized by the presence of depression or conduct disorder. The extent of depressive symptoms was significantly related to low scores on attribution style for positive events, but was not related to attributional style for negative events. Similarly, the adolescents with major depression differed significantly from the psychiatrically ill comparison group only on the positive events component, not on the negative. Pursuing the question of the role of attribution style as a vulnerability factor in depression, Asarnow and Bates (1988) and McCauley et al. (1988) suggested that negative attribution style is related to mood state, and is not present in children whose depression has remitted.

Very few studies of children's depressive cognitions have used longitudinal designs to test the causal role of negative thinking in depression, or have examined the stress-diathesis component of the models. Nolen-Hoeksema, Girgus, and Seligman (1986) studied depression symptoms in normal children at various testings over a one-year period, along with stressors and negative attribution style. They found a significant predictive relationship between prior attribution style scores and subsequent depression, and partial evidence of an interaction between stressful events and negative attribution style in predicting subsequent depression. In a one-month prospective study, Hops et al. (1990) found that negative attribution style predicted those who remained stably symptomatic and those who were initially symptomatic but improved, suggesting that negative attribution style may contribute to maintenance of symptoms. Similarly, low self-esteem predicted increased depression over time. The authors did not test the interaction of cognitions and stressors.

In another longitudinal study, Hammen and her colleagues examined changes in depression in a sample of children at risk for depression due to maternal affective disorder, medical illness, and comparison normal children. Hammen (1988) found that negative cognitions about the self, such as self-concept and negative self-schemas, predicted onset or change in depression over a six-month follow-up, and the effects of negative events and negative cognitions were additive. On the other hand, Hammen, Adrian, and Hiroto (1988) found that negative attribution style did not predict depression changes over this period, and there was no interaction of attribution style and negative events (although the interaction was predictive of *nondepressive* symptoms). Hammen and Goodman-Brown (1990) tested the hypothesis of differential vulnerability to specific stressors in the same high-risk sample, assessing children's "sociotropic" or "achievement" schemas. Children who had more stressful events that matched their schema type became depressed during the follow-up period, compared with those whose events did not match their schema type. However, the effect was most notable for the sociotropic children who experienced interpersonal events; achievement events were relatively rare for the group as a whole.

Commentary

Depressed children, like depressed adults, construe themselves, their worlds, and futures in negative ways that likely contribute to and sustain their dysphoria. However, studies of depressive cognition in children suffer from the same limitations as those of adult depressives: overreliance on measures of cognitions that are often transitory concomitants of depression, use of measures of limited psychometric quality (e.g. Robins & Hinkley, 1989), and methodologies that do not adequately test the hypotheses that cognitions may be vulnerability markers to depression. Additionally, most studies of cognition in children focus on rather simple, global, static constructs rather than specific processes that interact with environmental conditions, thus providing only limited understanding of the dysfunctions of the children that contribute specifically to depression.

In addition to these practical limitations, there are disconcerting conceptual limitations as well. Fundamental issues about the cognitive structures and schemas that are acquired in childhood and that establish the basis for subsequent behaviors and beliefs have been addressed only sparsely. Important links between mother-child attachment and subsequent cognitive representations of the self and of interpersonal relationships and behaviors have been addressed by some developmental psychologists and developmental psychopathologists, but have been rarely pursued in the context of the development of depression. Such directions would appear to be exciting and fruitful areas for further exploration (cf. Cicchetti & Schneider-Rosen, 1986; Digdon & Gotlib, 1985).

IMPLICATIONS FOR THEORIES OF DEPRESSION

1. Childhood and adolescent depression are relative latecomers to psychopathology, but with the development of changes in theories and diagnostic methods, we can now see that significant dysphoria and even clinical conditions affect many children and many more adolescents. Many of the psychological approaches to understanding depression in youth lag behind development of methods and concepts of adult affective disorders. Additionally, many of the theories and methods have been adapted from adult research with relatively little concern for a developmental focus tailored to the specific characteristics of children of different ages.

2. Many of the unique features of childhood depression that may distinguish it from adult conditions have not been addressed. Specifically, since childhood is the origin of the development of schemas about the self, the world, and others, as well as the beginning of acquisition of life skills for solving difficulties and coping with adversity, a more concentrated focus on such processes in normal children and in depressed youngsters would potentially contribute to the further understanding of adult affective disorder.

3. Issues of the continuity of mild and clinical depression, and of childhood, adolescent, and adult depression, are largely unexplored. Furthermore, as Rutter (1986) and others have noted, it is important to study how earlier experiences modify later ones, how depression and its related impairment in preadolescence may set the stage for maladjustment and depression at later ages. We also need to explore whether certain stressful experiences at certain ages and developmental stages are more predictive of later functioning than are those occurring at different ages.

4. It could be argued that most severe depression in children occurs in highly dysfunctional family situations, but is this also true of less serious

depression? It could also be argued that where there is a significantly depressed child there is also likely to be a depressed mother; further work is needed to explore the meaning of this common association, and to examine its genetic and psychosocial mechanisms.

5. As with adult depression, research on childhood depression has generally neglected the issue of specificity. What models are specifically predictive of depression, rather than anxiety disorders, or conduct problems, and the like? This problem is compounded by the considerable extent of psychiatric comorbidity in clinically depressed children, suggesting either that diagnostic entity models may not be as useful as dimensional models of symptoms, or that childhood experiences may shape the expression of symptomatology over time, from less differentiated to more differentiated forms.

6. The problem of high rates of comorbidity, along with the difficulty of parents and teachers in detecting dysfunctional internal states of children, make it difficult to identify depression in children. Much of childhood depression is likely to go unnoticed and, certainly, untreated. This may mean that by the time impairment or symptoms are noticed, they have had more negative consequences and are possibly more difficult to treat. It is an important question whether prevention efforts, based on early detection in community or high-risk samples, might alter the course of a child's development.

7. We might predict that depression of childhood or early adolescent onset means an especially pernicious course of development and symptomatology. As noted above, symptoms that interfere with the important developmental tasks of skill acquisition are likely to have continuing consequences. This suggests that depression of adult onset and adult depression of childhood onset may have different features not only in course of disorder, but also in vulnerability predictors and the influence of psychosocial factors.

8. There are many significant gaps in our understanding of the clinical features and course of childhood depression, as well as in our understanding of the psychosocial development and functioning of depressed youngsters. Such gaps can best be addressed in longitudinal designs, with extensive assessment across diverse domains. Much of the research reported to date has been relatively narrowly focused and cross-sectional. While such designs are appropriate in the beginning stages of research in new topics, it is now time that we move on to more complex studies and conceptualizations.

Chapter 3

Psychological Theories of Depression

In Chapter 1 we examined the clinical presentation and course of depression, as well as the epidemiology of this disorder. In this chapter we present various psychological theories of depression, all of which were proposed in an attempt to explain both the etiology of this disorder and the co-occurrence of the various symptoms of depression. As we shall see, there is considerable diversity among the major theories of depression with respect to their primary reliance on psychoanalytic, cognitive, or behavioral constructs in understanding this disorder. Nevertheless, we believe that there are also important commonalities among the theories, a point to which we will return more explicitly in Chapter 10.

We begin here with an examination of psychoanalytic theories of depression, and then turn to a discussion of behavioral and cognitive theories. We conclude with a presentation of more recent theories of depression that have attempted to integrate selected aspects of cognitive and behavioral theories. Finally, we would like to emphasize that our objective in this chapter is to present the reader with an overview of the major psychological theories of depression. Several of these theories have provided the impetus for a considerable body of empirical work. We will not attempt to discuss the results of these investigations in this chapter; rather, we will describe this research in subsequent chapters in the context of a general discussion of the nature of the cognitive and social functioning of depressed persons.

PSYCHOANALYTIC THEORIES OF DEPRESSION

Psychoanalytic conceptualizations of depression regard as central to this disorder the imagined or real loss of a valued or loved "object," through death, separation, rejection, or symbolically, through the loss of some ideal or abstraction. Typically, these "objects" are individuals who are significant early in a child's life—usually the parents, and most often the mother. Loss in early childhood is postulated to serve as a *diathesis*, a vulnerability factor that will lead to depression later in adulthood if the individual is confronted with a significant loss or disappointment. As we shall see later in this chapter, this diathesis-stress formulation of depression is characteristic not only of psychoanalytic theories, but of cognitive theories of depression as well.

In one of the earliest psychoanalytic formulations of depression, Abraham (1911/1985) gleaned his observations about depression from his treatment of six heterogeneous manic-depressive (bipolar) patients. Abraham theorized that individuals who are vulnerable to depression, or melancholia, experience a marked ambivalence toward other people, with positive and negative feelings alternating and reciprocally blocking expression of the other. Abraham postulated that this ambivalent form of relating has its origins in problematic object-relationships during childhood. Because of a tendency to experience pleasure in oral gratification, the depressive person experiences exaggerated dependency needs and excessive frustrations associated with oral behaviors, such as eating, drinking, and kissing. As a result of early and repeated disappointments and frustrations, the depressive person forms a permanent but unconscious linking of libidinal wishes with hostile destructive wishes. When the depressive experiences disappointments later in life, these feelings of hostility reemerge, leading to an episode of melancholia. The hostile feelings initially directed towards others (e.g. "I hate them") are projected onto others ("They hate me") and then internalized and directed towards the self. The depression-prone individual then justifies this self-denigration by magnifying some fault or defect. Interestingly, Abraham postulated that the unconscious destructive wishes of the depressed individual lead to overwhelming feelings of guilt, and that the loss of appetite so often seen in depressed persons is a defense against the hostile wish to "incorporate" the love object.

In a subsequent but similar formulation, Freud (1917/1961) expanded upon Abraham's postulations in explaining other depressive symptoms. In his classic paper, "Mourning and Melancholia," Freud compared depression with grief, but emphasized the importance of loss of self-esteem in depression. He noted that depressed persons exhibit symptoms similar to those present when one is in mourning following the experience of a significant loss. Unlike those in mourning, however, depressed persons appeared to be more self-denigrating and to lack self-esteem. They accuse themselves of being helpless, worthless, and inadequate. This observation led Freud to hypothesize that the denigration of the self is not actually directed at the self, but at a lost object, or person. As Freud wrote,

> If one listens patiently to the many and varied self-accusations of the melancholic, one cannot in the end avoid the impression that often the most violent of these are hardly at all applicable to the patient himself but that with insignificant modifications they do fit someone else, some person whom the patient loves, has loved or ought to love ... so we get the key to the clinical picture.

Thus, Freud theorized that the anger and disappointment that had previously been directed toward a lost object are internalized, leading to a loss of self-esteem and a tendency to engage in self-criticism.

Freud believed that the predisposition to this reaction to loss has its origins in a particular early childhood experience in which the young child experienced a loss of the mother, or of the mother's love. In order to lessen the impact of this loss, the child learns to internalize a representation of the lost object. The anger directed at the lost object, however, is now directed at a part of the child's own ego, thereby predisposing to future depressive episodes following significant losses. It is important to note that this formulation required the presence of relatively well-developed intrapsychic structures. Consequently, many analytically trained therapists believed that young children lack the capacity to be depressed.

A decade later, Rado (1928) postulated that, like children, persons vulnerable to depression are highly dependent for their self-esteem on the love and approval of others rather than on their own achievements. He pointed out that because of this elevated dependency on others, depressed persons are affected more than nondepressed individuals by disappointments and frustrations in their social environments. According to Rado, these frustrations lead first to hostility, which alienates others in the depressive's environment. The depressed person then attempts to regain the support of others through suffering, self-denigration, and other early symptoms of depression. If the depressive behavior does not win back the lost love and affection, these symptoms escalate to self-punishment, repentance, guilt, and depression. From this perspective, therefore, depression essentially represents an attempt to regain self-esteem following a significant interpersonal loss (see also Bibring, 1953).

Klein (1934) argued that a predisposition to depression was not due to early traumatic incidents such as losses, but rather, to the quality of the mother-child relationship in the first year of life. Klein suggested that if the child's experience with the mother did not promote feelings of being good, loved, and secure, the child would not be able to overcome ambivalence toward its love objects and would always be at risk for experiencing a depressive episode. For Klein, therefore, the predisposition to depression is a result of an early failure to overcome depressive fears and anxieties and to establish an optimal level of self-esteem. This formulation clearly paved the way for more contemporary object-relations theories, which emphasize the role of early mother-infant relationships in shaping the structure of personality and forming the basis of representations of the self and others that determine behavior and adjustment.

Building on Klein's (1934) work, Jacobson (1971) utilized an object-relations perspective to hypothesize that a fusion of the individual's self- and object-representations early in childhood result in the self-condemnation and self-reproach characteristic of depression. Anger and hostility are directed at the lost object and its internal representation, but through the process of fusion, the internal representations of the object and the self become indistinguishable. Consequently, the anger and hostility initially directed toward the lost object are experienced as self-condemnation and self-hate.

Further developing this object-relations perspective, Bowlby (1978, 1981) also emphasized the importance of early attachment experiences in predisposing an individual to later development of depression. Bowlby postulated that infants have an innate tendency to seek stimulation and promote attachment to significant objects who will provide protection and support. This tendency evolved through the process of natural selection. Bowlby suggested that early in the history of the human species, it would have been of survival value for helpless infants to seek the protective proximity of specific adults. Thus, infant behaviors such as crying, smiling, sucking, and grasping serve a care-eliciting function and help to ensure the development of attachment bonds.

Bowlby argued that a specific unbroken bond to a particular person is essential for nonpathological development. Bowlby believed that humans of all ages are vulnerable to impaired interpersonal relations if they do not develop strong attachment bonds early in their lives. Indeed Bowlby suggested that many psychiatric disorders have their origins in the inability to make and keep affectional bonds. The threat of loss of an important attachment figure, for example, creates anxiety and sadness. If attachment bonds (typically to the mother) are disrupted, either through actual separation or emotional unresponsiveness or inaccessibility, Bowlby postulated that individuals may become vulnerable to depression.

In essence, therefore, classical psychoanalytic theorists view depression as a failure of the normal mourning process, and describe a depressive syndrome composed of self-criticism, guilt, loss of libido, and low self-esteem. Furthermore, psychoanalytic theorists also emphasize the importance of loss in early childhood and, more recently, the quality of the mother-child relationship in the first year of life, as vulnerability factors for subsequent depression. Bowlby, in particular, believed that adult depression is related to the failure in early childhood to form a stable and secure attachment with the parents, or to the experience of actual loss of a parent, with associated feelings of helplessness and negative representations of the self and others.

BEHAVIORAL THEORIES OF DEPRESSION

In contrast to the focus of psychoanalytic theories of depression on early experiences and intrapsychic processes, behavioral theories attempt to explain depression essentially in terms of response and stimulus overgeneralization (cf. Rehm, 1990). For behavioral theorists, depression involves an overgeneralized response (e.g. loss of interest in a wide range of activities, loss of appetite, reduced interest in sex, low self-esteem) to a circumscribed stimulus (e.g. loss of a job). This problem of overgeneralization has been considered by a number of theorists but, as we shall see, there is no uniform agreement regarding their explanations.

Almost four decades ago, Skinner (1953) postulated that depression was the result of a weakening of behavior due to the interruption of established sequences of behavior that had been positively reinforced by the social environment. This conceptualization of depression as the result of an extinction schedule was reiterated by subsequent behavioral theorists. For example, 20 years later Ferster (1973) postulated that depression was a reduction in the frequency of emission of certain kinds of adaptive responses or activities which could be positively reinforced. Essentially, Ferster also suggested that the depressed individual was on an extinction schedule, receiving a reduced rate of reinforcement. He suggested that the depressive's failure to produce adaptive behaviors may be due to a number of factors, including (a) sudden environmental changes that require the establishment of new sources of reinforcement; (b) engaging in aversive or punishable behavior that preempts the opportunity for positive reinforcement; and (c) inaccurate observation of the environment, resulting in socially inappropriate behavior and a low frequency of positive reinforcement. Ferster invoked the concept of chaining to explain the generalizability of the response to the rather specific loss of reinforcement. Ferster argued that the loss of a central source of reinforcement led to a reduction in all behaviors that were "chained to," or organized around the lost reinforcer. For example, loss of a job might lead to a reduction in all of the behaviors that were chained to working. Thus an individual who lost his job might have difficulty getting up in the morning, seeing friends or colleagues, eating, planning recreational activities, and so on, if all of these behaviors were organized around his work, the central source of his reinforcement.

In a variant of this position, Costello (1972) distinguished between a reduction in the number of reinforcers available to the individual and a reduction in the effectiveness of available reinforcers. Costello argued that the loss of a single source of reinforcement does not easily account for the depressed person's general loss of interest in the environment. He proposed instead that depression was due to a disruption in a chain of behavior, likely caused by the loss of one of the reinforcers in the chain. Costello argued that the reinforcer effectiveness of all the components of the chain of behavior is contingent upon the completion of the chain. Thus, when a behavior chain is disrupted, there is a loss of reinforcer effectiveness associated with all of the components in the chain. Costello contends that the depressive's general loss of interest in the environment is a manifestation of this reduction of reinforcer effectiveness.

Lewinsohn and his colleagues (e.g. Lewinsohn, 1974; Lewinsohn, Youngren, & Grosscup, 1979) refined and elaborated these positions. They hypothesized that a low rate of "response-contingent positive re-inforcement" in major life areas, and/or a high rate of aversive experiences, leads to dysphoria and a reduction in behavior, resulting in the experience of depression. Lewinsohn suggested that there are three major factors that might lead to a low rate of reinforcement. The first involves deficits in the behavioral repertoire or skills of the individual that prevent the attainment of reinforcers or diminish the individual's ability to cope with aversive experiences. Thus, persons who suffer a social loss, such as widows and widowers, may lack the skills to form new reinforcing relationships. The second factor that might lead to a low rate of reinforcement is a lack of potential reinforcers in the individual's environment due to impoverishment or loss, or a surplus of aversive experiences. For example, a person who is confined to home while recuperating from a long illness may find little to do that is reinforcing. The death or departure of people who had provided social reinforcement, or loss of employment, would also result in a lack of reinforcement in the individual's environment. Finally, depression may result from a decrease in the person's capacity to enjoy positive experiences, or an increase in the individual's sensitivity to negative events.

Lewinsohn (1974) clearly focuses on the reduction of social reinforcement obtained by the depressed individual from significant others in his or her environment. Lewinsohn posited that depressed individuals may lack adequate social skills and may therefore find it difficult to obtain reinforcement from their social environment, leading them to experience a reduced rate of positive reinforcement. Libet and Lewinsohn (1973) defined social skill as, "... the complex ability both to emit behaviors which are positively or negatively reinforced, and not to emit behaviors which are punished or extinguished by others" (p. 304). An individual is considered to be socially skillful, therefore, to the extent that he elicits positive (and avoids negative) consequences from the social environment. Lewinsohn postulated that, because of insufficient positive reinforcement, depressed persons find it difficult to initiate or maintain instrumental behavior. Consequently, they become increasingly passive and inactive. This lack of rewarding interchanges with the environment is also assumed to result in the subjective experience of dysphoria.

Complementing this formulation, Coyne (1976b) contended that depression is a response to disruptions in the social field of the individual. Specifically, Coyne suggested that depression is maintained by the negative responses of significant others to the depressive's symptomatic behavior. Coyne maintained that depressed individuals create a negative social environment by engaging others in such a manner that support is lost, or at best, ambiguous (both supportive and hostile) reactions are elicited. Coyne postulated a sequence of behavior that begins with the depressed person's initial demonstration of depressive symptoms, typically in response to stress. Individuals in the depressed person's social environment respond immediately to these depressive symptoms with genuine concern and support. The depressive's behaviors gradually become demands, however, that are expressed with increasing frequency. Consequently, the depressive's behavior becomes aversive and elicits feelings of resentment and anger from other family members. At the same time, however, the depressed person's obvious distress also elicits feelings of guilt that serve to inhibit the open expression of this hostility. In an attempt to reduce both their guilt and anger, family members respond to the depressed person not only with veiled hostility, but with false reassurance and support. Being aware of, and feeling rejected by, these discrepant or incongruous messages, the depressed person becomes more symptomatic in an attempt to gain support, thus making it even more aversive for others to interact with him or her. This "deviation-amplifying" process continues to the point where people either withdraw from interactions with the depressive, or have the person withdrawn through hospitalization.

Finally, Coates and Wortman (1980) offered a similar formulation of the etiology of depression, but placed greater emphasis on the social comparison processes of depressed persons and the attempts made by others in the social environment to control directly the depressive's display of aversive symptoms. As in Coyne's (1976b) model, Coates and Wortman suggested that others initially react sympathetically to the depressed person and try to ameliorate the negative feelings through encouragement and distraction. These initial attempts at controlling the depressed person, however, may leave the individual feeling worse, doubting the appropriateness of his/her feelings and reactions. Over time others in the depressive's social environment become increasingly annoyed and frustrated with the depressive displays, and their initially supportive responses become more disjointed and ambiguous. The depressed person begins to emit more symptoms in order to regain the lost support and, as others' attempts to control the depressive's behavior become more overt and insistent, the depressed person is left feeling inadequate, isolated, and rejected. Thus, both Coyne and Coates and Wortman implicate the negative reactions of others in the maintenance of depression.

In sum, therefore, behavioral models of depression implicate a reduction in the rate or the effectiveness of positive reinforcement received by individuals from others in their environment in the etiology and/or maintenance of this disorder. Although this reduced rate or effectiveness of reinforcement can be due to a number of factors, most behavioral theories focus either on the overt behaviors of depressed individuals as deficient in their ability to obtain reinforcement, or on the behavioral reactions of others in their social environments as offering low rates of reinforcement to the depressed person. In contrast to these theories, which focus on behavioral aspects of depression, other theories emphasize the role of cognitive factors in the development and maintenance of this disorder. We turn now to an examination of cognitive theories of depression.

COGNITIVE THEORIES OF DEPRESSION

Cognitive formulations of depression differ from behavioral theories in two important respects. First, whereas behavioral models of depression focus on overt behaviors, cognitive formulations emphasize the importance of covert behaviors, such as attitudes, self-statements, images, memories, and beliefs. Second, cognitive approaches to depression consider maladaptive or irrational cognitions and cognitive distortions to be the cause of the disorder, or of its exacerbation and maintenance; negative affect, lack of motivation, physical symptoms, and other depressive behaviors are regarded as secondary manifestations resulting from maladaptive cognitions.

The last 15 years have witnessed a surge of research designed to examine cognitive aspects of depression. In particular, two models of depression that implicate cognitive factors in the etiology of this disorder have garnered the most theoretical and empirical attention. We will begin this section of the chapter by reviewing the basic tenets of Beck's (1967, 1976) cognitive theory of depression and Seligman's (1975; Abramson, Seligman, & Teasdale, 1978) learned helplessness model of depression. We will then present the hopelessness theory of depression, which is a recent revision of the learned helplessness model. Finally, we will then turn our attention to a discussion of self-control theory, self-awareness theories, and the differential activation theory of depression.

Beck's theory of depression

In developing his theory of depression, Beck (1967, 1976) drew heavily on his extensive clinical experience with depressed patients. Beck noted that depressed patients consistently engaged in negative thinking about themselves and their future; indeed, he commented on the masochistic nature of the dream material and free associations produced by depressed patients. Beck emphasized the primacy of this cognitive functioning in understanding not only the etiology and maintenance of depression, but processes involved in the treatment of this disorder as well. Beck's theory of depression focuses on three interrelated aspects of depressed individuals' cognitions: the "cognitive triad," cognitive distortions or faulty information processing, and negative self-schemas.

The cognitive triad refers to a depressotypic pattern of thinking in which depressed persons exhibit a negative view of themselves (e.g. "I'm no good"), their current situation (e.g. "My marriage is awful"), and the future (e.g. "Nothing will ever work out for me"). According to Beck, the existence of the cognitive triad is apparent through the misperceptions and misinterpretations by depressed persons of their environment. Depressives are postulated to perceive situations negatively, even when more positive interpretations are also plausible. Their interactions with their environments are misperceived in terms of defeat, and they expect failure when undertaking new tasks. Beck contends that the cognitive triad is responsible for many of the typical depressive symptom patterns, including deficits in affective, motivational, behavioral, and physiological functioning (cf. Beck, Rush, Shaw, & Emery, 1979, pp. 11–13).

Beck also suggests that depressed individuals demonstrate cognitive distortions through engaging in faulty information processing. More specifically, depressed persons are characterized by a number of common systematic errors in thinking, including arbitrary inference, selective abstraction, overgeneralization, magnification and minimization, personalization, and all-or-none thinking. Arbitrary inference, for example, describes a situation in which, in the absence of necessary evidence or even in the face of contrary evidence, depressed individuals draw negative conclusions about situations. Similarly, in selective abstraction depressed persons systematically focus on negative aspects of situations, and may perceive an entire event as negative by focusing on a minor negative component. For example, a depressed person might focus on one negative exchange within an entire conversation and interpret this as a sign of complete rejection. Magnification and minimization refer to the tendency of depressed individuals to exaggerate the significance of negative experiences while concurrently underestimating the significance or magnitude of any positive experiences. Finally, Beck noted that depressed individuals often demonstrated "automatic" responding, that is made responses that were based on insufficient reasoning or reflection, and that they lacked a critical attitude toward their depressive cognitions. According to Beck, many of the manifestations of depression, such as self-criticism, low self-regard, and escapist and suicidal wishes, are consequences of these reasoning errors.

Perhaps the most important construct in Beck's cognitive model of depression, however, is the negative self-schema, formulated by Beck to explain why depressed persons persist in self-defeating attitudes in the face of contradictory evidence. The concept of a "schema" has a long history in cognitive psychology (see, for example, Bartlett, 1932). Essentially, schemas are postulated to be memory representations that help to fill in missing details during retrieval operations. Since Bartlett's work, however, the schema concept has been used and altered in so many ways that there is probably no single accepted definition for the term. Beck (1964) defined a schema as:

> a structure for screening, coding and evaluating impinging stimuli. In terms of the individual's adaptation to external reality, it is regarded as the mode by which the environment is broken down and organized into its many psychologically relevant facets; on the basis of the matrix of schemas, the individual is able to orient himself in relation to time and space and to categorize and interpret his experiences in a meaningful way. (p. 564)

In general, most researchers and theorists would agree that a schema is a stored body of knowledge that affects encoding, comprehension, and retrieval of new information. The schema exerts this effect by guiding attention, expectancies, interpretations, and memory searches. It serves the function of efficiency and speed, but not accuracy, in information processing. Schemas are biased toward consistency and can therefore lead to errors of interpretation and selection of information so as to "fit" the pre-existing beliefs and propositions (cf. Fiske & Linville, 1980).

According to Beck's theory, schemas in the context of depression are cognitive processes that represent "a stable characteristic of (the depressive's) personality" (Kovacs & Beck, 1978, p. 530). Schemas are postulated to play a causal role in depression by influencing the selection, encoding, organization, and evaluation of stimuli in the environment in a negative and pessimistic direction, which leads subsequently to depressive affect (see also Sacco & Beck, 1985, p. 4). In a formulation reminiscent of those offered by psychoanalytic theorists, Beck (1967) postulates that schemas develop from early negative experiences in childhood: "During the developmental period, the depression-prone individual acquires certain negative attitudes regarding himself, the outside world, and his future ... The idiosyncratic attitudes represent persistent cognitive patterns, designated as schemas" (p. 290).

These schemas remain with the individual throughout his or her life, functioning as a vulnerability factor, or *diathesis*, for depression. They become reactivated when the individual is exposed to a relevant current stressor: "[schemas] may be latent but can be activated by specific circumstances which are analogous to experiences initially responsible for embedding the negative attitude" (Beck et al., 1979, p. 16). These reactivated schemas take the form of excessively rigid and inappropriate beliefs or attitudes about the self and the world, as well as unrealistic, often perfectionistic standards by which the self is judged. Because these schemas are hypothesized to influence the perception and structuring of experiences, depressed persons are postulated to be negatively biased in their perceptions of their environments. When these schemas are active, the depressed person attempts to interpret information from the environment so that it is consistent with the schemas, even if it means distorting the information to achieve congruence. Thus, positive stimuli may be selectively filtered out and negative or neutral information may be perceived as being more negative than is actually the case. Negative schemas, therefore, are postulated to play a critical role in predisposing an individual to depression.

Beck (1983) has also proposed that there are two major schematic subtypes of predisposition, or vulnerabilities, to depression. One subtype involves "autonomous" individuals, who are characterized by independence, high self-standards, and a high need for achievement. The other subtype involves "sociotropic" or dependent individuals, who are characterized by a high need for interpersonal closeness and security. Beck maintains that individuals in these two schematic subtypes will have their schemas activated only by relevant stressors. Thus, the schema of an autonomous individual may become activated by the loss of a job, whereas the schema of a sociotropic individual may become activated by the break-up of a relationship. As we shall soon see, however, other theorists disagree with the hypothesized importance of a match between diathesis and stress. Finally, it is noteworthy that, although Beck postulated the existence of these subtypes largely from his clinical observations, Arieti and Bemporad (1978) and Blatt and his colleagues (e.g. Blatt, D'Affliti, & Quinlan, 1976)—both from psychodynamic perspectives—have proposed conceptually similar subtypes of depression.

We noted earlier that cognitive theorists assign a primacy to cognitive factors in depression, and conceptualize the affective, behavioral, and physiological symptoms of this disorder as consequences of schema-based negative information processing. As Beck et al. (1979) state, "the patient's negative constructions of reality can be postulated to be the first link in the chain of symptoms" (p. 19). Although Beck et al. note that positive interpersonal relationships can counteract the depressives' self-critical tendencies, they clearly focus on depressed persons' perceptions of their relationships rather than on their actual interactions, and they consistently emphasize depressed persons' imperviousness to counter-schematic (i.e., positive) environmental feedback (e.g. Kovacs & Beck, 1978, p. 526)

The learned helplessness model of depression

A somewhat similar cognitive model, the reformulated learned helplessness model of depression (Abramson, Seligman, & Teasdale, 1978), originated with Seligman's (1975) theory of learned helplessness. Seligman advanced a model of depression based on results of his work with animals. Seligman and Maier (1967) found that dogs pretreated with inescapable shock were subsequently poorer at escaping shock in a shuttle box than were dogs pretreated with escapable shock or given no prior shock. These dogs rarely initiated attempts to escape, and would often passively endure the shock without overt signs of emotionality. Helpless behavior could apparently be learned through exposure to uncontrollable shock. This interference and the process underlying it were labelled "learned helplessness." Seligman claimed that learned helplessness could be produced in a variety of situations, with different types of uncontrollable events, and across a number of species. He argued that the main behavioral symptoms of learned helplessness—deficits in response initiation and in the ability to learn that responding produces reinforcement—result from the belief that responding and reinforcement are independent. Seligman suggested that these symptoms are evident in depression as well, and advanced the model of learned helplessness as an analog of this disorder, arguing that learned helplessness and depression have "parallel" etiology, symptoms, treatments, and prevention.

Seligman and his colleagues conducted a number of studies in which they attempted to induce learned helplessness in humans through exposure to uncontrollable stimuli (e.g. Hiroto & Seligman, 1975; Miller & Seligman, 1975). The results of these studies were comparable to those obtained in the animal studies: in general, subjects exposed to uncontrollable stimuli exhibited deficits in response initiation and learning. The learned helplessness theory, however, could not account for the loss of self-esteem in helpless subjects, for the generality of depression across situations, or for individual differences in the persistence of depression. Moreover, it was clear that not all people who are exposed to uncontrollable negative events become depressed; some became anxious, others angry, and some had little emotional reaction. These inadequacies in the application of the learned helplessness model to humans led to a number of reformulations of the model, each of which involved a significant shift in theory by introducing attributional concepts as mediators between the perception of noncontingency and expectations regarding future contingencies (e.g. Abramson, Seligman, & Teasdale, 1978; Miller & Norman, 1979). Although these reformulations are better able to accommodate data from humans, the importance they attach to higher cognitive processes renders parallels between human and infrahuman phenomena more uncertain (cf. Coyne & Gotlib, 1983).

The reformulation that has received the most empirical and theoretical attention is that outlined by Abramson, Seligman, and Teasdale (1978). These theorists postulated that mere exposure to uncontrollable stimuli is insufficient for deficits in cognitive, motivational, and emotional functioning to occur; they hypothesized that persons must expect that future outcomes are also uncontrollable in order for helplessness to be induced. "When a person finds that he is helpless, he asks *why* he is helpless. The causal attributions he makes determine the generality and chronicity of his helplessness deficits as well as his later self-esteem" (Abramson, Seligman, & Teasdale, 1978, p. 50). Thus, the theoretical sequence of the development of helplessness is

Objective noncontingency → *Perception* of present and past non-contingency → *Attribution* for present or past noncontingency → *Expectation* of future noncontingency → *Symptoms* of helplessness (Abramson, Seligman, & Teasdale, 1978, p. 52).

Abramson, Seligman, and Teasdale (1978) drew on Weiner, Frieze, Kukla, Reed, Rest, and Rosenbaum's (1971) dimensional structure in proposing that attributions of uncontrollability vary along three major dimensions: internal versus external locus of control, stable versus unstable conditions, and global versus specific attributions of uncontrollability. Each of these three dimensions is postulated to be related to a specific aspect of the depressive experience:

According to the logic of the reformulated model, different etiological factors are relevant for the production of different depressive symptoms. The cognitive and motivational symptoms result from the expectation per se that events will be uncontrollable. The tendency to attribute uncontrollable events to stable, global factors increases the likelihood that an expectation that events are uncontrollable will persist in the future and in new situations and thereby also contributes to producing cognitive and motivational deficits in depression. Alternatively, self-esteem deficits result from a tendency to attribute uncontrollable events to internal factors. Finally, depressive affect results from an expectation that an important goal is unattainable rather than from the expected uncontrollability of the goal. (Abramson & Martin, 1981, p. 123)

Thus, persons who are prone to experiencing depression derive their vulnerability from tendencies to attribute negative, uncontrollable, outcomes to internal, stable, and global factors and, to a lesser extent, positive outcomes to external, specific, and unstable causes (cf. Peterson & Seligman, 1984; Sweeney, Anderson, & Bailey, 1986). Moreover, these attributional tendencies, or "attributional style," collectively are viewed as a stable trait that has its origins in early childhood experiences. Therefore, individuals are expected to exhibit cross-situational and temporal consistency in their causal explanations for events, offering the same kinds of causal explanations for different bad events (cf. Brewin, 1985). Individuals with a "depressogenic" attributional style not only have learned through early experiences to believe that previous events in their lives were uncontrollable, but they expect that future outcomes, too, will similarly be out of their control. Indeed, the onset of a depressive episode is precipitated by the occurrence of a negative event that triggers the expectation of the uncontrollability of future negative events. Thus, as in Beck's model, these patterns of attributions are hypothesized to play a causal role in the development of depression.

Hopelessness theory of depression

Abramson, Metalsky, and Alloy (1989) have recently presented a revision of the reformulated learned helplessness model of depression (Abramson, Seligman, & Teasdale, 1978). Their "hopelessness theory" postulates the existence of a subtype of depression they refer to as "hopelessness depression." Essentially, Abramson, Metalsky, and Alloy (1989) postulate that hopelessness depression is a result of expectations that highly desired outcomes will not occur or that highly undesired outcomes will occur and that no response in one's repertoire will change the likelihood of occurrences of these outcomes. According to the hopelessness theory, the occurrence of negative life events serve as "occasion setters" for people to become hopeless. Abramson and his colleagues suggest that three kinds of inferences about the negative event can contribute to the onset of hopelessness. First, as in the reformulated learned helplessness model of depression, symptoms of hopelessness depression are likely to occur when people attribute important negative life events to stable and global causes. Second, hopeless depression is likely to occur when the individual views negative consequences of the event as important, not remediable, unlikely to change, and as affecting many areas of his or her life. Finally, Abramson and his colleagues emphasize the importance of the effects of the negative event with respect to inferred characteristics about the self, inferences a person draws about his or her own worth, abilities, personality, and so on.

Hopelessness will occur to the extent that individuals perceive themselves as unable to affect outcomes in their environments.

Abramson, Metalsky, and Alloy (1989) postulate the existence of a "depressogenic attributional style," a general tendency of some individuals to attribute negative events to stable, global factors and to view these events as very important. Individuals who exhibit this hypothesized depressogenic attributional style should be likely to become hopeless when confronted with a negative event. It is important to note that in the absence of a negative event, or in the presence of a positive event, these individuals should not be expected to develop hopelessness or to exhibit symptoms of hopelessness depression. Thus, the hopelessness theory, too, is a diathesis-stress theory of depression, in which the diathesis of a hypothesized depressogenic attributional style interacts with a stressful negative life event to produce hopelessness depression. Without the stress, the diathesis does not result in depressive symptoms.

In a formulation reminiscent of Beck's (1983) subtyping of autonomous and sociotropic individuals, Abramson, Metalsky, and Alloy (1989) suggest that the hypothesized depressogenic attributional style, too, represents a "domain-specific" vulnerability to depression. For example, individuals may be predisposed to make stable and global attributions for interpersonal-related, but not for achievement-related, negative events. In this case, an individual will exhibit symptoms of hopelessness depression when confronted by a negative life event in the interpersonal domain (e.g. break-up of a relationship), but not when faced with a negative achievement-related event (e.g. failure to get a job promotion). Thus, the hopelessness theory also requires that there be a match between the content areas of individuals' depressogenic attributional style and the negative life events they encounter in order for hopelessness depression to occur.

Self-control theory of depression

Rehm (1977) has proposed a model of depression that attempts to integrate behavioral and cognitive aspects of the disorder. Rehm draws heavily on Kanfer's (1977) model of self-regulation in formulating a self-control model of depression. In an attempt to understand the capacity of the human organism to develop means for regulating his own behavior in the absence of immediate environmental consequences, Kanfer proposed a three-stage, closed-loop learning model of self-regulation. In the first stage, self-monitoring, the individual observes his behavior and environment in order to later evaluate their relevancy and appropriateness for accomplishing his goal. In the second stage of self-regulation, self-evaluation, the information obtained through self-monitoring is compared with an internal standard for the desired behavior. Finally, following self-evaluation, the individual makes a judgment about the appropriateness of self-reinforcement, the third stage, usually contingent on the degree to which the behavior approximates the performance standard.

Rehm (1977) suggests that this model of self-regulation may serve as an heuristic model for the study of depressive etiology, symptomatology, and treatment. He proposed a self-control model of depression utilizing the same three component processes as those outlined by Kanfer. According to this model, specific deficits in self-monitoring, self-evaluation, and self-reinforcement may explain the various symptoms of depression. Specifically, Rehm postulated that the behavior of depressed persons could be characterized by one or more of six deficits in self-control behavior. First, with respect to self-monitoring, depressed individuals selectively attend to negative events that follow their behavior to the relative exclusion of positive events, a cognitive style that might account for the pessimism and gloomy outlook of depressed individuals. Second, depressed persons selectively attend to immediate consequences of their behavior to the relative exclusion of delayed outcomes, and therefore cannot look beyond present demands when making behavioral choices.

The third deficit in the self-control behavior of depressed persons involves self-evaluation, essentially a comparison between an estimate of performance (which derives from self-monitoring) and an internal criterion or standard. Nondepressed persons set realistic, attainable, explicit criteria for their behavior and objectively evaluate their ongoing actions by comparing their self-monitored behavior to these preset criteria. Rehm (1977) hypothesizes that depressed individuals, in contrast, set unrealistic, perfectionistic, global standards for themselves, making attainment improbable. As a consequence, depressed persons often do not succeed in reaching their goals and, therefore, evaluate themselves negatively and in a global, overgeneralized manner.

Depressed persons may also manifest a self-evaluation deficit with respect to their style of attribution. Consistent with Abramson, Seligman, and Teasdale's (1978) reformulated learned helplessness model, Rehm hypothesizes that depressed persons may not accurately attribute responsibility or causality for their performance, but may distort their perception of causality in order to denigrate themselves. If their performance is successful, for example, depressed persons may attribute their success to external factors such as luck and the simplicity of the task, thereby refusing to take credit for their success. Similarly, depressed persons may attribute the cause of an unsuccessful performance to internal factors such as lack of skill and effort, taking excessive responsibility for failure.

The final two possible deficits in self-control involve the constructs of self-reinforcement and self-punishment. Rehm (1977) postulates that depressed persons fail to administer sufficient contingent rewards to themselves to maintain their adaptive behaviors. This low rate of self-reward may account in part for the slowed rates of overt behavior, the lower general activity level, and the lack of persistence that typify depression. In addition, depressed persons are hypothesized to administer excessive self-punishment, which suppresses potentially productive behavior early in a response chain, resulting in excessive inhibition.

Problem-solving theory of depression

Nezu and his colleagues (e.g. Nezu, 1987; Nezu, Nezu, & Perri, 1989) have recently articulated a formulation of depression that implicates ineffective problem-solving skills in the onset and maintenance of this disorder. Nezu noted that a number of investigations have demonstrated an association between problem-solving deficits and depressive symptomatology, both in adults (e.g. Gotlib & Asarnow, 1979) and in children (e.g. Sacco & Graves, 1984). Given this association, Nezu and Ronan (1985) suggested that problem-solving skills may function to moderate the link between stress and depression (see Chapter 6). They hypothesized that effective problem-solving ability functions as a buffer against the potentially debilitating effects of negative life events. Moreover, Nezu has also postulated that problem-solving may moderate the association between a negative attributional style and depression.

According to Nezu's (1987) formulation, individuals with ineffective problem-solving skills are at increased risk for the development of a depressive episode. More specifically, Nezu contends that depression can result from deficiencies in any or all of five major components of problem-solving: problem orientation, problem definition and formulation, generation of alternatives, decision making, and solution implementation and verification. For example, individuals who experience difficulty with problem orientation might appraise a situation as a "threat" rather than as a "challenge," or may attribute the cause of the problem to internal, stable, and/or global factors (cf. Abramson, Seligman, & Teasdale, 1978). Similarly, individuals who are deficient in generating alternatives may generate a restricted range of alternatives, or may generate less effective alternatives than do their more skillful counterparts.

Regardless of the specific problem-solving deficit, Nezu (1987) suggests that the onset of depression occurs when an individual is confronted with a difficult situation. Nezu argues that if these problematic situations are not resolved, negative consequences are likely to occur, which themselves result in a decrease in the individual's reinforcement. To the extent that the individual experiences deficits in problem-solving skills, the resulting depressive episode will be severe and long-lasting. Moreover, Nezu also contends that deficits in problem-solving ability will increase relapse rates, due to the high probability of problems occurring in the future and remaining unresolved. Finally, as we shall discuss in Chapter 9, Nezu, Nezu, and Perri (1989) have developed a treatment for depression based on their formulation of the important role played by problem-solving deficits in the onset and maintenance of depression.

Self-focus theories of depression

Lewinsohn, Hoberman, Teri, and Hautzinger (1985) argued that both cognitive and reinforcement theories of depression have been too narrow and simplistic. They proposed a multifactorial model of the etiology and maintenance of depression that attempts to capture the complexity of this disorder. In this model, the occurrence of depression is viewed as a product of both environmental and dispositional factors. More specifically, depression is conceptualized as the end result of environmentally initiated changes in behavior, affect, and cognitions. Whereas situational factors are important as "triggers" of the depressogenic process, cognitive factors are critical as "moderators" of the effects of the environment.

The chain of events leading to the occurrence of depression is postulated to begin with antecedent risk factors, which initiate the depressogenic process by disrupting important adaptive behavior patterns. The general rubric of stressors at the macro (e.g. negative life events) and micro (e.g. daily hassles) levels are probably the best example of such antecedents. These stressors disrupt behavior patterns that are necessary for the individual's day-to-day interactions with the environment. Thus, for example, stressful life events are postulated to lead to depression to the extent that they disrupt personal relationships and job responsibilities. This disruption itself can result in a negative emotional reaction which, combined with an inability to reverse the impact of the stressors, leads to a heightened state of self-awareness. This increased self-awareness makes salient the individual's sense of failure to meet internal standards and leads, therefore, to increased dysphoria and to many of the other cognitive, behavioral, and emotional symptoms of depression. Finally, these increased symptoms of depression serve to maintain and exacerbate the depressive state, in part by making more accessible negative information about the self (e.g. Teasdale & Russell, 1983), and in part by reducing the depressed individual's sensitivity to others in their environment (e.g. Jacobson & Anderson, 1982).

Finally, it is important to note that Lewinsohn et al.'s (1985) model recognizes that stable predisposing individual differences may moderate the impact of the antecedent events in initiating the cycle leading to depression and in maintaining the depression once it begins. These constructs can be classified as vulnerabilities, which increase the probability of the occurrence of depression, and immunities, which decrease the probability of depression. Lewinsohn et al. suggest that vulnerability factors might include being female, having a history of prior depressions, and having low self-esteem. In contrast, examples of immunities include high self-perceived social competence, the availability of a confidant, and good coping skills. Finally, it is important to emphasize that Lewinsohn et al.'s model emphasizes the operation of "feedback loops" among the various factors. The feedback loops allow for either a "vicious cycle" or a "benign cycle." By reversing any of the components of the model, for example, the depression will be progressively ameliorated.

Pyszczynski and Greenberg (1987) recently proposed a self-regulatory perseveration theory of reactive depression that also emphasizes the central role of self-awareness, or self-focused attention, in the onset and maintenance of this disorder. This theory integrates aspects of psychoanalytic, cognitive, and behavioral theories of depression with Carver and Scheier's (1981) cybernetic model of self-regulation. Pyszczynski and Greenberg postulate a sequence of events that begins with the loss of a central source of self-esteem, such as the break-up of an important interpersonal relationship or the loss of a job. The loss must represent a central source of emotional security, identity, and self-worth (cf. Oatley & Bolton, 1985). Because of its importance, the loss not only undermines the stability of the individual's self-image, but further, leads to an increase in self-focus. This increased self-focus makes even more salient the significance of the loss.

Pyszczynski and Greenberg (1987) posit that the increase in self-focus leads to an increase in the internality of the attributions concerning the loss. This escalation of self-blame further increases the intensity of the negative affect experienced by the individual, and pushes the individual's self-image in a negative direction. This mounting negative affect and self-criticism may also interfere with the individual's social functioning, which exacerbates the negative cycle. Pyszczynski and Greenberg suggest that prolonged elevated self-focus following negative events represents a "depressive self-focusing style," which maintains and exacerbates the depressive symptomatology by magnifying the consequences of negative events (see Ingram, 1990, for an elaborated but similar self-absorption model of psychopathology, and Pyszcynski, Greenberg, Hamilton, and Nix, 1991, for a response to this elaboration.)

The Differential Activation Hypothesis

The final theory of depression that we will consider in this chapter is Teasdale's (1983, 1988) "Differential Activation Hypothesis." Teasdale distinguishes between vulnerability to the onset of depression, and vulnerability to the persistence of depression, and proposes the Differential Activation Hypothesis to account for individual differences in these vulnerabilities. Whereas other cognitive theories of depression posit stable cognitive factors that are present prior to the onset of depression (e.g. negative schemas, dysfunctional attitudes, negative attributional style), the Differential Activation Hypothesis focuses on patterns of thinking that are activated *in the depressed state*. Essentially, Teasdale points out that everyone experiences some life events that would be expected to produce at least mild or transient depression in most people. But only a minority of people go on to develop clinically significant depression. As Teasdale states:

> the patterns of thinking activated in the initial depressed state will determine whether that state remains mild or transient, on the one hand, or whether, on the other hand it becomes more severe (onset vulnerability). Differences in the patterns activated in more severe states will determine whether those states show remission or become persistent and chronic (persistence vulnerability). According to this hypothesis the original source of the depression may not matter too much—the crucial factor that determines whether the initial depression will intensify and persist is the pattern of thinking that exists, *once depressed*. (p. 251)

Teasdale (1988) suggests that, when faced with negative event, most individuals avoid entering into an escalating or self-maintaining vicious cycle of depression and negative thinking. In contrast, more vulnerable individuals exhibit patterns of thinking during the initial depressed state that may lead to more severe, clinical levels of depression. The cognitive constructs and self-representations that become accessible in the initial depressed state, for example, are likely more negative in these individuals than is the case in their less vulnerable counterparts. These thoughts, memories, and beliefs are stored in memory as a result of early learning experiences associating depressed affect with negative cognitions. These individuals may also have less social support and fewer coping resources than do less vulnerable individuals. As this negative thinking exacerbates the depressive symptomatology and the depression becomes more severe, the cognitive processing of these individuals becomes more negative, and adverse experiences and memories more easily accessible. Of course, this pattern of cognitive functioning serves to further worsen the depression, and the vicious cycle continues (see Ingram, 1984, for a similar description).

An important aspect of Teasdale's (1988) Differential Activation Hypothesis concerns the notion of a match between vulnerability and negative event. We noted earlier that Beck's and Abramson's cognitive models of depression posited that individuals might become depressed when faced with an event that is thematically relevant to their schema or vulnerability type. Beck (1983), for example, posited the existence of "autonomous" and "sociotropic" personality characteristics, and Abramson, Metalsky, and Alloy (1989) discussed the possible effects of "domain-specific" attributional tendencies. In contrast, the Differential Activation Hypothesis suggests that this matching of event to vulnerability subtype is not a necessary prerequisite to depression:

> the differential activation hypothesis views the increased accessibility of negative constructs and representations as a consequence of the depressed state reactivating the negative constructs that have been most frequently and prototypically associated with previous experiences of depression as a whole. It follows that a wider range of constructs would not be affected and, most importantly, that these constructs need not bear a particularly close relationship to the event that initially provoked the current depression. Even depressed moods originally resulting from fluctuations in some endogenous biological process would be expected to be associated with increased accessibility of a range of negative constructs and representations. (p. 255)

CONCLUDING COMMENTS

In this brief review of major contemporary models of depression, we have identified a number of themes—some that are specific to one model, and others that cut across a number of models. Our goal in writing this chapter was to present the basic ideas of several psychological theories of depression; we have not attempted here to evaluate their theoretical or empirical adequacy. In fact, the critical analysis of the status of some of these approaches will be the focus of several chapters to follow. Here, we will conclude with a brief overview of what we consider to be some of the most compelling of the ideas from the theories that were presented. Our contention is that a comprehensive theory of depression—even if it applies only to some forms of the disorder—ought to integrate multiple ideas and constructs that concern both the inner experiences of the depressed person and his or her transactions with the environment. Moreover, such a theory should also offer a sense of both the historical origin of depression and its future course. In this context, therefore, we propose that the following ideas are important and worthy of further consideration. Indeed, we shall return to these formulations in the final chapter of this book.

1. Cognitions are critically important in understanding the phenomenon of depression because they likely mediate the emotional impact of external circumstances. They characterize individual differences in peoples' interpretations of (and, therefore, reactions to) personal and environmental events and circumstances; consequently, they may be

significant in understanding individual differences in vulnerability to becoming depressed.

2. Negative cognitions about the worth and capability of the self may be necessary precursors to depressed mood. Once depressed mood occurs, other negative cognitions become highly accessible, and the availability of such associations may critically affect the severity and duration of the depressive syndrome.

3. There may be several kinds of cognitive vulnerability that operate on different levels. Depressogenic cognitive content, cognitive structures and processes, and deep, nonconscious memories and outcomes of early experience are but a few different types of possible cognitive vulnerabilities to depression.

4. The underlying beliefs, assumptions, and schemas that arise in the context of early parent-child attachment experiences may form the "working models" of the individual's world. As such, they represent critical cognitions and beliefs. It is likely that they influence not only interpretations and emotional reactions, but the entire range of skills, behaviors, and competencies that are available to the individual.

5. Stressful life events and adverse conditions are important instigators of depression by way of eliciting potentially depressogenic cognitions and deep representations of the self and the world.

6. While some cognitions about the self and the world may be distorted in depression, others are likely to be accurate. Depressed people often find themselves in truly negative circumstances. Moreover, some of these conditions may be partly of their own doing. Indeed, it is likely that stressors are not only a cause of distress, but are also a consequence of the way people conduct their lives. The reciprocity of this association represents a significant area for further investigation.

7. Stressors may have different meanings to different people, and individual differences may exist in vulnerability to these stressors. In particular, the interpersonal realm is a topic that is relatively poorly understood and underexplored with respect to depression.

8. There are at least three different levels at which interpersonal aspects of depression may be important: vulnerability due to interpersonal factors, the social skills and behaviors of the depressed person, and the effects of depression on social relationships. These levels should be examined systematically with respect to peer, family, and romantic relations.

9. Finally, while we have not included material in this chapter concerning biological aspects of depression, it is apparent from ongoing biological research that some depression vulnerability may result from dysfunctions in neuroendocrine functioning (although, to date, the complexities of such interacting systems have precluded exact specification). Early adverse life experiences and/or genetic factors may also contribute to such

vulnerability. Moreover, depressive experiences themselves may alter neuroendocrine functioning and biological vulnerability. Clearly, it will be important in further work to explore integrative biopsychosocial models, examining reciprocal relations among numerous variables.

Chapter 4

Assessment of Depression in Adults and Children

Advances in the diagnosis of depressive disorders, evolving from the Feighner Criteria, Research Diagnostic Criteria, and subsequent versions of the Diagnostic and Statistical Manual, have contributed enormously to the proliferation of research on mood disorders. In this chapter we review some of the techniques that have been developed to measure both diagnoses and symptoms of depression in adults. This is followed by a review of the relatively more recent developments in the assessment of children's depression.

ADULT MEASURES OF DEPRESSION

Interview measures for depression diagnoses and symptoms

Schedule for Affective Disorders and Schizophrenia

The Schedule for Affective Disorders and Schizophrenia (SADS) was developed by Endicott and Spitzer (1978) in an attempt to increase the reliability of interviewer-derived psychiatric diagnoses, and was originally based on the Research Diagnostic Criteria. With modification, of course, it can yield DSM-III-R diagnoses (but see the SCID, below). The SADS covers not only depression, but also such diagnostic categories as schizophrenia, anxiety disorders, and substance use disorders. There are three different versions of the SADS: the regular version, the lifetime version, and the change version. Of the three versions, it is the regular version that will likely be of most use to the practicing clinician; clinical research makes extensive use of all of the methods. Trained clinical interviewers can administer the semi-structured procedure with adequate interrater reliability (e.g. Endicott & Spitzer, 1978), and for some years the SADS has served as the major instrument in the US for establishing depressive diagnoses.

Structured Clinical Interview for DSM-III-R (SCID)

Spitzer and colleagues developed an updated version of the SADS, under contract to the National Institute of Mental Health, to cover the DSM-III-R (Spitzer, Williams, Gibbon, & First, 1990). It covers major diagnostic categories such as mood disorders, anxiety disorders, psychoses, eating disorders, somatoform disorders, and substance use disorders. There is also a version for personality disorders (SCID-II). The semi-structured probes are intended to cover both current and lifetime history of disorders, and clinical judgments are required so that it is assumed that interviewers have had clinical training. The SCID has undergone several modifications prior to the 1990 version, based on field trials and clinical/research experiences. Kappa coefficients and test-retest reliability have been derived from field tests in six sites, and are reported to be comparable to those of similar assessment methods such as the SADS and the DIS. However, the psychometric data have not yet been published by Spitzer and colleagues and are in preparation. The SCID will likely emerge as the most-used interview assessment method for diagnoses in clinical research. Meanwhile, Riskind, Beck, Berchick, Brown, and Steer (1987) have reported kappa of 0.72 (82% agreement) for major depressive disorder based on independent ratings of videotaped interviews of outpatients. This study also focused on the diagnosis of generalized anxiety disorder, and found similarly high interrater agreement for that diagnosis. The SCID will likely supplant the SADS in clinical research, owing to its basis in DSM-III-R diagnoses.

Diagnostic Interview Schedule (DIS)

This interview schedule was developed for use in the Epidemiological Catchment Area (ECA) studies, a multi-site survey of mental health problems in community adults (Robins, Helzer, Croughan, & Ratcliff, 1981). As a result of the need to have a method that could be applied by lay interviewers with minimal training, the DIS is highly structured and can be computer-scored to achieve diagnoses based on the DSM-III (now DSM-III-R). The DIS does not cover all diagnostic categories; in general, relatively rare disorders and personality disorders (except for antisocial personality disorder) are excluded. In a reliability study, 394 persons representing different diagnoses were independently reinterviewed by psychiatrists. Kappa coefficients comparing DIS-based diagnoses and clinician diagnoses were generally high. Kappa for major depressive disorder was 0.70; however, the DIS tended to underestimate major depression (see also Anthony, Folstein, Romanoski, Von Korff, Nestadt, et al., 1985 for problems in the reliability of DIS diagnoses). Attempts to clarify the sources of difficulty in the DIS procedure have continued, and in the final analysis it has been the basis of recent large-scale epidemiological data on mental health problems.

Hamilton Rating Scale for Depression

Although the recent advent of structured diagnostic interview schedules has altered the situation somewhat, the Hamilton Rating Scale for Depression (HRSD; Hamilton, 1960) remains the most frequently used interviewer rated measure of depression. It is important to note that this measure was not designed to yield a diagnosis, but rather, a depressive severity score in patients already diagnosed as depressed.

The HRSD contains 21 items covering mood, behavioral, somatic, and cognitive symptoms. By convention, only 17 of Hamilton's original 21 items are typically scored. The HRSD is most commonly administered by experienced clinicians, although a number of investigators have demonstrated that laypersons can be trained in a relatively short period of time to reach acceptable levels of administration. Furthermore, Endicott, Cohen, Nee, Fleiss, and Sarantakes (1981) have demonstrated that HRSD scores can be reliably derived from a SADS interview, so that the clinician may be able to obtain information for both of these measures through a single, comprehensive interview. The HRSD has been shown to be sensitive to change in the severity of depressive symptomatology over time, and consequently, is useful as a measure of the efficacy of therapy. Finally, we should note that Carroll, Feinberg, Smouse, Rawson, and Greden (1981) have developed a self-report version of the HRSD, the Carroll Rating Scale for Depression. The Hamilton scale has been extensively reviewed by Shaw, Vallis, and McCabe (1985).

Self-report measures of depression

There are numerous self-report instruments designed to measure depression or depressed affect. In fact, Moran and Lambert (1983) listed over 30 self-administered scales for the measurement of depression that had been reported in the psychological literature. Of these, only a handful have achieved widespread use, and it is these self-report measures of depression that we will describe below. Examples of items from commonly used scales are presented in Table 4.1. Below we discuss several scales at some length because of their frequent use (or misuse) in research. Additionally, because of their potential research application, we also note two self-report measures of *history* of depressive experiences.

Table 4.1   Examples of depression self-report scales

Beck Depression Inventory (BDI)

0   I am not particularly discouraged about the future.
1   I feel discouraged about the future.
2   I feel I have nothing to look forward to.
3   I feel that the future is hopeless and that things cannot improve.

0   I don't get more tired than usual.
1   I get tired more easily than I used to.
2   I get tired from doing almost anything.
3   I am too tired to do anything.

Center for Epidemiological Studies Depression Scale (CED-D)

	Rarely	A little	Moderate	Most
I felt that I could not shake off the blues even with help from my family and friends.	0	1	2	3
I talked less than usual.	0	1	2	3

Zung Self-Rating Scale for Depression

I have crying spells or feel like it.	A little of the time	Some of the time	Good part of the time	Most of the time
I feel hopeful about the future.	A little of the time	Some of the time	Good part of the time	Most of the time

---

Beck Depression Inventory

The Beck Depression Inventory (BDI) is probably the most frequently used self-report method of assessing depressive symptomatology. It was originally developed by Beck, Ward, Mendelsohn, Mock, and Erbaugh (1961) as an interviewer-assisted procedure, and consists of 21 items with four response choices each. Items were selected to represent the affective, cognitive, motivational, and physiological symptoms of depression, although it is well-known that the BDI emphasizes subjective symptoms to the relative neglect of somatic symptoms. Item categories include mood, pessimism, crying spells, guilt, irritability, sleep and appetite disturbance, and loss of libido. For each of these categories of symptoms, there is a graded series of four alternative statements, ranging from neutral (e.g. "I do not feel sad," "I don't feel disappointed in myself") to a maximum level of severity (e.g. "I am so sad or unhappy that I can't stand it," "I would kill myself if I had the chance"). The items are scored from 0 to 3, with the sum of the scores representing the total BDI score, which can range from 0 to 63. Generally, a total BDI score of 0–9 indicates a normal nondepressed state; 10–18 reflects a mild level of depression; 19–29 reflects moderate depression; and 30–63 indicates a severe level of depression (Beck, Steer, & Garbin, 1988). Note that these cutoffs are somewhat different from those often cited or in common use (e.g. Shaw, Vallis, & McCabe, 1985).

It is important to note that the BDI was not designed to yield a discrete diagnosis of depression; rather, it was constructed to measure depression as one single dimension of psychopathology that cuts across a wide variety of diagnostic categories. Its major focus, therefore, is on the depth or severity of depressive symptomatology, essentially defined by the combination of the number, frequency, and intensity of symptoms. Defining a subject group as "depressed" on the basis of scores above 9 or higher, would be an inappropriate use of the scale if the implication is that such a group is diagnosed depressed. As Kendall, Hollon, Beck, Hammen, and Ingram (1987) observed, the term depressed as applied to high-scoring research subjects should be replaced by the term "dysphoric" to describe subjects whose diagnostic status has not been established by clinical means using diagnostic criteria. Moreover, as Gotlib (1984) has noted, high scores may be highly correlated with other measures of psychopathology—at least in college students—so that nonspecific distress rather than depression as such may be captured in the BDI (as in other such self-report measures).

Beck, Steer, and Garbin (1988) recently reported that the BDI had been used in over 1000 research studies. Additionally, numerous studies of its psychometric properties have been reported. Beck, Steer, and Garbin (1988) performed meta-analyses of such studies to summarize features of the scale. Consistent with its unidimensional intent, high levels of internal consistency were obtained: mean coefficient alpha 0.86 for psychiatric populations, and 0.81 for nonpsychiatric samples. Test-retest stabilities across 10 studies ranged from 0.48 to 0.86 for patients across varying intervals, and from 0.60 to 0.83 for 5 nonpsychiatric samples. Given that mood is expected to change over time, the stabilities are respectable. Factor analyses have yielded numerous outcomes depending on method of extraction, but three related factors commonly emerge: sad mood/negative sense of self, psychomotor retardation, and somatic depression (Beck, Steer, & Garbin, 1988).

Validity studies indicate good concurrent validity in terms of correlations with other measures of depression severity; 35 such studies are reported by Beck, Steer, and Garbin (1988). Some studies have shown relatively poor discriminant validity between depression and anxiety using the BDI. Recently, however, Steer, Beck, Riskind, and Brown (1986) reported that diagnosed primary generalized anxiety patients scored lower on the BDI than diagnosed primary depressed patients.

Overall, the BDI has had an impressive career in clinical research, and has the advantage of communicability because it is commonly used, as well as established psychometric properties. If used appropriately as a screening instrument or as an indicator of severity (and change) in symptoms, it serves well.

Center for Epidemiological Studies Depression Scale

The Center for Epidemiological Studies Depression Scale (CES-D; Radloff, 1977) is a 20-item scale designed to measure the current level of depressive symptomatology in individuals from the general (i.e. nonpsychiatric) population. The items assess depressed mood, feelings of guilt, worthlessness, loneliness, and hopelessness, psychomotor retardation, concentration problems, and appetite loss and sleep disturbance, although there is a particular emphasis on affective symptomatology. For each item, respondents indicate on a four-point scale (0 to 3) how frequently they have experienced that symptom in the past week, ranging from "Rarely or none of the time" (less than 1 day) to "Most or all of the time" (5–7 days). Thus, total scores on the CES-D can range from 0 to 60. Radloff has suggested that a total score of 16, which demarcates the upper 20% of the score distribution in general population studies, may serve as a cutoff to differentiate "cases" of depression from noncases. Barnes and Prosen (1985) have suggested more specifically that scores below 16 indicate that the respondent is "not depressed"; scores from 16 to 20 indicate "mild depression," scores from 21 to 30 indicate "moderate depression," and scores of 31 and greater indicate "severe depression."

Like the BDI, the CES-D was designed to measure depression as one dimension of psychopathology that cuts across various diagnostic categories. Attesting to this unidimensional construction, Barnes and Prosen (1985) and Radloff (1977) have reported internal consistency coefficients of greater than 0.84. Despite this high reliability, however, the CES-D has consistently yielded three factors: Depressed Affect, Positive Affect, and Somatic/Retarded Activities (Radloff, 1977; Roberts, 1980). The presence of a Positive Affect not found in factor analyses of the BDI may be due to the inclusion of positively-worded items on the CES-D but not on the BDI. In fact, the separation of positive and negative affect on the CES-D is consistent with recent research suggesting that these are two independent dimensions rather than opposite ends of a single bipolar factor (e.g. Gotlib & Meyer, 1986; Watson & Tellegen, 1985).

The CES-D has been found to correlate significantly with other measures of depression (cf. Radloff, 1977; Weissman, Sholomskas, Pottenger, Prusoff and Locke, 1977), indicating acceptable convergent validity. Moreover, Weissman et al. reported the sensitivity of the CES-D (i.e. its capability to identify cases of depression) to be above 0.90, and its specificity (i.e. its ability to identify noncases) to be above 0.55. Despite these figures, however, the results of a number of studies suggest that the CES-D should not be used as a clinical diagnostic instrument. Boyd, Weissman, Thompson, and Myers (1982), for example, found that a significant proportion of the false positives on the CES-D received other psychiatric or medical diagnoses than depression. Lewinsohn and Teri (1982), too, found that a score of 17 or greater on the CES-D predicted a diagnosis of depression with only 34% accuracy; scores of 16 and less, however, classified subjects as nondepressed with an 82% accuracy rate. On the basis of their results, Lewinsohn and Teri suggest that the CES-D could be used as an initial screening instrument. Those persons scoring low on the CES-D would be considered to be nondepressed, while those scoring high would be subjected to a subsequent clinical interview. Interestingly, the results of other investigations suggest that even this is too liberal a use of the CES-D. Myers and Weissman (1980) and Roberts and Vernon (1983) found a false negative rate of between 36 and 40% in their samples of subjects; that is, 40% of the individuals identified as depressed by the Schedule for Affective Disorders and Schizophrenia (SADS) criteria scored below 16 on the CES-D. Myers and Weissman suggest that the CES-D is an effective screening device for research, but not for clinical practice, although in our view, this may not be a useful distinction. In a later section reported below under Child and Adolescent measures, we discuss the relative merits of the CES-D and BDI with adolescents.

MMPI-D Scale and D-30

The MMPI-D scale, one of the 10 clinical scales of the Minnesota Multiphasic Personality Inventory (Hathaway & McKinley, 1951), was originally developed to identify severely depressed patients. It consists of 60 statements to which patients respond true or false. The 60 items reflect various aspects of depressive illness, and were selected on the basis of their ability to identify a group of psychiatric patients exhibiting depressive symptomatology. Eleven items differentiated between depressed and nondepressed psychiatric patients, while the remaining 49 items discriminated between depressed patients and nondepressed, nonpatient, normals.

Certainly the MMPI is one of the most familiar psychological assessment instruments. Despite its empirical construction, however, the MMPI-D scale has been repeatedly criticized. For example, Snaith, Ahmed, Mehta, and Hamilton (1971) have questioned the construct validity of the scale, a challenge supported by the heterogeneity of its items and its complex and unreliable factor structure. In fact, Snaith et al. suggested that the MMPI-D scale may reflect personality factors rather than depressive illness. More recently, Nelson (1987) has suggested that using the MMPI-D scale for purposes of subject selection or group assignment may be misleading because one-third of the items on this scale, the "subtle" items, may play no role in defining depression. McNair (1974) has also expressed concerns about the lack of sensitivity of the MMPI to drug effects and the lack of a clear time reference period in the instructions.

In an attempt to address these drawbacks of the scale, Dempsey (1964) constructed the MMPI-D-30, a 30-item version of the MMPI-D scale. Although the MMPI-D-30 is a more nearly unidimensional depression scale than the MMPI-D scale, it still has limitations. For example, it shares with the MMPI-D scale the problem of heterogeneity of item pool and, like the BDI and the CES-D, does not sample from the entire range of depressive symptomatology, notably excluding items assessing somatic functioning. Finally, as Mayer (1977) notes, 25 items of the MMPI-D-30 are shared with Comrey's (1957) neuroticism factor and, consequently, it is unclear exactly what is being measured by this scale.

Zung Self-Rating Depression Scale

The Zung Self-Rating Depression Scale (SDS; Zung, 1965) consists of 20 items assessing symptoms of depression identified in previous factor analytic studies of the syndrome of depression. Ten of the items are worded symptomatically positive, and ten symptomatically negative. The 20 items assess "pervasive affect" (two items), "physiological equivalents or concomitants" (ten items), and "psychological concomitants" (eight items). Respondents indicate whether each symptom is true of themselves little or none of the time, some of the time, a good part of the time, or most of the time. The SDS yields a numerical score that can be used to indicate both the presence and severity of depressive symptomatology, regardless of specific diagnosis. It is important to note that no attempt was made to screen or evaluate potential items empirically before including them in the scale, and the final set of items was not tested for internal reliability. Blumenthal (1975), for example, reported that the positively worded items on the SDS load on a factor that is independent from the negatively worded, more "depressive" items, again, indicating the independence of positive and negative affect. Moreover, scores on the SDS correlate -0.28 with level of education, suggesting that individuals with more education are less likely to endorse depressive symptoms on the SDS (Glazer, Clarkin, & Hunt, 1981).

Carroll, Fielding, and Blashki (1973) have noted that the SDS lacks items assessing the depressive symptoms of guilt, retardation, hypochondriasis, and loss of insight, and that it cannot be used for purposes of differential diagnosis. Furthermore, Glazer, Clarkin, and Hunt (1981) have observed that normal adolescents and normal elderly persons both tend to score in the clinical range on this measure. Finally, although the SDS correlates moderately well with other self-report measures of depression, and particularly well with the BDI (cf. Schaefer, Brown, Watson, Plemel,

DeMotts et al., 1985; Zung, 1971), there is some evidence that it does not differentiate levels of severity within depressed populations, and is not sensitive over a wide range of clinical depression (Carroll, Fielding, & Blashki, 1973; Moran & Lambert, 1983). As Rehm (1976, p. 239) states, "The SDS is psychometrically unsophisticated ... (and its)... use in behavioral practice and research is questionable pending stronger psychometric support."

Depression Adjective Check Lists

The Depression Adjective Check Lists (DACL; Lubin, 1965, 1967/1981) are equivalent brief measures of depressed mood that were normed on depressed neuropsychiatric patients. The DACL consist of seven different lists of adjectives describing various feelings of depressed and elated mood. Each list contains 22 positive (depressed) and 10 or 12 negative (elated) adjectives, and respondents are required to check all of the words that describe their current feelings. The DACL are scored by adding all the positive words endorsed and the negative words not checked.

Normative data are available for samples of students, senior citizens, adolescent delinquents, and psychiatric patients. Reliability estimates for the DACL with normal (i.e. nondepressed) samples are typically greater than 0.80. The DACL have been found to distinguish between depressed and nondepressed persons, and to correlate modestly (0.27 to 0.70) with other self-report measures and clinical ratings of depression (e.g. Levitt & Lubin, 1975; Lubin, 1965; Tanaka-Matsumi & Kameoka, 1986). Furthermore, because of the large number of equivalent forms, the DACL are particularly suited for use in studies in which repeated measures of depressed mood are necessary. As Hammen (1981) notes, however, the greatest limitation of the use of this instrument is that it is a measure of depressed mood only; other aspects of the syndrome of depression, such as vegetative symptoms and cognitive dysfunction, are neglected. Indeed, Giambra (1977) factor analyzed the DACL and found the items to load on one factor alone, which he labelled "Affective Malaise."

Additional scales measuring depression

Costello–Comrey Anxiety and Depression Scales

Costello and Comrey (1967) developed the Costello–Comrey Depression Scale (CC-D) and the Costello-Comrey Anxiety Scale (CC-A) to assess an individual's predisposition to experience depression and anxiety, respectively, and to discriminate between these affective states. Items selected from a number of existing scales were administered to a large university sample and, on the basis of repeated factor analyses, dimensions representing depression and anxiety were identified. The final scales were composed of items whose factor loadings were found to discriminate between these two affective states. Correlations between the CC-D and CC-A have been found to range from 0.40 to 0.59. Items for these two scales are rated on nine-point scales and are worded in both positive and negative directions. The CC-D is comprised of 14 items. A split-half reliability of 0.90 was obtained for this scale when administered to a nonclinical sample. The CC-D has been found to correlate adequately with other self-report measures of depression in psychiatric populations (Mendels, Weinstein, & Cochrane, 1972). The CC-A is composed of nine items. A split-half reliability of 0.70 was reported for a university sample, and a correlation of 0.72 was observed for the CC-A scores of psychiatric patients obtained at admission and again at discharge (Costello & Comrey, 1967).

Millon Clinical Multiaxial Inventory

The Millon Clinical Multiaxial Inventory (MCMI; Millon, 1983) was developed to provide a comprehensive assessment both of enduring personality characteristics and of more acute clinical disorders in psychiatric populations. Each of the 20 scales on the MCMI was developed to measure a syndrome consistent both with current theories of personality and psychopathology and with current diagnostic practice (i.e., DSM-III). Item selection for the MCMI was based on a three-stage process involving clinical populations. Scales were constructed using items that not only successfully discriminated the target diagnostic group from an undifferentiated psychiatric population, but also, that covaried with other clinical scales in a manner consistent with current theories of personality and psychopathology. As a result, significant item overlap exists among the various scales.

The 175-item MCMI employs a true-false format, and actuarial base rate data are used in computing a patient's score on the various scales. Of particular relevance to the present chapter are the scales assessing depression and anxiety. The depression scale of the MCMI (MCMI-D) is a 36-item measure of the clinical syndrome of dysthymia, assessing cognitive, affective, and motivational symptoms of depression. This scale has been found to possess high internal consistency, acceptable test-retest reliabilites for intervals of one and five weeks (0.78 and 0.66, respectively), and moderate correlations with other self-report measures of depression (Millon, 1983; Goldberg, Shaw, & Segal, 1987). Goldberg, Shaw, and Segal have noted, however, that the MCMI-D scale does not assess vegetative depressive symptoms, such as appetite and weight loss, libido disturbance, and sleep difficulties. The 37-item anxiety scale of the MCMI (MCMI-A) assesses cognitive, behavioral, and physiological responses reflecting both generalized anxiety and specific phobias. This scale, too, has demonstrated high internal consistency, test-retest reliabilties of 0.80 and 0.68 for intervals of one and five weeks, respectively, and is moderately correlated with other measures of anxiety (Millon, 1983).

It is also important to note that substantial overlap exists between the items of the depression and anxiety scales of the MCMI, with a resulting intercorrelation of 0.93 for these two scales. In addition, the reader should be cognizant of the possible role that response bias might play in affecting scores on the MCMI-D and MCMI-A: only 4 of the 36 depression items, and 1 of the 37 anxiety items are keyed "False."

Symptom Checklist-90

The Symptom Checklist-90 (SCL-90; Derogatis, Lipman, & Covy, 1973) is a 90-item measure of symptomatic psychological distress designed for use with psychiatric and medical patients. It is an expanded version of the Hopkins Symptom Checklist, which itself was developed from the Cornell Medical Index. Each item on the SCL-90 is rated on a five-point scale ("not at all" to "extremely") to indicate the severity of the symptom over the past week. The inventory assesses nine clusters or primary symptom dimensions, in addition to providing three global indices of distress. Five of these nine clusters were identified on the basis of factor analyses, while the remaining clusters were rationally created. Of relevance to the present chapter is the 13-item depression scale and the 10-item anxiety scale. Items on the depression scale assess such symptoms as dysphoric mood, decreased motivation and interest, feelings of hopelessness, and thoughts of suicide. The scale has been found to have high internal consistency (coefficient alpha of 0.90) and test-retest reliability for a one-week period (Derogatis, Lipman, & Covy, 1973). With respect to concurrent validity, significant correlations have been reported between the SCL-90 depression scale and corresponding scales on other depression symptom inventories.

Profile of Mood States

The Profile of Mood States (POMS; McNair, Lorr, & Droppleman, 1971) was developed to assess short-term changes in six primary mood states. On the basis of repeated factor analyses conducted with samples of psychiatric patients and normals, dimensions labelled tension-anxiety, depression-dejection, anger-hostility, confusion-bewilderment, vigor-activity, and fatigue-inertia were identified. The 65 items on this checklist are each rated on a five-point frequency scale, ranging from "not at all" to "extremely," for a one-week time period. Reported internal-consistency coefficients for these dimensions range from 0.74 to 0.92, with test-retest reliabilities for a 20-day interval ranging from 0.65 to 0.74 (McNair, Lorr, and Droppleman, 1971). Separate male and female norms have been derived from a university health center sample. The POMS has frequently been employed to assess change in clinical outcome studies (e.g. McNair, 1974).

There is one caveat that McNair, Lorr, and Droppleman (1971) point out in their manual, but that seems to have been overlooked by investigators using this scale. For five of the six scales, the mood state measured by the scale is well described by the scale name. For the tension-anxiety scale, however, the authors are attempting to measure physical or muscular-skeletal tension rather than cognitive tension, anxiety, or the generalized feeling of nervousness and discomfort. Another difficulty with the use of the POMS is that the individual subscales are highly intercorrelated, so that general negative affectivity or distress, rather than "pure" mood states, may be assessed.

General Behavior Inventory

The General Behavior Inventory (GBI) was developed by Depue and his colleagues as a screening instrument to identify lifetime affective conditions in a nonclinical population, including a range of severity of symptoms from subclinical to syndromal (Depue, Slater, Wolfstetter-Kausch, Klein, Gopelrud, & Farr, 1981). The original version of the GBI aimed at identifying bipolar conditions; items attempted to characterize the intensity, frequency, and duration of specifically affective disorders symptoms, and to also capture the biphasic nature of bipolar conditions. The original GBI was subjected to careful validation procedures, and was shown to have sound psychometric features (Depue et al., 1981). Persons identified as at risk for bipolar disorder on the GBI had significant impairment of functioning over a 19-month follow-up compared to a control group (Klein & Depue, 1984).

A revised version of the GBI was subsequently developed to identify both bipolar and unipolar conditions in nonclinical samples based on lifetime symptoms (Depue, Krauss, Spoont, & Arbisi, 1989). The revised version, similar in format and structure to the original, contains 73 items, each rated on a 4-point frequency scale. Items include content covering depression, mania/hypomania, and biphasic fluctuations. Subjects receive two scores, one for depression and one for the combined mania/hypomania and biphasic items. The scores can be plotted on the two axes, and using empirically derived cut-scores, diagnostic estimates are derived. High scores on the depression scale would identify frequently recurrent or chronic-intermittent depression, but not simply infrequent episodic depression. In five large samples, coefficient alphas ranged from 0.90 to 0.96; test-retest reliabilities over 12 to 16 weeks were 0.71–0.74 based on two studies. In a large validation study of the revised version, Depue et al. (1989) screened a large group of students and interviewed high-scoring and comparison individuals. Indices of predictive power and specificity were in the high 0.80s and 0.90s, and sensitivity was 0.78 for unipolar and 0.76 for bipolar subjects. The great majority of unipolar and bipolar cases were thus correctly identified by their scores. Also, the unipolar and bipolar groups were relatively homogeneous and nonoverlapping. The authors conclude that the scale can be used as a screening instrument to identify potential subjects at risk for affective disorders. They note, however, that the validation has been based on college students, and studies need to be conducted on older samples that might include more nonaffective psychopathology to determine the utility of the cut-points in different samples.

Self-report questionnaire for diagnosing major depressive disorder

Zimmerman, Coryell, Corenthal, and Wilson (1986) developed the Inventory to Diagnose Depression (IDD) to be completed as a questionnaire. It contains 22 items covering symptoms with 5 choices per item varying in severity, scored as 0 (no disturbance), 1 (subclinical severity), and 2–4 (symptom present, varying in severity). Each symptom is also rated for its duration. The scale can then be scored using DSM-III criteria as to the presence of the requisite number of symptoms of sufficient severity, lasting for more than two weeks. The scale is reported to have adequate reliability, and concurrent validity based on DIS interviews (Zimmerman & Coryell, 1987). In a further validation study, Zimmerman and Coryell (1988) interviewed first-degree relatives of patients and also administered the IDD. They reported adequate kappa coefficients; agreement increased as the time interval between the two procedures decreased. Both the DIS and the IDD identified depression in the relatives of depressed patients. The psychometric data are clearly limited at this point. The authors express concern that the instrument not be used in place of diagnostic evaluations in clinical settings due to the risk of withholding appropriate treatment if the person does not "score" as depressed. However, it has research potential as a screening device. The authors also indicate that it can serve as a measure of the severity of depression covering the entire range of DSM-III symptoms, although its validity for this function remains to be demonstrated.

ASSESSMENT OF DEPRESSION IN CHILDREN AND ADOLESCENTS

Self-report measures of depression in children and adolescents

With the increased interest in childhood depressive disorders, there has been a proliferation of depression self-report questionnaires in the past few years. We begin by discussing two of the most widely used measures, with brief remarks concerning additional instruments, and then turn to a general discussion of issues in the self-report assessment of depression.

Children's Depression Inventory

The Children's Depression Inventory (CDI; Kovacs, 1983) was the first and is probably the most widely used self-report measure of depression in children. The CDI was developed from the Beck Depression Inventory, and was designed for use with school-age children and adolescents. It consists of 27 items assessing the presence and severity of an array of "overt" symptoms of childhood depression, such as sadness, anhedonia, suicidal ideation, and sleep and appetite disturbance, but it also includes items that tap oppositional behavior and school performance. Each item presents 3 choices, scored 0, 1, or 2 in severity level.

Considerable attention has been devoted to the psychometric properties of the scale, in keeping with increased attention devoted to childhood depression once it became clear that the syndrome could be identified in children using adult criteria. The studies address several issues that will be briefly discussed in the sections to follow.

First, what are the basic psychometric properties of the CDI? The scale appears to have solid internal consistency reliability, with coefficient alphas in the 0.80s or higher (Saylor, Finch, Spirito, & Bennett, 1984; Smucker, Craighead, Craighead, & Green, 1986). Also, test-retest reliability is adequate over varying durations, given true fluctuations in mood (e.g. Nelson & Politano, 1990; Saylor et al., 1984; Weiss & Weisz, 1988). Stability of scoring appears to differ by sample status (clinic-referred or nonreferred; reviewed in Kendall, Cantwell, & Kazdin, 1989). In a long-term follow-up Mattison, Handford, Kales, Goodman, and McLaughlin (1990) found fairly good stability of high scoring over several years, and low scorers consistently scored low.

In large-scale community samples of children and adolescents there do not appear to be significant age or gender effects in overall scores (although specific subsamples sometimes do show sex differences in patterns of scores), suggesting that the scale does not need to be normed separately for boys and girls, and those of different ages (e.g. Finch, Saylor, & Edwards, 1985). Smucker et al. (1986) suggested somewhat different test-retest stabilities for males and females, and interpreted them to mean that junior high school girls show more stable depressive symptoms, and their symptoms stabilize earlier, than do boys'. Several studies consistently have shown means of around 9, and a cut-off score of 19 defining the upper 10% (e.g. Doerfler, Felner, Rowlison, Raley, & Evans, 1988; Finch, Saylor, & Edwards, 1985; Kovacs, 1983; Smucker et al., 1986). A number of investigators have factor analyzed the CDI and, depending on the nature of the sample and methods of factor extraction, have reported between two and eight factors (e.g. Carey, Faulstich, Gresham, Ruggiero, & Enyart, 1987; Hodges & Craighead, 1990; Saylor, Finch, Spirito, & Bennett, 1984; Weiss & Weisz, 1988; Weiss, Weisz, Politano, Carey, Nelson, & Finch, 1991).

Second, does the CDI measure depression? In terms of concurrent validity, several studies have demonstrated that children in treatment score higher than do nonreferred children (e.g. Carey et al., 1987; Hodges, 1990; Romano & Nelson, 1988; Saylor, Finch, Spirito, & Bennett, 1984). On the other hand, most studies indicate that diagnosed depressed children do not differ significantly from children in the same treatment settings who do not have depressive disorders (e.g. Carey et al., 1987; Hodges, 1990; Kazdin et al., 1983; Saylor, Finch, Spirito, & Bennett, 1984; see Romano & Nelson, 1988, for an exception). Several investigators have noted that the CDI has reasonably good specificity but poor sensitivity; Hodges (1990), for instance, notes that although the CDI is good at identifying children who are not depressed, it is not very good at identifying those who are (see also Asarnow & Carlson, 1986; Saylor, Finch, Spirito, & Bennett, 1984). These researchers indicate that CDI scores are often elevated in children who also show symptoms of anxiety and conduct disorders. Perhaps increased concurrent validity would be demonstrated if the clinical samples were clearly separated into those with "pure" depression and those with another disorder not accompanied by depression. The questionable validity to date may reflect in part the highly prevalent comorbidity of depression and other disorders in children and adolescents.

Construct validity of the CDI has been reported in the form of associations between CDI scores and theoretically-predicted features of depression. Numerous studies, for instance, show significant correlations between CDI scores and low self-esteem, negative attribution style, external locus of control, and academic difficulties (e.g. Doerfler et al., 1988; Mattison et al., 1990; Saylor, Finch, Spirito, & Bennett, 1984).

Third, do the self-reported symptoms correspond to symptoms reported by others? In part, this is a question of validity of the measure, but it is also a question of the conceptualization of the phenomenon of depression. There is some indication of a significant association between psychiatric ratings of depression and self-reported CDI scores, at least in adolescents (Shain, Naylor, & Alessi, 1990). On the other hand, most of the studies show relatively poor agreement between self-reported CDI scores and those reported by parents, teachers, or peers (e.g. Doerfler et al., 1988; Kazdin et al., 1983; Saylor, Finch, Baskin, Furey, & Kelly, 1984). An exception to the nonconvergence finding was reported by Romano and Nelson (1988), who found good agreement between parents and their hospitalized children on the CDI. Part of this poor covergence is attributable to method variance (e.g. Kazdin et al., 1983; Saylor, Finch, Baskin et al., 1984). Some of the disagreement between sources, as noted previously in the discussion of interview methods, reflects differential accessibility to private, subjective experience; this issue is discussed more fully below.

Fourth, for what purpose is the CDI most useful? In view of the difficulties noted, most researchers acknowledge the limited utility of the CDI as a diagnostic measure. Instead, it is best used as a screening instrument indicating depressive symptoms and other kinds of distress (e.g. Carey et al., 1987; Hodges, 1990). Hodges and Craighead (1990) identified five factors of the scale, and suggested removal of items pertaining to the acting-out and oppositional conduct factor (and possibly the vegetative symptom factor), retaining three factors termed dysphoric mood, loss of personal and social interest, and self-deprecation. These factors were most clearly related to clinical depression in 6- to 13-year-olds.

CES-D scale for adolescents and children

The CES-D scale as developed for adults has sometimes been used to identify depressive symptoms in adolescents. Of the few such published studies, the most extensive is reported by Roberts et al. (1990), based on 2,000 students in grades 9 through 12 in western Oregon. Internal consistency reliabilities across samples were all above 0.87. Test-retest reliabilities over a one-month period were 0.49 for boys and 0.60 for girls.

Using the same cutoff score of 16 as recommended for adult samples, the overall prevalence of significant depressive symptomatology was 46% for boys and 58.6% for girls. While these figures are comparable to those reported by other investigators in samples of adolescents (e.g. Doerfler et al., 1988), they are more than twice the rates of 16–20% in adult samples using the same cutoff score. The issue of the validity of the scores for detecting clinical depression will be discussed below. Finally, it appears that the factor structure of the adolescent scoring on the CES-D is very similar to that of adults (Roberts et al., 1990).

Predictive and convergent validity of the CES-D have been assessed by comparing diagnostic evaluations to the CES-D scores, and by comparing the CES-D and BDI (or CDI) in adolescents. Roberts, Lewinsohn, and Seeley (1991) administered K-SADS diagnostic evaluations and Hamilton ratings for depression, the CES-D and BDI, and other questionnaires, to more than 1700 students in grades 9–12 in Oregon. Compared with diagnoses, both the CES-D and the BDI identified higher proportions of depressed students (major depression and dysthymia) than did the DSM-III-R criteria (e.g. the BDI identified 4% and the CES-D 12.1%, compared with major depression in 2.5% according to the DSM-III-R criteria). Overall, both the CES-D and BDI were considered to be relatively good at identifying true positives, but the false-positive rate was very high. Roberts, Lewinsohn, and Seeley (1991) also determined that brief, four-item scales of both the CES-D and BDI could be used as efficiently as the full scales, using clinical diagnosis as the criterion. The CES-D items included "felt depressed," "poor appetite," "felt sad," and "could not get going"; the BDI items were "feel sad," "blame myself," "cry," and "no appetite." However, neither scale should be used by itself to generate diagnostic information. In the final analysis of the instruments for assessing depression symptoms in adolescents, the authors favored the BDI because it identified 27% fewer false positives than did the CES-D. Somewhat similarly, Doerfler et al. (1988) compared the CDI and CES-D in children in grades 4–12. While the two measures correlated significantly (0.58), the CES-D cutoff of 16 identified 46% of the population in the "depressed" range. Thus, the CES-D appears to overrepresent the extent of depressive symptoms in child-adolescent populations.

Weissman, Orvaschel, and Padian (1980) modified the CES-D for use with children by making the items more readable, but limited information exists concerning its predictive validity. To address this issue, Fendrich, Weissman, and Warner (1991) administered the CES-D and provided psychiatric diagnostic evaluations of 166 children and adolescents at high or low risk for depression owing to presence or absence of major depression in one or more parents. Children who received diagnoses of major depression or dysthymia scored higher than all other children combined or with no diagnoses. However, those with anxiety, attention deficit, and conduct disorders also had elevated scores that were not significantly different from those with depressive diagnoses. Analyses indicated that the scale is most valid as a measure of depression for girls, and for those 12–18, compared with boys and younger and older children. The authors suggested that the scale may be limited in reliability and validity for children age 6–12. Also, the authors conclude that the scale measures current psychopathology in general, rather than depressive disorder in specific. If the scale is used as a screen with major depressive disorder as the criterion, the authors recommend using a cutoff of 15 to maximize sensitivity and specificity. A four-item screen performed nearly as well as the entire set of 20 items. Like most other investigators, Fendrich, Weissman, and Warner (in press) state that the instrument might function as a screen but should not be used as a substitute for clinical diagnoses.

Additional self-report measures of depression

Several recent reviews have detailed and compared the characteristics of other measures of childhood depression (e.g. Costello & Angold, 1988; Kazdin, 1990; Kendall, Cantwell, & Kazdin, 1989). These include the Child Depression Scale (Reynolds, Anderson, & Bartell, 1985), the Children's Depression Scale (Tisher & Lang, 1983), the Depression Self-Rating Scale (Birleson, 1981; Birleson, Hudson, Buchanan, & Wolff, 1987), and Reynolds Adolescent Depression Scale (Reynolds & Coats, 1986). Costello and Angold (1988) also review the Mood and Feelings Questionnaire (Angold, Costello, Pickles, et al., 1987). Recently, Lefkowitz, Tesiny, and Solodow (1989) developed a 12-item self-rating scale for children and adolescents based on items from the Peer Nomination Inventory for Depression (Lefkowitz & Tesiny, 1980). In addition, the Child Behavior Check List (Achenbach & Edelbrock, 1983) contains a depression factor, with different norms for children of different ages and gender; many of the items overlap with anxiety, however, and many symptoms of the depression syndrome are not included. In general, all of these instruments report satisfactory basic psychometric properties, but data supporting their use are limited.

Issues in the assessment of children's self-reported depression

Discrepancies in children's and informants' reports of symptoms

Numerous studies have reported relatively poor agreement among children, parents, teachers, and clinicians in the rating of children's symptoms and diagnoses. The disagreements appear to occur for a broad band of symptoms as well as depression specifically as measured on self-report instruments (e.g. Achenbach, McConaughy, & Howell, 1987; Doerfler et al., 1988; Moretti, Fine, Haley, & Marriage, 1985). Discrepancies also occur in the use of various interview procedures for diagnosing disorders in children, including the K-SADS, DICA, and DISC (e.g. Costello et al., 1988; Weissman, Wickramaratne, et al., 1987). They appear to occur in both community and clinical samples (e.g. Doerfler et al., 1988; Ivens & Rehm, 1988; Kazdin et al., 1983; Saylor, Finch, Baskin, et al., 1984), and in children of all ages, from preschool (Kashani, Holcomb, & Orvaschel, 1986) to late adolescence and early adulthood (Weissman, Wickramaratne, et al., 1987).

   In general, children tend to report more subjective and private symptoms than their parents do. Whereas overt behaviors and misconduct may be readily detected by parents and teachers, feelings of dejection, sadness, worthlessness, and experiences that children deliberately try to hide from parents are not perceived by parents. As a result, depression is likely to be underdiagnosed in children to the extent that such decisions are weighted by parent report.

Efforts to characterize the source of parent underreporting have focused mostly on demographic characteristics or on parents' own depressive symptoms. In general, few characteristics of the children's age, gender, family status, or psychiatric history have uniformly contributed to the parents' likelihood of reporting symptoms (e.g. Weissman, Wickramaratne, et al., 1987). The role of parental depression has been emphasized, with some investigators arguing that depressed or stressed mothers, for instance, exaggerate their children's problems (e.g. Forehand, Lautenschlager, & Graziano, 1986; Griest, Wells, & Forehand, 1979). On the other hand, some studies find no or few differences as a function of parental depression level (e.g. Ivens & Rehm, 1988), or that depressed mothers are relatively more sensitive in detecting their children's symptoms (e.g. Conrad & Hammen, 1989; Weissman, Wickramaratne, et al., 1987; see review by Richters, in press). Conrad and Hammen (1989) for instance, found that nondepressed women were especially inaccurate compared to external sources of information and, compared to depressed women, seemed to ignore, tolerate, or otherwise fail to detect actual problems in their children. Depressed women showed no evidence of indiscriminate reporting of symptoms in their children, and in fact distinguished accurately between children who did and did not have symptoms as reported either by children themselves or by clinician or teacher ratings.

The overall conclusion seems to be that for assessment of internal and private information, children's reports are essential. The various investigators of children's disorders urge that information be collected from various informants. With respect to diagnostic decisions, it might be well to adopt the strategy urged by Weissman, Wickramaratne, et al. (1987), who argue for giving preference to the child's report if choices of informants must be made. Ultimately, the choice of informants depends on the goal of the assessment, and the relative importance of specificity and sensitivity. Use of screening measures for depression that rely on self-report will likely identify larger numbers of children than if parent or teacher reports were used, but may yield high rates of false positives.

Theoretical issues concerning the content of self-report measures of childhood depression

There are several reasons to suspect that current self-report measures of depression are in need of refinement in order to improve their characteristics as measures of depression. First, developmental differences in the expression and experience of depression are not typically captured in the scales. Second, the psychometric studies of children's depression inventories indicate only modest correlations between different instruments purporting to measure the same construct. Costello and Angold (1988) point out that the content of the questionnaires overlaps only somewhat. Moreover, the actual DSM-III-R criteria for depression are relatively poorly sampled in the major instruments such as the CDI and CES-DC. Added to these considerations is the question of whether the various instruments should be construed as tapping depression as such, or whether they are measuring a broad band of internalizing problems or nonspecific negative affectivity (Wolfe, Finch, Saylor, Blount, Pallmeyer, & Carek, 1987).

For all of these reasons, it is reasonable to conclude that additional work is needed to develop instruments that are more specific to depressive disorders in children. Nevertheless, there is ample evidence that at least several of the instruments such as the CDI and CES-D, while not appropriately used as diagnostic instruments, may serve as effective screening devices for detecting psychopathology in children—some of which may signal diagnosable depressive disorders.

Interview assessment for depression in children and adolescents

With the advent of DSM-III diagnoses of depression in youngsters using adult criteria came the development of several interview-based schedules for diagnosing depressive disorders. We begin this section with a brief discussion of these interviews, and then present several procedures for interview assessment of the severity of depressive symptoms.

Schedule for Affective Disorders for School-Age Children (K-SADS)

Developed by Chambers, Puig-Antich, Orvaschel and colleagues, the K-SADS was modelled after the adult Schedule for Affective Disorders and Schizophrenia (Chambers, Puig-Antich, Hirsch, Paez, Ambrosini, et al., 1985). The K-SADS was based on Research Diagnostic Criteria for affective disorders and several other disorders of childhood, and is administered separately to the child and parent; a summary diagnosis is based on both sets of information. Depression symptoms are also rated for severity. Versions have been developed to assess lifetime history of disorder, as well as changes since a previous assessment (e.g. Orvaschel, Puig-Antich, Chambers, Tabrizi, & Johnson, 1982). Investigators have modified the format somewhat to include DSM-III-R diagnoses (e.g. Hammen, Gordon, et al., 1987). The procedure has been shown to yield reliable diagnoses of depressive disorders (e.g. Chambers et al., 1985), and is frequently used in clinical studies of depression in youth.

The Child Assessment Schedule

The Child Assessment Schedule (CAS; Hodges, McKnew, Cytryn, Stern, & Klein, 1982) is a structured psychological interview for the clinical assessment of children between the ages of 7 and 12. Diagnostic criteria for DSM-III-R are embedded within questions concerning 11 topic areas, such as school, friends, activities, family, fears, expression of anger, self-image, and others.

The CAS consists of two parts, and is modelled after adult diagnostic interviews. In the first part of the interview the child responds yes or no to approximately 75 questions. In the second part of the CAS, the clinician records her observations about the child after the interview has been completed. The CAS has been demonstrated to possess adequate interrater reliability with kappas above 0.70 for various diagnoses, and concordance with diagnoses obtained from the K-SADS. The CAS has been reported to discriminate among groups of child inpatients, outpatients, and normal controls (cf. Gotlib & Lee, 1989; psychometric characteristics are reviewed in Hodges, 1986).

The Interview Schedule for Children

The Interview Schedule for Children (ISC; Kovacs, 1978, 1983) is a structured interview that yields DSM-III diagnoses and ratings of depression symptom severity for children ages 8–13. Two forms of the ISC are available, permitting its use for both intake and follow-up assessment. Both the child and the parent are interviewed separately, and clinician ratings are based on information from both. The focus of the ISC is on the current phenomenology of the child's difficulties, encompassing major symptoms of psychopathology and severity of current condition, mental status, behavioral observations during the interview, and clinicians' impressions. Kovacs (1983) has reported high interrater reliability for the ISC.

Diagnostic Interview for Children and Adolescents (DICA)

Herjanic and Reich (1982) developed this schedule to be applied to children and adolescents. It is highly structured in format, with questions about symptoms yielding "yes," "no" and "sometimes" responses. The authors report satisfactory reliability and diagnostic agreement.

Diagnostic Interview Schedule for Children (DISC)

The National Institute of Mental Health DISC was developed by Costello, Edelbrock, and Costello (1985) to be administered by lay interviewers (or clinicians), so that it is suitable for applications to epidemiological surveys and community studies. Its format is highly structured, and includes some 200 questions coded as 0-1-2, corresponding to no, somewhat or sometimes, and yes. Versions are administered separately to the parent and the child. The DISC yields DSM-III diagnoses, and has been amended to include DSM-III-R criteria. The reliability and validity of the procedure have been established, including interrater reliability of scoring and diagnostic agreement, test-retest reliability (especially for older children), and discriminant validity based on referred and nonreferred children (summarized in Costello et al., 1988). A.J. Costello (1987) concludes that the reliability of the DISC is higher than that of other detailed interviews of its type, and that its validity is comparable or better. Nevertheless, as Weinstein, Noam, Grimes, Stone, and Schwab-Stone (1990) note in their review, agreement between clinician diagnoses and DISC-based diagnoses has been problematic, and some of the diagnostic categories, such as attention deficit, have not proven to be reliably diagnosed over time. However, convergent validity for affective disorders appears to be adequate, with consistency between interview- and self-reported questionnaire depressive symptoms on the CBCL or Youth Self-Report scale (Weinstein et al., 1990).

Interviews for symptom severity

Kazdin (1990) notes several interview-based schedules for rating depressive symptoms in children and adolescents. For instance, the Children's Depression Rating Scale (CDRS; Poznanski, Cook, & Carroll, 1979) was designed to be similar to the adult Hamilton Depression Rating Scale, although its 16 items are somewhat different in content. The authors report high correlations between scores on the CDRS in inpatient children and global depression severity ratings by psychiatrists. Other instruments include the Bellevue Index of Depression, modified by Kazdin et al. (1983), and the Children's Affective Rating Scale (McKnew, Cytryn, Efron, Gershon, & Bunney, 1979). On the whole, relatively less research has been devoted to interviews for severity of depression compared with self-reported symptoms, and psychometric information is sparse.

CONCLUDING COMMENTS

This chapter has reviewed some of the most widely-used methods of measuring the syndrome and symptoms of depression. Such methods are fairly well developed for adults; measures of symptoms and diagnoses in children and adolescents are less extensively studied, but considerable research has appeared in recent years. On balance, the methods for determining diagnoses of depression work well for adults, and for children provided that information from both parent and child sources is included in final decisions. The symptom measures, such as the BDI and CDI, are also satisfactory for certain goals such as identifying symptomatic subjects for further evaluation, or for measuring the severity of depressive symptoms (that may be embedded in the context of nonspecific distress). The self-report measures are not valid, however, as diagnostic instruments for identifying "depressed" subjects (cf. Gotlib & Cane, 1989).

It is now time to go beyond symptom measures, and to develop adequate instruments for measuring more about what depressed people *do*. To measure symptoms is to measure a very limited aspect of the experience of depression—and one that implies a somewhat static, mechanistic view of the person as someone who "has" symptoms. Instead, it would be valuable to turn some of our attention to questions about what depressed people "do" when depressed that may prolong, intensify, or maintain their depression.

One such partially successful effort has been the extensive work to develop measures of depressive cognitions. Such measures have proven stimulating to research testing particular theoretical models of depression. Yet, even in this realm, as we shall discuss in the following chapter, the definitions of what is meant by cognition have been rather narrow and require further development. However, certain other areas that are relevant lag far behind what has happened with depressive cognition. As Kazdin (1990) has noted with respect to children's depression, relatively little attention has been devoted to measures that involve observations of overt behavior. The same is true with adult depressed persons, whose actions while depressed undoubtedly contribute to events and relationships that have an impact on the course of the disorder. Thus, further measures of depressive interpersonal behaviors, such as family and intimate relationships, as well as work relationships, would be highly informative. Therefore, we urge the expansion of the domain of depression to include depression in people's lives. This is also crucial for the further study of childhood depression. As Kendall, Cantwell, and Kazdin (1989) recommended, we need assessment of multiple areas of functioning, including family functioning, peer interactions, and performance in school settings.

Chapter 5

The Cognitive Functioning
of Depressed Persons

The last decade has witnessed a surge of research designed to examine the role of cognitive factors in depression. As we saw in Chapter 3, there are a number of models of depression that have implicated cognitive factors in the etiology of this disorder. Two of these models in particular have garnered the most theoretical and empirical attention. In this chapter, therefore, we will focus primarily on the research that has been conducted in attempts to examine aspects of the cognitive models of depression formulated by Beck and his colleagues, and by Seligman and his collaborators. We will also discuss the recent trend among investigators interested in examining cognitive functioning in depression to utilize paradigms developed originally by researchers in experimental cognitive psychology. Finally, through an examination of this body of research, we will discuss the functional relation between cognition and depression, and will present a picture of the cognitive functioning of depressed persons.

Before we begin our analysis of this literature, we would like to make two brief points. First, there is little question that depressed persons experience considerable difficulty in the areas of thinking and concentration. In fact, impairment in cognitive functioning is listed in DSM-III-R as one of the core symptoms of major depressive disorder. In this context, there is a sizable body of empirical research examining the effects of depression on learning and memory functioning (see Wright and Salmon, 1990, for a detailed review of this literature). Certainly, a consideration of this type of cognitive functioning is unquestionably important in gaining a comprehensive understanding of depression. Nevertheless, it is clear that cognitive models of depression focus specifically on depressed persons' perceptions of, and responses to, valenced (i.e. positive and negative) stimuli and events. Therefore, in this chapter we will center our discussion around this aspect of cognitive functioning in depression.

Second, we should note that literally hundreds of investigations have been conducted examining cognitive aspects of depression. Obviously, it is beyond the scope of this chapter for us to present a detailed review of all of these studies. Therefore, in discussing the cognitive functioning of depressed persons we will not be exhaustive in our attention to the relevant literature; rather, we will present the results of representative work. Whenever possible, however, we will direct interested readers to more circumscribed reviews of relevant studies.

BECK'S COGNITIVE MODEL OF DEPRESSION

Beck's (1967, 1976) model of depression focuses on the "cognitive triad," faulty information processing, and negative self-schemas. As we described in Chapter 3, in the cognitive triad depressed persons are postulated to be characterized by a negative view of themselves, their experiences, and the future. Thus, depressed individuals are hypothesized to view themselves as inadequate and to believe that their world consists of obstacles too difficult to surmount; they are also hypothesized to view their future with a grim sense of hopelessness. With respect to faulty information processing, Beck postulates that depressed individuals demonstrate systematic errors in thinking, such as arbitrary inference, selective abstraction, and overgeneralization. This dysfunctional reasoning ability is theorized to result in an inaccurate appraisal of information from the environment. Finally, Beck postulates the existence of negative self-schemas in depressed individuals. These schemas are stable underlying cognitive structures originating early in childhood that, later in adulthood, affect the selection, encoding, and interpretation of environmental stimuli. When these schemas are activated by environmental stressors, depressed persons attempt to interpret information from the environment so that it is consistent with the schemas, even if it means distorting the information to achieve congruence. Consequently, depressed individuals may selectively filter out positive information, and may perceive neutral or negative information as being more negative than is actually the case.

Cognitive functioning of depressed individuals

Numerous studies have been conducted examining these three aspects of Beck's model of depression. Although the results of these investigations are not unanimous, there is little question that currently depressed persons differ from nondepressed individuals with respect to their cognitive functioning. For example, Beck postulates (as does Rehm, 1977) that depressed persons are characterized by a negative view of self. Consistent with these predictions, depressed persons have been found in a number of studies to demonstrate negative self-concepts (cf. Coyne & Gotlib, 1983; Segal & Shaw, 1986). Young, Moore, and Nelson (1981), for example, found that depressed subjects rated bogus negative personality descriptions as more valid than did nondepressed subjects. Lasher and Lynn (1981) similarly reported that depressed subjects demonstrated more negative self-evaluations on a role-playing task than did their nondepressed counterparts. Finally, depressed persons have been found to rate their performances on laboratory tasks more negatively than do nondepressed persons, despite equivalent objective performances (e.g. Friedman, 1964; Lewis, Mercatoris, Cole, & Leonard, 1980). In all of these studies, therefore, depressed persons have been found to demonstrate lower self-evaluations than do nondepressed persons. There is also some evidence to suggest, however, that this negative self-evaluation may not be specific to depression, but instead, may be characteristic of individuals exhibiting any form of major psychopathology (e.g. Gotlib, 1981, 1982).

Beck also postulates that depressed individuals perceive and interpret aspects of their environments more negatively than do nondepressed persons and recall these negative aspects more easily. In examining these postulates, researchers typically present depressed and nondepressed subjects with positive, neutral, and/or negative stimuli and ask the subjects both to rate the perceived valence of the stimuli and to recall the number of positive and negative stimuli they received. Some investigators have found depressed subjects, relative to their nondepressed counterparts, to perceive evaluative feedback as more negative and/or to recall receiving more negative feedback (e.g. Buchwald, 1977; Gotlib, 1981, 1983; Vestre & Caulfield, 1986). In contrast, other researchers have failed to find significant differences in the perceptions and recall of these two groups of subjects (e.g. Craighead, Hickey, & DeMonbreun, 1979; DeMonbreun & Craighead, 1977; Dennard & Hokanson, 1986).

A number of investigators have attempted to explain the discrepancies among these studies. Some researchers suggest, for example, that depression-associated differences in the perception of evaluative feedback are apparent only in research examining judgments concerning feedback about the self, and not with feedback about others (e.g. Hoen-Hyde, Schlottmann, & Rush, 1982; Wenzlaff & Berman, 1985). Other investigators emphasize the importance, when predicting subjects' perceptions of feedback, of considering the severity of the subjects' depression (Alloy & Abramson, 1988), the interaction of schema type and the nature of the feedback (e.g. Dykman, Abramson, Alloy, & Hartlage, 1989), and the interpersonal skill of the subjects (e.g. Dykman, Horowitz, Abramson, & Usher, 1991). Finally, Alloy and Abramson (1979), Golin and Terrell (1979), Lewinsohn, Mischel, Chaplin, and Barton (1980), and Johnson, Petzel,

Hartney, and Morgan (1983), among others, have reported data suggesting that it is *nondepressed* individuals who distort their environment in a positive direction, whereas depressed persons are accurate in their perceptions (see Alloy & Abramson, 1988, and Coyne & Gotlib, 1983, 1986, for more detailed examinations of the issue of "depressive realism").

Researchers have also examined Beck's postulation that depressed persons are characterized by enduring negative schemas and that they consequently engage in distorted thinking. The most widely used self-report measure of negative schemas is the Dysfunctional Attitudes Scale (DAS), developed by Weissman and Beck (1978).[1] The DAS is a 40-item inventory designed to measure depressogenic beliefs about the self hypothesized by Beck to represent a vulnerability to depression. Respondents indicate their agreement with statements primarily concerning self-worth contingencies (e.g. "I am nothing if a person I love doesn't love me," "I cannot be happy unless I know people admire me."). The content includes interpersonal as well as achievement themes. Scores range from 40 to 280, and nonpatients typically score 80–120, while depressed patients score 140–200. The scale has shown good internal consistency reliability, and correlates significantly with level of depressive symptoms (psychometric characteristics are reviewed in Hammen & Krantz, 1985; Merluzzi & Boltwood, 1989).

The results of investigations examining differences between currently depressed and nondepressed persons with respect to dysfunctional attitudes have been relatively consistent. Barnett and Gotlib (1990), Dobson and Breiter (1983), Gotlib (1984), Weissman and Beck (1978), for example, have all demonstrated that mildly depressed university students endorse significantly more dysfunctional attitudes on the DAS than do nondepressed students. Similar studies have found that depressed psychiatric patients also exhibit higher scores on the DAS than do normal controls (e.g. Hollon, Kendall, & Lumry, 1986), although the finding that they tend not to differ significantly from nondepressed psychiatric patients (e.g. Blackburn, Jones, & Lewin, 1987; Zimmerman, et al. 1986) suggests that an elevated level of dysfunctional attitudes may not be unique to depression.

In sum, the results of studies examining the cognitive functioning of currently depressed persons are largely consistent with Beck's formulation that depressed individuals are characterized by a negative view of the self, that they perceive, interpret, and recall aspects of their environments more negatively than do nondepressed persons, and that they engage in dysfunctional thinking. Beck's model goes further, however, in maintaining that dysfunctional cognitions should be relatively stable and that they should predict the onset of depression. The notion of stability implies that dysfunctional thinking should be evident in formerly depressed persons. Indeed, the fact that these "remitted depressives" have been vulnerable to depression in the past and are statistically at increased risk for future depressive episodes (Beck et al. 1979; Stern & Mendels, 1980) is consistent with Beck's postulation that they are characterized by a stable pattern of dysfunctional cognitions that leaves them vulnerable to episodes of depression. Unfortunately, the cross-sectional studies reviewed thus far do not permit an examination of the issue of the stability of dysfunctional cognitions or negative schemas, or of questions concerning the causal nature of the relation between dysfunctional cognitions and depression.

The temporal relation between depression and dysfunctional cognitions

A number of investigators have examined the stability of dysfunctional cognitions by assessing the cognitive functioning of remitted depressives. Eaves and Rush (1984), for example, found remitted depressives to exhibit more dysfunctional attitudes than did nondepressed controls. In contrast, however, a number of other studies have failed to differentiate remitted depressives from nondepressed controls with respect to their cognitive functioning (e.g. Blackburn & Smyth, 1985; Gotlib, Lewinsohn, et al., 1991; Hamilton & Abramson, 1983; Hollon, Kendall, & Lumry 1986; Rohde, Lewinsohn, & Seeley, 1990; Silverman, Silverman, & Eardley, 1984), although Reda, Carpiniello, Secchiarole, and Blanco (1985) have presented evidence indicating that a subset of dysfunctional cognitions may remain elevated in remitted depressives. Nevertheless, it is clear that the majority of the available evidence indicates that dysfunctional cognitions are time-limited to the duration of a depressive episode, returning to normal levels when the depression remits.

Other researchers have examined the causal role of dysfunctional cognitions in leading to the onset of a depressive episode. In a recent review, Barnett and Gotlib (1988b) noted that the results of this research are equivocal. Several studies have tried to predict future depression on the basis of current cognitive functioning. Rush, Weissenburger, and Eaves (1986), for example, administered the DAS to 15 depressed patients at discharge and followed the patients for six months. These investigators found that although scores on the DAS predicted level of self-reported depressive symptoms six months later, they did not predict either clinician ratings of depression or course of the disorder. O'Hara, Rehm, and Campbell (1982) found that dysfunctional attitudes measured during pregnancy did not significantly predict the subsequent severity of postpartum depression. Similar results were reported by Gotlib, Whiffen, Wallace, and Mount (1991), who found that dysfunctional attitudes assessed during pregnancy did not predict either the subsequent onset of postpartum depression or recovery from a depressive episode occurring during pregnancy.

A number of investigators have attempted to assess more explicitly the diathesis-stress aspect of Beck's formulations. These researchers have examined the ability of dysfunctional cognitions, considered in interaction with psychosocial stressors, to predict depression. Wise and Barnes (1986) and Olinger, Kuiper, and Shaw (1987, Study 2) both conducted cross-sectional studies and found the interaction of DAS scores and negative life events to predict depressive symptoms in a sample of university students. In a longitudinal investigation, Barnett and Gotlib (1988a) assessed female undergraduate students on two occasions three months apart. Although the interaction of the DAS with negative life events was not a significant predictor of subsequent depressive symptoms, dysfunctional cognitions did interact significantly with another stressor, low social support, to predict change in the severity of depression. This finding was replicated by Barnett and Gotlib (1990) in a larger sample of women. Interestingly, dysfunctional attitudes did not predict subsequent depressive symptoms, either alone or in interaction with low social support or negative life events, among men, suggesting that there may be gender differences in the development and maintenance of depression.

Finally, in a more comprehensive prospective investigation, Hammen, Marks, DeMayo, and Mayol (1985a) followed four groups of university students over a four-month period. Hammen et al. utilized a depth-of-processing incidental recall task (cf. Derry & Kuiper, 1981) and the Beck Depression Inventory to classify subjects as schematic-depressed, schematic-nondepressed, nonschematic-depressed, and nonschematic-nondepressed. The subjects were assessed periodically with respect to depression and the occurrence of life events. The results of this study indicated that schemas status was not a vulnerability factor for experiencing depression either as a symptom or a syndrome; in fact, initial depression status was the sole significant predictor of future depression. Contrary to the predictions of a cognitive diathesis-stress model of depression, the interaction of negative schematic functioning with negative life events did not predict subsequent level of depression. Thus, negative stressful events did not appear to "trigger" schemas to produce depression (see also Hammen, Marks, Mayol, and DeMayo, 1985b).

Overall, therefore, Beck's formulations that dysfunctional cognitions represent a stable aspect of depressed persons' functioning that interacts with stress to produce depression have received only equivocal support. While a number of explanations have been offered to account for the discrepant findings of these investigations (cf. Barnett & Gotlib, 1988b), it is apparent that the relations among stress, dysfunctional cognitions, and depression are more complex than Beck has postulated. In this context, there is recent evidence to indicate that dysfunctional cognitions may be activated, or "primed," not by stressful life events, but by dysphoric mood. For example, Miranda and Persons (1988) reported an association between the endorsement of dysfunctional attitudes and the experience of negative affect in formerly depressed individuals. Both formerly depressed and never-depressed subjects participated in a negative mood-induction procedure and then completed the DAS. Although the negative mood induction was effective for both groups, only the formerly depressed subjects endorsed more dysfunctional attitudes in response to the induction, suggesting the presence of depressogenic cognitive structures in these individuals that were primed by the induction of negative affect (see also similar work by Teasdale & Dent, 1987).

In a subsequent study, Miranda, Persons, and Byers (1990) reported that depressed subjects' scores on the DAS varied with their natural diurnal variation in mood. Specifically, subjects' DAS scores were more dysfunctional during their worst periods than during their best periods. Additional results from this study indicated that although the interaction of current mood and history of depression was a significant predictor of DAS scores in previously depressed subjects, no such relationship was found in never-depressed controls. In fact, differences between the formerly depressed and control subjects were apparent only in the presence of negative affective states. Thus, dysphoric mood may serve to trigger dysfunctional cognitions. The results of these studies are consistent with Teasdale's (1988) Differential Activation Hypothesis presented in Chapter 3, which emphasizes the importance of patterns of thinking that are activated once the individual is in a depressed state. Support for this hypothesis is, of course, preliminary; this does appear, however, to be a promising direction for further research.

THE LEARNED HELPLESSNESS MODEL OF DEPRESSION

A second major cognitive model of depression has been presented by Abramson, Seligman, and Teasdale (1978). Their reformulated learned helplessness model postulates that, because of their habitual style of explaining the causes of life events, or "attributional style," some persons are particularly vulnerable to developing depression. These people not only have learned to believe that previous events in their lives were uncontrollable, but they expect that future outcomes, too, will be similarly out of their control. Furthermore, Abramson, Seligman, and Teasdale postulate that persons who are prone to depression tend to attribute negative outcomes to internal, global, and stable factors and, to a lesser extent, tend to attribute positive outcomes to external, specific, and unstable causes. As in Beck's model, these patterns of attributions are hypothesized to play a causal role in the development of depression. Thus, according to the learned helplessness reformulation, the onset of a depressive episode is precipitated by the occurrence of a negative event that triggers the expectation of the uncontrollability of future negative events, and the attribution for the event to internal, global, and stable factors.

Attributions of depressed individuals

Initial investigations in this area typically compared the attributional styles of currently depressed and nondepressed individuals, or computed correlation coefficients between attributional style and severity of depressive symptomatology in an unselected sample. Many of the early studies examined the attributions of depressed and nondepressed subjects in response to laboratory success and failure experiences. Most of these investigations focused on the internality-externality dimension. With a small number of exceptions (e.g. Gotlib & Olson, 1983), most of these studies reported that depressed subjects made more internal attributions for failure than did nondepressed persons (e.g. Kuiper, 1978; Zuroff, 1981); group differences with respect to attributions for success are less consistent. As Coyne and Gotlib (1983) note, however, the results of these investigations for attributional dimensions other than internal-external tend not to support the predictions of the learned helplessness model.

As research in this area continued, investigators moved away from studies of attributions for laboratory success and failure and began to examine attributions of depressed and nondepressed subjects for hypothetical good and bad events. One of the most commonly used measures of attributions for this purpose is the Attributional Style Questionnaire (ASQ; Peterson, Semmel, von Baeyer, Abramson, Metalsky, & Seligman, 1982). This questionnaire presents subjects with 6 positive and 6 negative hypothetical events (although a more recent version contains 12 positive and 12 negative events). For each event, subjects are asked to write down the one major cause of the event. They are then asked to rate the cause along the three attributional dimensions of internal-external, stable-unstable, and global-specific, using seven-point likert scales. Because ratings along these three dimensions have only low to moderate reliability, and because the three scales are substantially intercorrelated within positive events and within negative events, Peterson (1991; Peterson & Seligman, 1984) has recommended that the three scales be combined into a single composite "attributional style" score within good and bad events. However, as Gotlib (1991), among others, has noted, the interpretation of this composite score is not at all clear.

Several studies using the ASQ have found internal, stable, and/or global attributions, and/or the composite score (although rarely all four) to be associated with level of depression. Seligman, Abramson, Semmel, and von Baeyer (1979), for example, found that mildly depressed students made more internal, stable, and global attributions for bad outcomes than did nondepressed students. Blaney, Behar, and Head (1980) also reported that depressed students made more stable and global attributions for negative hypothetical events than did their nondepressed counterparts; the two groups did not differ with respect to internal attributions. Similar results have also been reported in samples of psychiatric patients (e.g. Persons & Rao, 1985; Raps, Peterson, Reinhard, Abramson, & Seligman, 1982; Zimmerman, et al. 1986). Although there have been failures to replicate these results (e.g. Miller, Klee, & Norman, 1982), it is reasonably well established that, compared with nondepressed individuals, currently depressed persons tend to attribute hypothetical negative events more to internal, stable, and/or global causes. Indeed, authors of reviews and meta-analyses of this literature suggest that, in particular, the dimensions of internality and globality have received reasonable empirical support (cf. Coyne & Gotlib, 1983; Robins, 1988; Sweeney, Anderson, & Bailey, 1986).

Whereas these studies have focused on the attributions of depressed individuals for hypothetical events, other investigators have examined the causal explanations of depressed persons for actual stressful life events. Hammen and her colleagues have conducted a significant portion of the research in this area. For example, Barthe and Hammen (1981) found that students' perceived failure in an examination was associated with depression to the extent that they attributed their failure to lack of ability. No depression-associated effects were obtained in this study with respect to either internal or stable attributions for failure. In two other studies, Gong-Guy and Hammen (1980) and Hammen and Cochran (1981) also failed to differentiate depressives' from nondepressives' attributions for their five most stressful life events, although Hammen and Cochran noted a tendency for their depressed subjects to exhibit self-blame. Hammen, Krantz, and Cochran (1981) found that, although depressed students were more global in their attributions for romantic difficulties than were nondepressed students and endorsed more control, they did not differ with respect to either internality or stability. Finally, Cochran and Hammen (1985) reported that depressed elderly patients viewed their recent stressful life events as uncontrollable and as having been caused by external, rather than by internal, factors, although within the patient sample severity of depression was correlated with greater internality.

Other investigators have also assessed depressed persons' attributions for stressful life events. Feather and Barber (1983) examined adults' attributions for their unemployment, and found that depression was associated with perceived uncontrollability and ascriptions to internal causes. These researchers also noted, however, that situation-specific depressed mood about unemployment was related to attributions to external causes. Feather and Barber also reported that less than 7% of the variance in depression scores was accounted for by attributional variables. Devins, Binik, Hollomby, Barre, and Guttmann (1981) found that depression was unrelated to the attributions made by patients with end-stage renal disease for the control of dialysis they experienced. Similarly, Peterson, Rosenbaum, and Conn (1985) reported that they found no association between depressed mood and students' internal, stable, or global attributions regarding the causes of romantic breakups.

It is apparent from these studies, therefore, that the evidence in support of a "depressotypic" attributional style in response to stressful life events is equivocal. Some studies have found depression-associated effects for global attributions but not for internal or stable attributions. Interestingly, Feather and Davenport (1981) found that depressed subjects made *less* internal attributions for their lack of employment than did their nondepressed counterparts. As was the case with research examining predictions derived from Beck's model of depression, however, these cross-sectional studies do not address issues concerning the stability of attributional style or the causal nature of the relation between attributions and depression.

The temporal relation between depression and attributional style

The reformulated learned helplessness model conceptualizes depression as resulting from the kinds of attributions individuals make about negative events in their lives. Individuals who possess a trait-like tendency to attribute negative events to internal, stable, and global causes are hypothesized to be more likely to develop depressive symptoms in response to a stressful event than are individuals who tend to attribute negative events to external, unstable, and specific causes. These conceptualizations, as well as other related questions, can best be addressed through longitudinal research. For example, do individuals who later become depressed exhibit more negative attributional tendencies in their premorbid state than do control subjects who remain nondepressed? Does attributional style predict a subsequent change in depressive symptoms? Is a self-deprecating attributional style a stable cognitive trait that distinguishes control subjects from individuals who have had a previous episode of depression?

Several investigators have attempted to address these issues. In the first major study in this area, Lewinsohn, Steinmetz, Larson, and Franklin (1981) assessed the attributional functioning of 998 individuals and then followed them over the course of one year to examine whether attributional style predicts the onset of a depressive episode. Specifically, Lewinsohn et al. assessed subjects' internal and external attributions for success and failure. No differences were found in this study between the premorbid causal attributions of subjects who became depressed over the course of the study and the attributions of subjects who remained nondepressed. Similar results were subsequently reported by O'Hara, Neunaber, and Zekoski (1984), who found that attributional style, as assessed with the ASQ, during pregnancy did not predict the onset of an episode of depression postpartum. Although one can argue that these studies did not explicitly test the diathesis-stress hypothesis proposed by the learned helplessness reformulation (i.e. that it is the interaction of attributions with stress that leads to the onset of a depressive episode), Coyne and Gotlib (1986) have pointed out that, given the large number of subjects in these studies, this interaction would not mask a main effect for attributional style unless attributions and life events were strongly negatively correlated. In any case, the results of these studies suggest that a self-deprecating attributional style does not precede the onset of a depressive episode.

Other investigations have examined the effect of attributional style on change in level of depressive symptoms. Cutrona (1983), for example, examined causal attributions in a sample of women experiencing the birth of their first child. Cutrona found that attributional style measured during pregnancy accounted for about 10% of the variance in depressive symptoms following the birth. This finding held, however, only for women who had low symptom scores during pregnancy; attributional style was not a significant predictor of the postpartum symptoms of women with higher initial levels of depressive symptoms. This pattern of results suggests that attributional biases may influence depressed mood within a "normal" or nondepressed range; for women with mild to severe depression, the influence of attributional style was not significant. In a similar study, O'Hara, Rehm, and Campbell (1982) found that the ASQ significantly predicted improvement in depressive symptoms from pregnancy to the postpartum period; women who exhibited more self-deprecating attributions demonstrated less improvement than did women with fewer negative biases. Interestingly, this pattern of results is consistent with findings obtained by Lewinsohn et al. (1981), who reported that initially depressed subjects who improved had significantly fewer negative cognitions than did those who did not improve.

Two studies conducted by Metalsky and his colleagues also provide some support for the formulation that attributions mediate the relation between stressful events and depressed mood. In an early study, Metalsky, Abramson, Seligman, Semmel, and Peterson (1982) examined the interaction between attributional style and a stressful event among students. Metalsky et al. (1982) concluded that the relationship between internal and global attributions and future mood disturbance was significant only among subjects who had experienced the negative event. In a reanalysis of these data, however, Williams (1985) demonstrated that the correlation between attributional style and negative mood was not significantly greater among subjects who had experienced a negative event than it was among subjects who had not, suggesting, therefore, that the hypothesized interaction did not pertain. In a more recent study, Metalsky, Halberstadt, and Abramson (1987) again examined the predictive power of the interaction of students' attributional styles with the receipt of disappointing exam results. The results of this study suggested that attributional style had no effect on students' initial reactions to the receipt of a poor grade, nor on the severity of their mood disturbance during the entire course of the study. Four days following receipt of the grade, however, students with more negative attributional styles who had been disappointed in their grade continued to report some mood disturbance, whereas other students did not. These results appear to be similar to those reported by Cutrona (1983), suggesting that attributional style may be a useful predictor of certain parameters of normal fluctuations in mood experienced in response to negative life events.

These studies, therefore, have reported a significant relation between attributional style and subsequent mood. It is important to note, however, that a number of other investigations have failed to replicate this pattern of results. When initial symptoms were controlled statistically, attributional style was not found to predict the severity of symptoms of postpartum depression in community samples (e.g. Manly, McMahon, Badley, & Davidson, 1982; O'Hara, Neunaber, & Zekoski, 1984). Attributional style also did not predict the severity of depressive symptoms in samples of students (Cochran & Hammen, 1985; Peterson, Schwartz, & Seligman, 1981) or remitted depressives (Rush, Weissenburger, & Eaves 1986). As Barnett and Gotlib (1988b) note, these negative findings stand in contrast to the more positive results reported in two longitudinal studies with samples of normal children (Nolen-Hoeksema, Girgus, & Seligman, 1986; Seligman et al., 1984), both of which found attributional style to predict subsequent depressive symptoms. Nolen-Hoeksema et al. also found that the interaction of attributional style and life events was a significant predictor of subsequent symptoms. In a more recent longitudinal study, however, Hammen, Adrian, and Hiroto (1988) examined children at risk for depression due to maternal affective or medical disorder. These investigators found no association between changes in depression and initial attributional style, nor did they find an interaction of attributional style and negative life events. Although further research is clearly warranted in this area, it is possible that the processes involved in childhood depression may be different from those involved in depression among adults (cf. Digdon & Gotlib, 1985).

Finally, several investigations have examined the postmorbid attributional style of depressed patients. Two studies compared the attributional style of depressives with that of nondepressed controls both during and following the depressive episode (Eaves & Rush, 1984; Hamilton & Abramson, 1983). Similarly, two studies conducted cross-sectional comparisons of the attributional styles of groups of currently depressed, remitted depressed, and nondepressed subjects (Fennell & Campbell, 1984; Lewinsohn et al., 1981). In three of these four studies, and consistent with the cross-sectional literature, currently depressed patients were found to have a significantly more self-deprecating attributional style than were nondepressed controls (Eaves & Rush, 1984; Fennell & Campbell, 1984; Hamilton & Abramson, 1983). These differences, however, do not appear to be stable. Hamilton and Abramson found that patients' ASQ scores fell to normal levels following symptomatic recovery. Similarly, both Lewinsohn et al. and Fennell and Campbell found no significant difference between the attributional styles of remitted depressives and never-depressed controls. In fact, only Eaves and Rush found recovered patients to have a more self-deprecating attributional style than did control subjects. Thus, it appears that, following symptomatic recovery, formerly depressed people do not consistently exhibit a depressotypic attributional style, a finding that raises questions regarding the stability of attributional style.

In summary, research with adults has not consistently supported the causal hypotheses of the reformulated learned helplessness model. A self-deprecating attributional style has not reliably been found to be a temporal antecedent of depression, nor does it appear to predict an increase in depressive symptoms over time, although there is evidence of a predictive relationship between attributional style and negative affect among nondepressed adults. Finally, remitted depressives do not consistently exhibit more negative attributional biases than do control subjects. Thus, an abnormal attributional style does not appear to be characteristic of the cognitive functioning of either premorbid or remitted depressives. In fact, investigators have been largely unable to demonstrate the postulated robust, stable, attributional diathesis in people vulnerable to depression. As a caveat to this conclusion, however, we should note that virtually all of the longitudinal studies of the temporal relation of attributions and depression have used the ASQ to assess attributional style (the study by Lewinsohn et al., 1981, is a notable exception). As Barnett and Gotlib (1988b) note, there are psychometric difficulties associated with the ASQ. For example, the reliability coefficients of the individual subscales and of the composite score have been reported to be "too low, even for the experimental use of the measure" (Cutrona, Russell, & Jones, 1984,

p. 1046); test-retest correlations have also been reported to be relatively low (e.g. Cutrona, Russell, & Jones, 1984; Peterson et al., 1982). It is difficult to determine, therefore, whether the inconsistent results of research in this area are due to the psychometric problems of the ASQ or to a veridical lack of cross-situational consistency in subjects' causal attributions (cf. Cutrona, Russell, & Jones, 1984; Miller, Klee, & Norman, 1982). In either case, it is clear that further research with improved measures is urgently required before significant advances can be made in this area of investigation.

Considered collectively, therefore, although most studies have found that currently depressed persons demonstrate distorted perceptions and recollections of their environments and a negative attributional style, there are also a number of investigations in which these results have not been replicated. Furthermore, as we have noted earlier, there is no consistent evidence that these negative cognitions and dysfunctional attributions are present before the onset of a depressive episode, that they predict subsequent levels of depression, or that they remain elevated following recovery from a depressive episode. In particular, investigations utilizing the DAS and the ASQ largely fail to support Beck's and Abramson et al.'s formulations that dysfunctional attitudes or causal explanations, either alone or in combination with negative life events, represent stable vulnerability factors for future depressive episodes.

Part of the reason for this state of affairs may be that most of these studies have relied on gross measures to assess what are in actuality relatively fine aspects of cognitive functioning in depression. Virtually all of these investigations, for example, used data obtained through self-report measures to draw conclusions concerning the cognitive processing of depressed persons. Investigations examining perception and recall of environmental information, for instance, simply required depressed subjects to indicate on a questionnaire how many negative stimuli they recalled being presented to them in the experimental session. Coyne and Gotlib (1983) have argued that these measures may assess the influence of extra-laboratory experiences to at least the same extent that they do recall of experimental stimuli. Indeed, Nisbett and Wilson (1977) have reviewed evidence indicating that such self-reports are commonly inaccurate. Similarly, in studies using the DAS, respondents are required to endorse (or not endorse) negative statements on a questionnaire. As Zuroff, Colussy, and Wielgus (1983) and Ingram and Reed (1986), among others, have noted, self-report data are especially subject to the whims and diverse motivations of the participants in these studies. This point is particularly critical when the participants are depressed subjects, whom Coyne and Gotlib have speculated may be either more or less willing to endorse certain items on questionnaires than are their nondepressed counterparts. It is also evident that there is a tautology in the results of studies in which depressed subjects, who are typically selected for study by their willingness to endorse negative statements on such questionnaires as the Beck Depression Inventory, also endorse negative statements on other questionnaires, such as the DAS and the ASQ.

A related and conceptually more important concern involves the ability of any paper-and-pencil measure to assess the existence and functioning of schemas. Recall that schemas are hypothesized to represent automatically activated structures. Questionnaires such as the DAS and those used to measure perception and recall of experimental stimuli require subjects to make conscious and deliberate responses. Consequently, responses to these questionnaires are unlikely to reflect the operation of automatic functioning. As Spielman and Bargh (1990) note, the results of studies using questionnaires can also be explained by non-schematic cognitive processing, such as temporary priming or inadvertent activation of relevant constructs.

It is clear, therefore, that studies using introspective responses to questionnaire items as their primary source of information about cognitive functioning in depression may not be providing appropriate tests of cognitive theories of this disorder. In addressing this issue, some investigators have begun to use paradigms derived from cognitive-experimental psychology to assess the information processing of depressed persons. Thus, there is now a growing body of empirical studies that have utilized mood/memory recall tasks, Stroop color-naming tasks, depth of processing tasks, self-referent encoding tasks, stimulus recall tasks, and dichotic listening tasks to examine cognitive aspects of depression. As we shall see, the results of these investigations have been more consistent than those that have relied on self-report data; they may also be more promising in helping us to gain a better understanding of the cognitive functioning of depressed persons. We discuss these investigations in the following section.

INFORMATION PROCESSING APPROACHES

Both Beck's schema theory and more recent associative network theories (e.g. Bower, 1981; Ingram, 1984) predict that depressed persons demonstrate an attentional bias toward negative stimuli. Bower (1981), for example, posits that depressed mood activates a "depression node," which has associated with it in memory nodes of information concerning negatively valenced concepts and events. Thus, depressed individuals (who have activated depression nodes) are expected to have greater access to congruent (i.e. depressive) memories. Ingram (1984) similarly suggests that the experience of depression is accompanied by a heightened attention to negative aspects of an individual's experience (see also Teasdale, 1988).

There are two distinct literatures that are relevant to an assessment of these predictions. The first body of research that we shall consider concerns the effects of depressed mood on recall of positive and negative memories.

Depressed mood and memory

There are now numerous studies that have demonstrated that depressed individuals exhibit better recall for negatively- than for positively-valenced material. Interestingly, this differential recall pattern is the opposite of that found in samples of nondepressed subjects (cf. Blaney, 1986; MacLeod & Mathews, 1991; Singer & Salovey, 1988). In one of the first contemporary investigations in this area, Lloyd and Lishman (1975) required depressed patients to recall pleasant and unpleasant memories in response to a series of neutral "cue" words. Lloyd and Lishman found that response time to recall unpleasant memories was inversely related to severity of depression, reflecting an increased accessibility for negative memories in depressed patients. In a similar study, Clark and Teasdale (1982) required clinically depressed and nondepressed subjects to generate a memory in response to each of a number of neutral cue words. The depressed subjects generated a greater proportion of negatively valenced memories than did their nondepressed counterparts, although there were no group differences in response times to generate the memories.

These results suggest that depressed persons have greater access to negative memories than do nondepressed persons. It is possible, of course, that these findings are a function of depressed persons simply having a larger number of actual unpleasant memories from which to draw than do nondepressed controls. In a study designed, in part, to examine this possibility, Teasdale and Fogarty (1979) induced elated or depressed mood in college students and recorded their latencies to recall pleasant or unpleasant autobiographical memories in response to neutral stimulus words. Teasdale and Fogarty found that subjects in an elated mood recalled pleasant memories significantly more quickly than did subjects in whom a depressed mood was induced, although there were no mood-associated differences in recall time for unpleasant memories. Similar results were reported by Riskind, Rholes, and Eggers (1982), who also found faster retrieval of positive memories in "induced-happy" subjects; this effect was found for negative memories only in a sad mood created specifically with a small subset of self-devaluative Velten Mood Induction statements. Finally, Teasdale and Russell (1983) found that subjects in an induced depressed mood recalled fewer positive and a greater number of negative memories than did subjects in an induced elated mood.

Other investigators have examined the recall of depressed and nondepressed subjects for specific stimuli. McDowall (1984), for example, presented lists of pleasant and unpleasant words to clinically depressed and nondepressed subjects. On a subsequent free-recall task, McDowell found that the depressed patients recalled more of the unpleasant words than did the nondepressed controls, who recalled more of the pleasant words. Similar findings have been reported by Derry and Kuiper (1981) and Mathews and Bradley (1983).

There is also some evidence, although inconsistent, of mood-congruent encoding of information. For example, Bower, Gilligan, and Monteiro (1981) induced a happy or sad mood in subjects and then had them read a story involving both a sad and a happy character, with an equal number of sad and happy statements. Subjects returned the following day and, in a neutral mood, attempted to recall information about the story. Bower, Gilligan, and Monteiro found that material that was congruent with the subjects' mood at the time of encoding was recalled better: whereas 80% of the material recalled by the sad-mood-induced subjects were "sad" facts, only 45% of the material recalled by the happy-mood-induced subjects were "sad" facts. Interestingly, in a second study, Bower and colleagues found no effects of the subjects' mood at the time of retrieval.

Finally, we should note that, in addition to the mood-induction studies described above, there are data to indicate that these depression-associated patterns of memory functioning do not remain following clinical improvement. For example, Slife, Miura, Thompson, Shapiro, and Gallagher (1984) found that, while they were depressed, patients demonstrated a recall advantage for nonsense trigrams that they had rated as "disliked" over those they had rated as "liked." As their mood improved on completion of therapy, however, these subjects demonstrated the same recall advantage for the "liked" trigrams as was shown by the nondepressed controls. Similarly, Dobson and Shaw (1987) reported that the recall advantage for negative words demonstrated by depressed patients disappeared following treatment for those patients who improved. Interestingly, patients who did not demonstrate clinical improvement continued to display a bias in their recall of negative words.

It appears, therefore, that consistent with Beck's schema theory and with Bower's (1981) and Ingram's (1984) associative network theories, depressed persons demonstrate an attentional bias toward negative stimuli. Depressed persons have been found to recall more negative than positive memories, and to take longer to recall pleasant than unpleasant memories. In addition, a number of investigators have demonstrated that depressed subjects recall a greater proportion of negative than positive stimuli from lists they have seen earlier. Nondepressed persons, in contrast, typically exhibit the opposite pattern of recall. Interestingly, the recall biases demonstrated by depressed persons seem to normalize following recovery from a depressive episode, suggesting that these biases may not represent stable vulnerability factors in depression. This normalization may present more of a problem for Beck's model of depression than it does for network models, which tend to take more of a state perspective on depression.

The second body of research that is relevant to information-processing conceptualizations of depression involves the use of tasks derived from experimental cognitive psychology to examine the attentional functioning of depressed individuals.

Depression and attentional processing

One task that has frequently been utilized to assess attentional processing in depressed persons is a modified version of the Stroop color-naming task. In the original Stroop (1935) procedure, subjects were asked to name the colors of various types of stimuli, including a series of Xs, colored rectangles, and words. The stimuli were printed in different colors of ink, and the subjects' task was to quickly name the color of each stimulus. A consistent finding on the Stroop task is that subjects take longer to name the ink colors of color words (e.g. to respond with *blue* when presented with the word *green* printed in blue ink) than they do to name the ink colors of strings of Xs, colored rectangles, or non-color words. Stroop suggested that this differential response latency is due to response interference. That is, the automatic processing of the color word's meaning interferes with the competing response of naming the (different) ink color. Thus, the activation of the target word's color name must be suppressed in order to allow the subject to quickly name the ink color, resulting in a longer latency to name the ink color of color than of noncolor (i.e. task-irrelevant) words or stimuli.

A number of investigators have utilized this concept of response interference and have elaborated and expanded on the original Stroop task in elucidating parameters of cognitive functioning. In an early study in this area, for example, Warren (1972) found that he could increase subjects' response times on a Stroop task by first "priming" them with an oral presentation of words that were categorically similar to those subsequently presented on the task itself. Essentially, Warren found that subjects took longer to name the colors of words that were primed, and words that were categorically related to the primes (e.g. the words "uncle" and "cousin" with the prime "aunt"), than they did to name the colors of control stimuli. Based on this pattern of results, Warren suggested that the category designation of a word is activated as part of the word's encoding, and therefore, both the category and the word itself produce longer response times on the Stroop task through response competition.

Gotlib and his colleagues extended this application of the Stroop task to the study of cognitive aspects of depression. Beck's cognitive model of depression suggests that depressed persons are characterized by negative schemas that allow the rapid and more efficient encoding of depressive or negative stimuli. In an investigation examining this proposition, Gotlib and McCann (1984) reasoned that because of the operation of these schemas, depressed persons should be naturally primed to perceive negative aspects of their environment. Consistent with Warren's (1972) findings, this increased accessibility and attention to negative constructs should produce interference among depressed individuals when they are required to quickly name the colors of negative- or depressed-content words. Thus, depressed persons would be expected to demonstrate longer reaction times to name the colors of depressed- than of nondepressed-content words on the Stroop task because of response interference; a depressed word would be more likely to activate other depressed-content cognitions in depressed than in nondepressed subjects and, therefore, should interfere with the competing color-naming responses for depressed subjects.

Gotlib and McCann (1984) tested this formulation in two studies. In the first study, mildly depressed and nondepressed subjects participated in a modified Stroop color-naming task, quickly naming the colors of three types of words printed in different colors of ink. One group of 50 words (depressed-content) were adjectives that had been rated by depressed patients as most self-descriptive and by manic patients as least self-descriptive. A second group of 50 words (manic-content) were adjectives that had been rated by manic patients as most self-descriptive and by depressed patients as least self-descriptive. The final group of 50 words were of neutral content. The three types of words were matched for length and frequency of use. In the second study, Gotlib and McCann replicated this procedure in initially nondepressed subjects in whom either a depressed or an elated mood had been induced.

As predicted, in the first study Gotlib and McCann (1984) obtained a significant statistical interaction of group and word type. Whereas nondepressed subjects did not demonstrate differential response latencies across the three types of words, depressed subjects took longer to name the colors of depressed-content words than they did of either neutral- or manic-content words (see Figure 5.1). These results indicate that depressed persons find it difficult to ignore the content of depressed-content words, suggesting that depressed individuals differ from their nondepressed counterparts with respect to their relative accessibility of positive and negative cognitive constructs. Thus, the findings of this study are consistent with Beck's formulation of the operation of a negative schema in currently depressed individuals and, incidentally, with Bower's (1981) network theory of affect and cognition. Moreover, Gotlib and McCann's failure in Study 2 to replicate this pattern of results in subjects exposed to a negative mood induction

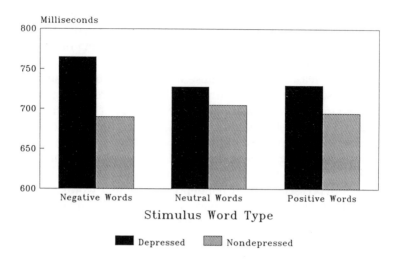

Figure 5.1   Color-naming response latencies: depressed and nondepressed subjects.
Source: adapted from Gotlib and McCann (1984)

procedure suggests that the effects are not due solely to transient mood
differences between depressed and nondepressed individuals.

In a subsequent investigation, Gotlib and Cane (1987) examined the
performance of diagnosed clinically depressed psychiatric patients on the
modified Stroop color-naming task. In addition, Gotlib and Cane also
attempted to alter the increased negative accessibility of the depressed
subjects by adding a cognitive priming procedure to the Stroop task.
Depressed and nondepressed subjects were required to name the ink colors
of half of the 150 stimulus words and then to complete a task designed
to prime either positive or negative categories. Subjects then completed
the second half of the Stroop task, naming the colors of the remaining
75 stimulus words. Consistent with Gotlib and McCann's (1984) findings,
Gotlib and Cane found that the depressed patients took longer to name
the color of the depressed-content than of the nondepressed-content words.
Gotlib and Cane also found that the priming task had no effect on subjects'
construct accessibility, suggesting that priming procedures designed to
produce small, short-term changes in construct accessibility may not be
sufficient to offset the larger accessibility differences associated with clinical
depression.

Finally, McCabe and Gotlib (1991a) conducted a study to examine the
generalizability of research using the Stroop task. Diagnosed depressed and
nondepressed subjects participated in a dichotic listening task. Subjects were
required to repeat or "shadow" neutral-content words presented to one
ear while attempting to ignore different positive-, negative-, and neutral-

content words simultaneously presented to the other ear. In addition, subjects simultaneously completed a separate, secondary, task in which they responded to an intermittent light probe by immediately pressing a button as soon as a light came on while continuing to shadow the dichotic material. The degree of attention necessary to perform this secondary task is considered an indication of schematic processing effects (cf. Bargh, 1982). Thus, if subjects are distracted (i.e. their attention is "caught") by certain stimuli presented in the unattended channel, their latency to respond to the secondary cognitive task will be increased. McCabe and Gotlib predicted that if depressed individuals are characterized by negative schemas, their reaction time to the secondary light-probe task would increase at those times that the words in the "to-be-ignored" channel are of negative content.

As predicted, McCabe and Gotlib (1991a) found that the reaction times of the depressed subjects to press a button in response to the light probe were significantly longer in the negative-content distractor condition than in the positive- or the neutral-content distractor conditions. In contrast, the nondepressed subjects did not demonstrate differential reaction times across the three conditions. These results indicate that the depressed subjects were more distracted by negative- than by positive- or neutral-content words presented in the unattended channel of the dichotic tape. This finding lends support to the results of our earlier studies using the visual Stroop task, and is consistent with Beck's formulation of the operation of negative schemas in depressed persons.

Other investigators have reported conceptually similar findings. Williams and Nulty (1986), for example, also utilized a Stroop procedure to assess construct accessibility in depressed subjects. These investigators presented neutral- and negative-content words and rows of 0s to currently depressed and nondepressed subjects. In addition, Williams and Nulty also had available data concerning these subjects' depression scores from one year earlier. Consistent with Gotlib and McCann's (1984) results, Williams and Nulty found that currently depressed subjects took longer to color-name the negative-content words than they did neutral-content words; no group differences were obtained with respect to response latencies to the rows of 0s. More interesting, however, was Williams and Nulty's finding that those subjects who were depressed both at the time of testing and one year earlier were more likely to demonstrate impaired color-naming of negative- versus neutral-content words than were subjects who were depressed on only one of the two occasions. This "chronicity" effect is consistent with Gotlib and McCann's formulation that Stroop interference reflects the effects on construct accessibility of stable depressive symptoms, rather than of more transient fluctuating affective disturbances. This effect also lends support to Beck's emphasis on the importance of enduring schemas.

Before we describe the results of information processing studies that have examined more explicitly the stability of negative schemas in depression, we should mention that two investigations have failed to find an attentional bias in depressed individuals. In a study of the attentional functioning of patients diagnosed with an anxiety disorder, MacLeod, Mathews, and Tata (1986) reported that depressed subjects did not deploy their attention differentially to emotionally negative words. In a similar study, Gotlib, MacLachlan, and Katz (1988) found that, compared with nondepressed subjects, mildly depressed subjects deployed their attention less frequently to positive words and more frequently to negative words. Additional analyses indicated, however, that these group differences were due to an attentional bias exhibited by the nondepressed rather than the depressed subjects. Compared to chance, the nondepressed subjects attended significantly more often to the positive-content words than to the negative-content words. In contrast, the depressed subjects showed no evidence of selective attention to a particular valence of word. Thus, Gotlib, MacLachlan, and Katz found that an attentional bias was exhibited by the nondepressed, but not by the depressed, subjects.

Although the results of this study are consistent with findings obtained by other investigators who have documented positive biases in nondepressed subjects and an "even-handedness" in the functioning of depressed subjects (e.g. Alloy & Abramson, 1979, 1988; Golin, Terrell, Weitz, & Drost, 1979; Lewinsohn et al., 1980; Raps et al., 1982), they seem to be inconsistent with the findings of the previous Stroop studies, in which depressed persons were found to respond differently to negative than to positive stimuli. MacLeod and Mathews (1991) suggest that these discrepancies may be due to the confounding effects in some of these investigations of anxiety, which is associated with a different pattern of attentional functioning than is depression (cf. Williams, Watts, MacLeod, & Mathews, 1988). Given the high comorbidity between depression and anxiety (cf. Lewinsohn et al., 1991; Maser & Cloninger, 1990), this is clearly an important issue to be addressed in future research.

Collectively, these results offer considerable support for Beck's postulation of the existence and automatic operation of negative schemas in currently depressed persons. Indeed, even the studies that found depressed persons to be characterized by an evenhandedness of information processing nevertheless reported differences between depressed and nondepressed subjects with respect to their cognitive functioning. As we noted earlier, an important tenet of Beck's cognitive model is that negative schemas are enduring, remaining as vulnerability factors for subsequent depression. One method of testing this formulation is to examine whether depression-associated differences in schematic processing remain after the depressive symptomatology remits, that is, whether negative schematic functioning is evident in remitted depressives.

This issue was addressed by Gotlib and Cane (1987) in the study described above. In this investigation, clinically depressed psychiatric patients were assessed on the modified Stroop task both when they were in episode and later when they had recovered symptomatically. Nondepressed nonpsychiatric subjects served as a time-matched control group. As we reported earlier, Gotlib and Cane found that while they were depressed, patients took longer to name the color of depressed-content than of nondepressed-content words, indicating that currently depressed individuals are characterized by negative construct accessibility. Gotlib and Cane also found, however, that this effect was evident only in the first session, at which time the depressed subjects were symptomatic and in hospital. In the second session, at which time the patients were no longer depressed, they did not demonstrate this differential construct accessibility (see Figure 5.2). Gotlib and Cane interpreted these results as indicating that negative schemas affect cognitive functioning only during the depressive episode, and that these schemas and the depressives' negative cognitive functioning may be most parsimoniously viewed as a concomitant rather than a cause or residual of depression.

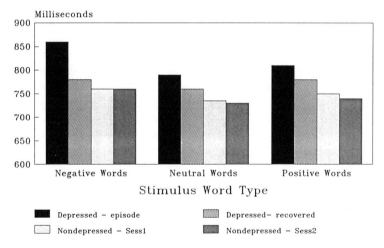

Figure 5.2   Color-naming response latencies: depressed and nondepressed patients. Source: adapted from Gotlib and Cane (1987)

The dichotic listening study conducted by McCabe and Gotlib (1991a) was also designed, in part, to examine the stability of negative schemas in depression. Recall that in this study depressed and nondepressed subjects shadowed neutral-content words presented in one ear while other positive-, neutral-, and negative-content distractor words were presented simultaneously in the other ear. At the same time, subjects were required to press a button in immediate response to a light flashing intermittently during this task. Subjects in this study were tested at two times: first, when the depressed subjects were symptomatic and, again, following recovery. As we noted earlier, when the depressed subjects were symptomatic, they were more distracted by negative- than by positive- or neutral-content words presented in the unattended channel of the dichotic tape. At Session 2, however, when these subjects were no longer depressed, they no longer demonstrated differential reaction times across the three distractor conditions. Indeed, analyses indicated that the depressed subjects were significantly less distracted by the negative-content words in the unattended channel in Session 2 than they were in Session 1. In contrast, the nondepressed subjects did not demonstrate differences in response latencies across the three types of words or between the two sessions.

The results of these two investigations suggest that, although depressed persons are characterized by negative cognitive functioning while they are symptomatic or in episode, their cognitive functioning appears to normalize following recovery. Furthermore, Williams and Nulty's (1986) results concerning subjects' BDI scores from a year prior to participation in their study suggest that individuals with recurrent depressions, compared to those with single or more sporadic episodes, may have stronger or more "entrenched" negative schemas *while they are symptomatic*, which might make it more difficult for them to recover from their depressive episodes (cf. Lewinsohn et al., 1981). In any case, these findings are consistent with the results of studies reviewed earlier assessing the stability and etiological role of dysfunctional attitudes and attributional style and, collectively, offer little support for the formulations of cognitive models of depression concerning the presence of a stable or "enduring" negative schema that plays a causal role in the onset of this disorder.

CONCLUDING COMMENTS

The results of these investigations of cognitive aspects of depression paint a reasonably consistent picture of the depressed person. There is little question that depressed individuals differ from their nondepressed counterparts with respect to their cognitive functioning. In numerous studies examining aspects of Beck's theory, for example, currently depressed persons have been found to perceive and recall environmental information more negatively, to evaluate themselves more negatively, and to maintain more dysfunctional attitudes than have nondepressed individuals. Similarly, the results of investigations conducted to examine the reformulated learned helplessness model of depression indicate that, compared to nondepressed persons, depressed individuals tend to attribute negative outcomes to internal and/or global causes, although the results of research assessing attributions for actual stressful events are the most equivocal in this area. Finally, findings from information-processing studies examining Beck's and associative network models of depression suggest that depressed persons are characterized, to a greater extent than nondepressed persons, by a tendency or readiness to attend to negative information from their environment.

Thus, across a variety of tasks and situations, currently depressed individuals demonstrate more negative cognitive functioning than do nondepressed persons. Moreover, the results of studies using information-processing methodologies make it unlikely that these depression-related patterns of cognitive functioning are due simply to a negative response style on the part of depressed subjects. Despite this robust negative cognitive functioning, however, research examining the more critical aspects of cognitive models of depression, that is, the causal role played by these cognitive styles and patterns in the development of this disorder, has not been so consistent. Indeed, on the basis of a review of longitudinal studies of cognitive functioning and depression, Barnett and Gotlib (1988b) concluded that there is little evidence of a stable cognitive vulnerability to depression and, therefore, little support for the causal hypotheses of cognitive vulnerability models of depression. A self-deprecating attributional style, a high number of dysfunctional attitudes, and a heightened attention to negative stimuli do not appear to be stable aspects of the depressed individual's functioning; rather, they seem to be cognitive abnormalities that wax and wane with the onset and remission of depression. They do not precede the onset of depression, nor do they consistently predict an increase in the severity of subsequent symptoms. Moreover, cognitive dysfunction is not typically evident following recovery from a depressive episode. Although a negative attributional style was found in some studies to be associated with the subsequent severity and longevity of dysphoria among children and nondepressed subjects, and to be involved in the process of recovery from depression, the results of most of the longitudinal studies simply do not support the postulates of existing cognitive models of depression.

Perhaps the most consistent negative finding among studies in this area of research involves the failure to demonstrate stability of cognitive dysfunction following a depressive episode. Investigations of dysfunctional attitudes, negative attributional style, and negative construct accessibility have most often found that formerly depressed patients do not differ from nondepressed controls with respect to their cognitive functioning. The fact that remitted patients have typically been found to exhibit normal, or nondepressed, self-schemas, attributional styles, and attentional processes suggests that their increased vulnerability for future depressive episodes is not adequately explained by current cognitive theories of depression. Some theorists have attempted to explain these negative findings by arguing that the kinds of longitudinal designs we have discussed in this chapter are inappropriate to assess cognitive vulnerability resulting from schematic processing (cf. Kuiper, Olinger, & Martin, 1990; Riskind & Rholes, 1984). These theorists argue that schematic processing should be conceptualized as "automatically activated" rather than as "automatically operating," and that schemas are inaccessible to measurement following symptomatic recovery from a depressive episode unless they are primed or activated by stressful experiences. In the absence of this activation, however, these schemas are not operational and do not guide information processing.

Reda et al. (1985), however, found that this was not the case. These investigators observed that although recovered depressives no longer endorsed the majority of the dysfunctional attitudes that they had held during their illness, a small number of these negative cognitions concerning dependence and autonomy did remain elevated and accessible postmorbidly. In addition, data such as those presented by Barnett and Gotlib (1990) suggest that dysfunctional cognitions are not primed by all negative events rated by subjects as being stressful. More specifically, the interaction between the DAS and a measure of the subjective stressfulness of the various life events experienced by subjects over a three-month period was not found to be a significant predictor of subsequent depression. Thus, there is evidence to suggest both that depressive schemas are accessible to measurement without a direct priming manipulation (but see also Miranda & Persons, 1988, and Miranda, Persons, & Byers, 1990), and that the interaction of stressful events and DAS scores is not a significant predictor of subsequent depression.

It is also possible that research has not supported the causal aspects of cognitive theories of depression because the sensitivity and/or specificity of measures of both dysfunctional cognitions and life events are too low to detect real effects. For example, Cane, Olinger, Gotlib, and Kuiper (1986) have recently demonstrated that the DAS measures at least two orthogonal dimensions: concerns regarding achievement and interpersonal evaluation. Interestingly, recent elaborations of cognitive vulnerability theories of depression have postulated the existence of two distinct superordinate schemas, or personality types, that seem to correspond to these substantive dimensions (Beck, 1983). Implicit in these theoretical developments is the recognition of the complexity of both vulnerability factors and personally relevant stressors. It may be that widely used measures of cognitive vulnerability such as the DAS and the ASQ must be modified to increase their sensitivity and specificity (although one must still explain discrepancies between the significant results of cross-sectional studies with these measures and the nonsignificant results of longitudinal investigations). Some modifications to these questionnaires have already been proposed (Metalsky, Halberstadt, & Abramson, 1987; Olinger, Kuiper, & Shaw, 1987), and the development of the Sociotropy-Autonomy Scale by Beck (1983) and the Depressive Experiences Questionnaire by Blatt and his collaborators (e.g. Blatt, Quinlan, Chevron, McDonald, & Zuroff, 1982) should also be viewed as steps in this direction.

Finally, paralleling this refinement of vulnerability measures are attempts to develop more precise life-event typologies (e.g. Hammen et al., 1985), with the expectation that a match between type of schema and type of life event would increase the power to predict the onset of subsequent depression. As we noted earlier, however, these "matching" studies have not been uniformly successful in this quest (cf. Hammen et al., 1985a,b; Small & Robins, 1988), although there are difficulties in the process of "typing" life events. For example, although raters may consider the loss of a job to represent an achievement event, the individual may perceive job loss to represent loss of contact with his colleagues at an interpersonal plane, and may respond to the loss on this level.

In closing, it is clear from the results of studies we have reviewed in this chapter that much more research is required before we have an adequate understanding of the functional role of cognition in depression. The current movement away from simple self-report measures of cognition toward more sophisticated assessments of information-processing styles may help to clarify some of the unresolved gaps in the empirical status of the concept of depression vulnerability. Nevertheless, there is another difficulty with cognition research that we have not addressed thus far. To date, cognitive approaches to the study of depression have been characterized by an extremely narrow focus on negativistic interpretations of events (their meaning, causes, and consequences) or on presumed pessimistic content in memory-based schemas. We believe that there are some crucial aspects of thoughts, beliefs, schemas, and the like that have considerable relevance to the psychopathology of depression that have yet to be studied. The considerable interest among developmental psychopathologists on the construct of attachment and related "working models" is a case in point. The idea of representations of the self and others, developing in the context of the mother-child relationship and having a pervasive and enduring influence on behavior, adjustment, and subsequent development, is clearly within the cognitive bailiwick. Such topics are too important to be left entirely to nonempirical object relations therapists, or to developmental psychologists who may not apply them to adult depression.

We contend that cognitively-oriented depression researchers have been too narrow in the types of cognitions they have studied, and in their neglect of investigations of the acquisition and development of maladaptive schemas, and of research examining the behavioral and emotional consequences of dysfunctional representations of the self and others (see Hammen, 1991a). It is our conviction that cognition must be considered within the context of the depressed person's interpersonal environment and social behavior—expressed not only in emotional reactions following interpretation of events, but also in behaviors and choices that influence the environment. In the following chapters, therefore, we turn to an examination of the interpersonal functioning of depressed individuals, including research on the development of depression vulnerability in the family and environmental context.

NOTE

[1]Readers should be aware that there are many other, less frequently used, self-report measures of dysfunctional thinking in depression (e.g. the Cognitive Bias Questionnaire: Krantz & Hammen, 1979; the Irrational Beliefs Questionnaire: Nelson, 1977; the Automatic Thoughts Questionnaire: Hollon & Kendall, 1980). Recent evidence suggests that these questionnaires collectively may assess the construct of Pessimism (ef. Gotlib, Lewinsohn, Selley, & Rodhe, 1991).

Chapter 6

The Social Functioning of Depressed Persons: I. Life Events, Social Support, and Interpersonal Behavior

Perspectives on the social functioning of depressed persons have not attained the status of cohesive theory in the same way that cognitive models have. Instead, there have been relatively isolated bodies of empirical research that implicate aspects of interpersonal functioning as important in understanding the etiology and maintenance of depression, as well as relapse of this disorder. Among these bodies of research are studies of stressful life events and depression, descriptive investigations of the social networks and social behaviors of depressed persons, studies of the marital and intimate relationship functioning of depressed individuals, and family and offspring studies related to depression. In this chapter we will focus broadly on the social context of depression, with a particular emphasis on stressors, social support, and interpersonal functioning. In the following chapter we focus more specifically on depression in the context of intimate relationships, including marriage, family, and childrearing aspects.

DEPRESSION AND STRESSFUL LIFE EVENTS

Large bodies of research suggest that stressful life events increase the likelihood of illness outcomes, including psychiatric distress. With respect to depression specifically, studies of both community residents and clinical patients have consistently demonstrated the existence of a significant relation between depression and life events (see reviews by Billings & Moos, 1982; Lloyd, 1980a,b; Paykel, 1979; Thoits, 1983a). These earlier studies were limited, however, by various methodological and conceptual shortcomings that contributed to relatively small associations between events and symptoms. More recently, theoretical and methodological refinements have provided more stringent tests, and investigators have been able to account for greater proportions of the variance in outcomes by including more mediating factors in their studies. Although it remains true that the majority of persons who experience even major negative events do not become clinically depressed, recent research suggests that for those individuals who are depressed, stressors may play a significant role in the timing of the symptoms and the course of disorder. In the following sections we present a selected review of research that is intended to highlight different theoretical and methodological perspectives on the link between stress and depression. Specifically, we present in some detail the work of Dohrenwend, Lazarus, Brown, Moos, and Lewinsohn and their colleagues. Following this presentation we discuss several recent developments in the attempt to clarify the depression-stress association.

Dohrenwend

The work of Bruce and the late Barbara Dohrenwend is especially noteworthy for its methodological rigor in attempting to establish a causal connection between life events and depression. The Dohrenwends attempted to develop a stressor assessment method that would reduce the confounding influence of symptoms, reporting bias, event-variation in categories, and subjective ratings. They developed a questionnaire with relatively specific, narrowly defined items, with symptom-related events omitted, and with objective weights. The Psychiatric Epidemiology Research Instrument (PERI; Dohrenwend, Shrout, Egri, & Mendelsohn, 1980) can serve as a checklist with follow-up interviewing to establish the occurrence and timing of the event. Using this method, Dohrenwend, Shrout, Link, Martin, and Skodol (1986) demonstrated that, compared with nondepressed community controls, depressed patients experienced a significantly greater number of events in the year prior to the depressive episode in three *a priori* categories: fateful loss events, physical illness and injury, and events disruptive of the social support network.

In a further refinement, Dohrenwend and colleagues attempted to clarify the causal link between depression and stressors. Shrout, Link, Dohrenwend, Skodol, Stueve, and Mirttznik (1989) argue that the contextual threat measures of events (to be discussed below), or those that take subjective appraisal into account, may strengthen the associations of depression and stress but obscure the causal direction. The source of the difficulty is the possibility that psychopathology influences the occurrence of events. As a stringent test, Shrout et al. examined the occurrence of 12 "fateful" loss events—defined as major negative events that were outside the control of the person. Interviews verified that these events were indeed fateful and disruptive. These investigators compared the frequency of occurrence of these events in the year prior to onset of major depression in a patient population and in a community control sample. Shrout et al. found that the odds of a depressed patient experiencing one or more such events was 2.5 times greater than was the case for individuals in the control group.

In addition to their conservative test of the causality hypothesis by using events beyond the person's control, another feature of the Dohrenwend group's approach is its de-emphasis of individual differences in cognitive appraisal. It is not that the authors do not believe that such individual differences occur, but rather, they emphasize the normative impact of major loss events on depression. Nevertheless, various kinds of trait-like individual difference variables are very much a part of their risk factor approach. Indeed, Dohrenwend et al. (1986) present preliminary data supporting the role of personality variables such as mastery/helplessness, locus of control, denial, Type A personality, and masculinity-femininity—all assessed as traits. Moreover, their overall model hypothesizes possible genetic vulnerability due to parental disorder, and weak social support networks, in addition to stressful events impinging on vulnerable personality characteristics. Dohrenwend et al. (1986) also note that they suspect that childhood bereavement may be a risk factor, and plan to incorporate this element in future work. Clearly, therefore, their depression model is expanding to include a full array of contextual (including internal) mediators of events. Nevertheless, the specifically cognitive aspects of the process have not been elaborated, and remain implicit. The major contribution to date of the Dohrenwends' stress model appears to be the elegant and rigorous test of the role of negative fateful events in provoking depression.

Lazarus

At the other end of the conceptual continuum involving appraisal processes is the work of Richard Lazarus. His work, evolving over several decades, has come to epitomize the emphasis on appraisal as a determinant of the impact of stressors. Indeed, viewed from his perspective, stress is a product of appraisal, conceptualized as a transaction between the person and the environment (e.g. Lazarus & Folkman, 1984, 1987). Necessarily, therefore, stress is best measured not on "objective" checklists, but through subjective reactions to events. Such reactions are constantly changing due to feedback from the events and from one's assessment and use of coping options. Assessment, therefore, is a complex process of attempting to measure what the stakes are, what the coping options are, and what types of coping are used. In turn, the primary and secondary appraisals of events are viewed as consequences of a variety of environmental and person variables (including values, self-esteem, and a host of other cognitive contents). Lazarus opposes the use of both simple life event checklists on the one hand and contextual threat ratings on the other. Both are viewed as reducing complex contextual factors into overly simplistic single scores. Moreover, Lazarus argues that major episodic life events as such are relatively rare. Accordingly, it is more important, both theoretically and empirically, to evaluate the impact of minor stressors—specifically, daily stressful encounters called Daily Hassles (cf. Kanner, Coyne, Schaeffer, & Lazarus, 1981). Lazarus and his colleagues have reported evidence of the utility of their multivariate approach to assessing stress in context, predicting health and mood symptoms as a consequence of daily hassles (see Lazarus, 1990, for a detailed review of these studies).

The advantages of Lazarus' model of stress may lie not so much in its empirical base, or even in Lazarus and his colleagues' contribution to depression research (because he does not study depressive phenomena as such). Rather, the most important element of Lazarus' model arguably is the concept of the person-environment transaction. While many have been critical of Lazarus' methods, arguing that he confounds measurement of stress with outcomes (e.g. Dohrenwend & Shrout, 1985), Lazarus makes a strong argument both for the impact of persons on environments and for individual differences in appraisal processes as mediators of outcome. On the other hand, Lazarus has also been criticized for disavowing the importance of personality traits or dispositional approaches to appraisal (e.g. Ben-Porath & Tellegen, 1990), and for describing the environment only in terms of what the subject reports on a questionnaire (e.g. Brown, 1990). Thus, questions of what factors determine appraisal, including objective features of the environment, are relatively ignored in Lazarus' approach (see also Moos & Swindle, 1990, for further commentary).

Brown

George Brown's British studies have focused specifically on the relations between stressful life events and depression, and present a very different conceptual and methodological focus than do those of Dohrenwend and Lazarus. In his seminal study of community women in the Camberwell district of London, Brown (Brown & Harris, 1978) described the contextual threat methodology for assessing the objective impact of an event by understanding the context in which it occurs. Objectivity is retained by having independent raters who have no knowledge of the respondent's actual reactions to the event rate the objective impact of the event as it would appear to a typical person under identical circumstances. Interviews are conducted to obtain detailed information about each event and the circumstances in which it occurs (the Life Event and Difficulty Schedule). The purpose of obtaining knowledge of the context of the event is to convey information about the likely meaning of the event. Thus, if a person responded "yes" on a checklist to death of a pet, its impact might be greatly misperceived unless one knows that the pet was the elderly respondent's only "social" relationship. Meaning—a cognitive construct—is inferred from information about the environmental context of the event rather than from asking the individual.

Brown has demonstrated that negative events judged to have major impact occur significantly more frequently preceding depressive episodes than they do in samples of nondepressed women (Brown & Harris, 1978). Subsequently, refinements of the theoretical model and empirical tests have demonstrated that predictability of depression is improved by including information concerning: (a) whether the events "matched" ongoing difficulties; (b) level of commitment to particular roles or activities; and (c) role conflict (Brown, Bifulco, & Harris, 1987). For instance, Table 6.1 illustrates findings from one of Brown and colleagues' recent studies. The table shows the extent to which major events that match a person's "vulnerabilities," defined as preexisting ongoing difficulties or areas of life in which the person is especially invested (commitment), increase the likelihood of depression (Brown, Bifulco, & Harris, 1987).

Brown's work has also presented a conceptual framework and supporting empirical data involving life event occurrence in the context of reduced social support, ongoing or chronic strains, and even childhood factors that increase vulnerability by altering self-esteem and general appraisal of the self and the world. For instance, as we shall discuss in greater

Table 6.1 The role of "meaningful" life events as precipitants of depression: examples from the research of George Brown

	Women with depression onset	
Severe Event Occurred		
Matches Prior Difficulty	46	
Does Not Match Prior Difficulty	14	$p < 0.001$
Severe Event Occurred		
Matches Prior Commitment	40	
Does Not Match Prior Commitment	14	$p < 0.01$

Prior Difficulty: ongoing (at least 2 years) of problems in a particular area, rated most severe (1–3) on 6-point scale of unpleasantness.
Prior Commitment: degree of dedication and enthusiasm for each of 5 areas, children, marriage, housework, employment, activities outside the home. Rated as 1 (marked commitment) on 4-point scale.
Source: Adapted from Brown, Bifulco, and Harris (1987).

detail in the next chapter, Brown and his colleagues have demonstrated that early childhood loss that is accompanied by poor parental care often predicts adult depression as a response to major stressors, especially through a path that includes early pregnancy and marital separation (e.g. Bifulco, Brown, & Harris, 1987; Harris, Brown, & Bifulco, 1986, 1987). Thus, Brown's work includes a broad characterization of context, involving not simply the contemporary environment, but also the early childhood psychological environment in which parenting quality is associated with children's cognitive representations of the self that, in turn, influence the types of relationships and subsequent social supports the person may have (e.g. Brown, Andrews, Harris, Adler, & Bridge, 1986).

Brown's work is certainly methodologically elegant and rich in capturing the actual features of the environmental context. Nevertheless, it is not without its critics. For instance, the contextual threat method of assessment is labor-intensive, and such critics as Tennant, Bebbington, and Hurry (1980) have contended that the judgments that go into the objective threat ratings may include unsystematic information that ought to be measured independently. Furthermore, Brown's approach to measuring "meaning" is indirect in the sense of inferring how the respondent ought to have felt, rather than in direct assessment of his or her cognitions about the event. Nevertheless, the model and the methods are powerful tools for predicting depression from knowledge of various environmental and personal characteristics.

Lewinsohn and Moos

The contributions of Lewinsohn and Moos and their colleagues are somewhat similar in their emphasis on multiple risk factors in large community surveys. Stressors are but one ingredient in an array of social-family support, cognitive, and coping variables that have been shown to predict depressive symptoms in previously nondepressed individuals, or the course of disorder in persons who have been depressed. For instance, Billings, Cronkite and Moos (1983) and Holahan and Moos (1991) have presented increasingly complex models of multiple factors predicting depression. In their most recent report, for instance, Holahan and Moos used causal modelling techniques in a sample of 254 adults to demonstrate that the relations between personal and social resources and depression are different for those experiencing high versus low stress. For instance, under high stressor conditions, personal and social resources affect coping, and coping predicts psychological outcome over a four-year follow-up period. Resources include self-confidence, easy-goingness, and family support, and these resources in turn predict effective (approach rather than avoidance) coping under high stress conditions. In contrast, under low levels of stress the resource factors predict depression directly. Research on a sample of clinically depressed individuals at a four-year follow-up assessment also indicated that coping style was related to outcome. Swindle, Cronkite, and Moos (1989) found that problem-solving coping was related to less current depression, while emotion-focused coping was related to more current depression. Family conflict was a significant predictor of depression over the follow-up period. Moos and his colleagues rely on self-report questionnaire measures of various constructs including life stress and coping, and typically use statistical methods to control for the possibility of depressive symptoms influencing responses.

Lewinsohn and his group in Oregon have also been active in testing the operation of complex psychosocial models of depression in large community samples. Lewinsohn's research is unique for including samples across the life span, from adolescents to older adults, and for including structured clinical diagnostic evaluations of depression status in community samples. Lewinsohn's recent investigations also typically involve prospective designs. For example, Lewinsohn, Hoberman, and Rosenbaum (1988) collected baseline data from nearly 1000 residents of two Oregon counties and then interviewed a large subset of them an average of eight months later (including the symptomatic and a random sample of the nonsymptomatic respondents). The baseline assessment included extensive sampling of stressful life events, social supports and interpersonal functioning, cognitive vulnerability variables, pleasant activities, and sociodemographic characteristics. Lewinsohn, Hoberman, and Rosenbaum found that both major and minor life events, and chronic conditions such as marital strain and unemployment, were among the predictors of developing a diagnosable depression. Being female, young, and having had a previous episode of depression were also among the important predictors of developing a clinically significant episode of depression. Cognitive vulnerability factors in general did not predict the onset of depressive episodes, with the exception of self-dissatisfaction. Interestingly, however, cognitions were associated with the prediction of elevated self-reported depression scores.

The Lewinsohn group has also demonstrated the importance to depression of psychosocial factors, including stressful life events, in adolescent community samples. For instance, Allgood-Merten, Lewinsohn, and Hops (1990) found that stressors were associated with both current and future depression. Girls were more likely to report stressors than boys, and also girls' depressive reactions to stressors were mediated by body image. Girls generally were more negative about their appearance, and the relative lack of such concern on the part of boys may have shielded them from depression responses to stressors.

Cognitive vulnerability and life events

As we noted in Chapter 5, most of the cognitive theories of depression have become more explicitly stress-diathesis models as they have evolved over time. For example, Beck's (1967, 1976) cognitive model of depression, Abramson, Seligman, and Teasdale's (1978) learned helplessness model of depression, and Abramson, Metalsky, and Alloy's (1989) hopelessness model all postulate a cognitive vulnerability to depression that is activated by stressful life events. As a consequence of the relatively recent emphasis on the stress portion of the diathesis stress models, there is surprisingly little data testing the role of cognitive vulnerability interacting with stressors (the major exception to this conclusion—hypotheses concerning the congruence between vulnerability and type of stressor—will be reviewed in a separate section later in this chapter).

There have been several studies that have attempted to test Beck's hypothesis that individuals with depressive vulnerability due to dysfunctional, depressogenic attitudes would be more prone to depression onset following stressful life events than would nonvulnerable controls. Several short-term longitudinal studies have failed to find evidence of the utility of the interaction of events and cognitive vulnerability to predict depression (e.g. Barnett & Gotlib, 1988a, 1990; Hammen et al., 1985a; Power, 1988). Interestingly, cross-sectional studies have also provided only mixed results for the cognitive vulnerability–stressful event interaction (e.g. Robins & Block, 1988; Wise & Barnes, 1986; see Barnett & Gotlib, 1988b, and review and commentary by Haaga, Dyck, & Ernst, 1991, for more detailed presentations of these studies). Also, earlier forms of attribution models of depression that involved causal analyses of specific stressful conditions have been reviewed in more detail elsewhere (e.g. Hammen, 1985).

Commentary

This brief analysis of the theoretical and methodological approaches to life stress and depression research by some of the major investigators in the field indicates that despite differences, there is nonetheless considerable congruence. The empirical association between stressors and subsequent depression is consistent, and the case for a causal relationship is strengthened by use of prospective designs and methods that attempt to limit the potential confounding of personal characteristics with event occurrence. Moreover, the various investigators have helped to improve the prediction of depression by focusing not solely on stressors, but by also including cognitive and social resource factors in their predictive equations. Interestingly, there has been only limited support for the specific interaction of vulnerability cognitions and life events, but it is clear that much research remains to be done in this regard. We shall have more to say about the social resource and support factors in subsequent sections of this chapter. For now, however, we shall proceed to explore two additional elements of life stress research that bear on the cognitive and social functioning of depressed persons.

VULNERABILITY TO INTERPERSONAL LIFE EVENTS

A theme that recurs in many formulations of the etiology of depression is loss. As we noted in Chapter 3, loss of a loved person is a central theme both in early psychoanalytic formulations of depression, and in current developmental psychopathology models such as those of Bowlby. Certainly the loss of a significant relationship is a calamity for most individuals, although normal bereavement does not typically evolve into clinically significant depression. Nevertheless, certain individuals seem to be especially likely to experience depression following the loss of a personal relationship. Moreover, there appears to be a particularly strong empirical association between "social exit" or "fateful loss" events (many of which involve loss of a person) and depression (e.g. Brown, Bifulco, & Harris, 1987; Paykel, 1979; Shrout et al., 1989).

The concept of loss has also come to be applied to the stressful event–depression field in terms of an expanded definition involving loss of meaning or loss of something of value to one's self-concept (e.g. Finlay-Jones & Brown, 1981). It is argued that the key psychological ingredient determining whether someone will experience depression following a negative event is the appraisal of the meaning of the event as signalling loss of self-worth, a belief that something essential for one's experience of being valued has been lost with no means of replacing it (e.g. Oatley & Bolton, 1985; Thoits, 1983b). In Brown's terminology, this construct is also referred to as "hopelessness" (Brown & Harris, 1978; Brown, Bifulco, & Harris, 1987). In this context, depression is the specific outcome, rather than some other psychiatric problem, because the belief that one lacks worth and efficacy is central to the experience of depression. In this section we explore further these related concepts. We also attempt to examine individual vulnerability to depression in response to specific types of life stress (commonly interpersonal stressors).

Sociotropy-autonomy and specific life event vulnerability

As we noted earlier, one attempt to improve the statistical association between life events and depression has involved a consideration of the mediating effects of cognitive vulnerability. Thus, depression would be predicted to occur to the extent that an individual appraises an event to mean devaluation of the self and deprivation of essential psychological supplies. Another person experiencing the same event but lacking such an interpretation would not be expected to become depressed (or perhaps would become only mildly and transiently dysphoric). Both psychodynamic and cognitive formulations of depression have hypothesized that, whereas some persons organize their sense of worth and mastery around interpersonal relatedness, other persons experience worth as related to the achievement of goals and the maintenance of autonomy, freedom of choice, and mobility (Arieti & Bemporad, 1980; Beck, 1983; Blatt et al., 1982). Although differing greatly in theoretical accounts of the mechanisms involved, there is agreement that negative events that involve interpersonal loss or conflict would be especially challenging for some people, while negative events that involve failure or goal frustration would be particularly difficult for others. Moreover, these theorists hypothesize that the type of depressive experience occasioned by the matching of negative events and individual vulnerability will also differ.

Several studies, using very different methodologies and designs, have tested the hypothesis of specific vulnerability to domains of life events that match the vulnerability. These studies differ, for example, in the measure of specific cognitive vulnerability, variously using the Sociotropy-Autonomy Scale, the Depressive Experiences Questionnaire, the Dysfunctional Attitudes Scale, or other procedures for indexing schema structure. The studies also differ in sample and design, with some based on college students and others based on clinical samples of depressed patients, and some using retrospective designs while others utilize cross-sectional or prospective methodologies. Finally, the studies also vary in terms of both the kind of stressful life event assessment or experimental manipulation and the type of instruments used to assess depression. Consequently, given the heterogeneity of the methods, the extent of consistency that exists in the findings is striking.

One of the first such studies was reported by Hammen et al. (1985b), who used a cognitive memory task—recall for recent personal events— to identify subjects for whom interpersonal events were most salient and subjects for whom achievement/autonomy events were most salient. Using a prospective design with college students interviewed monthly for four months for life event occurrence based on a contextual threat interview, as well as a clinical interview for assessing depression, Hammen et al. found support for the specific vulnerability model. In particular, for the interpersonally-vulnerable individuals, depression was more strongly associated with negative social- than achievement-oriented events. The effect was also apparent for the achievement-oriented students experiencing negative achievement events, but was less pronounced. Two other studies using college students tested in cross-sectional designs, one correlational and the other an experimental manipulation of stress, obtained conceptually similar results in reporting that dependent or sociotropic subjects were more reactive to social failure or social events than were achievement-oriented students (Robins & Block, 1988; Zuroff & Mongrain, 1987). In general, the association of depression and negative sociotropic events was higher for high sociotropic subjects than for autonomous subjects. The predictions for autonomous subjects, however, were not supported.

Subsequently, several studies of relapse in clinical patients have been conducted, measuring vulnerability with Beck's Sociotropy-Autonomy Scale, a self-report questionnaire measuring adherence to values, preferences, and attitudes reflecting the importance of interpersonal or autonomy themes. Hammen et al. (1989) studied patients prospectively for six months following assessment of vulnerability type. Hammen et al. found that unipolar depressed patients were more likely to experience onset, as well as more severe depression, if they experienced more events that matched their sociotropy-autonomy status. Sample sizes were too small to determine if the effect also held separately for the sociotropic and autonomous subgroups. Interestingly, Hammen et al. also reported that a sample of bipolar patients did not show an association between symptoms and the matching of events and vulnerability type in a six-month observation period.

Speculating that six months is insufficient to see changes in symptom status in most bipolar patients, Hammen, Ellicott, and Gitlin (in press) extended the follow-up period to an average of 18 months. These investigators found that onset was not related to matched events, but that symptom severity was predicted by sociotropy, interpersonal events, and their interaction. There was no such effect, however, for autonomy or achievement events. Robins (1990) has also reported support for a congruence of Sociotropy-Autonomy type and life events in a clinical sample. He assessed patients' retrospective recollections of recent life events, and found that high sociotropic patients reported significantly more interpersonal events than negative autonomy-related events. The opposite pattern, for high autonomous patients, was not observed, however.

Segal, Shaw, Vella, and Katz (1992) used the Dysfunctional Attitudes Scale to assess specific vulnerability, and followed a sample of remitted depressed patients for one year. Relapse was predicted by the interaction of self-criticism scores and negative achievement events over the period prior to relapse. The predicted effect for dependency-oriented patients was not significant, except when only the events in the two months before onset were counted. The authors speculate that interpersonal events are often immediate losses and have an immediate impact, whereas achievement-related events might involve worsening of ongoing difficulties over a period of time.

Although somewhat beyond the scope of this chapter, it is noteworthy that sociotropy and autonomy represent not only vulnerability to specific types of stressors, but also different types of depressive symptoms. Building on partially supported hypotheses reported by Robins, Block, and Peselow (1989), Robins and Luten (1991) developed a somewhat different version of the SAS and an expanded list of clinical features of depression. They found that patients who scored high on autonomy (and low on sociotropy) had clinical features associated with endogenous depression, while sociotropic patients had features of nonendogenous reactive depression (but only for men). Thus, quality of the depressive symptoms and features of the syndrome might be affected by the nature of cognitive vulnerability reflective core values.

We should also note that some studies have examined the relation between level of sociotropic or dependent values and depression, irrespective of the role of stressful life events. Viewed as a personality style, there appears to be evidence of "dependency" as a correlate of depression. For instance, Nietzel and Harris (1990) conducted a meta-analysis on studies that used the Depressive Experiences Questionnaire, the Interpersonal Dependency Inventory, and the Sociotropy-Autonomy Scale. These authors concluded that dependency needs are especially strongly related to depression, suggesting a pernicious pathway to this disorder. Comparable analyses involving self-criticism characteristics and depression showed them to be less substantial. This conclusion is in keeping with some of the evidence that will be presented in later chapters on the particular role of dependency in depression vulnerability.

Commentary

There is a growing body of evidence indicating that the link between stressful life events and depression is strengthened by determining individual vulnerability to specific types of events. Vulnerability in this sense is a cognitive process referring to the interpretation of the meaning of the event for the person's worth. To date, however, there is no direct evidence demonstrating that sociotropic or autonomous subjects actually interpret different domains of events in different ways or that such interpretations involve self-worth, so that the mechanism by which the "congruency" process functions remains to be delineated.

Although the focus on the interpersonal and achievement domains appears consistent with a variety of clinical perspectives, this does not mean that other types of individual vulnerability are unimportant. Indeed, it is likely that highly idiosyncratic areas of vulnerability could be located for most individuals. In any event, it is striking that interpersonal events and interpersonal vulnerability have received the strongest support in their presumed association with depression. Events concerning social relatedness, conflict, loss, and disruption appear to have depressive consequences for many individuals. It appears that some of the recent methods for assessing the salience of interpersonal values and goals have the potential for helping to predict well ahead of time the circumstances under which certain individuals will experience depression.

STRESS GENERATION AND THE COURSE OF DEPRESSION

A discussion of stressful life events and depression would be incomplete if we focused only on the direction of causality that goes from event occurrence to depressive outcome. Because of the improvements in the methods of testing the causal link from negative events to depression, we now have enough confidence in the strength of this empirical association to risk addressing the other direction of the relationship. Until recently, the possibility that characteristics of the person might affect the occurrence of stressors was regarded as a methodological nuisance. Although this has been widely speculated about, or at least acknowledged clinically (e.g. Depue & Monroe, 1986), most investigators took the stance that such processes were unwanted confounds in understanding the etiological significance of life events for depression (see also Monroe & Simons, 1991). In view of the emphasis on fully understanding the context of event occurrence espoused by many of the life event theorists discussed earlier, it seems useful to consider the other side of the coin: do people at risk for depression actually cause, or partly cause, negative events?

Hammen, Burge, and Adrian (1991) recently addressed this issue, comparing life events assessed by contextual threat interviews over a one-year period in several groups of women who were demographically similar: unipolar depressed, bipolar, medically ill, and nonpsychiatric normal women. Based on total stress summed across objective threat ratings for each event, Hammen, Burge, and Adrian found that the unipolar women had significantly more stress than did the normal women. But what was particularly striking was the pattern of events considered to be either independent (i.e. outside the woman's control or contribution) or dependent (i.e. at least partly due to the woman's behavior or characteristics). Although the groups did not differ on independent stress, the level of dependent stress was higher for the unipolar women. Moreover, compared to women in the other groups, the level of dependent stress among the unipolar women was specifically higher for interpersonal events, and especially for conflict events. Unipolar women appeared to have suffered an excess of stress, due largely to their own contribution, as a result of conflicts with others, including friends, family, bosses, neighbors, teachers, and landlords. Table 6.2 presents the group means for the comparisons.

Table 6.2   Mean objective threat rating totals by group

Group	Type of event category			
	Total all events	Independent	Dependent	Interpersonal
Unipolar	12.7	3.6	8.8	6.3
n = 14	(12.5)	(3.2)	(9.6)	(7.0)
Bipolar	9.1	3.6	5.5	3.2
n = 11	(6.0)	(2.7)	(4.8)	(3.2)
Medically ill	11.6	6.6	5.1	3.0
n = 13	(6.5)	(6.1)	(5.5)	(4.3)
Normal	7.6	4.4	3.3	2.0
n = 22	(7.6)	(5.9)	(3.7)	(2.8)

Standard deviations are in parentheses.
Source: Adapted from C. Hammen (1991b). The generation of stress in the course of unipolar depression. *Journal of Abnormal Psychology*, **100**, 555–561.

Additionally, Adrian and Hammen (in press) recently reported that the children of unipolar women showed a similar pattern of generation of interpersonal events in a study of their events over a three-year follow-up period. Although they did not differ significantly from the bipolar offspring in conflict events, the children of unipolar women showed the highest levels of dependent events overall, including categories of both family and peer conflict, compared to all other groups.

What factors might contribute to the generation of stressors? One approach to understanding stress generation in subjects at risk for depression concerns their families of origin. As we have noted throughout this book, depression tends to run in families. Indeed, in the following chapter we document the consistent finding that many depressed people come from families they report to have been punitive, rejecting, and unsupportive. Therefore, it is possible that such early childrearing experiences set the stage for difficulties in interpersonal relationships and for poor acquisition of skills for resolving interpersonal conflict. In our own studies of depressed women and their families (Hammen, 1991a), and in the work of George Brown (e.g. Bifulco, Brown, & Harris, 1987), depressed women from adverse childhoods are seen to marry early, perhaps marrying unsuitable men who have psychiatric conditions, with subsequent marital conflict and separation, as well as various chronic strains associated with economic disadvantage and raising children. Each of these steps can be understood as a series of stressful life events that contribute to further symptoms. Alternatively, the whole context can be understood as dysfunctional transactions between the person and her environment that are bidirectional. Hammen (1991a) presented a model, tested and supported by structural equation methods, in which women's own backgrounds contributed to their stressful circumstances, which in turn contributed to dysfunctional parenting, leading to children's diagnoses.

In a separate prospective study of unipolar depressed outpatients, Hammen, Davila, et al. (1992) predicted that stressful life events and chronic strains would mediate the relationship between family history of psychopathology, early onset of symptoms, and depression severity. Data were consistent with the model, and support the formulation that adverse personal and family psychiatric history sets the stage for a vicious cycle of stressors and depression. Although we do not rule out genetic explanations, we also speculate that early onset of symptoms and having parents with psychopathology impair the person's acquisition of important social and problem-solving skills. As a result, vulnerable individuals generate stressors and fail to resolve stressful situations, in turn leading to a more pernicious, severe course of depression with recurring symptoms (and more stressors).

Results from these studies strongly suggest that if we wish to understand the context of depression, it is necessary to understand not only that people react to negative events by becoming depressed, but also that they may contribute to the event occurrence. Because the specific types of events that the unipolar women in the first study experienced in excess involved interpersonal conflict, we must consider what it is that such women might be doing and thinking that contributes to stressor occurrence. It seems likely that both dysfunctional cognitive and interpersonal patterns are implicated in stress generation. In the next few sections of this chapter, therefore, we explore in detail the topic of interpersonal functioning in order to learn more about the social difficulties of depressed persons.

SOCIAL NETWORKS AND SOCIAL SUPPORT

There is a mounting body of research indicating that depressed persons have smaller and less supportive social networks than do their nondepressed counterparts. For example, in one of the first investigations in this area, Pattison, de Francisco, Wood, Frazier, and Crowder (1975) found that whereas nondepressed individuals reported knowing between 20 and

30 people, "neurotic depressed" patients reported knowing only 10 to 12. Moreover, the social networks of the depressed patients also appeared to be less integrated than were those of the nondepressed subjects, in that fewer of the people listed by the depressed patients knew one another. Finally, the depressed patients were more likely to nominate people who lived far away or who were dead, thereby suggesting that their significant others are not as available to them as is the case for nondepressed persons.

Subsequent investigations have replicated and extended these findings. Brim, Witcoff, and Wetzel (1982) found that depressed inpatients reported having less frequent and less helpful contact with members of their social networks than did nondepressed control subjects. Similarly, Brugha, Conroy, Walsh, Delaney, O'Hanlon, et al. (1982) found that a sample of outpatients, most of whom were depressed, recalled having smaller networks and fewer nonfamily contacts than did nondepressed controls. The patients also reported spending less time interacting with the person they nominated as their primary attachment figure and, perhaps as an explanation of this finding, were also more likely to perceive these interactions as negative. Finally, Henderson, Byrne, and Duncan-Jones (1981) found that depressed subjects not only reported having fewer close friends and fewer contacts outside of the household than did matched nondepressed controls, they also judged a higher proportion of their interactions with these individuals to be negative.

Other investigators have also reported that depressed people, and particularly depressed women, experience their interpersonal relations to be less emotionally supportive than do nondepressed persons (e.g. Billings, Cronkite, & Moos, 1983; Dean & Ensel, 1982). For example, Gotlib and Lee (1989) conducted a study which examined the social functioning of depressed psychiatric outpatient women, nondepressed psychiatric outpatients, and nondepressed community controls. As can be seen in Figure 6.1, the depressed women in this study reported that they engaged in fewer social activities and had fewer close relationships than did subjects in both of the nondepressed groups. The depressed women also rated the quality of their significant relationships more poorly than did the nondepressed women, and reported that there were arguments in their families over a greater number of issues than was the case for subjects in either of the nondepressed groups. The results of this study are consistent with the findings reviewed earlier indicating that depressed persons perceive their social networks to be smaller and less supportive than do nondepressed persons. Moreover, because the depressed patients differed from both the nondepressed patients and the nondepressed community controls, these results also suggest that perceptions of smaller and less supportive social networks may be specific to depression, rather than characteristic of psychopathology in general.

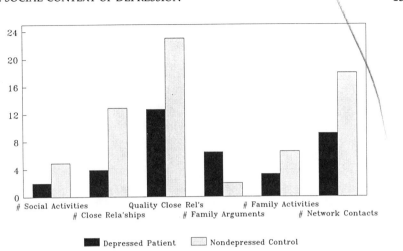

Figure 6.1   Social functioning of depressed and nondepressed patients. Source: adapted from Gotlib and Lee (1989)

While it is tempting to conclude from this research that depressed persons experience difficulties with their social networks, it is important to note that in most of these investigations the data were obtained only once, while the individuals were depressed. As we noted in Chapter 3, a number of theorists have postulated that, congruent with their mood, depressed individuals exhibit negatively distorted perceptions of their environment (cf. Beck et al., 1979). Indeed, several studies have demonstrated that negative mood states facilitate the perception and/or recall of negatively-toned information (e.g. Bower, 1981; Gotlib, 1983; Gotlib & Cane, 1987). It is possible, therefore, that findings indicating that depressed subjects report negative perceptions of their social environments reflect transient mood-related perceptions rather than stable veridical perceptions (cf. Gotlib, Mount, Cordy, & Whiffen, 1988). The results of a number of investigations, however, suggest that this is not a viable explanation.

Several researchers have conducted longitudinal assessments of the social functioning of depressed subjects. In these studies, subjects are typically examined first when they are depressed, and again when they are no longer symptomatic. The results of these investigations suggest that the negative characterizations by depressed persons of their social functioning are not the result of a reporting bias. For example, Billings and Moos (1985a,b) and Gotlib and Lee (1989) both found that although there was some increase in the number of social contacts reported by depressed individuals one year following their depressive episode, they continued to report restricted social networks when they were no longer symptomatic. At both assessment times, depressed subjects reported having fewer friends and fewer close relationships than did nondepressed controls. In addition, while formerly depressed subjects reported a higher quality in their significant relationships at follow-up than they did while they were depressed, their family interactions continued to be marked by arguments and negativity. The results of these studies also suggest that depression affects meaningful social relationships to a greater extent than it does superficial relationships. Billings and Moos (1985b), for example, found that although formerly depressed persons did not differ from nondepressed controls with respect to levels of superficial relationships, they continued to report having fewer close relationships. Indeed, one of the "risk factors for nonremission" identified by Billings and Moos was few close social relationships at intake.

Using a different methodology to examine the possibility of negative distortion of depressed persons in describing their social networks, Billings, Cronkite, and Moos (1983) compared the reports of depressed patients with those of a nondepressed family member. They found no evidence that the depressed patients were more negative about their social environments. In fact, there was good concordance between the depressed individuals and their family members with respect to estimating the size of the depressed person's network and the number of close relationships. Reporting similar findings, Lee and Gotlib (1991a) presented data indicating that mothers' negative perceptions of their children, almost a year following their depressive episodes, are corroborated by clinicians' ratings. Finally, in a recent review, Richters (in press) concluded that there was little evidence of negative distortion in depressed mothers' ratings of behavioral problems in their children. In sum, therefore, it appears that the association of depression and social dysfunction is not an artifact of distorted perception or recall.

Several investigators have attempted to examine more explicitly the nature of the relation between depression and social dysfunction. For example, a number of researchers have demonstrated that perceptions of low social support antedate the onset of depression (e.g. Cutrona, 1984; Monroe, Imhoff, Wise, & Harris, 1983; see Barnett & Gotlib, 1988b, and Oatley & Bolton, 1985, for more detailed reviews of these studies). Other theorists have posited, however, that low social support in and of itself is insufficient to result consistently in depression. Thus, some investigators have examined the more complex formulation that we alluded to earlier in this chapter, that low social support leads to depression by increasing people's vulnerability to the debilitating effects of stressful life events. In one of the first studies to suggest that social support may moderate the relationship between life events and depression, Nuckolls, Cassel, and Kaplan (1972) investigated the roles of stressful life events and social support with respect to birth complications. Nuckolls, Cassel, and Kaplan found that, of those women who reported high life change scores, those who also reported receiving high social support experienced fewer birth complications than did those who reported low support. A number of subsequent investigations have now demonstrated that low social support is most strongly associated with subsequent depression when it occurs in the presence of stressful life events (e.g. Cutrona & Troutman, 1986; Monroe, Bromet, Connell, & Steiner, 1986). Indeed, Brown and Harris (1978) and Costello (1982) reported that the lack of a supportive intimate relationship was a critical risk factor for depression, especially when individuals were experiencing major stressors in their lives (Brown & Harris, 1978). It is likely that social resources help individuals cope more effectively with stress, which results in a reduced incidence of depressed mood. Consistent with this formulation, as we noted earlier, research suggests that support is associated with the use of effective coping strategies, such as problem-focused coping, that are less related to the development of depressive symptoms (Billings, Cronkite, & Moos, 1983; Billings & Moos, 1984; Holahan & Moos, 1991).

Finally, it is important to note that decreased social support can result not only from a reduction in network size, but from the nature or quality of the interactions with network members as well. Recent studies suggest that "social support" should not be conceptualized simply as low levels of supportiveness in relationships; rather, it must also include the presence of negativity in the relationships. In fact, negative features of social relationships appear to be more strongly related to measures of perceived support and the presence of psychological symptoms than do positive features (e.g. Coyne & Bolger, 1990; Pagel, Erdly, & Becker, 1987). Indeed, the negative, conflictual features of relationships appear to be significantly related to the presence of depression. Whereas the degree of negativity and distress caused by stressful interpersonal relationships was found to predict the development of depression, the presence of helpful relationships was not (Kiecolt-Glaser, Dyer & Shuttleworth, 1988; Pagel, Erdly, & Becker, 1987). Perhaps the most convincing data indicating that negative features of social relationships are more influential than are positive features come from a study of 3000 adults in the Epidemiologic Catchment Area Study (Weissman, 1987). Weissman reported that the negative effect of being involved in a relationship and being unable to talk to one's spouse was more strongly related to the risk for depression than was the positive effect of being able to communicate well with one's spouse.

Commentary

There is ample research to indicate that the social networks of depressed people are smaller and less supportive than are those of their nondepressed counterparts. The reason for these differences between depressed and nondepressed persons with respect to their social networks, however, is not clear. Based on our earlier discussion concerning the stress generation of depressed persons, one likely explanation for the greater negativity in the social networks of depressed individuals is that people who are depressed behave in ways that lead to problematic interpersonal relationships and, consequently, to a loss of social support. In the following section of this chapter, therefore, we will begin our examination of the literature assessing the interpersonal behavior of depressed persons. We shall first review studies that have assessed the interactions of depressed individuals with strangers and friends. Then, in the following chapter, we shall turn our attention to studies of the marital and family relationships and interactions of depressed persons.

THE SOCIAL BEHAVIOR OF DEPRESSED PERSONS

Although the situation is changing slowly, it remains the case that most of the interactional/observational studies of depressed persons have assessed one-time encounters of depressed individuals with strangers. These studies of the social behavior of depressed persons derived their impetus primarily from Lewinsohn's (1974; Lewinsohn, Biglan, & Zeiss, 1976) social skills formulation of depression. As we discussed in Chapter 3, Lewinsohn postulated that depressed individuals demonstrate deficits in social skill. More specifically, Lewinsohn suggested that depressed persons do not emit responses that are reinforced by others in their environment. The resultant low rate of response-contingent positive reinforcement received from others leads to depression. Researchers testing this formulation have typically examined the behavior of depressed persons engaged in social interactions.

A number of investigators have identified various social skills deficits associated with depression. Gotlib and Asarnow (1979), for example, found depressed persons to be less skillful than were their nondepressed counterparts at solving interpersonal problems. Other researchers have reported similar findings indicating that, in both group and dyadic interactions, depressed persons are less socially skillful than are nondepressed individuals. Specifically, depressed persons have been found to speak more slowly and more monotonously (Gotlib & Robinson, 1982; Libet & Lewinsohn, 1973), and to take longer to respond to others' verbalizations (Libet & Lewinsohn, 1973; Youngren & Lewinsohn, 1980). Gotlib (1982) found depressed psychiatric patients to maintain less eye contact and to use more awkward hand movements than did nondepressed, nonpsychiatric control subjects. Jacobson and Anderson (1982) found depressed subjects to make more inappropriately timed verbal responses than did their nondepressed counterparts. Finally, several investigators have demonstrated that, compared with nondepressed controls, the content of depressed people's conversations is more self-focused and negatively toned (Blumberg & Hokanson, 1983); in an interpersonal situation depressed persons tend to communicate self-devaluation, sadness, and helplessness (Biglan, Hops, Sherman, Friedman, Arthur, & Osteen, 1985; Hokanson, Sacco, Blumberg, & Landrum, 1980). Not surprisingly, given this pattern of interpersonal behavior, depressed individuals have also been found to judge themselves to be less socially competent than do nondepressed persons (Gotlib & Meltzer, 1987). Considered collectively, therefore, these studies indicate that depressed individuals exhibit an interpersonal style in social situations that is markedly more negative than that demonstrated by nondepressed persons.

Investigators have recently broadened the scope of these findings by examining the behavior of persons interacting with depressed individuals. The impetus for many of these studies was provided by Coyne's (1976b) interpersonal description of depression. As we outlined in Chapter 3, Coyne contended that depressive symptomatology is maintained or exacerbated by the responses of others with whom the depressed person interacts. Researchers assessing the validity of Coyne's interpersonal description of depression have typically examined people's responses to depressed individuals. In the first empirical test of this formulation, Coyne (1976a) examined the reactions of undergraduate females to telephone conversations with depressed and nondepressed female psychiatric outpatients. He found that subjects who had interacted with a depressed patient reported feeling significantly more depressed, anxious, and hostile following the interaction than did subjects who had interacted with a nondepressed patient. Subjects who had interacted with a depressed patient were also more rejecting of their partner. These results are consistent with the hypothesis that behavior of depressed persons is aversive and capable of inducing negative affect in others. Equally important is the finding that the behavior of the depressed patients also resulted in other people rejecting opportunities for further interaction, a situation that clearly restricts the interpersonal contact available to the depressed person.

Subsequent investigations have corroborated these initial findings. Hammen and Peters (1977), Winer, Bonner, Blaney, and Murray (1981), and Gotlib and Beatty (1985) all found people to respond more negatively to transcripts describing a depressed person than they did to a description of a nondepressed individual. Similarly, Boswell and Murray (1981) found students to exhibit more negative mood and greater rejection in response to audiotaped interviews with depressed psychiatric inpatients than they did with tapes of nondepressed persons. Employing a different methodology, Hammen and Peters (1978) and Howes and Hokanson (1979) examined the behaviors and perceptions of subjects interacting with confederates portraying a depressed role. These researchers reported that subjects rated themselves as more depressed following the interaction than did subjects who had interacted with a "nondepressed" confederate. Compared with "nondepressed" confederates, "depressed" confederates also elicited more silences and directly negative comments, a lower rate of overall verbal responding, more personal rejection and less interest in further interaction.

In an important study, Yarkin, Harvey, and Bloxom (1982) told half of their subjects that the woman they were watching on a videotape was facing depressing circumstances and was worried about her mental health; the remaining subjects were given no information about the woman. When subjects were subsequently given an opportunity to interact with the woman, those who were told that she was depressed sat further away, maintained less eye contact, engaged in more negatively toned conversation, and spoke with her for a shorter period of time. Thus, the expectations subjects held about their partner were sufficiently powerful to affect their overt behavior. In fact, Cane and Gotlib (1985) have drawn on findings from these and other investigations in suggesting that a consideration of others' expectations may be critical in understanding how the negative interpersonal effects of depression are maintained and exacerbated.

Two investigations have examined the behavior of strangers engaged in actual face-to-face interactions with a depressed person. Gotlib and Robinson (1982) and Gotlib and Meltzer (1987) assessed the behavior, mood and perceptions of individuals engaged in dyadic interactions with depressed and nondepressed persons. Subjects who interacted with depressed individuals were found to emit more negative verbal and nonverbal behavior during the interactions than were subjects who interacted with nondepressed individuals, and also perceived themselves to be less socially skillful. Interestingly, the behavioral differences were present from the first three minutes of interaction. In a similar study, Strack and Coyne (1983) had subjects interact with either depressed or nondepressed individuals. Strack and Coyne found that, following the conversation, subjects who had interacted with a depressed individual reported feeling more depressed, anxious and hostile, and were less willing to interact again with their partners than were subjects who had interacted with a nondepressed person. Interestingly, the depressed individuals were significantly more rejecting of the subjects with whom they interacted than were the nondepressed individuals, and also correctly anticipated more rejection from their partners.

The results of these studies suggest, therefore, that depressed persons have an aversive interpersonal style to which others respond with negativity and rejection. Although there have also been negative results reported by some investigators (e.g. King & Heller, 1984; McNiel, Arkowitz, & Pritchard, 1987), Gurtman (1986) recently concluded that rejection of depressed persons is reasonably consistent across studies and methodologies. It is important to note, however, that virtually all of this research has been conducted with analog populations or procedures, not only in the use of nonclinical samples, but also in the sense that the interactions occur between strangers. It is not clear whether the results of studies conducted in a laboratory setting examining brief encounters between strangers and dysphoric college students, or confederates pretending to be depressed, are generalizable to clinically significant levels of depression occurring in the context of more intimate relationships.

In an intriguing attempt to begin to address this issue of generalization, Hokanson and his colleagues (e.g. Hokanson, Rubert, Welker, Hollander, & Hedeen, 1989; Howes, Hokanson, & Loewenstein, 1985) examined the mood and social behaviors of pairs of college roommates over the course of an academic year. Howes, Hokanson, and Loewenstein had initially unacquainted roommates complete the Beck Depression Inventory immediately before they moved in together, and again during their first, fifth, and eleventh week of cohabitation. On the basis of these BDI scores, Howes, Hokanson, and Loewenstein selected three groups of roommate pairs for analysis: (a) those pairs in which one roommate scored 12 or above on the BDI throughout the study (unremitted group); (b) those pairs in which one roommate scored 12 or above on the pretest but scored 7 or below on each of the subsequent assessments (transient-remitted group) and (c) those pairs in which one person scored 7 or below on the BDI on all administrations (nondepressed control group). The most striking finding reported by Howes, Hokanson, and Loewenstein was that the roommates of the unremitted depressed persons displayed a progressive increase in their own BDI scores over the course of the investigation. Other results of this study indicated that both the depressed roommates and their nondepressed partners perceived the depressed partner to become increasingly dependent over time, while the nondepressed partner became increasing managerial and responsible (Hokanson, Loewenstein, Hedeen, & Howes, 1986). Indeed, Hokanson et al. suggested that the nondepressed partner's increased caretaking behavior may reinforce and exacerbate the depressed roommate's dependent behavior.

In different analyses, Hokanson et al. (1989) found that diagnosed depressed students reported reduced social contact with their roommates, low enjoyability of such contact, and elevated levels of experienced stress. Replicating the results of their earlier work, Hokanson et al. (1989) found that the roommates of depressed students reported low ratings of enjoyability of contact with their roommates and strong aggressive-competitive reactions toward their depressed partners. Indeed, Hokanson, Hummer, and Butler (1991) reported that unremitted depressed subjects perceived the highest levels of hostility and the lowest levels of friendliness in their roommates. Similar results were also reported by Burchill and Stiles (1988), who found that, compared with roommates of nondepressed students, roommates of depressed students indicated more rejection, dislike, and avoidance of their roommates, and higher levels of depression themselves.

Finally, Rosenblatt and Greenberg (1991) examined depressed individuals (selected on the basis of elevated scores on the BDI) and their best friends. These investigators found that the best friends of depressed persons themselves had higher scores on the BDI than did the best friends of nondepressed control subjects. To examine whether depressed people might choose more depressed friends because they feel better after talking with a depressed than a nondepressed person, Rosenblatt and Greenberg conducted a second study in which they examined depressed and nondepressed subjects' mood following interactions with either a depressed or a nondepressed partner whom they did not know. The results of this second study indicated that, compared with the nondepressed subjects, depressed subjects experienced more negative mood after conversing with nondepressed partners. More specifically, depressed subjects who had interacted with a nondepressed partner reported more anxiety and hostility following the interaction than did any of the other three types of subject-partner dyads. Thus, it may be the case that depressed individuals prefer interacting with other depressed individuals.

CONCLUDING COMMENTS

In this chapter we have considered the social functioning and interpersonal experiences of depressed individuals, and the nature of the role of stress in this disorder. It is clear from our review that theorists in this area are developing increasingly more sophisticated accounts of the nature of the association between stress and depression. Ideally, researchers will similarly design and conduct more refined investigations of the stress-depression link; indeed, it appears from the evidence we have reviewed here that this reciprocal relation between theory and empirical findings in this area is in fact progressing.

It is also clear from our review that depressed persons are characterized by marked difficulties in their interpersonal functioning. Compared with their nondepressed counterparts, depressed individuals report having smaller and less supportive social networks. In interactions with strangers, roommates, and friends depressed people have been found to be less socially skillful than are nondepressed people, and to elicit more negative responses from others around them. Furthermore, several studies have demonstrated that depression in one person can result in increases in negative affect in others with whom they interact, in decreases in others' enjoyability of time spent with the depressed person, and in changes in the interpersonal dynamics of their relationship. Interestingly, there is some evidence that depressed persons themselves may feel worse following interactions with nondepressed partners, perhaps leading to increasingly more negative emotions and interactions. Certainly, the findings that depressed persons both engender negative affect and rejection in nondepressed others, and feel worse following these interactions, is consistent with our suggestion that depressed persons generate some of the stress in their lives, especially interpersonal conflict.

Considered collectively, therefore, the results of these studies are important in beginning to elucidate the nature of the social functioning and interpersonal experiences of depressed persons, as well as the role of stress in the etiology and maintenance of depression. To examine these issues more closely, in the following chapter we turn our attention to investigations explicitly assessing the marital and family relationships of depressed individuals and the psychosocial functioning of children of depressed parents.

Chapter 7

The Social Functioning of Depressed Persons: II. Marital and Family Relationships

As we saw in Chapter 6, over the past decade there has been increasing attention paid, at both a theoretical and an empirical level, to the interpersonal functioning of depressed persons. Investigators have examined the nature and quality of the social support available to depressed persons, and have assessed their social behavior in interactions with strangers, roommates, and friends. This recent focus on interpersonal functioning has also led researchers to begin to examine both the role of more intimate relationships in the etiology, course, and treatment of depression, and the potentially negative impact of depression on close relationships. In this context, investigators have begun to examine the marriages of depressed individuals, the relationships of depressed persons with their children, and the psychosocial functioning of offspring of depressed parents.

In this chapter we will examine the current state of knowledge concerning the relation between depression and marriage, and between depression and impaired family functioning. We will also examine the psychosocial functioning of children of depressed parents, and will discuss possible mechanisms by which the offspring of depressed parents might experience emotional and behavioral difficulties. We begin with a brief examination of the literature documenting an association between depression and marital status. Following this discussion, we examine empirical studies that document the pervasiveness of the relation between depression and marital distress, and we consider a number of explanations for this association. Finally, we turn our attention to an examination of the family relationships, parenting, and children of depressed persons.

DEPRESSION AND MARITAL STATUS

Over the past 40 years, epidemiologists have consistently demonstrated a significant relation between psychiatric disorder and marital status (e.g

Bebbington, 1987; Lavik, 1982; Odegaard, 1946). Despite the relatively coarse and insensitive nature of marital status as an independent variable, a stable pattern of results has emerged from these investigations. With remarkably few exceptions, the highest rates of psychological distress, and particularly depression, have been reported for unmarried individuals (i.e. separated, divorced, widowed, and never married), while currently married persons evidence the lowest rates of distress (e.g Bachrach, 1975; Blumenthal, 1967; Gove & Tudor, 1973; Rushing, 1979). Interestingly, this ordering of the unmarried reporting more depressive symptoms than do the married remains essentially unaffected by the type of sample examined (e.g psychiatric outpatients, psychiatric inpatients, unselected community residents) or the social class of the sample.

   Although it is clear that there is a consistent relationship between marital status and depression, the meaning and reasons for this association are not well understood. As Pearlin and Johnson (1977) note, relatively little research has been aimed directly at understanding why married people are more likely to be free of depression than are their unmarried counterparts. Nevertheless, there are three major hypotheses that have been proposed to account for differences in the incidence of depression as a function of marital status. The *selection hypothesis* proposes that individuals who display depressive symptomatology are less desirable and, therefore, are less likely to marry than are their emotionally healthier counterparts. Moreover, if such people do get married, they are hypothesized to be less able to stay married. In contrast, the *causation hypothesis* posits that marriage itself either protects the individual from depression or is an etiological factor in the disturbance. Thus, the different lifestyles associated with the various marital statuses are hypothesized to produce different levels of stress, resulting in different rates of emotional disorder. Finally, the *utilization hypothesis* proposes that the relationship between marital status and depression is essentially spurious, a function of unmarried individuals having higher rates of treatment for depression than do married people despite equivalent levels of depressive symptoms.

   As Gotlib and McCabe (1990) note, there is mixed support for all of three of these formulations. The utilization hypothesis, that unmarried individuals are more likely to seek psychological treatment than are married persons, is rendered less tenable by the results of studies with unselected community samples that do not rely on treatment seeking (e.g Amenson & Lewinsohn, 1981). The selection hypothesis, that individuals who exhibit symptoms of psychopathology are less likely to get married than are their emotionally healthier counterparts, seems less applicable to depression than to schizophrenia and alcoholism. Finally, the causation hypothesis, that being married protects against depression, has found support in Brown and Harris' (1978) finding discussed earlier that the presence of a confidant decreases the risk of depression. Pearlin and Johnson (1977) examined the relation between life strains and depressive symptoms in a large sample of married and unmarried persons. Pearlin and Johnson found that being unmarried increased both individuals' chances of experiencing hardship, and the probability of their being psychologically hurt by such experience as well. They concluded that marriage can help people cope more effectively with economic and social strains and stressors.

We must also note, however, that the protective function of marriage appears to operate more strongly in males than in females (e.g Ensel, 1986; Gove, 1972). As we noted earlier, it has been well documented that females generally exhibit higher rates of depression than do males (e.g Amenson & Lewinsohn, 1981; Weissman & Klerman, 1977). More specifically, however, these gender differences seem to be largest among married persons (e.g Radloff, 1975; Roberts & O'Keefe, 1981; Weissman & Boyd, 1983). Thus, whereas marriage appears to be beneficial for men, married women have been found to exhibit higher levels of depression than have both unmarried women and married men. For males, therefore, marriage seems to provide a buffer against the development of depression, whereas for females, marriage appears to exacerbate the disturbance (cf. Cleary & Mechanic, 1983). The most widely accepted explanation for this marriage-gender interaction is that traditional gender roles mediate the relation between marital status and psychopathology (cf. Gotlib, Whiffen, Mount, Milne, & Cordy, 1989; see Gove, 1972, for an extended discussion of this issue).

Although these theories each provide a partial explanation of the relationship among marital status, gender, and depression, it is clear that the construct of marital status fails to consider the quality of the marital relationship, which may mediate the association between marriage and depression. Indeed, in a large household survey, Renne (1971) found that both males and females who are dissatisfied with their marriages are more depressed than are their separated and divorced counterparts. As we shall see in the following sections, research examining the quality of the marital relationships of couples in which one spouse is suffering from depression clearly indicates that these marriages are characterized by elevated levels of tension and distress; indeed, spouses in such marriages are at increased risk for divorce (Merikangas, 1982). Thus, it is to this issue of the association of depression and marital distress that we now turn our attention.

DEPRESSION AND MARITAL DISTRESS

In recent years there has been considerable interest in the relation between marital distress and depression. The results of a number of diverse investigations have documented a consistent association between marital dysfunction and depression. Rush, Shaw, and Khatami (1980), for example, suggest that in at least 30% of couples experiencing marital problems, one spouse is clinically depressed. Similarly, Weissman (1987) reported that the six-month prevalence rate of major depression in a community sample of maritally distressed wives was 45.5%. Moreover, a growing body of literature is also demonstrating not only that treatment outcome is less favorable in couples who are experiencing marital distress, but further, that relapse is more likely for those depressed patients who return to unsatisfying marriages (cf. Hooley, 1986; Hooley & Teasdale, 1989). Indeed, Merikangas (1984) found the divorce rate in depressed patients two years after discharge to be nine times that of the general population.

Other investigators have also reported a significant association between marital distress and depression. Ilfeld (1977), for example, found that more than 25% of the variance in depression scores in a community survey were accounted for by the stresses of marriage and parenting. Coleman and Miller (1975) and Crowther (1985) both obtained significant positive correlations between self-report measures of depressive symptomatology and marital distress in psychiatric samples. Similarly, Hoover and Fitzgerald (1981) found that both unipolar and bipolar patients reported greater conflict in their marriages than did nondepressed controls.

Weissman and her colleagues (e.g Rounsaville, Weissman, Prusoff, & Herceg-Baron, 1979; Weissman & Paykel, 1974) reported comparable results in an intensive study of 40 moderately to severely depressed female outpatients. Weissman found that these patients reported greatest impairment as wives and mothers, expressing problems in the areas of affection, dependency, sexual functioning, and communication. The depressed women reported that their marital relationships were characterized by friction, hostility, and a lack of affection. Indeed, Weissman and Paykel's findings led them to conclude that, "... the marital relation was a significant barometer of clinical status" (p. 94). Freden (1982) obtained similar results based on interviews with 91 depressed men and women and 109 nondepressed controls in Sweden. Freden found that whereas 40% of the depressed subjects reported that they were unable to talk to their spouse about almost anything, only 7% of the nondepressed controls reported having a similar communication problem. Finally, Gotlib and Whiffen (1989b) examined the marital relationships of couples in which the wife met diagnostic criteria for clinical depression. These investigators found that depressed women and their husbands both reported greater dissatisfaction in their marriages than did a group of nondepressed control couples.

The results of these investigations clearly underscore the pervasiveness of the relation between depression and marital disturbance. It is important to note, however, that because these studies are cross-sectional, it is impossible to determine the causal nature of this association. For example, it may be the case that the impact of a depressive episode leads to subsequent marital distress. Alternatively, marital distress might lead one or both spouses to experience depression (cf. Gotlib & Hooley, 1988). In the following sections, therefore, we will briefly discuss the results of studies related to these two possibilities, and will then turn to an examination of the broader family relationships of depressed persons.

Depressive episodes lead to marital distress

One explanation for the association of depression and marital distress is that an episode of depression in one spouse leads to marital distress in the couple, due perhaps to the stresses of living with a depressed partner. In the previous chapter we reviewed the results of a number of studies indicating that depressed individuals can in fact induce negative affect and behavior in others with whom they interact (e.g Gotlib & Robinson, 1982; Marks & Hammen, 1982). Consistent with these findings, there is also converging evidence from a variety of sources to indicate that living with a psychiatrically disturbed person exerts a significant toll on the individual's spouse and family (e.g Clausen & Yarrow, 1955; Krantz & Moos, 1987; Noh & Avison, 1988). Targum, Dibble, Davenport, and Gershon (1981), for example, found that over half of the spouses of bipolar depressed patients indicated that they regretted having married. More recently, Noh and Turner (1987) reported that the perception of the psychiatric patient as a burden was a significant correlate of psychological distress among their spouses. Indeed, Coyne, Kessler, Tal, Turnbull, Wortman, and Greden (1987) found that 40% of the spouses of depressed persons were themselves sufficiently distressed to warrant referral for psychotherapy.

A number of investigators have conducted direct observations of the marital interactions of depressed persons. In one of the first of these studies, Hinchliffe, Hooper, and Roberts (1978) examined 20-minute interactions of 8 male and 12 female depressed inpatients and their spouses while in the hospital. These interactions were compared with the interactions of nonpsychiatric surgical patients and their spouses, and with the interactions of the depressed patients with opposite-sex strangers. Hinchliffe, Hooper, and Roberts found that, compared with the interactions of the nondepressed controls, the conversations of couples with a depressed spouse were marked by greater conflict, tension, and negative expressiveness. Their interactions were also characterized by a greater number of interruptions and a greater frequency of pauses. Interestingly, the interactions of the depressed patients with their spouses were also more negative than were their interactions with the strangers.

These results lend support to Gotlib and Colby's (1987) contention that the interpersonal difficulties of depressed persons are more pronounced in close relationships. That interactions with depressed individuals take a toll on their spouses is also supported by data indicating the presence of hostility in the marital interactions of depressed persons. Arkowitz, Holliday, and Hutter (1982), for example, found that following interactions with their wives, husbands of depressed women reported feeling more hostile than did husbands of psychiatric and nonpsychiatric control subjects. In a similar study, Kahn, Coyne, and Margolin (1985) reported that couples with a depressed spouse were more sad and angry following marital interactions, and experienced each other as more negative, hostile, mistrusting and detached than did nondepressed couples. Hautzinger, Linden, and Hoffman (1982) assessed the interactions of 26 couples seeking marital therapy, 13 of whom had a depressed spouse. The couples in each group were matched on the severity of their marital difficulties. Hautzinger, Linden, and Hoffman found that the communication patterns of the depressed couples were more disturbed than were the communications of the nondepressed couples. Specifically, the interactions of the depressed couples were more uneven, negative, and asymmetrical, and were more concerned with discussing emotional difficulties.

Biglan and Hops and their colleagues (e.g Biglan et al., 1985; Hops, Biglan, Sherman, Arthur, Friedman, & Osteen, 1987) compared the marital interactions of couples who were neither depressed nor maritally distressed with those of two groups of couples in which the wife was clinically depressed. In one of these two groups the couples were also reporting marital distress, while in the other the level of marital distress was relatively low. Biglan et al. found that, regardless of level of marital distress, depressed women exhibited higher rates of depressive affect and behavior and lower rates of problem-solving behavior than did either their husbands or the nondepressed control spouses. Moreover, in examining the conditional probabilities of these interactional behaviors, Biglan and Hops found that the depressed wives' dysphoric displays served to reduce the likelihood of their husbands' aversive behaviors. We should note, here, however, that recently Nelson and Beach (1990) obtained this pattern of results with nondepressed-distressed couples, and Schmaling and Jacobson (1990) failed to replicate these results with a sample of depressed couples. It is clear, therefore, that this finding remains tentative until it is clarified by additional research.

Three studies conducted in our laboratory provide further evidence of the negative marital interactions of depressed persons. Kowalik and Gotlib (1987) had depressed and nondepressed psychiatric outpatients and nondepressed nonpsychiatric controls interact with their spouses while simultaneously coding both the intended impact of their own behavior and their perceptions of their spouses' behavior. Compared with the nondepressed controls, the depressed patients were found to code a lower percentage of their messages as positive and a higher percentage as negative, indicating that they perceived the interactions and their spouses as problematic. Interestingly, however, behavioral ratings made by observers did not differentiate among the three groups of subjects and spouses. In a subsequent study, Ruscher and Gotlib (1988) examined the effects of depression and marital distress on the marital interactions of mildly depressed couples from the community and nondepressed control couples. The results indicated that, compared with nondepressed couples, couples in which one partner was depressed emitted a lower proportion of positive verbal behaviors and a greater proportion of negative verbal and nonverbal behaviors (see Figure 7.1). Further analyses on these data indicated that the depressed spouses emitted more negative behaviors than did spouses in any of the other groups. Interestingly, this pattern of results was no longer significant when level of marital satisfaction was covaried, suggesting that the negative interactions may be a function of either depression or marital distress. Finally, Gotlib and Whiffen (1989a) examined marital satisfaction and interpersonal behavior in groups of depressed psychiatric inpatients, nondepressed medical patients and nondepressed community controls. Subjects and their spouses completed measures of marital satisfaction and then participated in a 20-minute marital interaction task. Both the depressed and the medical patients and their spouses reported significantly lower marital satisfaction than did the community control couples. Furthermore, during the marital interaction, couples in both patient groups smiled less,

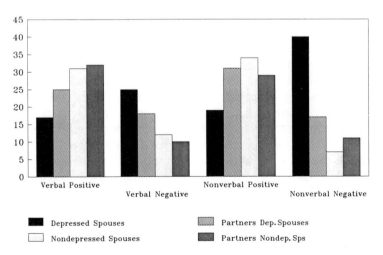

Figure 7.1   Interactional behaviour of depressed and nondepressed couples. Source: adapted from Ruscher and Gotlib (1988)

exhibited less pleasant facial expression, and maintained eye contact less frequently than did the nonpatient control couples.

The results of these studies suggest, therefore, that depressed persons and their spouses perceive their marital interactions to be marked by tension and hostility, and may behave negatively in interactions with their partners (cf. Gotlib & Whiffen, 1991). These data, juxtaposed with those concerning the responses of strangers to depressed individuals, provide tentative support for the hypothesis that depression can lead to marital distress. Depressive behavior seems consistently to be experienced by others as aversive, and can lead to dysfunctional interactions. Given this position, it is informative to consider the results of studies that have examined the marital relationships of depressed persons following recovery from depression.

In a four-year follow-up of Weissman and Paykel's (1974) depressed women, Bothwell and Weissman (1977) found that marital problems persisted, even though the women were no longer severely depressed and had improved in the other areas of functioning. Consistent with this finding, Schless, Schwartz, Goetz, and Mendels (1974) found that the vulnerability demonstrated by depressed patients to marriage- and family-related stresses persisted after symptomatic recovery. Finally, Hinchliffe, Hooper, and Roberts (1978) found that, although the marital interactions of depressed males improved following symptomatic recovery, the depressed women and their spouses continued to demonstrate high levels of tension and negative expressiveness following hospital discharge. It appears, therefore, that the marital relationships of depressed persons do not improve immediately following one spouse's recovery from a depressive episode. As we shall see later in this chapter, this pattern of residual interpersonal difficulties has also been found with the children of depressed parents.

Marital distress leads to depressive episodes

An alternative explanation for the consistent association of depression and marital distress is that marital distress may lead to, rather than result from, depression. From this perspective, marital distress may precede the onset of a depressive episode, or may affect the course of depression. There is considerable evidence to indicate that marital distress may precede a depressive episode. Paykel, Myers, Dienelt, Klerman, Lindenthal, and Pepper (1969), for example, found that the most frequent life event reported by depressed women preceding the onset of their depression was an increase in arguments with their spouses. Similarly, Weissman and Paykel (1974) also found that an increase in marital disputes was the most frequently reported event among their sample of depressed women prior to requesting treatment. Brown and Harris (1978) interviewed large samples of community-living women and depressed patients and their relatives.

Brown and Harris reported that the lack of a confiding, intimate relationship with a spouse or boyfriend was one of four factors that were associated with women becoming depressed when faced with major life events or chronic difficulties (see also Costello, 1982). Finally, Freden (1982) found that depressed persons reported perceiving their spouses as being excessively demanding and burdensome, particularly during the period prior to the onset of their depressive episodes.

These data, therefore, are consistent with the hypothesis that marital dysfunction may precede depressive episodes. Results from other investigations suggest that marital difficulties may affect the course of depressive disorders. For example, both Sims (1977) and Rounsaville et al. (1979) found that those psychiatric patients whose symptoms appeared to be precipitated by marital difficulties demonstrated the poorest outcomes in treatment. More specifically, Rounsaville et al. reported that those women entering treatment who also had marital problems showed less improvement in their symptoms and social functioning, and were more likely to relapse following individual therapy. Interestingly, resolution of these marital disputes resulted in both a decrease in depressive symptoms and a reduced likelihood of relapse.

The importance of family relationships in the course of depressive disorder has also been underscored in a study by Vaughn and Leff (1976b). These investigators interviewed the family members of schizophrenic and depressed patients around the time of the patients' hospitalizations. On the basis of the extent to which they expressed critical, hostile, or emotionally overinvolved attitudes to the interviewer when talking about the patient, relatives were classified as either high or low in expressed emotion (EE; see Hooley, 1985, for a review of this construct). Vaughn and Leff found that patients who returned from the hospital to live with high EE relatives were significantly more likely to relapse during a nine-month follow-up period than were patients who returned home to live with low-criticism family members.

More recently, Hooley and her colleagues (e.g Hooley, Orley, & Teasdale, 1986; Hooley & Teasdale, 1989) replicated this association between spouses' high levels of EE and relapse in their unipolar depressed partners. Interestingly, although the spouses of depressed patients were as critical of their partners as were the relatives of the schizophrenics in Vaughn and Leff's (1976b) study, Hooley, Orley, and Teasdale found the depressed patients to relapse at lower rates of relatives' criticism than did the schizophrenic patients. Indeed, both Vaughn and Leff and Hooley, Orley, and Teasdale found that the level of spouses' criticism associated with depressed patients' nine-month relapse rates was lower than the levels of criticism typically associated with relapse in studies involving schizophrenic samples (e.g Brown, Birley, & Wing, 1972).

It appears, therefore, that there are data to support both these directions of influence for the association of depression and marital distress. We have reviewed results of studies indicating that depressive episodes can lead to marital distress; we have also presented evidence indicating that marital distress can precede depressive episodes, and may also affect the course of a depressive episode. Although some investigators have utilized longitudinal designs in attempts to distinguish empirically between these two causal explanations (e.g Ulrich-Jakubowski, Russell, & O'Hara, 1988), it is arguably inappropriate to view them as competing; it is likely, in fact, that both formulations would be supported in any large sample of depressed married persons.

Moreover, it is also possible that a third factor, such as underlying characterological disorders or adverse early interpersonal experiences, may place individuals at increased risk for the development of both depression and marital distress (cf. Gotlib & Hooley, 1988). As we shall see in Chapter 10, it is possible that dysfunctional early childhood relationships between parents and children predispose to depression vulnerability by way of cognitive schemas and dysfunctional interpersonal behaviors.

In addition to the impact of depression on marital satisfaction, and of satisfaction on depression, there is yet another facet to consider: the association between depression and dysfunctional mate selection. There is growing evidence that depressed individuals marry others with diagnosable psychiatric conditions (Hammen, 1991a; Merikangas, Weissman, Prusoff, & John, 1988; Rutter & Quinton, 1984). Moreover, while it is certainly likely that some distress in the spouse is a consequence of being married to a depressed person (as we have discussed in this chapter and in Chapter 6), there is also evidence that disorders in the spouses may have existed prior to marriage, or that vulnerability to disorder existed in the spouses before marriage. For instance, Hammen (1991a) in the UCLA study of children of depressed mothers, and Merikangas et al. (1988) in the Yale high-risk study, independently determined that the ill spouses of depressed patients themselves had family histories of psychopathology. Thus, at least indirectly, evidence suggests that spouse disorders were independent of those of the depressed spouse.

While not unique to affective disorders, this pattern of *assortative mating* has particular implications for an interpersonal approach to depression. As Rutter and Quinton (1984) and Hammen (1991a) have shown, elevated rates of psychopathology in spouses are associated with high rates of family discord or chronic relationship stress. For instance, marrying someone with a disorder such as alcoholism or antisocial personality disorder is highly likely to contribute to episodic and ongoing stressors. Additionally, the risk to children for disorder increases as a function of having two ill parents (e.g Hammen, 1991a; Merikangas, Prusoff, & Weissman, 1988).

A depressed parent who has children with disorders is further likely to experience stressful, depressing conditions. For those with particular interpersonal vulnerability or dysfunctional interpersonal conflict resolution skills, dysfunctional mates (and children) probably translate into increased risk for depression. It remains an intriguing question why depression-vulnerable people may select mates with disorders. We speculate that the process of mate selection is greatly influenced by one's cognitive representations of the self and others that arise in the context of attachment to caretakers in childhood.

In the following sections we discuss in greater detail the early experiences of depressed adults, and examine the relationships of depressed persons with their children.

PARENT-CHILD RELATIONSHIPS AND DEPRESSION

Depression runs in families, and many depressed children and adults come from dysfunctional families. In this section we attempt to explore the data supporting these assertions and to examine the family context of risk and vulnerability for depression. In the final analysis, we will contend that for many people, depression is a disorder of interpersonal relatedness. The key to understanding vulnerability to depression for such persons is the nature of early parent-child relationships, in their contribution to cognitions about the self, others, and the world, as well as in the behaviors that come to reflect such representations. We begin our discussion by briefly examining the literature that focuses on the relation between early parental loss and adult depression, and then turn our attention to research assessing the adverse effects of problematic early parental experience.

Depressed patients' reports about their childhoods

Parental loss

The issue of whether early loss of a parent places an individual at increased risk for depression later in life has been the focus of a longstanding controversy. Since Freud first commented on the similarity between bereavement and depression, investigators have conducted research designed to examine this relationship more systematically, typically comparing rates of early parental loss among groups of adults differing with respect to the presence of depression. Data generated from these investigations have been equivocal. For example, Brown (1961) found that

41% of a large sample of depressed adult psychiatric patients had lost a parent through death before the age of 15, an incidence twice that of a control group of general practice patients and three times that of the general population in England. Similarly, Frommer and O'Shea (1973) found that women who had experienced separation from or the death of either parent before age 11 had an incidence of postpartum depression that was twice as great as that of women who had not (see also Roy, 1981, and Pfohl, Stangl, & Tsuang, 1983).

Other investigators, however, have not been able to replicate these findings. For example, Munro (1966), Abrahams and Whitlock (1969), Jacobson, Fasman, and DiMascio (1975), and Perris, Holmgren, Von Knorring, and Perris (1986) all found no differences between depressed psychiatric patients and matched nondepressed controls with respect to the loss of a parent in childhood. Reflecting this perplexing state of affairs, two reviews of this research concluded that there is an association between parental loss and depression (Lloyd, 1980a,b; Nelson, 1982), while two others concluded that no such relationship exists (Crook & Eliot, 1980; Tennant, Bebbington, & Hurry, 1980).

The results of three recent studies suggest that these contradictory findings may be understood by considering the quality of parental care that followed the loss. Harris, Brown, and Bifulco (1986) found that early maternal loss was frequently followed by inadequate parental care. In fact, Harris, Brown, and Bifulco noted that once lack of parental care was taken into account, maternal loss no longer predicted onset of depression in adulthood. On the basis of this finding, they suggested that it is lack of parental care, rather than simple parental loss, that is the vulnerability factor for experiencing depression in adulthood. These findings were subsequently replicated by Bifulco, Brown, and Harris (1987).

Finally, conceptually similar results were reported by Breier, Kelsoe, Kirwin, Beller, Wolkowitz, and Pickar (1988), who examined factors relevant to the development of psychopathology, largely depression, in a sample of 90 adults, all of whom had experienced the loss of a parent between the ages of 2 and 17 years. Diagnostic interviews were admininistered, and psychopathology in first-degree relative and quality of early upbringing were also assessed. Subjects also underwent a neuroendocrine assessment. On the basis of the diagnostic interviews, subjects were divided into two groups: those with a psychiatric history during adulthood (77% of the sample) and those with no history of psychiatric disorder during adulthood (23% of the sample). Only four subjects were experiencing symptoms and signs of a current psychiatric disorder at the time of their participation in this study.

Breier et al. (1988) found that the subjects who had a history of psychiatric disorder reported a poorer quality of early home life than did subjects without a psychiatric history. The subjects with a psychiatric history also had higher plasma cortisol and β-endorphin levels than did the no-psychiatric history subjects. Interestingly, a discriminant function analysis indicated that the quality of early home life alone correctly classified 80% of the subjects in this study as having or not having a history of psychiatric disorder.

These studies underscore the likely importance of the quality of early parental care in placing individuals at risk for depression. It is to this literature that we now turn.

Adverse early environment

Although some individuals are ill-treated by people who are not members of their immediate family, most of the available data on early life and depression concern family life. Unfortunately, there is a paucity of longitudinal research in which children and their families are assessed, and the children followed into their adult years to assess childhood predictors of depression. Consequently, in examining the childhood environments of adults who experience episodes of depression, we must rely in large part on retrospective research. As we shall see, the results of studies in this area are remarkably consistent in suggesting that the early lives of depressed adults were marked by inadequate parenting.

A number of theorists have emphasized the importance of early adverse experience in placing an individual at risk for the subsequent development of a depressive disorder. With respect to psychoanalytic theory, for example, Bibring (1953) maintains that a predisposition to depression is caused by insufficient parental love during childhood. More recently, Beck (1967) has argued that depression in adulthood results from negative cognitions about the self, the world, and the future. These cognitions are postulated to have their origins in the early interactions of the child with his or her parents. Finally, Blatt (1974; Blatt & Homann, 1992) suggests that anaclitic and introjective depressions are due to failures during childhood to establish good relations with the parents and to develop adequate representations of the parents.

Recent empirical investigations have converged to suggest that depressed individuals have had more aversive childhoods than have nondepressed persons. Munro (1966) examined perceptions of early parent-child relationships in samples of depressed patients and general hospital patient controls, and found that the depressed patients' "relations with a parent figure were consistently strained or unhappy ... during at least part of childhood" (p. 445). Raskin, Boothe, Reatig, Schulterbrandt, and Odle (1971) administered the Children's Report of Parental Behavior Inventory (CRPBI; Schaefer, 1965) to depressed patients and matched nondepressed controls.

Compared with the nondepressed controls, the depressed patients in this study rated their parents as less positively involved in their children's activities, less loving and affectionate, and more negatively controlling. Corroborating these results, Jacobson, Fasman, and DiMascio (1975) found that compared with normal controls, depressed patients reported greater parental rejection and abuse, higher parental discord, and less parental affection. The more severe inpatient cases reported the worst abuse.

In a large, multisite study, Crook, Raskin, and Eliot (1981) examined the reports of early parental behavior by 714 depressed adult inpatients and 387 nondepressed, nonpatient controls. All subjects completed the CRPBI, and extensive information concerning the social history of the subjects was collected by trained social workers through interviews with relatives and knowledgeable others. Crook, Raskin, and Eliot found that the depressed patients described both their mothers and fathers as more rejecting, controlling through guilt, demonstrating hostile detachment, and instilling persistent anxiety than did the controls. These reports were in large measure corroborated by the social workers.

Studies utilizing nonclinical or community samples have produced similar results. Blatt, Wein, Chevron, and Quinlan (1979), for example, examined the relation between severity of depressive symptoms and parental descriptions among college students. Using a variety of formats and measures to assess representations of parents, Blatt et al. found that depression was related to perceptions of the parents as lacking in nurturance, support, and affection. In a prospective community study Andrews and Brown (1988) found that working-class mothers who reported lack of adequate parental care or a high degree of antipathy from their mothers were more likely than other women to become clinically depressed following a severe life event. Another recent community study in which subjects were interviewed involved a sample of 200 individuals from a larger epidemiological project (Holmes & Robins, 1987, 1988). The subjects were selected according to a lifetime diagnosis, that is whether standardized diagnostic criteria were met for depression or alcoholism at any time in the person's life. Fifty subjects, mostly women, met the criteria for depression and 50, mostly men, met the criteria for alcoholism. Fifty men and 50 women with no lifetime diagnosis of either syndrome were selected as controls. Holmes and Robins found that harsh parental discipline in childhood was significantly related to both major depressive disorder and alcohol disorder (but see also Lewinsohn & Rosenbaum, 1987).

Gotlib et al. (1988) examined the perceptions of early parenting of women with mild levels of postpartum depression. Depressed and nondepressed women completed the Parental Bonding Instrument (PBI; Parker, Tupling, & Brown, 1979), indicating their early perceptions of their mothers. The PBI is a well-validated questionnaire measure of two dimensions of parental characteristics: care versus indifference/rejection, and overprotection versus encouragement of independence (see Parker, 1981). Gotlib et al. found that, compared to a control group of nondepressed women, depressed subjects recalled their mothers to have been less caring and more overprotective. Using a larger, independent sample of subjects, Gotlib, Whiffen, et al. (1991) found that women who were diagnosed as depressed in the postpartum period reported less maternal and paternal care and greater maternal overprotection than did women who were not depressed in the postpartum period. Indeed, in this study perceptions during pregnancy of early parental care were a significant predictor of the onset of depression in the postpartum.

In sum, the results of these studies indicate that depressed individuals are more likely than are nondepressed persons to report early relationships characterized by low care, high overprotection, and hostile and abusive behaviors. In a recent meta-analysis of the literature examining perceived parental rearing practices in depressed and anxious patients, Gerlsma, Emmelkamp, and Arrindell (1990) reached similar conclusions. On the basis of their review, they concluded that phobic disorders and neurotic depressions (but not bipolar depressions) were related to a parental rearing style of less affection and more control, a style labelled "Affectionless Control." There seems to be little question, therefore, that depression in adulthood is consistently associated with reports of problematic early experiences.

The validity of retrospective reports

Given the emphasis in most cognitive theories of depression on negative perception and recall of environmental stimuli, there have been questions raised concerning the validity of these retrospective reports of depressed adults. Indeed, a number of psychologists have suggested recently that depressed patients' accounts of their childhoods are unreliable. For example, Burbach and Borduin (1986, p. 146) state that "the validity of retrospective data obtained from depressed patients and their families is questionable at best." Gerlsma, Emmelkamp, and Arrindell (1990, p. 270) similarly suggest that mood biases in the recall of autobiographical memories "seriously question(s) the stability of parental rearing style measurement." Finally, Lewinsohn and Rosenbaum (1987, p. 618) conclude more forcefully, "retrospective memory should probably never be construed to represent what really occurred."

The results of empirical investigations addressing this issue, however, suggest that the retrospective reports of depressed persons of problematic early family environments may, in fact, be accurate. Parker (1981), for example, compared the reports of parenting behaviors of depressed persons and their mothers, and found a significant degree of correspondence between these two sources of information. In a subsequent study with monozygotic and dizygotic twins, Parker (1986) reported mean levels of sibling agreement on the PBI subscales of about 0.70. Oliver, Handal, Finn, and Herdy (1987) compared ratings of parental childrearing by depressed and nondepressed siblings in a college sample. Although these investigators found that the relatively depressed subjects did indeed report more negative perceptions of their parents, the reports were consistent with those of their nondepressed siblings. Finally, several studies have demonstrated that depressed patients continue to report adverse early family environments even when they are no longer symptomatic (e.g Abrahams & Whitlock, 1969; Gotlib, Mount, et al., 1988; Plantes, Prusoff, Brennan, & Parker, 1988) and, in the Gotlib, Whiffen, et al. (1991) study, perceptions of early parenting quality obtained when subjects were not depressed predicted onset of depression six months later (see Brewin, Andrews, & Gotlib, in press, for a more detailed discussion of these studies and the general issue of the validity of retrospective reports.) Considered collectively, these studies suggest that patients' reports of adverse interpersonal environments may not be biased, and should be taken seriously.

Ratings of parenting quality in samples of depressed children

In Chapter 2 on depression in children and adolescents, we reviewed the comparatively sparse data on family functioning. In several community surveys of mildly or nonclinically depressed youngsters, there was evidence of relatively negative parent-child relationships (e.g Garrison et al., 1990; Hops et al., 1990; Kandel & Davies, 1986; Kaslow, Rehm, & Siegel, 1984; Lefkowitz & Tesiny, 1985). Indeed, in Larson et al.'s (1990) study of children's and adolescents' daily ratings of their activities, there was a strong tendency of relatively depressed youngsters to want to avoid their families, suggesting a problematic relationship.

Relatively few studies of clinical samples have included systematic information on the nature of the parent-child relationship. A small number of earlier exceptions typically involved clinician ratings or observations of family disruption. These studies commonly reported negative, critical communications and/or family adversity involving abuse or lack of care by a biological parent (e.g Kashani & Carlson, 1987; Kovacs et al., 1984a; Puig-Antich et al., 1985a,b). Clearly, more direct observation studies of clinically depressed youngsters and their parents—as well as nondepressed patient controls—are needed.

Overall, therefore, the data available on parenting of depressed adults or children suggest some negativity or disturbance in the relationship.

However, reliance on indirect methods, such as retrospective report or clinician ratings, makes it difficult to characterize the elements of dysfunction that are relevant to depression. Moreover, many of the studies lack appropriate comparison groups to establish the specificity to depression of particular types of parent-child dysfunction. Finally, the causal role of parent-child discord has not been established, since the characteristics of the depressed subject may have contributed to the negativity of the relationship, as well as the reverse.

Outcomes of children of depressed parents

One of the strongest pieces of evidence suggestive of an association between family life and depression vulnerability comes from studies of the offspring of depressed parents. In this section we briefly review this growing body of research. In the following section we present studies that specifically implicate the parenting practices of depressed patients as significant elements of children's risk for depression.

Research on the offspring of depressed parents has been reviewed by Hammen (1991a), Downey and Coyne (1990), Gelfand and Teti (1990), Goodman (1992), and Gotlib and Lee (1990). There are relatively few such studies, and several of them originated as comparison groups in high-risk studies of children of schizophrenic parents. Most of the studies are somewhat limited by methodological shortcomings. Among these are sample selection and control or comparison group problems. Some of the early studies failed to separate unipolar and bipolar groups, many studies compared depression groups only with normals, and some of the studies included parents in the acute phase of depression or when hospitalized so that the "typical" effect of depression in the parent was obscured. Studies sometimes included only mildly depressed, or confounded mild and severe depression in the same sample. Many samples mixed depressed fathers and depressed mothers (or both were depressed), and the samples varied widely in the ages of children studied. Hammen et al. (1987) included chronically medically ill, bipolar, and normal women, compared with unipolar depressed women with recurrent depression not tested in the acute phase. Klein et al. (1988) included a medical comparison, as did Lee and Gotlib (1989a,b, 1991a), who also included a group of nondepressed psychiatric control subjects. Such designs permit analyses of the effects that are specific to depressive disorder rather than characteristic of chronic disorder of a medical nature. Another difficulty of much of the research concerned assessment; many studies did not include direct psychiatric evaluation of the children, or utilized only limited assessment of children's functioning. Relatedly, most of the studies did not examine potential mediators of the children's risk, presumably based on the assumption of genetic transmission of a depressive disease. Finally, only a few of the studies provided longitudinal follow-ups of children's functioning to evaluate the long-term status of children's adjustment. For example, Lee and Gotlib (1989b) had a six to eight week follow-up, Lee and Gotlib (1991a) had a ten-month follow-up, Billings and Moos (1986) had a one-year follow-up, Hammen et al. (1990) reported a three-year follow-up, and the Weissman project has now reported a two-year follow-up (Warner, Weissman, Fendrich, Wickramaratne, & Moreau, 1991).

Despite these methodological and conceptual limitations, the results of investigations of offspring of depressed parents are remarkably consistent. Across the direct interview studies, for example, rates of disorder in the children were quite high, ranging from 41% (Orvaschel, Walsh-Allis, & Ye, 1988) to 77% lifetime disorder (Hammen et al., 1987). For example, the lifetime diagnoses of the 96 children included in the Hammen study—based on interviews at the entry into the study—are reported in Table 7.1. Lee and Gotlib (1989a) found that clinicians rated the children of depressed mothers as demonstrating more severe psychiatric symptoms both on the Child Assessment Schedule (Hodges, Kline, Stern, Cytryn, & McKnew, 1982) and on the Global Assessment Scale for Children (Rothman, Sorrells, & Heldman, 1976) than they did the children of the nondepressed control mothers. Other investigators have reported more specifically that rates of major depression in children of depressed parents were especially high, although conduct/opposition disorder, anxiety disorders, and substance use disorders were also elevated. Hammen et al. (1990), for instance, found that the cumulative probability of major depression in the unipolar offspring was 0.67, and many of these children were also severely impaired academically and socially. The problems of the majority of affected youngsters tended to be chronic or intermittent over the period of observation.

These findings clearly indicate that depression in a parent affects the entire family, with a considerable risk for children to develop disorders themselves. It is difficult, however, to attribute the children's dysfunction directly to parental depression, in that many families with a depressed adult also experience a host of nonorthogonal risk factors (Walker, Downey, & Nightingale, 1989). Among these are chronic stressful conditions associated with the parent's disorder and characteristics, assortative mating, marital conflict, parent-child conflict, and the like. We would argue, therefore, that depression vulnerability needs to be considered in context, and certainly the interpersonal and stress contextual factors are complex and multifaceted. In the following section, we attempt to explore one element of the family context, the quality of the parent-child relationship as a potential mediator of children's risk for depression.

Table 7.1   Past diagnoses of child by maternal group

	Group								
	Unipolar ($n = 22$)		Bipolar ($n = 18$)		Medical ($n = 18$)		Normal ($n = 38$)		
Diagnosis	N	%	N	%	N	%	N	%	x^2(3, N = 96)
Any disorder[a]	17	77	12	67	8	44	9	24	19.16[***]
Affective disorders	10	46	3	17	3	17	3	8	12.74[**]
Major depression	9	41	3	17	2	11	3	8	11.19[**]
Dysthymia	3	14	0	0	1	6	0	0	7.46[+]
Mania/hypomania	0	0	0	0	0	0	0	0	0.00
Behavior disorders	4	18	6	33	1	6	3	8	7.85[*]
Attention deficit	2	9	1	6	1	6	2	5	.40
Conduct disorder	4	18	5	28	0	0	3	8	7.80[*]
Alcohol use	0	0	1	6	0	0	0	0	4.38
Drug use	1	5	0	0	0	0	1	3	1.48
Anxiety disorders	5	23	3	17	2	11	4	11	1.91
Separation anxiety	1	5	2	11	2	11	2	5	1.25
Overanxious	1	5	0	0	1	6	1	3	1.11
Other	3	14	1	6	0	0	1	3	4.67

a.   Does not include episodes of minor depression.
[***] $p < 0.001$.
[**] $p < 0.01$.
[*] $p < 0.05$.
[+] $p > 0.05 < 0.10$.
Source: From Hammen, C. (1991). *Depression Runs in Families: The social context of risk and resilience in children of depressed mothers*. New York: Springer-Verlag.

Impairment of parental functioning in depressed women

Genetic contributions to children's risk

Given the findings discussed above, there is little question that children of depressed parents themselves are at elevated risk for the development of depression and other disorders. There are various potential explanations for this increased level of risk. One of the most common and widely accepted explanations implicates the genetic transmission of some as-yet unknown biological defect. With respect to unipolar (i.e. nonbipolar) depression, there is clear evidence of increased incidence of depression in the relatives of depressed probands (e.g Weissman, Merikangas, Wickramaratne, Kidd, Prusoff, et al., 1986, reviewed in Goldin & Gershon, 1988; Hammen, 1991a,b). Although these patterns are consistent with a genetic explanation, they are also inconsistent with any simple mode of transmission. Such studies are not, of course, definitive proof of genetic factors, since they are also compatible with psychosocial explanations operating through the family environment. Studies of identical and fraternal twins have indicated higher concordance for affective disorders in the former than in the latter, but there is clearly less-than-perfect concordance in those who share identical genetic make-up. Linkage studies, highly vaunted in psychiatric and behavior genetic research, are unlikely to yield clear evidence for unipolar disorders because of the apparent heterogeneity of depression and the probability of polygenic modes of transmission (Blehar, Weissman, Gershon, & Hirschfeld, 1988).

In view of these limitations, there is ample reason to vigorously explore psychosocial factors in risk for depressive disorders (e.g Blehar et al., 1988; see also Reiss, Plomin, & Hetherington, 1991). Such investigations may help both to clarify some of the diversity in etiological mechanisms, and to characterize potential subgroups of depressives. Moreover, whatever biological or nonbiological factors may influence the origin of depression, it is clear that psychosocial processes are important determinants of the course, severity, and response to treatment. Therefore, without minimizing a potential genetic contribution to disorder in children of depressed parents, we argue that a strong case can also be made for the influence of cognitive social learning factors, in the form of parent-child interactions.

Indirect reports of depressed parent functioning

Until relatively recently the only information available on parent-child relationships in families of depressed patients was based on parent report. The seminal studies by Weissman and her colleagues that we discussed earlier, based on interviews of depressed women, indicated that they had more friction and less positive involvement in their relationships with children (Weissman, Paykel, & Klerman, 1972; Weissman & Paykel, 1974). Even following recovery from an episode of depression, the women reported continuing interpersonal dysfunction in their relationships with children, family members, and others. More recently, numerous studies of women with elevated depression scores have indicated that such women view their children's behaviors more negatively than do nondepressed women, with the implication that they exaggerate the children's problems or are more intolerant of them (e.g Forehand, Wells, McMahon, Griest, & Rogers, 1982; Griest, Forehand, Wells, & McMahon, 1980; Webster-Stratton & Hammond, 1988).

Research by Moos' group has consistently implicated quality of family relationships as factors in both adult and child depression. For instance, both the initial cross-sectional study (Billings & Moos, 1983) and the one-year follow-up investigation (Billings & Moos, 1986) indicated that children's physical and psychological functioning, as reported by the parents, was associated with parental reports of family arguments (which presumably included parent-child conflict). Similarly, in the Stony Brook High Risk offspring study, which employed depressed patient parents as comparisons with schizophrenic parents, Weintraub (1987) reported that adverse family functioning, including conflict and problems in parenting skills, was related to child adjustment. Little detail was presented concerning the specific patterns associated with depressed parent families. Overall, however, the Stony Brook project emphasized nonspecificity of children's outcomes by parent diagnosis.

Considered together, therefore, these studies provide some general, albeit imprecise, information implicating dysfunctional parent-child relationships in diverse samples of subclinically and clinically depressed parents.

Observations of depressed mothers and their young children

A recent generation of research has provided specific information about the quality of parent-child interactions, based on observational studies. Starting with infancy, some of the earliest high-risk investigations reported that clinically depressed women have difficulties with their interactions with their babies. They appeared to clinicians to be overwhelmed, anxious, unresponsive, and uninvolved (e.g Anthony, 1983; Cohler, Grunebaum, Weiss, Hartman, & Gallant 1977; Davenport, Zahn-Waxler, Adland, & Mayfield 1984; Sameroff, Seifer, & Zax, 1982).

More specific observational information has recently been reported by developmental psychologists and others, examining the behaviors of nonpatient samples of mothers with elevated depression scores. Livingood, Daen, and Smith (1983), for example, observed such women to display less unconditional positive regard toward their newborns than did nondepressed mothers, although the two groups did not differ on contact and stimulation. The results of studies conducted by Field and her colleagues (Field, 1984; Field, Sandberg, Garcia, Vega-Lahr, Goldstein, & Guy, 1985; Field et al., 1988; Field, Healy, Goldstein, & Guthertz, 1990) similarly indicate that, compared with their nonsymptomatic counterparts, depressed mothers are less active, less playful, and less contingently responsive in face-to-face interactions with their three- to six-month-old infants. Bettes (1988) reported that symptomatic mothers were delayed in speech directed toward their infants. In fact, Bettes emphasized that the mean response delay of the depressed women in her study was sufficiently long to suggest disengagement from the child. Finally, Fleming, Ruble, Flett, and Shaul (1988) found that, compared to nondepressed mothers, women with postpartum depression showed less reciprocal vocalization and affectionate contact with infants.

These studies indicate that depression interferes with responsiveness of mothers toward their infants; the results of other studies raise perhaps more serious concerns in suggesting that some depressed mothers may, in fact, be explicitly negative in interactions with their infants. Lyons-Ruth, Zoll, Connell, and Grunebaum (1986), for example, reported that relatively depressed low-income mothers displayed covert hostility and flattened affect with their year-old babies. Cohn, Matias, Tronick, Connell, and Lyons-Ruth (1986) and Field et al. (1990) also reported angry and intrusive behaviors displayed by depressed mothers toward their babies. Cohn, Campbell, Matias, and Hopkins (1990) did not find unresponsiveness in depressed women, but did find greater negativity toward their infants (especially boys). The infants themselves were more negative in the interactions.

What does research suggest about babies' responses to depressed mothers? Studies of simulated depression indicated that infants react with protest (Cohn & Tronick, 1983). Field (1984), however, found that only babies of nondepressed women reacted, whereas infants of the depressed women did not change. In a later study, Field et al. (1990) observed that the infants of depressed mothers "matched" their mother's state particularly when she was negative, and less so when she was positive toward them. Whiffen and Gotlib (1989a) observed that the infants of women with postpartum depression displayed lower cognitive development on the Bayley Scales, and also showed more negative emotional reactions during the testing periods.

Fewer observational studies have been conducted with toddler-age offspring of depressed women. Radke-Yarrow, Cummings, Kuczynski, & Chapman (1985) observed children between the ages of one and four years interacting with their unipolar or bipolar mothers. These investigators found that more children of women with affective disorders, compared to those of normal mothers, displayed insecure attachment. Mothers of insecurely attached children also showed less positive and more negative affect toward them. Breznitz and Sherman (1987) observed the toddlers at ages two to three years, and reported that the children and their mothers with affective disorders spoke less to each other than did nondepressed control mothers and children. The depressed mothers also responded more slowly to the children's speech. Kochanska, Kuczynski, Radke-Yarrow, and Welch (1987) observed the same children and their mothers during a naturalistic observation focused on "control" episodes in which the mothers attempted to influence the children's behaviors. Women with affective disorders were less successful than were normal mothers in resolving these conflict situations, commonly avoiding confrontation when the child resisted.

In a sample of disadvantaged black women, Goodman and Brumley

(1990) compared depressed, schizophrenic, and normal mothers interacting with their young children. The depressed mothers were not as impaired as the schizophrenic mothers, but compared to normal women they were significantly less responsive and involved, and used less structure and discipline. Children's IQ and aspects of their social behavior were related to maternal responsiveness, positive affect, and interest. Mills, Puckering, Pound, and Cox (1985) observed depressed community women in England and their two- to three-year-old toddlers. Using a concept similar to "responsiveness," Mills et al. (1985) found that the depressed women were less responsive and reciprocal in their interactions than were nondepressed women. The children with the greatest levels of behavior problems had mothers with the lowest proportions of reciprocated interactions.

Considered collectively, these studies provide consistent evidence of reduced maternal responsiveness in depressed women. In turn, the infants and toddlers in these studies displayed a variety of dysfunctions apparently associated with maternal behavior. Although the direct observations are an important advantage of these studies, their cross-sectional designs limit the conclusions we can draw concerning the consistency and stability of maternal interactions, and the developmental consequences to children over time.

Observations of depressed mothers and school-age children

Webster-Stratton and Hammond (1988) observed mothers of three- to eight-year-old clinic-referred children. The women with elevated BDI scores made more critical statements directed toward their children than did nondepressed mothers, but did not differ on any other variables. As we noted earlier in this chapter, Hops et al. (1987) collected extensive observation data in the homes of maritally distressed or nondistressed depressed or nondepressed women, carefully coding interaction sequences of exchanges between the women, their husbands, and children. The results were interpreted to suggest that the mothers' sadness served to suppress aggressive affect by other family members, and the latter behavior suppressed mothers' dysphoric affect. While functional in the short run, the patterns were seen as mutually aversive interchanges with maladaptive consequences in the long run. Panaccione and Wahler (1986) observed relatively dysphoric mothers interacting with their preschoolers. Level of maternal depression was associated with mothers' negative interactions with the child, including disapproval and shouting, as well as with negative perceptions of the child.

The most extensive analysis of mother-child interactions involving clinically diagnosed unipolar depressed mothers and school-age children has been reported by Hammen and her colleagues. These investigators conducted systematic observations of a conflict discussion task involving unipolar depressed women and their children, and similar pairs from bipolar, medically ill, and normal families. Gordon, Burge, Hammen, Adrian, Jaenicke, & Hiroto (1989) reported group comparisons for several maternal interaction variables: positive interactions (agree, confirm, praise), negative interactions (disagree, criticize, disconfirm), and ability to stay focused on the task (task productive comments, off-task comments). Overall, the unipolar depressed women were found to be the most negative and critical, the least positive and confirming, and had the most difficulty sustaining the task focus. Indeed, they differed significantly from all three of the other groups on these variables. Subsequently, Hammen, Burge, and Stansbury (1990) and Burge and Hammen (1991) found that the quality of the mother-child interaction predicted the children's subsequent functioning at a six-month follow-up assessment. Affective quality of the interactions was particularly related to children's adjustment. The relative negativity of the mothers' comments (based on combined positive and negative interaction variables) was significantly related to children's diagnoses of depression (but not nondepressive disorders), school behavior, and academic performance. The quality of maternal task productivity was also related to school behavior.

In an effort to further understand the characteristics of dysfunctional interactions in the families, Hammen examined the predictors of maternal interaction quality. Burge and Hammen (1991), for example, demonstrated that whereas chronic stress was uniquely related to the affective quality of the interaction, depressed mood was especially related to task productivity. That is, women who are stressed due to chronic aversive conditions may be relatively more critical and impatient with their children. We can speculate that these women lack the luxury of being able to enjoy and be tolerant of their children when they are demoralized, worried, and preoccupied by financial, work, and relationship difficulties. Women whose mood is depressed—whether or not they are in a "clinical" depression—seem to be unable or unwilling to stay focused on resolving a conflict. It may be that they cannot sustain their attention; alternatively, they may simply be attempting to avoid conflict. In any case, these processes are by no means unique to, or limited to, depression, and can occur in women with other kinds of psychiatric disorders (such as manic-depression) and women whose lives are particularly stressful (chronically medically ill or otherwise stressed women).

Another issue involving the parenting interactions of depressed women and their children concerns the perhaps implicit assumption that the mothers' characteristics are the cause of the interaction problem. As a related point, it is often assumed that depressed women, because of their depressive cognitions, may exaggerate their children's shortcomings and fail to appraise their behaviors realistically. Results of analyses from the Hammen UCLA study fail to support either of these prevailing assumptions. First, several analyses suggested that the mothers and children have important reciprocal influences on each other. Hammen, Burge, and Stansbury (1990b) used causal modelling analyses to demonstrate that characteristics of both the mother and child influenced their interactions with each other, and the reciprocal interactions during the conflict discussion task were a predictor of the child's outcomes. Conrad and Hammen (1989) also demonstrated that mothers whose children actually had behavior problems (both internalizing and externalizing) interacted more negatively with them than they did with their children whose behaviors were normal. Finally, Hammen, Burge, and Adrian (1991) analyzed the temporal relations between mothers' and children's symptoms and diagnoses over a longitudinal course (of up to three years). Hammen, Burge, and Adrian discovered a significant association in the timing of symptoms, which was especially clear for onsets of major depression in families of unipolar women. The symptoms of the mothers and children apparently affected the other person. For all of these reasons, we think that it is essential to view the depressed mother-child relationship as a reciprocal one in which each person affects the other.

Another goal of the Hammen project was to clarify the accuracy of depressed women's perceptions of their children. Conrad and Hammen (1989) compared the ratings, made by relatively depressed and nondepressed women, of their children, against ratings from other sources, such as interviewers, teachers, and the child's own self-reports. Across most measures and informants the pattern was consistent: depressed women made distinctions in their views of their children that corresponded to their actual problems. In contrast, the nondepressed women did not see their symptomatic children as having problems. Rather than negative biases in depressed mothers, if anything the biases appeared in the nondepressed women. It appears that the depressed women were the most accurate. Anderson and Hammen (1991a) examined a subset of sibling pairs in which one had psychiatric diagnoses and the other did not. Examination of the mother-child interactions of these pairs indicated that the more symptomatic siblings had a significantly more negative interaction with the mother. Thus, the mothers were making important discriminations, and interacted more negatively only with those children who had problems. Given that many such youngsters were very difficult and oppositional, the mothers probably found it difficult to sustain positive interactions with them. Again, we emphasize the reciprocity of the relationships, and also underscore the likelihood that depressed mothers may not be invariably dysfunctional in their parenting roles. They may have difficulties with their difficult children, but may interact relatively positively with their well-functioning children.

CONCLUDING COMMENTS

It is clear from the studies reviewed in this chapter that depression disrupts close interpersonal relationships—between adults and spouses, and between parents and children. When a family member is depressed, the other members are also likely to be negatively affected. Their negative reactions, in turn, may influence the maintenance, rate of recovery or relapse of the depressed person (see also review by Keitner & Miller, 1990). Moreover, marital and family relations typify an important process in depression: the ways in which depressed persons are likely to engender the very stressful events that trigger or exacerbate their depression.

Not only are the marriages of depressed individuals characterized by tension and discord, often ending in divorce, but the psychosocial functioning of the children of depressed parents is frequently impaired. Such difficulties undoubtedly contribute to further depression, and contribute to vicious cycles of depression and rejection. Thus, although the interpersonal behavior of depressed women may be typified by difficulties in positive affect and responsivity toward their children, such effects are undoubtedly not unidirectional, at least not once they are initially established.

It is unclear whether the difficulties in the spousal or parent-child relationships in depressed families are specific to depression, or represent more general problems that arise in families in which there are other psychopathologies or adverse conditions. Lee and Gotlib (1991b), for example, have argued that children who experience parental marital discord, divorce, and parental psychopathology all demonstrate similar psychosocial difficulties. There is also a great deal that remains unclear about what depressed mothers do that affects their children, and what it is about depression that may affect the mothers' parenting. Thus, the mechanism of transmission or the processes underlying the difficulties in the offspring of depressed parents represents a critical direction for further research (cf. Goodman, 1992). Moreover, because depression is multifaceted, the various manifestations such as apathy, irritability, withdrawal, or negativism need to be studied for their potentially different consequences for parenting.

It is also crucial to examine the context in which maternal depression occurs. The quality of the marital relationship, for instance, and the intriguing issue of assortative mating, are just two examples of contextual factors that influence depression and parenting. Moreover, the effects of maternal depression at different developmental stages of the children's lives require further analysis. We would speculate that impaired mother-infant interactions have profound consequences, but there are doubtless many adaptation skills that may be impaired at other points of development.

Considerably more research is needed to identify some of the crucial tasks that may suffer if the mother is depressed, such as attachment, emotion regulation, self-concept, social competence, and problem-solving skills, to name but a few. Finally, we also require further exploration of how depression, rather than some other disorder, comes to be the outcome of certain parenting processes.

In short, there are numerous unresolved issues concerning both marital and mother-child interactions, and vulnerability for depression. Indeed, particular kinds of depression may be especially susceptible to interpersonal difficulties. As we indicated in the previous chapter, some individuals may be especially vulnerable to negative interpersonal events. Moreover, in a reciprocal manner, there may also be maladaptive interpersonal behaviors and cognitions that contribute to the occurrence of negative interpersonal events. Considerably more research is needed to clarify the nature of the social skills and interpersonal vulnerabilities of depressed people. In the final chapter we discuss one area in particular—attachment—that holds promise for providing a framework to address many of these questions. Before we present this discussion, however, in the following two chapters we examine cognitive and interpersonal approaches to the treatment of depression.

Chapter 8

Treatment of Depression:
I. Cognitive Approaches

Cognitive therapy for depression has been one of the success stories of therapy in the past 15 years. Along with antidepressant medications, it has offered hope and relief to legions of persons who otherwise were considered difficult and unrewarding patients. The relentless negativism, lack of energy, and low motivation of depressed persons had long thwarted many traditional therapists. It is impossible to estimate how many persons treated by dynamic approaches found that, when they did not improve after all of the appropriate exploration of childhood and interpretations of deep-seated conflicts, they were told that they were resisting and must really *want* to be depressed (or *want* to resist the therapist).

On the other hand, the behaviorism of the precognitive therapy era was grounded largely in narrow learning models of operant or classical conditioning. There was little attention to, or even a discounting of, thoughts, states of mind, beliefs, perceptions, and other "mentalistic" phenomena. Moreover, orthodox behavioral interventions seemed to work best for uncomplicated behaviors, and often even the most dramatic gains did not generalize from one setting to another, or persist over time. Thus, behaviorism as practiced in its most orthodox forms, also had little to offer to depressed persons—although certain applications developed specifically for depression proved to have some success, as explored in the next chapter (e.g. McLean & Hakstian, 1979; Zeiss, Lewinsohn, & Munoz, 1979).

Against this background, new voices—often influenced by the then-popular humanistic psychotherapies—began to express ideas about new models, new techniques, and new goals for therapy (see Mahoney, 1974). In this milieu, Aaron Beck, a psychiatrist, and his students—mostly psychologists—evolved a novel therapy for the treatment of depression, at approximately the same time that other cognitive therapies were in development for treatment of a wide variety of other problems in living (Beck et al., 1979). Beck's unique contribution, first articulated in the 1960s, was that depression is fundamentally a disorder of thinking (Beck, 1967).

Given this observation, the therapy set out to modify the thinking directly. In this chapter we attempt to review in a very brief way the methods of cognitive therapy, followed by an evaluation of its effectiveness from controlled studies and a discussion of its mechanisms of action. Then we discuss some of the new developments and unresolved issues of cognitive-behavioral therapy, as well as a few alternative cognitive approaches to the treatment of depression.

METHODS OF COGNITIVE THERAPY

Like most other cognitive therapies, Beck's cognitive-behavioral therapy integrated ideas from all of the dominant models of the time. From the dynamic approaches came the idea that certain underlying maladaptive beliefs and assumptions were rooted in childhood and family experiences (although it is unnecessary for the treatment of such dysfunctional thoughts to explore their childhood origins). From behaviorism came the emphasis on empiricism, on treatment of the "symptoms" as the problem, and a focus on systematic modification of behavior by direct means. From humanistic psychotherapies, the "Third Force," came the emphasis on the phenomenology of the client's own experiences, on a collaborative therapist-client relationship, and the teaching of "awareness," specifically focused on inner dialogues and automatic thoughts. In this context the contribution of Albert Ellis' emphasis on direct challenges to maladaptive beliefs must be acknowledged. Beck's here-and-now approach assumed that the depression is the problem to be tackled first, because depression causes the lack of energy or motivation, or pessimism that interferes with solving the real-life difficulties that contribute to the person's depressive thoughts. There is an emphasis on homework to practice adaptive behavior changes and to collect information for the testing of hypotheses, as well as a systematic effort to identify and then alter maladaptive thoughts. The therapist and client maintain a relationship of "collaborative empiricism," working together to collect data, test hypotheses, and refine methods. The therapy is intended to be relatively brief, initially developed and tested in a roughly 20-session format.

Some of the key ingredients of the therapy are behavioral activation, graded task assignments, thought-catching and cognitive restructuring, identification and challenging of underlying maladaptive beliefs, and problem-solving and specific behavioral techniques as needed to deal with particular life difficulties. While most of these concepts are practiced in one form or other in most cognitive therapies, Beck's behavioral activation and thought-catching/challenging interventions are somewhat unique to this method.

Behavioral activation employs the well-known commonsense idea that being active is an antidote to depression. It assists the client in identifying pleasurable or mastery activities and then helps the person to overcome obstacles to performing them, followed by accurate assessment of their value. Often depressed individuals fail to participate in previously enjoyable activities because of a loss of interest and pleasure, or they anticipate that activity would be too difficult, take too much energy, or would fail to produce pleasure. Thus, the therapist attempts to avoid merely cajoling or nagging the person (in the way that well-meaning friends and relatives might) and, instead, urges the client to experiment with activity and discover for herself whether activities make a difference—even a small and temporary difference—in mood. The therapist and client collaborate to identify possibly pleasurable or meaningful activities, and then anticipate and deal with possible actual or cognitive obstacles to undertaking them. In combination with this technique, graded task assignments help clients to engage in successively more rewarding yet demanding activities that lead to increased pleasure or mastery experiences. While it is assumed that feelings of pleasure or sense of accomplishment are "antidepressant," clients are encouraged to demonstrate this empirically for themselves. Behavioral activation and graded task assignments are especially likely to be employed to treat the depression syndrome directly, usually at the initial stages of treatment.

Thought-catching of "automatic negative thoughts" is the fundamental tool for changing maladaptive, depressogenic thoughts. Clients are taught to observe the link between thoughts and feelings, and to clarify their own emotion-related thoughts. Using a written form typically divided into three columns, individuals keep records of emotion-arousing experiences, the automatic negative thoughts associated with them, and in the third column, their realistic thoughts or challenges to the maladaptive thoughts. In Table 8.1 we present an example of this format.

Several techniques are taught to clients to challenge each negative thought, such as "is there a distortion?", "what's the evidence?", "is there another way to look at it?", and "so what?" Usually, one or more of these challenges helps the client to replace the dysfunctional thought with a more realistic one. Often the realistic thoughts lead to specific behavioral activities to try out new ways of behaving, or collecting behavioral data to test out one's beliefs. The negative thoughts are hypothesized to occur at different levels, ranging from surface level interpretations of events ("if he didn't call me it means he doesn't like me"), to deeper, pervasive, underlying beliefs and assumptions ("if someone doesn't like me it means I'm no good"). Later stages of therapy would be more likely to deal with the deeper level assumptions and schemas. The thought-catching and cognitive restructuring assignments are used to deal with ongoing,

Table 8.1 Example of thought-catching and cognitive restructuring (the three-column technique of Beck et al., 1979)

Event	Automatic negative thoughts	Rational replies
My boyfriend is losing interest in me.	He'll leave me.	*What's the error?* I can't read his mind or foresee the future. *What's the evidence?* He doesn't call as much. But he's been busy. *Get more evidence?* I could ask him. *Another way to look at it?* If he's losing interest, it doesn't mean he'll leave me. Maybe we can improve things. *So what?* Even if he did leave me, I guess I could survive. I've been single before.
	I'll be rejected. It means I'm undesirable. No one will ever love me. I'll always be alone.	

daily emotion-arousing situations, and also to identify patterns of recurring "silent assumptions" and dysfunctional beliefs that are also subject to challenge.

Therapist characteristics of warmth, genuineness, and positive regard are assumed to be essential ingredients of the effectiveness of the therapy. Also, the transactions between the client and therapist are considered to be important to the extent that they offer the opportunity to observe, characterize, and alter maladaptive thoughts and behaviors that contribute to the client's difficulties. Such interactions are seen not as symbolic but as real relationships often characterized by faulty beliefs and related dysfunctional behaviors. Details of the techniques of cognitive-behavioral therapy for depression are described more fully in Beck et al. (1979). Applications of the methods written for the layperson as self-help tools appear in books by David Burns (e.g. *Feeling Good: The New Mood Therapy*, 1980). Therapists are also encouraged to review Jacqueline Persons' (1989) *Cognitive Therapy in Practice: A Case Formulation Approach*.

Assessment of cognitions

Before turning to a discussion of the efficacy and mechanisms of cognitive therapy for depression, it is important that we comment on some of the major instruments for assessing cognition. As we noted in Chapter 5, when they were originally developed many of the more widely-used instruments were based on the assumption that they captured some enduring, depressogenic thinking tendencies. Unfortunately, content and process, product and cause were often indistinguishable in the terminology of early research. Subsequently, important distinctions were drawn among four types of cognition: cognitive structure (how information is represented internally), cognitive propositions (content that is stored in the cognitive structures), cognitive operations (processes of encoding, storage, and retrieval), and by-products of schemas and operations (the conscious thoughts and interpretations) (Merluzzi & Boltwood, 1989).

Most of the available assessment instruments purport to assess either the by-products or the propositions (or schemas). As an example of the first type, the Automatic Thoughts Questionnaire (ATQ; Hollon & Kendall, 1980) attempts to measure the frequency of 30 negative ruminations or automatic thoughts ("I can't finish anything"). The scale has been found to have good internal consistency reliability, and convergent validity; it correlates highly with symptoms of depression (reviewed by Hammen & Krantz, 1985; Merluzzi & Boltwood, 1989). DeRubeis, Evans, Hollon, Garvey, Grove, and Tuason (1990) note that the scores range from 30 to 150, and most nonpatients score 40–60, and depressed patients score 90–130. Its major disadvantage, and one acknowledged by its authors, is that it appears to be concomitant of depression rather than a vulnerability factor.

Two similar measures, the Dysfunctional Attitudes Scale (DAS; Weissman & Beck, 1978) and the Attribution Style Questionnaire (ASQ; Peterson et al., 1982) were reviewed in more detail in Chapter 5. Briefly, the DAS is a 40-item self-report instrument intended to assess the underlying negative beliefs and attitudes, or schemas, that give rise to depressive interpretations of the self and life events. As we noted earlier, although the DAS differentiates currently depressed from nondepressed persons, it does not appear to be independent of mood (e.g. Hamilton & Abramson, 1983; Silverman, Silverman, & Eardley, 1984). Moreover, the DAS may assess cognitions that are associated with general psychopathology, so that an elevated level of dysfunctional attitudes may not be specific to depression. There is some empirical support, however, for the possibility that the DAS nevertheless is useful as a predictor of relapse (e.g. Rush, Weissenburger, & Eaves 1986; Simons, Murphy, & Levine, 1984). The ASQ has been widely used to assess tendencies toward depressogenic causal analyses of events (see Hammen & Krantz, 1985, and Merluzzi & Boltwood, 1989, for reviews of psychometric properties of the ASQ). Like the DAS, the ASQ has also shown evidence of mood-dependent elevations rather than functioning as a stable measure of dysfunctional cognition (e.g. Hamilton & Abramson, 1983).

Overall, as this brief review indicates, measures of depressive cognitions have generally correlated with depressive symptoms, and they may certainly serve useful purposes in therapy, to illustrate depressive thinking and to indicate particular content areas of difficulty. Their roles as measures of underlying schemas or vulnerability predicting depression onset or recurrence, and their function as indicators of mechanisms of change in cognitive therapy (discussed below), are more problematic.

RESEARCH EVALUATING THE EFFECTIVENESS OF COGNITIVE THERAPY FOR DEPRESSION

The research on the treatment of depression with cognitive therapies is too extensive to present analyses of individual studies. Several excellent reviews of the efficacy of cognitive therapies for depression have appeared in recent years (Dobson, 1989; Hollon & Najavits, 1988; Hollon, Shelton, & Loosen, 1991; Nietzel, Russell, Hemmings, & Gretter, 1987; Rehm, in press; Robinson, Berman, & Neimeyer, 1990). Among them, the reviews have identified cognitive-behavioral analogue studies, actual clinical trials comparing cognitive therapy with other psychotherapies and/or antidepressant medications, various kinds of cognitive therapies for depression, and a few dismantling studies attempting to characterize key ingredients. The meta-analysis review studies represent one approach to evaluating the efficacy of the therapy, but another approach is a comprehensive study based on large-sample clinical populations, comparing the major treatment modalities with pill placebos, conducted at multiple sites. Therefore, we will also discuss the NIMH collaborative study (Elkin, Parloff, Hadley, & Autry, 1985). Based on these extensive evaluations, the results have been surprisingly mixed.

Nietzel et al. (1987) analyzed 31 studies evaluating the effects of various treatments for unipolar depression that employed the Beck Depression Inventory as the outcome measure, but included broadly-defined cognitive therapies. Their conclusion was that while psychotherapy in general produces moderately significant clinical improvement in depression, there were no differences between types of therapies—once age and initial BDI score were controlled. A considerably rosier outcome for cognitive-behavioral therapy was reported in Dobson's (1989) meta-analysis of 28 studies specifically testing Beck's cognitive treatment for depression, using the BDI as the outcome measure. Dobson (1989) concluded that cognitive therapy is significantly better than no therapy, behavior therapy, or pharmacotherapy or other forms of psychotherapy. The effects appeared to hold regardless of duration of treatment. The analysis did not include follow-up evaluation.

Robinson, Berman, and Neimeyer (1990) provided perhaps the most comprehensive review of therapies for the treatment of depression, including cognitive, cognitive-behavioral, behavioral, medication, and general verbal therapies. The authors indicate that they included 58 studies, of which 47 were not included in Dobson (1989). This covered a broad array of different types of cognitive therapy for depression. A number of interesting conclusions emerged from their calculations of effect sizes. First, treatments for depression overall were superior to no-treatment control groups. However, when such control groups were subdivided into wait-list and placebo controls the effects of treatment were not significant for comparisons with placebo controls. Second, comparisons between types of treatment indicated that cognitive-behavioral interventions were superior to general verbal and to behavioral methods, but did not differ from cognitive-only treatments. Third, therapist allegiance to a particular model had a sizable impact on therapy outcome. When the effects of ratings of allegiance were taken into account statistically, there was no evidence for the superiority of any one form of therapy for depression. Fourth, psychotherapy treatments were superior to pharmacology interventions. However, again when therapist allegiance was controlled, the differences were eliminated. Finally, the authors noted that by posttreatment, patients' depression level was typically reduced significantly; however, it remained in the mild depression range and was significantly higher than that of normative samples.

Taken together, these results temper the claims of some cognitive-behavioral researchers for the clear superiority of cognitive-behavioral methods. Instead, it appears that treatment gains are real, but may depend to a large extent on experimenter enthusiasm for a particular method. Moreover, relatively sparse data exist on the efficacy of specifically cognitive-behavioral procedures in comparison to other, perhaps nonspecific, techniques.

Hollon and Najavits (1988) also sounded a somewhat cautious note, but generally concluded that Beck's cognitive therapy for depression was effective for the acute treatment of depression. They note that cognitive therapy alone has proven to be as effective as tricyclic antidepressant therapy. Unlike Robinson, Berman, and Neimeyer (1990), Hollon and Najavits (1988) suggested that the combination of cognitive therapy and tricyclic antidepressants is superior to antidepressants alone. Hollon and Najavits (1988) also indicated that cognitive therapy has clear superiority to pharmacological treatment in the prevention of relapse/recurrence. They noted that four of five studies that used follow-ups indicated such superiority, noting that relapse occurs in more than 60% of medication-treated patients without maintenance, compared with 30% for cognitive therapy. Hollon and Najavits (1988) noted that relatively few studies have investigated predictors of outcome of cognitive therapy. However, in general, outcomes tend to be worse for older female patients who are unemployed, nonendogenous, neurotic, and/or chronically depressed.

In their most recent review, Hollon, Shelton, and Loosen (1991) draw somewhat more cautious conclusions about the efficacy of cognitive therapy in comparison to antidepressant medications. Such a comparison is of critical importance, since medications represent the most typical treatment option of persons with clinically significant depression. Hollon, Shelton, and Loosen (1991) currently conclude that the designs of most outcome studies comparing cognitive therapy with pharmacotherapy have been inadequate to permit firm conclusions. Specifically, few such comparisons have included pill placebo treatments which would permit a clearer basis for evaluating the effectiveness of medications. In the absence of such controls, it is possible that the drug-treated patients have not been particularly responsive. Thus, concluding that cognitive therapy differs from medication treatment may be an inadequate test of the effectiveness of cognitive therapy. Moreover, the authors note that few of the medication studies have provided optimal pharmacotherapy in terms of dosage, duration of treatment, or use of supplemental medications.

Noting these shortcomings, Hollon, Shelton, and Loosen (1991) reviewed studies including a few not available to previous reviews. Their conclusion was that there is little to suggest the superiority of cognitive therapy to tricyclic antidepressants; the studies that do seem to indicate such superiority can be seen to have implemented the drug treatments inadequately. Moreover, in the NIMH collaborative study to be discussed below, cognitive therapy did not do very well in a design that executed the pharmacotherapy as well as any previous study and also contained a placebo condition. For these reasons, Hollon, Shelton, and Loosen (1991) believe that it is premature to conclude that cognitive therapy is equal to tricyclic pharmacotherapy. They note that there is no reason to think that it will prove to be less effective, but that further research is needed to support the claim of comparability. Similarly, the authors conclude that there is no clear evidence of the superiority of the combination of cognitive and pharmacotherapy compared to either modality alone, despite some trends suggesting such superiority. Larger-scale studies should be conducted to pursue this question, since the smaller studies have made it difficult to detect differences.

Finally, Hollon, Shelton, and Loosen (1991) address the issue of whether cognitive therapy prevents relapses, as some of the earlier reviews had concluded. Certainly the issue of maintenance of gains is a crucial one for cognitive therapy, since it claims to teach tools to clients to help them resist succumbing to maladaptive negative interpretations of themselves or life events. The authors' tentative conclusion is that cognitive therapy does appear to be superior to pharmacotherapy in protection against relapse/recurrence. However, cognitive therapy might mostly prevent relapse rather than recurrence. It has been speculated that the natural course of a depressive episode may last 6–9 months beyond the remission of symptoms, a period during which the person is vulnerable to relapse. Pharmacotherapy might merely suppress the symptoms in the short run, and if discontinued after remission, would leave the patient open to relapse of symptoms. Thus, cognitive therapy might show superiority compared to what amounts to the premature withdrawal of medication. The test of long-term effectiveness of treatment would be its effects on recurrence, the development of new episodes. To date, however, studies have not followed-up patients long enough to determine such outcomes.

The NIMH Treatment of Depression Collaborative Research Program (Elkin et al., 1985) recently reported results of its multisite large-scale study. The design compared two brief psychotherapies, cognitive therapy (Beck et al., 1979) and interpersonal psychotherapy (Klerman, Weissman, Rounsaville, & Chevron, 1984), with imipramine plus clinical management, and pill placebo plus clinical management. In the study 250 outpatients with major depression were assigned to one of the four conditions for 16 weeks.

Overall the results have been a disappointment to the proponents of cognitive therapy (Elkin, Shea, Watkins, Imber, Sotsky, et al., 1989). In general, both psychotherapies and the medication treatment were equally likely to result in reduced symptoms. However, the placebo condition was also fairly effective. Typically, across the various analyses, the imipramine did best, and the placebo worst, with the two psychotherapies in between. On mean scores the groups tended not to differ, but on outcomes measured by recovery rates, interpersonal therapy and medication were superior to placebo, but cognitive therapy was not. Also, interpersonal therapy to some extent, and imipramine to a large extent, were especially effective with the more severely depressed and impaired patients. For the less depressed participants the treatments (including placebo) did not differ. Clearly, the contribution of the "clinical management" portion of the pill placebo treatment was strong, at least for the less severely depressed persons, suggesting the possibility that nonspecific effects such as contact with a therapist may be powerful. The comparisons with the placebo condition, partially indicating differential effectiveness of the treatments, somewhat obscure the fact that there were no significant differences on scores between cognitive and interpersonal therapy. Thus, the results are perhaps best interpreted to mean that both cognitive and interpersonal therapy compared very well to the "standard reference treatment" (imipramine) for the most part. The investigators also note that there were several differences between treatment sites, and interactions between treatments and sites. For instance, cognitive therapy did extremely well at one site, but poorly at another. Whether these differences were related to different patient characteristics or other factors is being explored.

One possibility—and an argument for the relatively unspectacular showing of the cognitive therapy—is that the training and supervision of cognitive therapists may have been less adequate than that of other modalities. For example, Hollon and Najavits (1988) have speculated that the cognitive therapy typically involved recruiting and training therapists more accustomed to other modalities, while the medication/clinical management and interpersonal (psychodynamic) therapies were more familiar to practitioners' standard methods. Thus, newly trained cognitive therapists working in a somewhat unfamiliar modality, supervised only monthly, might have been at a relative disadvantage. Further fine-grained analyses of therapist and subject variables are promised, and also the effectiveness of the various treatments at follow-up remain to be reported.

Range of applications of cognitive therapy

It might be noted that the review and meta-analysis studies reported typically aggregate their analyses across widely different subject populations. For instance, cognitive therapy for depression—in its various forms—has been applied to depressed elderly populations (e.g. Beutler, Scogin, Kirkish, Schrtelen, Corbishley, et al., 1987; Gallagher & Thompson, 1982; Steuer, Mintz, Hammen, Hill, Jarvik, et al., 1984), as well as to juvenile populations (Lewinsohn, Clark, Hops, & Andrews, 1990). While cognitive therapy has been most commonly studied in treatments of outpatients, it has also been shown to be more effective (in combination with standard medication treatment) for *inpatients* than standard treatment alone in proportions of treatment responders and maintenance of gains during 6- and 12-month follow-ups (Miller, Norman, & Keitner, 1989). It has been applied to individuals mostly, but also to marital couples, and in groups (and comparisons of group and individual therapy formats has led to discrepant conclusions—e.g. Nietzel et al., 1987; Robinson, Berman, & Neimeyer, 1990). Cognitive therapy for depression has even been administered by computer and shown to be as effective as therapist-administered treatment, and both treatments were superior to a wait-list control (Selmi, Klein, Greist, Sorrell, & Erdman, 1990). Despite the range of applications and the apparent ease with which cognitive therapies can be adapted to fit different groups, it remains to be shown what patient characteristics predict response to treatment. Further research is clearly needed to determine whether certain individuals or groups are preferentially responsive to cognitive treatment, or should be treated with a different modality.

Commentary

As this brief review indicates, cognitive therapy for acute depression is widely practiced, and has proven to be effective—often after only relatively brief periods of treatment. What is not so clear, however, is its comparative efficacy when contrasted with well-executed medication treatment or short-term interpersonal therapy. In most studies it appears to do as well as its competitors, but earlier claims of its outright superiority have not been sustained by the NIMH collaborative study. With respect to maintenance of gains, there is clearer evidence of its ability to prevent or delay relapse—at least in trials comparing it to nonmaintenance pharmacotherapy. However, its ability to actually prevent or attenuate new episodes has not been established in the relatively brief follow-ups used in most studies.

It is clear, therefore, as Hollon, Shelton, and Loosen (1991) and others have noted, that additional research with large samples is needed to pursue some of these basic questions. Additionally, and perhaps even more importantly, individual predictors of responsiveness to the various treatments should be studied.

Despite the qualifications on statements of cognitive therapy's superiority, it is apparent that medication treatment is not the only effective method for reducing depressive symptoms. Thus, persons with medical conditions that contraindicate antidepressants—or those who cannot tolerate the side-effects or simply resist the use of medications—have psychotherapy options available. However, matching the best treatment to the person's clinical and personal characteristics would likely improve the performance rates of both the antidepressant and brief psychotherapy treatments.

To date, the NIMH collaborative study gives the clearest indication that severity of the depression might be one basis for selecting medication, but this finding needs to be replicated—especially in view of a recently reported study by Thase, Simons, Cahalane, McGeary, and Harden (1991). These investigators studied differences in cognitive therapy outcome for moderately- and highly-symptomatic depressed outpatients. They found that cognitive therapy showed significant reductions in symptoms for both groups—however, the more severely depressed group did not show as complete remission of symptoms as did the moderately depressed group. Thase et al. (1991) conclude that cognitive therapy can be effective even with severely depressed persons, although it might be even more effective to provide longer durations and more intensive interventions than the standard 16-week, 20-session protocol.

There does not appear to be a case, however, for choosing medication therapy on the basis of endogenous or nonendogenous symptoms (Joyce & Paykel, 1989). Other clinical features including family history of possible genetic loading, age of onset, or perhaps presence of anxiety symptoms, should be studied for their differential prediction of treatment outcome. Similarly, a variety of personal characteristics including skill deficits, personality disorders, and other traits, might prove to be a basis for selecting patients preferentially suitable for cognitive therapy.

One of the great gaps in the outcome literature is the question of the mechanisms of change, and the role of cognitive changes as a mediator of clinical improvement. This topic is pursued in the next section on issues and developments in cognitive therapy for depression.

ISSUES AND DEVELOPMENTS IN COGNITIVE THERAPY FOR DEPRESSION

Mechanisms of change in cognitive therapy

Rehm (in press) is among those who have observed that many of the head-on comparisons between treatments for depression indicate no clear winners. While some of the nondifferences in efficacy may result from methodological problems such as small sample sizes that are insensitive to subtle treatment effects, he notes several common ingredients that cut across different treatments. Such commonalities shared by the methods may contribute to their success but make it hard to distinguish among them. Rehm (in press) notes four shared nonspecific mechanisms: provision of a clear rationale, high degree of structure and specific action plans, instigative approaches in terms of motivating and homework-oriented, and provision of progress feedback. Such mechanisms are speculated to provide specific means of change, and to provide evidence that change is occurring (and therefore alters beliefs in one's ability to change).

Relatively few empirical studies of the role of specific techniques within cognitive therapy have been conducted. Teasdale and Fennell (1982) showed that changing chronically depressed patients' distorted thoughts led to improved mood, compared to a control condition in which simply exploring the thoughts did not. Persons and Burns (1985) tested the effects of changing automatic negative thoughts and the quality of the patient-therapist relationship in a small sample of anxious and depressed patients. They found a highly significant relationship between the amount of change in negative thoughts and mood change, and also a significant association between mood change and quality of relationship. The two therapeutic ingredients made separate and additive contributions to mood change. DeRubeis and Feeley (1990) explored the predictors of change in 25 depressed patients treated with cognitive therapy. Raters made judgments of the extent to which the therapists created facilitative conditions (e.g. warmth, empathy), developed a positive therapeutic alliance, and adhered to methods of cognitive therapy. The latter ratings were subdivided into two categories, representing "concrete" symptom-focused methods, or "abstract" discussions of principles. Only the specific, concrete interventions predicted improvement; neither abstract discussions nor traditional therapist-client relationship characteristics were related to change. This study suggests, therefore, that there is something about the specific cognitive therapy interventions that relates to change.

The role of cognitive change

Several additional studies have examined general, rather than session-specific changes in cognition, as related to therapy outcome. An initial study of the specificity of cognition change as a mediator of mood change was reported by Rush, Beck, Kovacs, Weissenburger, and Hollon (1982), who found that cognitions did mediate change for cognitive therapy patients but not for those treated with tricyclic antidepressants. On the other hand, Simons, Garfield, and Murphy (1984) and Zeiss, Lewinsohn, and Munoz (1979) found that cognitive changes were as likely to occur in noncognitive interventions as in cognitive therapy. Similarly, the recent NIMH collaborative treatment study failed to find mode-specific differences in outcome measures in the different treatment groups (Imber, Pilkonis, Sotsky, Elkin, Watkins, et al., 1990). That is, the Dysfunctional Attitude Scale—a putative measure of the operative mechanism of cognitive therapy—was as likely to show changes in medication or interpersonal therapy as in cognitive therapy.

One interpretation of the nonspecificity of cognitive change in cognitive therapy is that cognitions do not mediate change. Such an interpretation would certainly undercut the primary assumption of cognitive therapy. However, Hollon, DeRubeis, and Evans (1987) argue that such an interpretation is premature in that the analyses fail to make a distinction between cognitions as consequences of therapy and as causal determinants of outcome (causal specificity versus consequential specificity). Hollon, DeRubeis, and Evans argue for the plausibility of a causal specificity/consequential nonspecificity model: cognitive therapy produces cognitive changes that cause changes in depression (that in turn also alter cognitive processes), whereas other outcomes of other modalities are not mediated by cognitive changes, even though mood changes they produce may alter cognitions. As Hollon and colleagues point out, some of the previous studies such as Simons, Garfield, and Murphy (1984) cannot rule out the possibility that cognitive variables were mediators in one treatment method and consequences of change in the other. Indeed, it is very difficult to develop tests of the competing roles of cognition. Cross-sectional analyses of equivalently powerful treatments make it very difficult to distinguish cause from effect, especially when the depressive symptoms and the mechanisms of effective treatment are reciprocally related. Hollon, DeRubeis, and Evans urge the use of causal modelling analyses as one way to provide greater clarity concerning mechanisms of change.

An alternative strategy to address the issue was recently reported by DeRubeis et al. (1990), based on the Hollon et al. study comparing cognitive therapy and imipramine. DeRubeis and colleagues measured the amount of cognitive change (on several questionnaire measures such as the Dysfunctional Attitude Scale, the Hopelessness Scale, and the Attribution Style Questionnaire) from pretreatment to mid-treatment. Then, they used regression analyses to predict change in depression from mid-treatment to posttreatment as a function of cognitive change. The results indicated the significant group by cognitive change interactions, with the cognitive therapy group, but not the medication treatment group, showing depression change as a function of cognitive change. The authors conclude that the cognitive processes did play a mediating role of symptom change in cognitive therapy, but that it was not a causally sufficient role. The imipramine treatment group showed as much depression reduction as did the cognitive therapy, but its effects apparently were not mediated by cognitive change. The authors speculate that cognitive therapy is effective to the extent that clients learn to monitor and alter cognitions, apply these techniques and see change occur. Thus early cognitive change predicts further cognitive activity leading to symptom change. On the other hand, pharmacotherapy-treated subjects may alter their cognitions initially (such as beliefs that pills produce change) but such early cognitive change does not produce later cognitive activity and symptom change.

A question that is related to the issue of cognitive mechanisms of change is whether successful therapy actually alters the core, dysfunctional schemas of depressed patients. As indicated in Chapter 5, several studies have suggested that changes in dysfunctional attitudes are state-dependent concomitants of mood change, while others have suggested that level of dysfunctional attitudes is a predictor of relapse/recovery independent of mood. Recently, Whisman, Miller, Norman, and Keitner (1991) examined cognitions and symptom levels during 6- and 12-month follow-ups in a sample of depressed patients who had been treated as inpatients. Patients who had received cognitive therapy in addition to standard medication and milieu therapy reported significantly less cognitive bias and hopelessness, and lower DAS scores at the six-month assessment, compared to standard treatment only. Notably, however, the groups did not differ on concurrent symptom levels. The authors interpret the results to indicate specific effects due to cognitive therapy, and speculate that such changes may help to explain the success of cognitive therapy in lowering relapse rates during follow-ups.

These results are consistent with the "compensatory change" hypotheses of Barber and DeRubeis (1989), who discuss several possible mechanisms of change originally described by Hollon, Evans, and DeRubeis (1988). One model is "accommodation," meaning that cognitive therapy effects a change in the basic cognitive schemata, either in content or process or both. Barber and DeRubeis argue that process change is unlikely, since there is no evidence that depressed and nondepressed people actually process information differently. With respect to content change these authors argue that measures of cognition such as the DAS or ATQ have offered ambiguous evidence that they represent underlying schemas, and instead may reflect mood-dependent states. Moreover, as several studies of cognitive therapy compared with other forms of treatment have indicated, changes in cognitions are not specific to cognitive therapy. For these reasons, the authors do not think that "accommodation" is the best explanation for changes in cognitive therapy.

A second possible model of change is "activation-deactivation" in which the maladaptive schemas are not *changed*, but are deactivated while more adaptive schemas are activated. The authors argue that while this might be a good model for explaining changes induced by antidepressant medication, it alone does not seem to fit with the apparent success of cognitive therapy in preventing relapses. This leaves a third model of change which Barber and DeRubeis (1989) favor: "compensatory skills." According to this model, cognitive therapy does not alter the tendency to think in depressive ways, but rather provides a set of skills that help individuals to deal with the thoughts when they do arise. Such a model is consistent with Teasdale's (1985) hypothesis that the availability of coping skills helps cognitive therapy patients overcome "depression about depression." Barber and DeRubeis argue that, eventually, with repeated practice, there may gradually be accommodation of the underlying schema so that it becomes less negative. However, these authors doubt that short-term therapy as typically practiced will produce such changes. Moreover, they argue that outcome studies have not really assessed compensatory skills, and that such evaluation might provide a more accurate method of gauging the mechanisms of change.

Who does best in cognitive therapy?

Relatively little empirical evidence exists to characterize patients who do best in cognitive therapy. Three studies have suggested that pretreatment symptom severity predicts worse outcome at termination (Elkin et al., 1989; Simons, Lustman, Wetzel, & Murphy, 1985; Thase et al., 1991). Cognitive characteristics, such as learned resourcefulness on the Self-Control Schedule, have been shown to predict better outcome (Murphy, Simons, Wetzel, et al., 1984; Simons et al., 1985). A recent study of coping styles and homework compliance partially supported this finding. Burns and Nolen-Hoeksema (1991) had patients rate their coping strategies and their willingness to try suggested activities. Overall more resourceful coping strategies did not predict outcome of cognitive therapy. However, willingness to try the suggested coping activities, and therapist-rated compliance with homework assignments, made separate and additive contributions to improvement. The authors note that contrary to their expectations, patients who used more active coping strategies were not better candidates for cognitive therapy. They also note that the data do not prove that it is the homework that contributes to success, since compliance with assignments may also indicate more general cooperativeness and motivation to change.

Other studies indicate that greater DAS scores predicted worse outcome at termination (Keller, 1983) and at a one-year follow-up (Simons et al., 1986). The NIMH treatment of depression collaborative study recently attempted to identify individual predictors of outcome (Sotsky, Glass, Shea, Pilkonis, Collins, et al., 1991). They found that good responses to cognitive therapy were related to lower initial cognitive dysfunction (DAS), briefer duration of the current episode, absence of a family history of affective disorder, later age of onset, and more prior episodes of depression. Taken together, the few studies suggest that presence of high levels of cognitive dysfunction do *not* indicate preferential response to cognitive therapy; in fact, if anything, high levels of cognitive dysfunction may predict poor outcome.

Commentary

Data are relatively sparse on the question of which ingredients of cognitive therapy are especially effective, and whether the changes in mood that are produced can accurately be attributed to modification of cognitive processes. It is highly likely that so-called nonspecific ingredients account for considerable change in outcome. Nevertheless, the direct assault on the maladaptive thinking of depressed persons probably adds to the effectiveness of the treatment—although it is unclear whether such efforts actually *reduce* maladaptive thinking or instead provide tools to *cope* with it and its effects. Additional studies are needed to study the mechanisms of change in cognitive therapy; as Hollon, Shelton, and Loosen (1991) have noted, the needed studies are technically challenging.

NEW DEVELOPMENTS IN COGNITIVE THERAPY FOR DEPRESSION

Treatment-resistant depressions

It has become clear over the years since the development and application of Beck's original cognitive therapy methods that some patients are more difficult to treat than others. Indeed, many of us came to wonder where all the relatively uncomplicated cases of major depressive episode—commonly highly effectively treated in a brief period—went. Whether it is an illusion or an actual reflection of changing case-loads, many practitioners have noted an increase in the number of chronically depressed cases, or those with depression of childhood origins, or those with significant personality disorders along with depression. In such instances, the highly structured brief therapy, with its requirements of considerable client effort and cooperation, has not seemed to be sufficiently effective or has met with "resistance."

In addition to the apparent changes in client characteristics, two additional developments have implications for the next generation of cognitive therapy. One is the increasing focus of cognitive theory on deep or early schemas and core maladaptive assumptions—in contrast to more surface negative cognitions about everyday events and circumstances. The evolution of cognitive models and vulnerability hypotheses and methods of analyses were discussed more fully in Chapter 5. Increasing emphasis has been given to the much harder-to-change basic schemas about the self and the world, with the attendant recognition of their childhood origins typically arising in the context of dysfunctional family life.

The other theme that requires recognition as an influence on new developments in cognitive therapy is the growing influence (or resurgence) of interest in psychodynamically oriented therapy. Nowadays, in the form of object relations theories, there is considerable emphasis on depression as a result of maladaptive experiences in the early mother-child relationship, often involving separation-individuation and its consequences for the formation of an adaptive sense of self.

In part as a consequence of these developments there are three new developments in cognitive therapy to consider. These are not meant to suggest that they are separate and independent developments, nor that they are the only ones. Nevertheless, the following three sections are intended to highlight some likely areas of further research and development in cognitive therapy and cognitive theories of depression.

Cognitive therapy for personality disorders

There has been a recent proliferation of discussions of how to do cognitive therapy for personality disorders (e.g. Beck & Freeman, 1990). Excursions into personality disorders represent a natural extension for cognitive therapies in the sense that such disorders may be conceptualized as maladaptive beliefs and schemas organized around particular content. For example, Beck and Freeman and their associates (1990) hypothesize that each of the personality disorder types is grounded on particular maladaptive beliefs that are coupled with characteristic behavioral strategies. Thus, the dependent personality is organized around the belief "I am helpless" and the coping strategy of seeking or maintaining attachment to others; the obsessive-compulsive believes "Errors are bad. I must not err," and coping strategy is to aim for perfection.

Chronic and treatment-resistant depressions may profit from the application of some of the newly-modified principles of cognitive therapy as applied to personality disorders. Not only are the modifications aimed at dealing with difficult cases, but also, as we indicated in Chapter 1, many such intractably depressed persons may have underlying Axis II conditions.

The major modifications of cognitive therapy to apply to such cases of coexisting personality disorders concern duration and pace of therapy, additional use of the client-therapist relationship, alternative ways to structure collaboration, and identification and focus on core maladaptive schemas. Obviously, such therapy is longer and slower-paced because the core maladaptive schemas and their strategic behavioral goals might prove to be obstacles to some of the traditional ways that cognitive therapy generates change. For instance, clients with personality disorders might have a great deal of difficulty performing homework assignments because they lack self-regulatory skills or have poor collaborative skills, have extremely self-defeating expectations of change, or are fearful of change— among numerous such obstacles traditionally termed "resistance." The therapy needs to identify such obstacles and work to overcome them. The therapeutic relationship itself often becomes a focus of resistance as well as a tool for identifying and working with dysfunctional schemas. A variety of techniques are recommended to challenge maladaptive deep beliefs and to build underdeveloped schemas and behaviors. As we shall see below, some of these ideas are being incorporated into alternative cognitive therapy approaches.

Attachment theory and constructivistic cognitive therapies

In 1983 the Italian psychotherapists Guidano and Liotti wrote a book that attempted to integrate certain psychodynamic formulations of psychopathology with a cognitive conceptual model and cognitive interventions. Their work based many of its key formulations on Bowlby's (1969, 1981) attachment theory of the development of views of the self and others in the context of the early mother-child relationship. Basically, most forms of psychological disorder are viewed as pathologies of attachment, leading to maladaptive views of the self and the world. Preexisting cognitive structures—schemas—have profound effects on subsequent action and cognition. Guidano and Liotti particularly emphasize self-theories held by the client as exerting a profound effect on the person's behaviors. Therapeutic interventions are aimed at identifying maladaptive cognitions, including eventually the deep, core cognitions about the self. The authors appear to support use of a variety of intervention tools, including increasing awareness of the illogical and maladaptive aspects of the client's beliefs and behaviors, behavioral rehearsals and skill acquisition, and use of imagery.

Guidano and Liotti present case studies for application of their cognitive-attachment theory model to a variety of emotional disorders. As yet, however, there are no empirical data available to test key hypotheses.

Interpersonal schemas in cognitive therapy

Recently Safran (1990a,b; Safran & Segal, 1990) has made a similar effort to integrate cognitive and dynamic formulations, linking cognitive theory with interpersonal process theories. The fundamental hypothesis is that interpersonal relationships, including the therapeutic process, are commonly the source of growth and change in psychotherapy. Often, too, personal relationships are the source of difficulties for many persons in treatment, including depressed patients. Safran uses the concept of "interpersonal schema" as an integrative construct. Grounded in cognitive theoretical notions of schemas as generalized cognitive representations or knowledge structures that guide the processing of information and the activation of behavior, the focus is on the organization and content of interpersonal representations. Bowlby and others (e.g. Bowlby, 1969) have argued that interpersonal relatedness is a wired-in need system with profound effects on personality development. Bowlby has postulated that infants learn fundamental representations of themselves and others— "working models"—from the nature of the mother-infant attachment process. Safran uses the term interpersonal schema to characterize the self–other representations that are formed in the attachment process, and considers such schemas to operate like a program for maintaining relatedness (Safran, 1990a, p. 93).

The interpersonal schema consists of information, strategies, and propositions about relationships and the ways to achieve and maintain connectedness with others; such schemas include affective, and expressive-motor information as well as conceptual information concerning relationships. Because the schema process serves the goal of efficiency and speed of processing information, rather than accuracy of information, the schema often guides the selection, interpretation, or retrieval of information that fits the schema, to the relative neglect of inconsistent information. Thus, bias in information processing may help to perpetuate the schema. A dysfunctional schema may thus be enduring regardless of disconfirming information. Moreover, a maladaptive schema may result in dysfunctional behavior that might even elicit negative behavior from others that actually confirms the schematic propositions.

Safran (1990a) terms these processes cognitive-interpersonal cycles, as illustrated in the following example: "I can't trust men to be reliable" is a belief that might be sustained by a woman's selective perception of men's actions. A woman who holds such a belief might treat her boyfriend as if she does not believe him or treats him with criticism or withdrawal when she imagines he has let her down in some way. Eventually, the boyfriend might become angry, discouraged, and disinterested in her and, in effect, leave the relationship, thereby "confirming" her expectation of men's unreliability. According to Safran (1990a), the more maladjusted the person, the more likely he or she will elicit similar responses from a range of different people. Moreover, he would argue that the interpersonal deficits might not necessarily be grossly impaired behavior, and might be difficult to detect in standardized behavioral measures. Instead, the schemas and their related dysfunctional behaviors might unfold in somewhat subtle interchanges. Although many examples are given of *depressed* patients' dysfunctional schemas, Safran's theory is actually broad-based in application, hypothesizing that all clinical problems stem from interpersonal schemas that are problematic (1990b).

The therapy that Safran (1990b; Safran & Segal, 1990) proposes is aimed at using cognitive constructs and methods to identify and alter the dysfunctional "working models" or interpersonal schemas and the cognitive-interpersonal cycles in which people evoke schema-consistent reactions from others. An important step is the assessment of interpersonal dysfunction—often subtle and nonverbal nuances of style. Safran (1990b; Safran & Segal, 1990) advocates the use of the therapist's own analysis of process—feelings, thoughts, and actions experienced by the therapist that are monitored closely during interactions. It is assumed that many of the problematic features of the interpersonal life of the client will be played out with the therapist, and close attention to the interpersonal nuances in the therapy hour can be used to identify dysfunctions and to clarify the underlying cognitions. The therapist communicates his or her awareness of dysfunctional behaviors and possible underlying thoughts, and such communication is intended to provide feedback and to facilitate exploration.

An important next step after identification of maladaptive interpersonal schemas is disconfirmation of the erroneous cognitions. This process can occur in the therapy session, and should also be extended to the out-of-session world of the client, testing out beliefs and behaviors that came to light during the therapy process. The client is thus expected to be an active collaborator in the change process, and to carry out homework tasks between sessions.

Safran (1990a,b) presents numerous hypotheses to be tested empirically. To date, however, neither the interpersonal schema therapy nor specific tenets of the model have been tested. It appears that both the Guidano and Liotti (1983) and Safran and Segal (1990) elaborations of cognitive therapy have similar, important contributions to make in the direction of encouraging additional effort to treat and change core maladaptive schemas about the self or others. Beck's therapy for depression certainly attempts such change, but has neither elaborated the nature of the maladaptive core schemas nor emphasized methods of changing such fundamental belief systems. The integration with attachment models is a useful theoretical advance, and provides a cognitive framework for construing the structure, content, and operation of early-acquired and constructivistic schemas. The real challenge for cognitive models will be to develop methods of assessing such processes, and to continue the tradition of empirically-based validation of theories and methods.

CONCLUDING COMMENTS

Cognitive therapy for depression has been shown to be an effective, relatively brief therapy for the acute treatment of depression. As such, it appears to offer an alternative to medication for certain depressed persons whose health status or psychological preferences may preclude use of psychotropic medication. The evidence in support of the effectiveness of cognitive therapy in preventing relapse, or possibly even recurrences of depression, is especially promising and, in that regard, it might represent an improvement over psychopharmacological interventions. Appropriate caution is due, however, because the results of studies examining the relative effectiveness of cognitive therapy compared to other modes of treatment are equivocal, and are sometimes based on designs that offer less than optimal administration of alternative treatments or placebo controls. Moreover, additional outcome studies are needed to provide definitive answers to basic questions, such as which patients are most suited to cognitive therapy, and to tackle the thorny issue of whether cognitive therapies succeed because they alter cognitive processes.

Both the somewhat mediocre showing of cognitive therapy in the NIMH collaborative study and the increasing appearance or recognition of treatment-resistant depressed patients provide additional challenges to the model. In particular, compared with the somewhat simplistic early formulations of depression and of cognitive therapy, it seems important at the present time to flesh out some of the issues concerning schema acquisition, content, mechanisms, and change. Some of the most promising possibilities that are currently being discussed concern the integration of schemas about the self and others that are acquired in the early mother-child relationship. Going beyond the vague and untested hypotheses of object relations models, attachment-theory perspectives emphasize cognitive structures that presumably can be measured and relevant interventions tested. Somewhat less developed are the methods for altering basic schemas; indeed, evidence of the utility of new integrated methods and of the validity of the proposed mechanisms is lacking altogether. It is a particular challenge to cognitive therapy to demonstrate that the systematic methods of identifying and altering core schemas work better than other forms of supportive-expressive psychotherapy. It is to be hoped that the evolving integration of cognitive models with interpersonal content will continue the tradition of cognitive-behavioral theories' emphasis on empirical evidence. In the following chapter we examine more explicitly interpersonal and behavioral approaches to the treatment of depression, and then in Chapter 10, we present an integrative cognitive-interpersonal formulation of this disorder.

Chapter 9

Treatment of Depression: II. Behavioral and Interpersonal Approaches

As we have seen in Chapters 6 and 7, over the past decade researchers have gained a growing appreciation of the significance of interpersonal relationships of depressed persons in contributing to the onset and maintenance of depression, and to the process of recovery from this disorder. In particular, the quality of the marital and family functioning of depressed persons has been implicated in depression, affecting the onset and course of depression, as well as relapse. There is little question that depressed persons are characterized by problematic interpersonal functioning. At a broad level, for example, we reviewed studies indicating that depressed individuals have smaller, less integrated, and less supportive social networks than do their nondepressed counterparts (e.g. Brim, Witcoff, & Wetzel, 1982; Gotlib & Lee, 1989). We also presented evidence that a lack of supportive interpersonal relationships may be implicated in the etiology of depression (e.g. Barnett & Gotlib, 1988b; Brown & Harris, 1978; Costello, 1982; Gotlib, Whiffen et al., 1991). With respect to more intimate relationships, we presented the results of studies that have demonstrated that the marital and family functioning of depressed persons is characterized by tension and hostility (e.g. Biglan et al., 1985; Gotlib & Whiffen, 1989a,b; Ruscher & Gotlib, 1988), and that the presence of negative marital interactions increases the likelihood of depressed patients' relapse (e.g. Hooley, Orley, & Teasdale, 1986). Finally, we noted that a number of investigations, encompassing a diverse range of methodologies, have found that children of depressed mothers demonstrate problematic psychosocial adjustment and functioning (e.g. Hammen, 1991a; Hammen et al., 1987; Lee & Gotlib, 1989a,b, 1991a).

Given the negative interactions of depressed persons with their social environments and the pervasiveness of their difficulties in interpersonal functioning, a number of interventions for depression have been developed that focus explicitly on improving the social skills and interpersonal relationships of depressed patients. Indeed, there are several investigations that have reported the successful treatment of depression using behaviorally and/or interpersonally oriented therapies, as well as therapies explicitly involving the spouse and family of the depressed patient. In this chapter, we will first examine behavioral approaches to the assessment of depression and of the social functioning of depressed persons. We will then discuss the principles and effectiveness of interpersonally focused therapies for depression. Finally, we will consider various therapeutic approaches designed explicitly to involve the spouse and/or the family of the depressed patient in the assessment and treatment of depression, and will examine the results of investigations conducted to assess the efficacy of marital/family oriented therapy for depression.

BEVHAVIORAL APPROACHES

Behavioral assessment of depression

In Chapter 4 we discussed issues and procedures relevant to the assessment of depression. We described diagnostic strategies that utilized both clinician ratings and self-reports of depressive symptoms. Behavioral approaches to the assessment of depression typically focus on overt features of the disorder, such as psychomotor and verbal behavior. In addition, however, given the focus of behavioral theories of depression on environmental contingencies, behaviorally oriented clinicians and researchers also attempt to assess aspects of the environment, and of the person-environment interaction, that may be related to the onset or maintenance of depression. Thus, behavioral assessment may include an examination of such factors as the social skills of the depressed individual, the behaviors of others with whom the depressed patient interacts, and the activities and reinforcers available to the depressed person.

For example, in assessing the social skills of depressed persons, Becker and Heimberg (1985) recommend that a clinical interview be conducted in which the interviewer and the depressed patient role play problematic target situations identified by the patient. During this role playing, the interviewer should carefully observe the patient's performance, in terms of speech content, volume, tone, eye contact, posture, and so on (see also Lewinsohn, Biglan, & Zeiss, 1976). In addition, standardized role play tests such as the Behavioral Assertiveness Test (Eisler, Hersen, Miller, & Blanchard, 1975) can serve to augment the situations provided by the patient. For more severely depressed inpatients, Williams, Barlow, and Agras (1972) developed an observer-rated scale to assess the patients' behaviors on the hospital ward. Essentially, this scale assesses depressed patients' verbal behavior, social interactions, smiling, and motor activity, such as reading, sewing, and grooming. This measure yields a longitudinal record of the patients' depressed behaviors, and correlates highly with clinician ratings of depression severity. Interestingly, Williams, Barlow, and Agras reported that scores on this instrument were more predictive of relapse of depression one year later than were scores on the BDI or the HRSD.

Becker and Heimberg (1985) also recommend that a clinical interview be devoted to an examination of the depressed patient's life circumstances. More specifically, patients should be asked about interpersonal difficulties they may be experiencing in different settings, such as work, school, marital and/or family relationships, and social encounters with friends or strangers. The purpose of this interview is to identify behavior settings and individuals that appear to be associated with changes in the patient's mood. The patient's perception of this link between environmental characteristics and mood is critical to the success of therapy, which is aimed at altering the functional relation between the patient and the environment. Thus, Becker and Heimberg emphasize the importance of obtaining detailed descriptions of these settings and individuals, often using roleplaying procedures to gather this information.

Behavioral therapists may also require depressed patients to maintain a daily event log. These logs or diaries can be useful in assessing the response consequences of the depressed patient's social behaviors and in providing information about the patient's social environment and the available social reinforcers. In a more systematic attempt to facilitate behavioral programs designed to increase the amount of positive reinforcement received by depressed persons, MacPhillamy and Lewinsohn (1971) developed the Pleasant Events Schedule (PES), an inventory designed for use in assessing, tracking, and modifying positive activity level in depressed persons. The PES consists of 320 items describing interactions with the environment that many people find to be pleasant (e.g. being with friends, being told I am loved, seeing beautiful scenery, going to a restaurant). The patient first rates each item on a three-point scale indicating the frequency of each event's occurrence during the past month. Each item is then rated a second time with respect to the subjective enjoyability of the event. The frequency ratings are assumed to measure the individual's rate of engagement in person-environment interactions, while the subjective enjoyability ratings are assumed to reflect the individual's potential for positive reinforcement. The cross-products of the frequency and impact ratings provide a measure of the total amount of positive reinforcement the patient has experienced over the past month. In addition, scores or profiles on the PES can be used to provide an individualized list of potential target pleasant activities for change.

In general, therefore, behavioral approaches to the assessment of depression focus not only on the observation of overt aspects of the disorder, but on the relationship between depressed individuals and others in their social environments. As we shall see later in this chapter, there are also a number of structured instruments for the assessment of the marital and family interactions of depressed persons. Before we describe these measures, however, we turn to an examination of behavioral or interpersonal approaches to the treatment of depressed individuals.

Behavioral treatment of depression

Given the focus of behavioral theories of depression on environmental contingencies and reinforcers, a major goal of behaviorally oriented therapies for depression involves increasing the positive reinforcement received by the depressed individual. In this context, a number of different behavioral treatment approaches have been described, all of which share this common goal (cf. Antonuccio, Ward, & Tearnan, 1989; Hoberman, 1990). Moreover, as Hoberman and Lewinsohn (1985) note, there are a number of other commonalities associated with behavioral approaches to the treatment of depression. For example, patients are usually required to monitor activities, mood, and thoughts. Patients are encouraged to set achievable goals in order to ensure successful early experiences, and to give themselves rewards for reaching their goals. Finally, most behavioral approaches involve training designed to remedy various performance and skill deficits of depressed patients (e.g. social skills training, assertiveness training), and most programs are time-limited, designed to run from between four and twelve weeks.

Increasing pleasant activities

Lewinsohn and his colleagues (e.g. Lewinsohn, Sullivan, & Grosscup, 1980; Libet & Lewinsohn, 1973) have underscored the significant relation between depression and low rates of positive reinforcement. As we noted in Chapter 3, these investigators have posited that depression may be due, in part, to a low rate of response-contingent positive reinforcement. In fact, Libet and Lewinsohn (1973) demonstrated that depressed persons emit fewer interpersonal behaviors than do nondepressed persons and elicit little social reinforcement from others with whom they interact (see also Gotlib & Robinson, 1982). Lewinsohn, Sullivan, and Grosscup (1980) developed a 12-session, highly structured behavioral program aimed at changing the quality and quantity of depressed patients' interactions with their environments. Specifically, through the use of such techniques as relaxation training, cognitive self-management, stress management, and feedback, Lewinsohn, and his colleagues taught depressed patients to manage and reduce the intensity and frequency of aversive events and to increase their rate of engagement in pleasant activities. They reported that this program of decreasing unpleasant activities and increasing engagement in pleasant activities was effective in reducing level of depression (see also Hammen & Glass, 1975; Turner, Ward, & Turner, 1979; Zeiss, Lewinsohn, & Munoz, 1979).

Based on this finding of a positive relationship between an increase in pleasant events and improvement in depression, Lewinsohn (Brown & Lewinsohn, 1984; Lewinsohn, Antonuccio, Breckenridge, & Teri, 1987) developed a psychoeducational group treatment for depression also aimed, in part, at increasing engagement in pleasant events. The Coping With Depression (CWD) course is a structured, eight-week, 12-session, treatment program that includes relaxation training, scheduling training, constructing thinking strategies, stimulus control strategies, self-change strategies, structured exercises, identifying and increasing pleasant activities, and social skills training. Group time is divided among lectures, assignment and review of homework tasks, discussion, role play, and structured tasks. In general, this treatment focuses on the acquisition of skills in four specific areas: relaxation training, increasing pleasant activities, changing aspects of thinking, and improving the quality and quantity of social interactions.

Several outcome studies have demonstrated the efficacy of this program. For example, Brown and Lewinsohn (1984), Steinmetz, Lewinsohn, and Antonuccio (1983) and Hoberman, Lewinsohn, and Tilson (1988) all found that the CWD course was more effective in the treatment of depression than was a wait-list control condition, and was as effective as individual behavior therapy. Interestingly, Hoberman, Lewinsohn, and Tilson found that positive perception of group cohesiveness was a significant predictor of treatment outcome, attesting to the efficacy of the group format of this approach. More recently, Lewinsohn, et al. (1990) developed an adolescent version of the CWD course, consisting of 16 two-hour sessions over eight weeks. Groups of depressed adolescents are taught to control their depressed mood through skills such as relaxation, increasing pleasant events, increasing social skills, and interpersonal problem-solving and conflict resolution. Lewinsohn et al. found that the CWD course, both with and without parental participation, was effective in the treatment of depressed adolescents. Finally, the efficacy of the CWD course has been demonstrated with elderly depressives, and as a preventative program for individuals at risk for the development of depressive episodes (see Hoberman, 1990, for a review of these studies).

Social skills therapy

Given the consistent finding of poor social skills of depressed persons (e.g.

Gotlib, 1982; Libet & Lewinsohn, 1973; Youngren & Lewinsohn, 1980), a number of investigators have described behaviorally oriented treatment programs for depression that focus explicitly on the training of social skills. One such treatment program for depression has been described by Becker, Heimberg, and Bellack at the Mood Disorders Clinic of Albany Medical College (e.g. Becker & Heimberg, 1985; Becker, Heimberg, & Bellack, 1987; Bellack, Hersen, & Himmelhoch, 1981). This program is based on the following assumptions:

1. Depression is a result of an inadequate schedule of positive reinforcement contingent on the person's nondepressed behavior.
2. A meaningful portion of the most salient positive reinforcers in the adult world are interpersonal in nature.
3. A meaningful portion of the noninterpersonal rewards in adult life may be received or denied, contingent on the person's interpersonal behavior.
4. Therefore, any set of treatment techniques that helps the depressed patient increase the quality of his or her interpersonal behavior should act to increase the amount of response-contingent positive reinforcement and thereby decrease depressive affect and increase the rate of "nondepressed behavior" (Becker & Heimberg, 1985, p. 205).

Becker and Heimberg also suggest that inadequate interpersonal behavior may be due to any of a number of factors, such as insufficient exposure to interpersonally skilled models, learning of maladaptive interpersonal behaviors, insufficient opportunity to practice important interpersonal routines, decaying of specific behavioral skills due to disuse, and failure to recognize environmental cues for specific interpersonal behaviors.

Given this context, Becker, Heimberg, and Bellack (1987) describe assessment and treatment procedures that focus jointly on decreasing depressive symptoms and enhancing expressive and receptive interpersonal communication skills. With respect to assessment, Becker, Heimberg, and Bellack recommend the use of a clinical interview both to determine a psychiatric diagnosis and to assess the patient's life circumstances and experience of interpersonal difficulties. As we noted earlier, Becker, Heimberg, and Bellack attempt to identify those behavior settings and interaction partners that seem to have a strong functional relation to the patients' mood. Information is gathered about the patient's interpersonal relationships and about significant others in the patient's life. This clinical interview is augmented by a videotaped behavioral role-play test to assess level of social skill, and by a variety of self-report questionnaires measuring interpersonal behavior and depressive symptoms. Becker, Heimberg, and Bellack recommend the use of such instruments as the BDI, the HRSD and the Raskin Depression Scale to assess depression, and the Wolpe–

Lazarus Assertiveness Scale and the Social Adjustment Scale to measure social behavior.

This social skills training program is composed of four general components: social skills training, social perception training, practice, and self-evaluation and self-reinforcement. Becker, Heimberg, and Bellack (1987) utilize strategies and techniques that involve instruction, feedback, social reinforcement, modelling, behavioral rehearsal, and graded homework assignments in a highly structured format. Because social skills tend to be situation-specific, training is provided in each of four problem areas: interactions with strangers, with family members, with friends, and at work or school. Becker and his colleagues suggest that treatment across these different social contexts maximizes the likelihood that social skills will generalize across a variety of situations.

The training program focuses primarily on three specific behavioral repertoires that appear to be particularly relevant to depressed individuals: negative assertion, positive assertion, and conversational skills. *Negative assertion* involves behaviors that allow persons to stand up for their rights and to act in their own best interest. Thus, training in negative assertion skills involves learning how to refuse unreasonable requests or demands, how to request that others change their behavior when it infringes on the patients in some important way, and how to compromise and negotiate solutions. *Positive assertion* and *conversational skills* involve the performance of behaviors that should enhance the patients' social attractiveness to others. Positive assertion refers to the expression of positive feelings about others, such as affection, approval, praise, and appreciation, as well as offering appropriate apologies. Training in conversational skills involves initiating conversations, asking questions, making appropriate self-disclosures, and ending conversations gracefully. In all of these areas depressed patients are given direct behavior training as well as training in social perception. Patients are encouraged to practice the skills and behaviors across different situations. Finally, depressed patients are trained to evaluate their responses and behaviors more objectively and to administer appropriate self-reinforcements.

Treatment takes place over 12 weekly one-hour sessions followed by six to eight maintenance sessions over a six-month period. The first session involves an overview of treatment; sessions 2 and 3 consist of training in the first problem area; sessions 4 and 5 involve training in the second problem area plus the introduction of social perception training and self-evaluation and self-reinforcement; sessions 6, 7, and 8 consist of training in the third problem area; sessions 9–11 in the fourth problem area; and session 12 involves a summary of the entire treatment. The emphasis of the six to eight sessions in maintenance treatment is on problem-solving and review.

Bellack and his colleagues have demonstrated the efficacy of this approach in the treatment of depression. For example, Bellack, Hersen, and Himmelhoch (1983) and Hersen, Bellack, Himmelhoch, and Thase (1984) randomly assigned 120 female unipolar depressed patients to four individual treatment conditions: social skills training plus amitriptyline, social skills training plus pill placebo, amitriptyline alone, and dynamic psychotherapy plus pill placebo. Patient in the social skills conditions received 12 weekly one-hour sessions of social skills training. Over the following six-month period, patients were seen for six to eight additional sessions of social skills training, focused on problem-solving and review. Patients in the psychotherapy condition received an identical number of sessions of psychodynamic psychotherapy.

The results of this project indicated that, prior to treatment, the depressed patients demonstrated significant deficiencies in speech duration, voice tone, posture tonus, gaze, Request/Compliance content, and overall assertiveness. Following treatment, patients who received social skills training (with amitriptyline and placebo) showed the greatest improvement in their assessed level of social skill. Indeed, these patients performed better on every measure of social skill than did patients in the other two treatment groups. More important, perhaps, these gains were maintained at the six-month follow-up assessment. Patients in all four treatment groups demonstrated significant improvement in their level of depression following treatment; there were no significant differences among the groups with respect to degree of clinical improvement. Interestingly, however, Bellack et al. found that social skills training resulted in fewer dropouts and a higher proportion of completely remitted patients than did the other treatments.

A similar approach to the treatment of depression that also focuses on the training of social skills has been described by McLean (1976, 1981). McLean views depression as resulting from individuals' perceived loss of control over their interpersonal environment. Consequently, treatment for depression is aimed at training in coping and social skills. The major task of therapy is to help depressed patients interact with their environment in a manner that leads to more frequent positive personal and social recognition. McLean outlines a structured, time-limited treatment program aimed at improving social behaviors that are incompatible with depression. Graduated practice and modelling are used to effect improvements in the following six skills areas: communication, behavioral productivity, social interaction, assertiveness, decision-making and problem-solving, and cognitive self-control. Patients are required to engage in daily skill development activities and to use structured log sheets to monitor their achievements. Patients are also prepared for the experience of future depressive episodes, and contingency plans for coping are established and rehearsed with the patients.

McLean and Hakstian (1979) assessed the efficacy of this behavioral treatment with 178 unipolar depressed outpatients, randomly assigned to four treatment conditions: behavior therapy, "traditional" insight-oriented psychotherapy, relaxation training, and amitriptyline. Treatment was conducted over a period of ten weeks. The results of this investigation indicated that behavior therapy was superior to the other treatments on nine of the ten outcome measures administered immediately following treatment, and on seven of the ten outcome measures at a three-month follow-up assessment. Patients in the behavior therapy condition also had the lowest drop-out rate. Data from a two-year follow-up of these patients reported by McLean and Hakstian (1990) indicate that this pattern of results is stable: over a 27-month follow-up period, behavior therapy patients were found to be significantly improved in mood, more socially active, and more personally productive than were patients in the other treatment conditions, particularly in the relaxation therapy condition.

Self-control therapy

Self-control therapy for the treatment of depression is probably the most-studied cognitive-behavior therapy application specifically for depression outside of Beck's methods. Self-control therapy emphasizes progressive goal attainment, self-reinforcement and contingency management strategies, and behavioral productivity (Antonuccio, Ward, & Tearnan 1989). This approach to therapy for depression was developed from Rehm's (1977) self-control model of depression, outlined in Chapter 3. Briefly, Rehm suggests that depression is associated with deficits in self-monitoring, self-evaluation, and self-reinforcement. More specifically, the model hypothesizes six deficits that contribute to depression: selective attention to negative experiences to the neglect of positive experiences; attention to immediate rather than delayed consequences; stringent standards for self-evaluation; negative attributions; insufficient contingent reinforcement to achieve long-term goals; and excessive self-punishment. Consequently, these areas of functioning are the focus of self-control therapy.

Self-control therapy is a structured, time-limited, group-format treatment approach. It consists of six to twelve sessions divided into three parts, each focusing on one of the three deficit areas described above. With respect to self-monitoring, patients are required to maintain a daily record of positive experiences and their associated mood. Patients graph events and mood to provide explicit feedback on the association between positive mood and positive events. In the self-evaluation phase, patients are taught to develop specific, overt, and attainable goals in terms of positive activities and behavioral productivity. Large goals are decomposed into smaller, more easily attainable subgoals. In addition, patients assign points to these subgoals, and keep a tally of their points as they meet their goals. Finally, in terms of self-reinforcement, patients are taught to identify reinforcers and to administer these rewards to themselves as they accomplish their specific goals. At the end of treatment patients are encouraged to continue using these self-control skills.

Rehm has demonstrated the efficacy of this self-control treatment for depression in a number of studies. In fact, Rehm (in press) reviewed eight studies conducted by himself or colleagues, and reported that self-management therapy was superior to both waiting list and placebo controls in six studies, and equal to placebo treatment in two. For example, in one of the first tests of the efficacy of this therapy, Fuchs and Rehm (1977) reported that self-control treatment was more effective than was nonspecific group therapy or a wait-list control condition in reducing depression in a sample of 36 clinically depressed women. Moreover, this improvement was maintained at a six-week follow-up assessment. Rehm, Fuchs, Roth, Kornblith, and Romano (1979) found that self-control therapy was more effective in the treatment of 24 depressed patients than was assertion skills training (see also Roth, Bielski, Jones, Parker, and Osborn, 1982). Interestingly, as Rehm (1990) notes, the effectiveness of this treatment does not depend on the inclusion of all three components; outcomes do not seem to be affected by the omission of the self-evaluation or self-reinforcement portions of the program. Finally, self-control therapy appears to be equally effective in altering cognitive and behavioral aspects of depression (cf. Rehm, 1990), suggesting a nonspecificity of treatment effects (cf. Zeiss, Lewinsohn, & Munoz, 1979).

Problem-solving therapy

In Chapter 3 we described a problem-solving model of depression formulated by Nezu (1987; Nezu, Nezu, & Perri, 1989). This model focuses on transactional relations among major negative life events, current problems, problem-solving coping, and depressive symptomatology. These four variables are postulated to be constantly interacting, and each variable can influence the others to produce and/or maintain depression. In general, however, Nezu and his colleagues focus most explicitly on the link between poor social problem-solving skills and depression. In the context of the treatment of depression, therefore, these investigators have described in detail strategies and procedures designed to reduce depressive symptomatology through training in problem-solving skills.

Nezu, Nezu, and Perri (1989) outline four goals of problem-solving therapy for depression: (a) to help depressed individuals identify previous and current life situations that may be antecedents of a depressive episode; (b) to minimize the negative impact of their depressive symptoms on current and future coping attempts; (c) to increase the effectiveness of their problem-solving efforts at coping with current life situations; and (d) to teach general skills that will enable clients to deal more effectively with future problems, thereby preventing future depressive reactions.

In attaining these goals, Nezu, Nezu, and Perri (1989) describe a problem-solving treatment for depression that focuses primarily on training in the five major problem-solving component processes of problem orientation, problem definition and formulation, generation of alternatives, decision making, and solution implementation and verification. Training in problem orientation focuses on providing patients with a positive and constructive set to problems in living and problem-solving as a means of coping with them. Training in the remaining four problem-solving components involves didactics and practice. Nezu, Nezu, and Perri present in detail a structured 10-week intervention program in which such therapeutic techniques as instruction, prompting, modelling, behavioral rehearsal, homework assignments, shaping, reinforcement, and feedback are utilized to increase problem-solving ability and decrease depressive symptomatology. Training in maintenance and generalization are also built into this program.

There is a considerable body of literature suggesting that problem-solving therapy may be efficacious for the treatment of depression. For example, preliminary results reported by Caple and Blechman (1976) and Shipley and Fazio (1973) indicated that problem-solving may be an important component of an effective treatment program for depression. Hussian and Lawrence (1981) subsequently presented data indicating that problem-solving training alone was superior to a social reinforcement approach in the treatment of depression. Nezu (1986) demonstrated that training in problem-solving skills was more effective in reducing depressive symptomatology than was either a problem-focused discussion group or a waiting list control condition. Finally, in a larger and more systematic study, Nezu and Perri (1989) replicated these results, reporting that problem-solving therapy was more effective in reducing depression than was an abbreviated form of problem-solving therapy (without training in problem orientation) or a waiting list control condition. Furthermore, a six-month follow-up assessment revealed that these gains were maintained after the completion of treatment. Considered collectively, these studies indicate that training in problem-solving skills may represent an effective approach to the treatment of depression.

Commentary

There is little doubt, therefore, that there are a number of effective behavioral treatment programs for depression that focus on changing the patient's interactions with the social environment. Interestingly, these programs are diverse, focusing variously on helping depressed patients to engage more frequently in pleasant activities, to sharpen their social skills, to become more accurate in self-monitoring, less stringent in self-evaluation, and more liberal in self-reinforcement, and to learn more effective coping and social problem-solving skills. Despite this diversity, it is clear that a primary goal of virtually all of these programs involves increasing the amount of positive reinforcement received by depressed patients; it is also clear that attainment of this goal typically leads to a significant reduction in depressive symptomatology. While there have been several attempts to dismantle the components of these therapies in efforts to examine the mechanisms responsible for change, there is not the level of progress that has been achieved in studies of cognitive therapy for depression. There is little question that this will be an important direction for researchers in this area to pursue.

These behavioral treatments have focused on the interactions of depressed persons with others in their social environment. Consequently, it is not surprising that investigators and therapists have recently directed their attention to improving the quality of the more intimate relationships between depressed individuals and their spouses and children. It is to this literature that we now turn.

MARITAL AND FAMILY THERAPY FOR DEPRESSION

Drawing on the findings reviewed in Chapter 7 concerning the marital and family functioning of depressed patients, a number of investigators have broadened the scope of behaviorally oriented interventions for depression to include an explicit focus on the spouse and/or family (cf. Gotlib, Wallace, & Colby, 1990). Indeed, there are now several distinct intervention programs for depression that have been developed specifically for the treatment of depression occurring within the context of a problematic marital or family environment. In this section of the chapter, we discuss strategies for the marital/family assessment and treatment of depression, and present the results of studies designed to examine the efficacy of this approach to intervention.

Assessment

The goals of assessment from a marital/family perspective are to describe the marital and family environment, to identify problematic patterns of interaction among family members, to pinpoint the areas of functioning on which treatment should focus, and to obtain baseline measures of marital/family functioning in order that treatment progress can be monitored and followed. Stuart (1980) has outlined five criteria for adequate marital and family assessment. First, the assessment should be relevant to the therapy, and should not slow down the treatment process. Second, in order to achieve convergent validity the assessment should be multidimensional, making use of different ratings from different participants. Third, assessment should be tied to theory, rather than a randomly selected battery of measures. Fourth, the assessment should be "situation-specific," examining functioning in the marital or family environment. Finally, the assessment should itself provide useful information for the couple or family, independent of the treatment program.

Despite the fact that these criteria were outlined more than a decade ago, there is not yet a great deal of information about the mapping of different marital and family systems to therapeutic strategies. Nevertheless, there are several instruments and procedures available that offer the therapist a relatively quick and comprehensive overview of the couple or family's relationship. These measures provide information concerning the couple or family's satisfaction with their relationships, specific significant areas of conflict, and the structure of the family and roles of the family members; they can also highlight important potential targets for intervention.

With respect to marital functioning, the Dyadic Adjustment Scale (Spanier, 1976) is probably the most frequently used measure of marital adjustment. This scale consists of 32 items, and is composed of four factors: dyadic satisfaction, dyadic cohesion, dyadic consensus, and affectionate expression. Several investigations have demonstrated that the Dyadic Adjustment Scale is a psychometrically reliable and valid measure that discriminates happily married from unhappily married and divorced samples (e.g. Jacobson & Margolin, 1979; Spanier, 1976), and couples with a depressed spouse from nondepressed couples (e.g. Gotlib & Whiffen, 1989b).

Two less frequently used but nonetheless valuable measures to assess marital functioning are the Areas of Change Questionnaire (AOC; Weiss, Hops, & Patterson, 1973) and the Impact Message Inventory (IMI; Kiesler, 1984). The AOC focuses on the spouses' perceptions of strengths and weaknesses in their relationship. Spouses are required to indicate which of 34 specific relationship behaviors they would like to see changed (e.g. spending money, sexual needs). Discrepancies between the partners can be calculated, and potential targets for intervention can be identified. The IMI is a 60-item self-report measure of the impact of one person's interpersonal style as experienced by another person (e.g. a spouse). It is composed of 15 subscales (e.g. Dominant, Hostile, Agreeable, Nurturant) that fall on the two dimensions of Friendly-Hostile and Dominant-Submissive. Gotlib and Whiffen (1989) and McCabe and Gotlib (1991b) both reported that the IMI differentiated the interpersonal impact of depressed patients from that of nondepressed persons and, interestingly, the impact of spouses of depressed patients from that of spouses of nondepressed subjects.

In addition to these measures of marital functioning, there are a number of questionnaires designed to assess the functioning of the family. For example, the Family Environment Scale (FES; Moos & Moos, 1981) was designed to measure the interpersonal relationships among family members and the social-environmental characteristics of families. The FES is a 90-item inventory composed of 10 subscales assessing three underlying domains or dimensions of family functioning: Relationships, Personal Growth, and System Maintenance. The FES also yields Incongruence scores for members of the family, which reflect the extent of disagreement among family members with respect to their perceptions of their family's functioning. This score can be particularly useful in assessing a family with a depressed member. In fact, several studies have used the FES to examine the family environments of depressed individuals. Mitchell, Cronkite, and Moos (1983) found that depressed patients reported less family support than did nondepressed controls. Similarly, McCabe and Gotlib (1991b) found that couples in which the wife was diagnosed as depressed reported more problematic family functioning on the FES than did nondepressed couples. Other self-report measures of family functioning include the Family Adaptability and Cohesion Evaluation Scales (FACES; Olson, Portner, & Bell, 1982) and the McMaster Family Assessment Device (FAD; Miller, Epstein, Bishop, & Keitner, 1985).

There are also a number of observational procedures available for the direct assessment of the interactions of depressed patients with their spouses and families. For example, Weiss, Hops, and Patterson (1973) developed the Spouse Observation Checklist (SOC) as an aid for couples themselves to collect direct-observation data in their home environments. The SOC covers 12 categories of behavior, including companionship, sex, affection, communication, and spouse independence. Each spouse is instructed to check all behaviors engaged in by their partner, and to indicate whether the behaviors were experienced as pleasing or as displeasing. Thus, the SOC permits the identification of those behaviors that are most important to the satisfaction of each spouse. Other direct observation procedures are designed for use by external raters. The Marital Interaction Coding System (MICS; Hops, Wills, Patterson, & Weiss, 1972) and the Kategoriensystem für Partnerschaftliche Interaction (KPI; Hahlweg, Reisner, Kohli, Vollmer, Schindler, and Revenstorf 1984) are two frequently used observer-rated systems for the coding of marital interactions. In addition, a broader system, the Living in Familial Environments Coding System

(LIFE; Arthur, Hops, & Biglan, 1982) was developed expressly to study the interactions of depressed women and their families. It was adapted from the MICS, with the addition of depression-relevant content codes and seven codes for scoring affective behavior. The content codes cover such behaviors as elicit self-disclosure and worry, whereas the affective codes are used to score concomitant neutral, happy, caring, irritated, depressed, sarcastic, and whiny affect. In all three observational systems, couples or families with a depressed member have been found to differ from nondepressed couples and families (e.g. Biglan et al., 1985; Nelson & Beach, 1990; Ruscher & Gotlib, 1988).

Finally, the results of several recent studies have underscored the importance of assessing the attitudes of family members concerning the patient's depression. In an early study in the area of schizophrenia, Vaughn and Leff (1976a) interviewed family members of schizophrenic patients at or around the time of the patients' hospitalizations. On the basis of the extent to which they expressed critical, hostile, or emotionally overinvolved attitudes when talking about the patient, relatives were classified as high or low in expressed emotion (EE; see Hooley, 1985, for a review of this construct). Vaughn and Leff found that schizophrenic patients who returned from the hospital to live with high-EE (i.e. critical) relatives were significantly more likely to relapse during a nine-month follow-up period than were patients who returned home to live with low-criticism family members.

This relation between spouses' high levels of EE and subsequent patient relapse was recently replicated by Hooley, Orley, and Teasdale (1986) with a sample of unipolar depressed patients. Interestingly, Hooley and colleagues found that depressed patients relapsed at lower rates of relatives' criticism than did the schizophrenic patients in Vaughn and Leff's (1976a) study, suggesting that depressed patients may be even more sensitive than are schizophrenic patients to criticisms of family members. In assessing EE, most researchers have used a version of the Camberwell Family Interview (CFI; Vaughn & Leff, 1976b). The CFI is a one- to two-hour semi-structured interview of a significant family member. An audiotape of the interview is rated for hostility, criticality, and emotional overinvolvement. Interestingly, Hooley and Teasdale (1989) recently demonstrated that depressed patients' responses to a single-item question concerning how critical they considered their spouses to be of them ("perceived criticism") were more strongly predictive of subsequent relapse than were EE scores derived from the CFI with the patients' spouses.

In sum, therefore, there are a number of measures available for the assessment of depression occurring within a marital or family context. Clarkin and Haas (1988) emphasize the importance of conducting a systematic assessment in each of three domains of functioning. Indeed, they consider such an assessment to be an integral part of family/marital treatments for depression. First, Clarkin and Haas contend that evaluation of individual symptomatology, cognition, and role functioning is essential in helping to gain a comprehensive picture of the nature of the patient's affective disorder. Second, these investigators suggest that an assessment of the illness-related perceptions, cognitions, and behaviors of the spouse and other family members is essential both in providing information concerning the family's response to the patient's depressive symptoms and in helping to identify specific targets for intervention and family involvement. Finally, Clarkin and Haas recommend that therapists identify maladaptive interpersonal communication patterns and problem-solving behaviors that might contribute to or maintain the affective disorder within the context of the marriage or family.

Therapy

Although the treatment of depression from a marital/family perspective is a relatively recent undertaking, a growing body of empirical literature is attesting to the promise of this approach. In an early series of case studies, Lewinsohn and his colleagues described an approach to the treatment of depression that focuses on reestablishing an adequate schedule of positive reinforcement for the individual by increasing the quality and range of interpersonal interactions. Lewinsohn postulated that providing depressed patients and their spouses with feedback about their interpersonal behaviors in the home can lead to a decrease in the level of depression and an improvement in their social relationships. Thus, Lewinsohn and Atwood (1969) and Lewinsohn and Schaffer (1971) present cases in which feedback about interpersonal behavior between a depressed woman and her husband was used in combination with conjoint marital therapy to effect behavior change. The results demonstrated significant decreases in the women's MMPI-Depression scores and improvement in their marital communication and family interactions.

   In a subsequent controlled investigation, McLean, Ogston, and Grauer (1973) examined the effects of behaviorally-oriented conjoint marital therapy on the valence of the marital communications of depressed outpatients and their spouses. McLean, Ogston, and Grauer compared a non-treatment control group of depressed couples with a group of couples who received behavioral marital therapy (BMT). Twenty married depressed outpatients received either BMT with their spouses or "treatment as usual," which typically involved medication, group therapy, individual psychotherapy, or some combination of these treatments. Couples in the

BMT treatment group received eight, one-hour, weekly sessions with male and female co-therapists. During these sessions they received training in social learning principles, and the spouses were given feedback regarding each others' perceptions of their verbal interactions. Using behavioral contracts, spouses were taught how to communicate to their partners changes they desired in their relationships and how to monitor the feedback they were giving to their spouses. Couples in the BMT condition were also given "cue boxes" to use at home. These boxes were small battery-powered devices containing red and green button-operated lights and an electric counter. They were designed to provide immediate positive and negative feedback to spouses while interacting, without necessarily interrupting their conversation. Spouses pressed the red light when they considered their partner to be negative in reaction to their discussion, and the green light when they perceived their spouse to be positive.

Prior to beginning treatment, patients were assessed with the Depression Adjective Checklist (DACL), were tape-recorded at home with their spouse discussing their problems, and were asked to list five target behaviors that were attributed to the patient's depression. Both at the end of treatment and at a three-month follow-up couples indicated any changes they noted in these five target behaviors. McLean, Ogston, and Grauer (1973) found that, overall, patients in the BMT group demonstrated greater improvements than did the control patients. Both at the end of treatment and at the three-month follow-up period, couples in the BMT group reported significantly greater reductions in their DACL scores and greater improvements in their problematic interpersonal behaviors. In contrast, couples in the comparison group exhibited only minor improvement in these areas. Finally, couples who received marital therapy demonstrated more adaptive verbal behavior, including a significant reduction in the frequency of their negative perceptions of their partner's behaviors and their verbal interchanges.

In a widely cited investigation of the effectiveness of marital therapy in the treatment of depression, Friedman (1975) conducted a 12-week therapy program designed to assess the separate and combined effects of amitriptyline and "marital and family-oriented psychotherapy" in depressed patients. Subjects were male and female depressed outpatients whose spouses agreed to make regular visits to the clinic. Patients were randomly assigned to one of four treatment conditions: drug therapy and marital therapy, drug therapy and minimal contact, marital therapy and placebo, and placebo and minimal contact. A total of 150 depressed patients completed the full course of treatment. In the drug treatment groups, patients received amitriptyline hydrochloride for the first ten weeks of treatment, while the last two weeks were drug-free in order to assess withdrawal reactions. Patients in the marital therapy conditions had twelve hours of contact with a therapist using marital- and family-oriented psychotherapy. Finally, patients in the minimal contact group received seven, half-hour, individual sessions with a physician.

Several assessment measures were utilized to evaluate outcome at the end of treatment, including a Psychiatric Rating Scale, a Global Improvement Clinical Scale, a self-report Inventory of Psychic and Somatic Complaints, a Family Role Task and Activity Scale, and a Marital Relations Inventory. Essentially, Friedman (1975) found that both drug and marital therapy were more effective than were their respective control conditions (placebo drug and minimal individual contact). However, there also appeared to be differential effects of these two types of treatment. Whereas drug therapy was associated with early improvement in clinical symptoms, marital therapy was associated with longer-term improvement in the patient's participation and performance in family role tasks, the reduction of hostility in the family, and improvement in the patient's perceptions of the quality of the marital relationship. Overall, for most of the outcome measures, the combined drug-marital therapy group demonstrated the greatest improvement. In discussing these results, Friedman stated that it is possible that "the marital therapy approach is more effective and quicker to achieve a positive effect with neurotically depressed married patients than is either individual or peer group therapy" (p. 634). Although there are methodological difficulties inherent in this study (see Beach, Sandeen, & O'Leary, 1990), the results are nevertheless encouraging of further examination of marital therapy in the treatment of depression.

The usefulness of including the spouse in therapy was also examined in a retrospective study of 100 couples in which one partner was diagnosed with a primary affective disorder (PAD). Greene, Lustig, and Lee (1976) examined 40 unipolar depressed, 42 bipolar depressed, and 18 unipolar manic patients and their spouses. All PAD spouses received psychotherapy and/or somatotherapy, while the therapist offered supportive psychotherapy to the non-PAD spouse. The major emphasis of Greene, Lustig, and Lee's approach was to utilize the non-PAD partner as an "assistant therapist," with the goal of stabilizing the marriage. They reported that approximately 10% of the couples receiving this treatment achieved stabilization for at least 15 years. Given this low baserate, combined with Greene, Lustig, and Lee's perception that marriage to an individual with a PAD often involves serious risks around suicide and emotional instability, the authors caution that they typically advise against marriage when there is a history of a primary affective disorder in one of the potential spouses.

Davenport, Ebert, Adland, and Goodwin (1977) also reported on the effectiveness of couples therapy in the treatment of bipolar affective disorder. Sixty-five married bipolar patients who had been previously hospitalized for an acute manic episode were followed-up for between two and ten years after their discharge from hospital. The patients and their spouses were arbitrarily assigned to one of three groups at the time of discharge: a couples' psychotherapy group with lithium maintenance, a lithium maintenance group with no regular psychotherapy, and a home community aftercare group. Each couples' group consisted of 3–5 couples who met for approximately 90 minutes per week with male and female cotherapists. The focus of therapy, conducted with cotherapists, was on couple interactions and the acquisition of more adaptive behaviors. Davenport et al. found the overall outcome to be quite poor for those couples who did not receive the couples' therapy. Patients in the lithium/no psychotherapy and home aftercare groups demonstrated high rates of rehospitalization and marital failure; in fact, three of these patients committed suicide. In contrast to this pattern of functioning, none of the twelve patients in the couples' group required rehospitalization or experienced marital failure. Although there were a number of demographic differences among these groups that must be taken into account, Davenport et al. conclude that bipolar patients and their spouses can benefit from participation in a homogeneous conjoint marital therapy group.

In a report of the effectiveness of marital therapy for the treatment of depression, Waring, Chamberlaine, McCrank, Stalker, Carver, et al. (1988) describe an ongoing investigation in which they use essentially the same four treatment groups as did Friedman (1975). Waring et al. report results from 12 couples who had completed ten weeks of therapy sessions. The subjects were all dysthymic women whose husbands agreed to participate in treatment. Patients received either doxepin or a placebo drug crossed with either minimal contact or cognitive marital therapy, selected for its focus on the intimacy between couples and the use of self-disclosure to improve intimacy. Waring et al. found that all patients showed an improvement in depressive symptomatology and an increase in reported intimacy. In addition, there was a trend for these effects to be most pronounced for patients in the cognitive marital therapy condition. On the basis of these results, Waring et al. suggest that the simple presence of dysthymic women's spouses in therapy may itself be beneficial.

More recently, Beach, Sandeen, and O'Leary (1990) have described a program of therapy based on their marital discord model of depression. Consistent with the literature we reviewed in Chapter 7, Beach, Sandeen, and O'Leary suggest that a discordant marital relationship may play a powerful role not only in the development and maintenance of depression, but in the promotion of recovery and maintenance of gains. They note that marital discord is associated with verbal and physical aggression, increased marital conflict, and reduced spousal support; they suggest further that this marital stress and lack of marital support may mediate the relation between marital discord and depression. Finally, Beach, Sandeen, and

O'Leary propose that the long-term presence of depressive symptoms may exacerbate marital discord.

On the basis of these formulations, Beach, Sandeen, and O'Leary (1990) outline a brief (15-session) structured program of marital therapy for the treatment of depression. They divide their therapy into three phases. In the first phase the therapist focuses on the identification and rapid elimination of extreme stressors within the marital relationship, and on the reestablishment of joint positive activities and cohesion for the couple. Beach, Sandeen, and O'Leary suggest that successful completion of this phase of therapy should result in a substantial elevation of mood for the depressed patient and increased expressions of positive feelings on the part of both spouses. The second phase of treatment focuses on restructuring the spouses' day-to-day communication, interaction, and problem-solving. Successful completion of this phase of treatment should increase the couple's stability, mutual support, and intimacy. Finally, in the third phase of therapy the couple is prepared for termination. The therapist helps the couple to identify and prepare for likely high-risk situations that may produce future marital discord or episodes of depression. The therapist also helps the couple to attribute the gains they have made in treatment to their mutual caring and love.

The efficacy of this approach to the treatment of depression has now been assessed in a number of studies. In a preliminary investigation, Beach and O'Leary (1986) described the clinical outcome for eight couples in which the wife met diagnostic criteria for unipolar depression. Couples were randomly assigned to one of three groups: conjoint behavioral marital therapy, cognitive therapy for the depressed spouse only, or a wait-list control group. The marital therapy treatment focused on improving communication and problem-solving skills, increasing positive instrumental behaviors, and gaining insight into the reasons for the development of marital discord. In contrast, the cognitive therapy condition focused on examining the manner in which the patients structured their worlds, and how this in turn influenced their affect and behavior. Couples in the wait-list control group were told that they could request therapeutic consultation, although none did during the 14 weeks of treatment.

Beach and O'Leary (1986) assessed depressive symptoms and marital discord at every second week throughout treatment by having subjects complete the Beck Depression Inventory and the Dyadic Adjustment Scale. Couples also completed these measures one week after the last session and at a three-month follow-up. The results of this study indicated that both active treatment conditions were more effective than was the wait-list condition in reducing depressive symptoms, and did not differ significantly from each other. In addition, however, couples in the behavioral marital therapy condition also reported significantly more rapid and larger increases in marital functioning than did couples in either the cognitive therapy or the wait-list control groups, and similar data were obtained for their husbands. Finally, Beach and O'Leary found this pattern of results to persist at the three-month follow-up assessment. Because this study is based on only eight couples, it is inappropriate to draw firm conclusions about the differential effectiveness of these intervention approaches. Nevertheless, it is noteworthy that whereas wives receiving behavioral marital therapy and individual cognitive therapy both showed clinically significant reductions in depressive symptomatology, only those wives receiving the conjoint marital therapy also showed a marked reduction in marital dissatisfaction.

O'Leary and Beach (1990) recently reported the results of an expanded version of this study. Thirty-six couples in which the wife received a DSM-III diagnosis of major depression or dysthymic disorder and in which at least one spouse scored in the discordant range on the Dyadic Adjustment Scale were randomly assigned to conjoint marital therapy, cognitive therapy for the depressed spouse only, or a wait-list control group. Both therapy conditions involved 15–16 weekly sessions. As was the case in the earlier study, O'Leary and Beach found that, at the end of treatment, patients in both therapy groups demonstrated a significant reduction in depressive symptomatology; in contrast, patients in the waiting list control group did not change. In addition, only patients who received marital therapy also demonstrated higher marital satisfaction scores at the end of treatment.

At a one-year follow-up, patients in the marital therapy and the cognitive groups did not differ on depressive symptoms. Patients who had received marital therapy, however, continued to report greater marital satisfaction than did patients in the cognitive therapy condition. Finally, O'Leary and Beach reported that, at the end of treatment, 67% of the individual therapy patients and 83% of the marital therapy patients no longer met the study criteria for depression (see Figures 9.1 and 9.2). Moreover, 25% of the individual therapy patients and 83% of the marital therapy patients had at least 15-point increases in their marital satisfaction scores from pre- to posttherapy. This general pattern of results was also evident at the one-year follow-up assessment. O'Leary and Beach suggest that the fact that the marital therapy subjects demonstrated as much change in depression as the cognitive behavior therapy subjects reflects the impact that marital satisfaction can have on depression. They suggest further that when significant marital discord is found in conjunction with clinically significant depression, marital therapy may be the most effective and appropriate treatment. Indeed, the primary advantage of marital therapy documented in this study is its ability to effectively reduce depressive symptomatology while enhancing marital satisfaction (although recent work by O'Leary, Riso, & Beach, 1990, suggests that marital therapy may not be as effective in

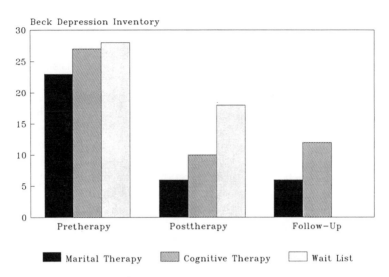

Figure 9.1 Changes in depression. Source: adapted from O'Leary and Beach (1990)

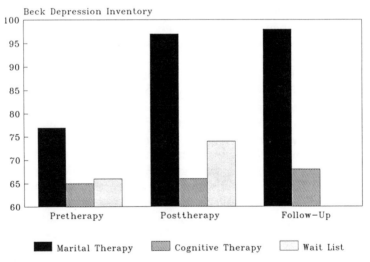

Figure 9.2 Changes in marital adjustment. Source: adapted from O'Leary and Beach (1990)

discordant-depressed couples in which the depressive symptoms preceded the onset of the marital difficulties).

Similar results were recently reported by Jacobson, Dobson, Fruzzetti, Schmaling, and Salusky (1991). Sixty depressed women and their spouses were randomly assigned to receive 20 sessions of conjoint behavioral marital therapy (BMT), 20 sessions of cognitive therapy focusing on the depressed spouse alone (CT), or a combination of these two treatments (CO). In the BMT condition, depressed women and their spouses were told that because depression occurs in an interpersonal context, both members of the marital dyad must be included in therapy. The treatment focused on behavioral exchange principles, and on training in communication and problem-solving. In the CT condition, depressed women were seen alone and were treated with Beck et al.'s (1979) cognitive therapy, which involves the assessment and modification of dysfunctional beliefs, thoughts, and attitudes that may have precipitated or maintained the depressive episode. Finally, in the CO condition, depressed wives attended the CT sessions alone, but were accompanied by their husbands for the BMT sessions. Typically, this treatment condition began with individual treatment and then involved both spouses in therapy.

Consistent with O'Leary and Beach's (1990) results, Jacobson et al. found that all three treatments led to a reduction in depression severity, as measured with the BDI and HRSD. Interestingly, BMT was found to be less effective than CT in reducing depressive symptoms for couples who did not report marital distress before therapy; for maritally distressed couples, the BMT and CT conditions were equivalent. In contrast, BMT, both alone and in the combined condition, was most effective in increasing marital satisfaction. Finally, improvement in depression was related to improvement in marital satisfaction only in the BMT condition, which focused exclusively on enhancing the quality of the marital relationship. In the two other therapy conditions, in which relationship enhancement was not the sole target of treatment, improvement in depression was unrelated to changes in marital functioning (see Figure 9.3). Thus, BMT appears to be effective in the treatment of depression primarily in cases in which the couples report marital distress prior to treatment. This finding underscores the heterogeneous nature of depression, and provides empirical support for Beach, Sandeen, and O'Leary's (1990) suggestion that marital therapy may be most effective in the treatment of those depressions occurring in the context of marital discord.

Two recently developed interpersonal approaches to the treatment of depression have yielded promising results. Klerman et al. (1984) describe their Interpersonal Psychotherapy (IPT) for depression, which is based on the assumption (corroborated by the findings of empirical investigations reviewed in Chapters 6 and 7) that depression can result from, and lead to, difficulties in the interpersonal relationships among depressed persons and their significant others. IPT, therefore, attempts both to alleviate depressive symptoms and to improve interpersonal functioning by "clarifying, refocusing, and renegotiating the interpersonal context associated with the onset of depression" (Weissman & Klerman,

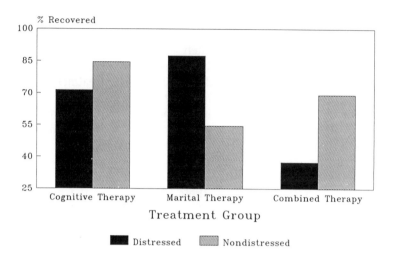

Figure 9.3   Clinical significance of BDI change: pretest to posttest. Source: adapted from Jacobson, Dobson, Fruzetti, Schmaling, and Salusky (1991)

1990). IPT is a brief, weekly therapy taking from 12 to 16 weeks to complete. The first goal, relieving acute depressive symptoms, is addressed through educating the patient about the nature and course of depression. Psychopharmacological approaches may be used in conjunction with IPT to achieve more rapid symptom reduction.

The second goal, improving the depressed patient's interpersonal functioning, is accomplished by exploring with the patient one or more of the following problem areas commonly associated with the onset of depression: grief, role disputes, role transition, or interpersonal deficit. Information is gathered concerning the patient's functioning in these areas. Klerman et al. (1984) discuss specific goals and procedures to deal with each of the four problem areas. In general, however, IPT therapists make use of nondirective exploration, encourage expression of affect, teach the patient more effective methods of interpersonal communication, and attempt to alter depressive behaviors. It is important to note that, despite its name and focus, IPT is conducted with patients individually, rather than conjointly with their spouses or other family members.

A number of studies have now been conducted examining the efficacy of IPT in the treatment of major depression. DiMascio, Weissman, Prusoff, Neu, Zwilling, and Klerman (1979) and Weissman, Prusoff, DiMascio, Neu, Goklaney, and Klerman (1979) have demonstrated that IPT is as effective as pharmacotherapy in reducing depressive symptomatology, and is more effective than pharmacotherapy in improving interpersonal functioning. Furthermore, at a one-year follow-up, patients who had received IPT alone or in combination with pharmacotherapy demonstrated significantly better social functioning than did patients who had received only pharmacotherapy (Weissman, Klerman, Prusoff, Sholomskas, & Padian, 1981). Frank, Kupfer, and Perel (1989) demonstrated that IPT was more effective than maintenance imiprimine in reducing the recurrence of new episodes in the treatment of chronic recurrent depressions. Of the patients receiving maintenance medication, 50% experienced a recurrence of depression by 21 weeks. In contrast, it took 61 weeks for 50% of the patients receiving IPT to experience a recurrence of depression. As we discussed in greater detail in the previous chapter, recent data from the NIMH Treatment of Depression Collaborative Research Program indicate that although IPT was as effective as cognitive therapy and pharmacotherapy in the reduction of depressive symptoms, patients treated by IPT achieved more rapid gains in interpersonal functioning (Elkin et al., 1989). Interestingly, IPT also had the lowest attrition rate in the study.

Foley, Rounsaville, Weissman, Sholomskas, and Chevron (1989) recently reported results of a study designed to compare the effects of IPT conducted with and without the explicit involvement of the depressed person's spouse. Foley et al. randomly assigned 18 depressed outpatients to either individual IPT or a newly developed couple format version of IPT. In sessions with the spouse, the functioning of the couple is assessed in five general areas: communication, intimacy, boundary management, leadership, and attainment of socially appropriate goals. Particular difficulties in any of these areas are noted, and treatment is focused on bringing about improved functioning in these areas.

Foley et al. (1989) found that the inclusion of the spouse in cases where there were ongoing marital disputes was well received by patients and, even in their small sample, resulted in marginally greater improvement in the marital relationship than did the standard individual format for IPT. On the other hand, both formats produced significant and comparable reductions in symptoms of depression. These results suggest that the findings obtained by O'Leary and Beach (1990) and replicated by Jacobson et al. (1991) may be generalizable to other couple formats as well. That is, direct attention to dyadic processes in structured directive couples therapy may enhance marital functioning while providing relief of depressive symptomatology that is comparable to standard individual treatments. Because follow-up data were not reported, this study does not address the relative merits of the two formats with respect to the maintenance of treatment gains. Nevertheless, it appears that continued examination of conjoint IPT is warranted.

The second interpersonal approach to therapy for depression is Inpatient Family Intervention (IFI; Clarkin, Haas, & Glick, 1988), developed for the treatment of depressed inpatients. This intervention is a brief psychoeducational and problem-focused family treatment aimed at helping patients and their families to accept and understand the current illness and hospitalization, and at identifying possible precipitating stressors, both within and outside of the family. IFI also attempts to identify family interaction patterns that may produce stress for the patient, and to help the family plan strategies to minimize potential future stresses.

The strategies and techniques utilized to achieve these goals involve psychoeducation, task-oriented interventions, and problem-solving. Given the brief nature of this intervention and the hospitalized status of the patients, little emphasis is placed on psychodynamic or structural family therapy strategies. Depressed patients and relevant family members meet regularly during the patient's hospitalization, with a family therapist and the patient's primary therapist acting as cotherapists.

In the first report of the efficacy of IFI, Glick, Clarkin, Spencer, Haas, et al. (1985) randomly assigned 54 schizophrenic and 47 depressed inpatients either to standard hospital treatment, which included individual, group, and milieu activities, and somatic therapy, or to standard treatment plus IFI. The IFI patients participated in at least six one-hour family sessions. The goals of these sessions included the identification of precipitating and/or future stressors, identification of stressful family interactions and strategies for dealing with these interactions, and acceptance of the need for continuing treatment. Glick et al. reported that, at discharge as well as at the six-month follow-up, there were no significant treatment differences for the depressed patients. The schizophrenic patients with good prehospital functioning, however, demonstrated a more favorable response to IFI, exhibiting better global outcomes at discharge.

In the second report on a somewhat larger sample, Haas, Glick, Clarkin, Spencer, Lewis, et al. (1988) provided greater detail concerning group differences in treatment outcome at discharge. Although IFI was found to be generally more effective than standard hospital treatment, female patients, particularly depressed female patients, appeared to benefit more from this form of treatment than did male patients. This pattern of results was also maintained at 6- and 18-month follow-ups, at which time female schizophrenic and depressed inpatients and their families demonstrated greater improvement with IFI than did their male counterparts (Clarkin, Haas, & Glick, 1988; Spencer, Glick, Haas, Clarkin, Lewis, et al., 1988). Finally, Clarkin, Haas, and Glick (1988) note that IFI was more effective in the treatment of bipolar than of unipolar depressed patients. In general, therefore, IFI seems most effective in the treatment of female schizophrenic and bipolar depressed inpatients.

Finally, Gotlib and Colby (1987) recently presented an interpersonal systems approach to the conceptualization of depression, and outlined explicit strategies and procedures to be used in assessing and treating depressed patients and their spouses. In terms of assessment, Gotlib and Colby suggest that three specific aspects of depressed patients' functioning be examined in a comprehensive assessment: the symptomatology manifested by the patients, their current cognitive functioning, and the nature and quality of their current interpersonal behavior. As we noted in Chapter 4, a number of psychometrically sound measures are available to assess these aspects of the patients' functioning. For example, to assess depressive symptomatology, clinicians can use the SADS, complemented by the self-report BDI. The cognitive functioning of depressed patients can be assessed with the DAS and the ASQ. Finally, there are a number of measures available to assess various aspects of the depressed patient's interpersonal functioning, some of which we discussed earlier in this chapter, as well as others, such as the self-report Social Support Questionnaire (Sarason, Levine, Basham, & Sarason, 1983) and the clinician-rated Social Adjustment Scale (Weissman & Paykel, 1974). In addition to the use of these measures, the clinician should also observe the interactions of patients and their spouses and families, both to gain a more complete understanding of the nature and quality of the depressed patients' interactions and to identify potential targets for intervention.

In terms of treatment, Gotlib and Colby (1987) emphasize that the principles and strategies utilized by the therapist to alleviate the patients' depression should focus on both cognitive and interpersonal functioning. Briefly, with respect to cognitive functioning, as we noted in the previous chapter, the therapist must recognize that depressed individuals demonstrate increased attention and sensitivity to negative aspects of their environment. A major goal in working individually with depressed patients, therefore, is to attenuate this accessibility to negative stimuli. This goal is typically accomplished through education and making the patients aware of how they are processing information, and of how this manner of processing affects their perceptions of their interactions with others. It is also important to help depressed individuals become more accurate in monitoring their own and other people's behaviors. Keeping daily records and increasing the number of pleasurable experiences in which they engage are useful procedures in meeting this objective.

Treatment strategies and procedures aimed at improving the depressed patients' interpersonal functioning are more complex. Gotlib and Colby (1987) conceptualize depression as involving not only the depressed person, but also people with whom they have an intimate relationship (most typically, their spouses and families). Consequently, attempts to alleviate the depression also often involve concomitant changes in the interpersonal system. It is to the therapist's benefit, therefore, to have a working knowledge of principles of General Systems Theory (GST; von Bertalanffy, 1968). GST is based on a group of assumptions regarding the organizational properties of systems. According to this theory, a complex interactional system (e.g. a couple or a family) is more than a collection of separate parts. Consequently, a system can only be fully understood by examining the relations among the various components. No part of a system can move or change without affecting all of the other elements in the system. Indeed, a deviation in the behavior of one family member is often a reaction to some change in another member's behavior, which in turn leads to additional changes. Seen from this perspective, the development of problems is conceptualized as interactional rather than intrapsychic in nature, and all members of the family system, rather than only the depressed patient, are viewed as being involved in the maintenance and modification of the depression.

Gotlib and Colby describe a number of intervention strategies and procedures, derived from systems theory, in outlining an interpersonal systems approach to the treatment of depression. The primary goal of this therapy is to stimulate new patterns of communication and behavioral sequences that interrupt the depression-maintaining interactions that brought the depressed person into therapy. In general, therefore, interpersonal systems therapy focuses on the present rather than on historical events, with the therapist adopting an active, problem-solving approach to treatment. The therapist typically broadens the focus of treatment from the depressed patient in order to involve as much of the system (i.e. the marital dyad or the family) as possible in therapy.

Finally, Gotlib and Colby (1987) specify circumstances under which the spouses or relatives of depressed individuals should be involved in therapy and describe the effective use of a number of techniques and procedures that the systems-oriented therapist can utilize to initiate change in depressed patients and their families. They describe such therapeutic procedures as joining, enactment, reframing, restructuring, altering family boundaries, and emphasizing the couple's or family's strengths. Although additional empirical work is required to refine these techniques and to further validate the efficacy of this intervention, the results of preliminary work utilizing this interpersonal systems approach to the treatment of depression are promising.

CONCLUDING COMMENTS

We have attempted in this chapter to provide the reader with an overview of principles, strategies, and procedures involved in behaviorally- and interpersonally-oriented approaches to the assessment and treatment of depression. These approaches to intervention have not received as much empirical and theoretical attention as have the cognitive therapies we reviewed in the previous chapter. Thus, issues that have been at the center of debates in the cognitive therapy literature, such as those concerning mechanisms of action of therapy, specificity and generalizability of treatment effects, range of application of treatment, and differential efficacy of treatment for various patient characteristics, have not yet been explored systematically with these approaches to treatment.

One important issue that clearly warrants attention in future investigations involves the differential importance of marital discord and depression in affecting the efficacy of interpersonally-oriented therapy. On the basis of the results of their research, Beach, Sandeen, and O'Leary (1990) suggest that marital therapy for depression will be ineffective in the absence of marital discord. Indeed, data reported by Jacobson et al. (1991) corroborate this position. Nevertheless, in those couples who are experiencing both depression and marital distress, it will be essential to ascertain the relative contribution of these two constructs to the success of treatment (cf. O'Leary Riso, & Beach, 1990). Similarly, there is little question that the functional relation between depression and interpersonal difficulties varies from patient to patient (although O'Leary, Riso, and Beach, 1990, present data indicating that most depressed, maritally distressed women believe that their marital difficulties preceded and caused their depression). It will be important, therefore, that the causal nature of this relation be assessed more systematically with respect to its impact on the outcome of therapy.

There are other issues that must also be addressed by investigators interested in examining the efficacy of interpersonal therapies for depression. For example, we do not know what subtypes of depressed patients' interpersonal therapies are most effective. Similarly, we do not know under what conditions cognitive therapies might be best integrated with interpersonal interventions (cf. Gotlib & Colby, 1987; Safran, 1990a,b). Furthermore, given the broad interpersonal context of marital and family approaches to the treatment of depression, it is clear that we have barely begun to examine the range of effects of these therapies, not only with respect to the patients' depression, but in terms of the patients' interpersonal functioning, their relationships with their spouses and children, and the impact of treatment on the children's psychosocial functioning. Finally, in this chapter we have reviewed research examining the efficacy of interpersonally-oriented interventions in alleviating depression. The use of interpersonal therapies in the prevention of depression is an area of investigation that also warrants serious consideration.

Despite the recency of interpersonal approaches to the treatment of depression, it is clear from our review that therapy focusing on altering the relationship between depressed patients and their social environment, and interventions involving the spouse or family of the depressed patient in therapy, represent promising directions in the treatment of this disorder. From the results of studies reviewed in Chapter 8, it is apparent that individual cognitive therapy has repeatedly been demonstrated to be effective in reducing patients' levels of depressive symptomatology. The results of investigations reviewed in this chapter, however, suggest that cognitive therapy may be less effective in ameliorating difficulties in marital and family functioning. In contrast, marital therapy has been demonstrated in several studies to achieve both symptom relief and a reduction in marital discord, particularly when the discord preceded the onset of the depression. Moreover, the few studies that have reported data addressing the long-term effectiveness of marital therapy suggest that the initial improvement in interpersonal functioning is maintained for at least one year. These data are important, given the results of studies implicating marital and family discord in relapse of depression. For example, it is possible that through its positive influence on family functioning, interpersonal therapy may prove to be more effective than individual therapy in the prevention of further depressive episodes. This hypothesis, of course, awaits additional research.

In the context of the review of cognitive and interpersonal functioning in depressed persons that we have presented in the past several chapters, we now turn to the final chapter, in which we present a cognitive-interpersonal formulation of depression.

Chapter 10

Toward a Cognitive-Interpersonal Conceptualization of Depression

In this final chapter we will present an approach to the understanding of nonbipolar depression that draws on, and integrates, theory and research that we have reviewed throughout this book concerning the cognitive and interpersonal functioning of depressed persons. We will outline a framework that considers both cognitive and interpersonal aspects of depression, and that emphasizes distinctions among processes and factors involved in vulnerability to depression, in the etiology and maintenance of depression, in recovery from this disorder, and in relapse of depression. We will also examine the utility of this framework for addressing some of the issues and implications that we raised in Chapter 1, particularly those involving the elevated incidence of depression among women. Finally, we will discuss what we believe are fruitful directions that should be taken by investigators examining psychological aspects of depression in order that the field might make significant and integrative advances.

PROPOSITIONS BASED ON RELEVANT RESEARCH AND THEORY

Several general propositions form the assumptive basis of more specific hypotheses of an integrated cognitive-interpersonal model of depression.

1. *Cognitive mediation.* We assume that depression commonly results from negative interpretations of events and circumstances and beliefs about the worth and efficacy of the self. Depressed mood is a specific consequence—as well as a cause—of such negative cognitive content and processes. Vulnerability to depression occurs, in part, as a product of schematically organized representations of the self, others, and the world that emphasize personal inadequacy, devaluation or lack of responsiveness from others, and inability to obtain desired goals. Cognition is also implicated in coping reactions.

2. *Context and transactions.* Depression arises in a context of social and

environmental resources and behavioral competencies. These resources and competencies have been neglected in cognitive and biological formulations of depression. While negative cognitions may be the immediate trigger of depressed mood, the environmental context may activate the cognitions. Further, the extent of depression and its duration are determined in part by the individual's transactions with the environment, including reciprocal influences between behaviors and cognitions of the person and of other people and events in the environment. Vulnerability to depression, in part, is a function of the environment that has been created by the person and by the available skills and resources, of which interpersonal relations are especially important.

3. *Triggering events and circumstances*. Most depressions are reactions to events and circumstances. As we noted in Chapter 6, such circumstances may be contributed, at least in part, by the person, particularly in his or her interpersonal transactions with others. Events, whether they are episodic major events, fateful occurrences beyond a person's control, ongoing life difficulties, or even minor daily hassles, have their impact through the person's interpretations of their meaning and access to personal and environmental resources.

4. *Biological factors*. The contribution of biological factors to vulnerability to depression is assumed, but poorly understood at this time. It is likely that individual variations in neurohormonal processes influence the degree and duration of depressive reactions. Such processes may be genetically transmitted, or may arise from neurochemical changes and sensitivities arising from early traumatic experiences. The interaction of biological and psychological processes is an important area for future study.

5. *Heterogeneity of depressive processes*. It is assumed that there are multiple kinds of unipolar depression; consequently, it is also assumed that there are various etiological pathways to depression. The approach we describe in this chapter is potentially most relevant to early-onset, recurring depressions; in contrast, late-onset, single-episode, or mostly biologically-instigated depressions might involve only some of these processes. We cannot specify the precise range of application of the present model, in part because of limitations in our knowledge of subtypes of depression. Indeed, it is important that we take the heterogeneity of depression into account and acknowledge that the present approach is not intended to apply to all nonbipolar depression.

DEVELOPMENT OF DEPRESSION

In discussing the development of nonbipolar depression, we must emphasize the importance of distinguishing among four potentially different sets of factors and processes: (a) those factors that may place an individual at elevated risk or vulnerability for the development of nonbipolar depression; (b) those processes involved in the onset of a depressive episode; (c) those processes responsible for maintaining an episode of depression; and (d) those factors responsible for recurrence of depression. In making these distinctions, we will propose a formulation of depression, presented graphically in Figure 10.1. We begin our discussion with an examination of vulnerability factors that may place an individual at increased risk for depression.

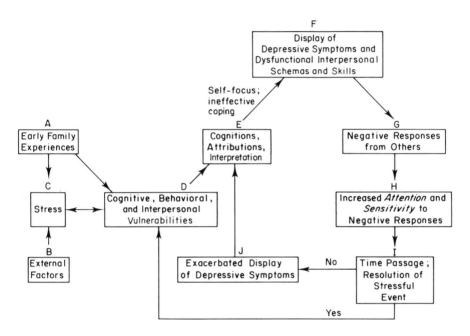

Figure 10.1   Cognitive-interpersonal conceptualization of depression

Vulnerability to depression

In this section of the chapter we discuss psychological factors and processes that may place individuals at elevated risk for experiencing one or more episodes of depression (Box D in Figure 10.1). Because we will focus in a later section on factors involved proximally in the onset of a depressive episode, we will concentrate in this section on more distal factors.

We offer three general propositions concerning vulnerability to depression:

1. *Adverse parent-child experiences contribute to the acquisition of negative cognitive representations (schemas, or working models) of the self and others.*
2. *Such negative schemas and exposure to dysfunctional parenting profoundly affect interpersonal behaviors and skills.*
3. *Childhood experiences contribute to the formation of goals and propositions concerning what is necessary for the attainment of self-worth and satisfaction.*

As a consequence of these processes the developing child acquires schemas about the self, others, and the world that have the potential for negative emotional consequences. The individual also acquires interpersonal skills and motives that may also contribute to the risk for depression to the extent that: (a) dysfunctional relationships may be entered; (b) dysfunctional conflict resolution skills may be acquired; and (c) inadequate skills for attaining gratification and support may be developed. Furthermore, the individual may acquire vulnerability to certain types of negative events, in the sense of overvaluing certain kinds of goals, or defining one's worth and competence in terms of particular outcomes. In the following sections we briefly review theory and research that support these propositions. We also attempt to indicate where there are important gaps in the research, and suggest areas in which further study is required in order to establish the empirical validity of the current framework.

The results of research we reviewed earlier in this book clearly suggest that individuals who become depressed have experienced more adverse early family environments than have nondepressed persons (Box A in Figure 10.1). Several early studies implicated the early loss of a parent as a significant risk factor for depression (e.g. Brown, 1961; Frommer & O'Shea, 1973). As we discussed in Chapter 7, the results of more recent research suggest that the quality of care that replaces a loss may be more important in placing an individual at risk for depression later in life than the loss itself (e.g. Bifulco, Brown, & Harris, 1987; Breier et al., 1988). Indeed, even in situations in which there was not a loss of a parent, researchers have found that the early family environments of persons who developed an episode of depression were more negative than were those of nondepressed controls (e.g. Blatt et al., 1979; Crook, Raskin, & Eliot, 1981; Gotlib, Whiffen, et al., 1991; Hammen, 1991a). Moreover, this pattern of results does not appear to be due simply to a negative response bias on the part of depressed persons (cf. Brewin, Andrews, & Gotlib, in press; Gotlib et al., 1988).

Given these data, there is little question that the early experiences of persons who are later to become depressed are more difficult than are the early experiences of individuals who remain nondepressed. These early adverse experiences, therefore, appear to represent a vulnerability factor for depression, placing individuals at increased risk for the development of this disorder. In this context, it becomes important to try to understand the *processes* or *mechanisms* by which these early experiences may function as risk factors. For example, one significant implication of early loss of a parent or inadequate early care is that the infant or child may develop weak or insecure attachments to the parents, and it may be this inadequate early attachment that places individuals at risk for subsequent depression. A second, but related, implication is that early adverse interpersonal experiences lead to the development of specific personality characteristics that render individuals particularly susceptible to developing episodes of depression later in life. We discuss these two possibilities in greater detail below.

Attachment difficulties and subsequent depression

As we described in Chapter 3, Bowlby (1969, 1978, 1981) proposed that the formation of intimate emotional bonds is a basic and biologically necessary aspect of human nature. Such attachments ensure proximity of the helpless infant to the protective mother and, therefore, provide for the security and survival of the infant. The nature of the attachment bond between the infant and primary caregiver determines major elements of the child's personality and development through its contribution to the formation of cognitive representations of the self and others in the world ("working models"). To the extent that the caregiver (usually the mother) is reliably available, sensitive, and responsive to the infant's needs, she provides a secure base for the developing child's exploration of the world, and protection from overwhelming stress. She also reflects back to the child that he or she is accepted, valued, and worthwhile. Provided a safe base from which to explore and a positive view of the self as reflected in the mother's attitudes, the child presumably experiences him- or herself as desirable and competent, and views others as trustworthy and responsive. Accordingly, the child's behaviors reflect such internal representations, and are exploratory, independence- and mastery-oriented, and prosocial. The interactions between positive expectations and competence experiences unfold developmentally over the life span, influencing not only childhood development but also adult experiences such as work and romantic attachments, profoundly influencing not only competence, but also persistence and problem-solving ability.

Depression is viewed as the child's reaction to "loss" of the parent through separation or emotional unavailability; the security of the child's attachment determines the response to such a loss. An insecurely attached child, who acquires negative working models of the self and the world (conceptually similar to negative schemata) as a result of maternal rejection or inconsistent maternal responsiveness, would experience parental loss as more devastating than would a child whose secure base is well established.

Moreover, the quality of the cognitive representations of the self, as reflected in the mother's behaviors and attitudes toward the developing infant, establishes the degree of vulnerability to depression due to self-devaluation and negative expectations of the self's ability to achieve important goals. An insecurely attached infant might become an anxious or avoidant toddler, whose mastery, social competence, and problem-solving capabilities are impeded because of cognitive representations of the self as undesirable, and of the world and others as depriving, rejecting, or unreliable.

Based on this theoretical formulation, we speculate that *attachment difficulties and/or other adverse early experiences result in negative cognitive schemata or working models, and in personality characteristics involving elevated dependency needs, both of which may serve to increase the risk of subsequent depression.*

Certainly, Bowlby's emphasis on the mother-child bond as a fundamental element in psychological adjustment was hardly novel. Nevertheless, it departs from more traditional psychoanalytic or object relations formulations both by emphasizing the acquisition of cognitive representations as mediators of the effects of parenting, and by encouraging empirical and systematic evaluation of relevant hypotheses. Subsequent to Bowlby's formulations, numerous investigators have confirmed important elements of the model. For instance, Ainsworth and her colleagues developed the "Strange Situation," a behavioral method for operationalizing infants' attachment quality, by observing separation and reunion behaviors as expressions of the child's felt security (e.g. Ainsworth, Blehar, Waters, & Wall, 1978). Presumably a stressful situation, separation-reunion provides an opportunity to observe the child's experience of the degree to which he or she can rely on the attachment figure as a source of security by assessing the level of distress, reactions to the mother when she returns, and ease of being comforted.

Other investigators have used this paradigm and have demonstrated that attachment quality is relatively stable from infancy through preschool, and is related to various indicators of adjustment and competence in the child (e.g. Egeland & Farber, 1984; Erickson, Sroufe, & Egeland, 1985; Main, Kaplan, & Cassidy, 1985; Sroufe, 1979; a complete review of the attachment research is beyond the scope of this chapter, but see Bretherton & Waters, 1985, and Greenberg, Cicchetti, & Cummings, 1990). Type of attachment pattern is also predictable from quality of maternal responsiveness (e.g. Ainsworth et al., 1978; Egeland & Farber, 1984; Waters, Vaughn, & Egeland, 1980): more secure patterns of attachment are associated with sensitive, responsive parenting, while insecure attachment patterns are associated with rejecting, hostile, rigid, unexpressive behaviors.

It is instructive to note that gender differences in attachment that have been reported by investigators in this area are consistent with the elevated prevalence of depression among women. Typically, insecure attachment is associated in boys with avoidance, and in girls with anxiety. These two types of attachment have implications for functioning in interpersonal relationships. For example, males, who are avoidant, will tend to deny the significance of relationships, and will be (superficially, at least) unaffected by difficulties in interpersonal functioning. In contrast, females, who are anxious, will be hypervigilant and extremely sensitive to perceived problems in their social relationships. Females, therefore, will also tend to be more dependent in terms of their personality characteristics. This differential pattern of functioning will continue to be reinforced by traditional socialization practices.

Bowlby and others have emphasized the continuity of attachment-based characteristics of intimate relationships throughout the lifespan (e.g. Ainsworth, 1989; Bowlby, 1969, 1978, 1981, 1988; Main, Kaplan, & Cassidy, 1985). Although the person's internal working models are constantly affected by his or her transactions with the world, it is assumed that attachments with parents and with intimate partners in adolescence and adulthood continue to reflect the imprint of the early attachment experiences with the primary caregiver. Indeed, some support is emerging for attachment classification beyond childhood and its predicted correlates (e.g. Bartholomew & Horowitz, 1991; Collins & Read, 1990; Hazan & Shaver, 1987; Kobak & Sceery, 1988; Main, Kaplan, & Cassidy, 1985).

Nevertheless, many issues remain unresolved. For example, it is not clear which patterns of insecure attachment can be identified and reliably rated (reviewed in Cummings, 1990; see also Bartholomew, 1990). There is also controversy about what methods are appropriate for identifying adult attachment characteristics, ranging from psychodynamically-inferential interviews to self-report questionnaires.

Another unresolved matter concerns the specific association between parent-child attachment quality and vulnerability for depression. Recent research involving attachment relationships between depressed mothers and infants, including samples at risk due to maternal affective disorder, have found evidence of insecure attachment in such offspring. Radke-Yarrow et al. (1985) found a higher proportion of insecurely attached children among unipolar and bipolar depressed women compared with nondepressed women (see also Zahn-Waxler, Cummings, Iannotti, & Radke-Yarrow, 1984). Other investigations of families at risk due to sociocultural disadvantage or child maltreatment have also found evidence of relatively high proportions of insecurely attached children (e.g. Carlson, Cicchetti, Barnett & Braunwald, 1989; Egeland & Sroufe, 1981; Lyons-Ruth et al. 1986; Spieker & Booth, 1988). In addition to being stressed by socioeconomic conditions, many of the women in these studies were also depressed. Presumably the depressed mother is emotionally unavailable and therefore unresponsive or even rejecting of her infant's or child's efforts to elicit proximity and connection (cf. Lee & Gotlib, 1991b). Several of the studies have reported that the insecure attachment of the children in these high-risk situations is accompanied by signs of dysphoria and internalizing disorders, as well as some instances of externalizing and conduct disorders.

Despite the evidence of dysfunction in insecurely attached children, and of insecure attachments in offspring of depressed and stressed mothers, there is as yet no direct link between attachment and depressive disorders in children and adults. Nevertheless, the research that we reviewed in Chapter 7 concerning the recalled and observed dysfunctional parenting associated with depressive symptoms in children and adults is clearly consistent with this approach. Recently, Cummings and Cicchetti (1990) have specifically articulated a developmental psychopathology theory of depression with origins in the dysfunctional attachments of children and their mothers.

As Cummings and Cicchetti (1990) note, the case of the attachment approach to depression will be strengthened if it can be demonstrated that the cognitive and emotional sequelae of early insecure attachment contribute to later depression. Specifically, we need to examine the links among depressogenic cognitions, attachment, and later symptoms. Bowlby's model emphasizes the cognitive representations of the self and others that are formed in the context of the mother-child relationship (and see also Main, Kaplan, & Cassidy, 1985, for further elaboration of the cognitive emphasis). To date, however, there has been relatively little systematic development of measures of cognitive representations of the mother, the self, the world, and others. Although there have been inferential methods based on interviews (e.g. Kobak & Sceery, 1988; Main, Kaplan, & Cassidy, 1985), further development of alternative and more accessible methods is clearly required.

Research linking parenting, self-concept, and stress

Most of the research that supports a developmental psychopathology model of depression has not specifically used an attachment theory base. However, work by Brown and his colleagues, and also by Hammen and her colleagues, supports the value of linking early childhood experiences with stressors and subsequent depression. For instance, Brown, Bifulco, and Harris (1987; see also Harris, Brown, & Bifulco, 1987) determined that risk for depression was increased not only by exposure to severe proximal life events (Box B in Figure 10.1), but also by several additional (and more distal) predisposing factors. Among these factors were early loss of a parent that was accompanied by poor care, and subsequent premarital pregnancy, marital distress, and negative evaluation of the self.

Hammen (1991a; Hammen, Burge, Brown, & Stansbury, 1991) extended the study of children of depressed women to include intergenerational transmission of depression, and found support for a complex causal model of depression. The depressed woman's exposure to dysfunctional (psychiatrically ill—mostly depressed) parents predicted her own maladaptive parenting and her marriage to a man with diagnosable disorder. These factors, in turn, predicted children's social competence and children's own stressful life events, which in turn predicted their depressive symptomatology. We might further speculate that the children of depressed women who became symptomatic are themselves at risk for maladaptive parenting and dysfunctional marriage. It is also noteworthy that children's self-concepts were significantly related to both their perceived and observed relationship with their mothers (Jaenicke, Hammen, Zupan, Hiroto, Gordon, et al., 1987).

Although comprising limited evidence, these studies underscore the importance of linking adult depression to early childhood experiences and to the role of the latter in contributing to adverse life events. Adverse life events may include dysfunctional parenting and marital relationships, thus providing a mechanism for understanding why depression runs in families. A second mechanism that might account for the link between early childhood experiences and adult depression involves the role of certain personality characteristics in rendering individuals particularly susceptible to developing episodes of depression later in life. In the following section we explore this possibility in greater detail.

Personality characteristics and depression

The depressive personality has a long theoretical and clinical history in psychiatry (Phillips, Gunderson, Hirschfeld, & Smith, 1990). More recently, psychoanalytic theories of object relations as well as theories of social-cognitive development are consistent with the position outlined above that the child's relationships with his or her parents result in the development of working models of the self and of relationships with others. As we noted, early aversive childhood experiences of depressed individuals may have resulted in the development of self-schemas that are characterized by low self-worth, and may have led these individuals to develop expectations of interpersonal negativity and rejection. According to both psychodynamic and social-cognitive theories of the self, such negative cognitive/affective structures may leave individuals with chronically low self-esteem, persistent interpersonal problems, and at risk for developing depression when faced with life stressors. Indeed, developmentally acquired traits, such as interpersonal dependency and labile self-esteem, have been identified in clinical case studies as being characteristic of the personalities of people who are prone to depression (see reviews by Chodoff, 1972; Hirschfeld,

Klerman, Chodoff, Korchin, & Barrett, 1976). Vulnerable individuals are hypothesized to depend primarily on the love and attention of others for the maintenance of their fragile self-esteem. When these extreme dependency needs are frustrated, the resulting threat to self-worth is defended against by increasing demands for support, or by denying interpersonal dependency and developing obsessive, perfectionistic tendencies. Thus, these two traits of dependency and perfectionism are thought to share a common etiology of excessive dependency needs.

As we discussed in Chapter 6, a number of theorists have implicated these two personality traits in attempts to explain why individuals differ in their reactions to stressful life events. Beck (1983), for example, has labelled these traits "sociotropy" and "autonomy," and argues that these traits may predispose individuals to develop depression in response to specific types of life stressors. Sociotropy refers to the beliefs, attitudes and goals that draw an individual to other individuals. Thus, sociotropic individuals, typically females, place a great deal of importance on interpersonal relationships and judge their self-worth according to the amount of acceptance and affection they receive from others. When confronted with a threat to the stability of interpersonal relationships (e.g. separation, threatened rejection), or an interpersonal loss (e.g. the break-up of a love relationship, the death of a loved one), such individuals are at risk for developing depression (Beck, 1983). Indeed, Hirschfeld and his colleagues have demonstrated that depressed persons are more interpersonally dependent than are nondepressed persons (e.g. Hirschfeld, Klerman, Clayton, & Keller, 1983; Reich, Noyes, Hirschfeld, Coryell, & O'Gorman, 1987; see Barnett & Gotlib, 1988b). Moreover, even after they are no longer symptomatic, remitted depressives continue to report elevated emotional dependency.

In contrast to sociotropy, autonomy refers to beliefs and attitudes concerning achievement, personal freedom, and control over the environment. Autonomous individuals are likely to evaluate their self-worth in terms of personal accomplishments and control over their environment. When confronted with a threat to independence or autonomy (e.g. loss of a job, failure to achieve a desired goal), such individuals are at risk for developing depression (cf. Beck, 1983).

Descriptions of a similar dichotomy of traits associated with depression have been presented by other theorists. Although the personality styles identified by these theorists appear to be similar, different terms have been used to describe them. For example, Blatt and his colleagues (e.g. Blatt, 1974; Blatt, D'Affliti, & Quinlan, 1976) discuss anaclitic, or dependent, and introjective, or self-critical traits, and Arieti and Bemporad (1980) conceptualize these traits in terms of "dominant other" and "dominant goal." Although the tendencies characterized by these two traits are postulated to be dominant modes of personality, they may nevertheless coexist within a single individual. Both personality modes are hypothesized to predispose an individual to depression. These theorists suggest that whereas the dependent person is particularly at risk when sources of interpersonal support are threatened, the autonomous individual is sensitive to setbacks in goal attainment.

In sum, therefore, there is reasonably consistent evidence indicating that persons who become depressed have an elevated incidence of adverse early experiences in which there is early perceived loss or lack of emotional support that is experienced by the child as being outside of his or her control. For some individuals these childhood experiences might involve parental death or separation at an early age; for others, they may consist of parental discord, rejection, emotional neglect, or abuse. These experiences lead to attachment difficulties, with the child developing the kinds of "working models" or cognitive "schemas" concerning the self and others that we have argued may represent one prerequisite or vulnerability factor for the development of depression. Indeed, as we shall see, these schemas are critical factors in the onset and maintenance of this disorder.

In addition, we have argued that these adverse early experiences may lead the individual to develop certain personality characteristics, such as elevated dependency needs, that also increase the risk for the subsequent development of depression. We also assume, based in part on studies of attachment and children's social adjustment and on data concerning child and adolescent correlates of depression, that interpersonal behaviors are also adversely affected. This impairment may take the form of an inadequate repertoire of skills for social problem-solving or for achieving and maintaining supportive and gratifying social relationships. Finally, because these characteristics are relatively stable factors, these vulnerable individuals are clearly at risk for experiencing multiple episodes of depression, a point consistent with the recurrent nature of this disorder. We turn now to an examination of processes involved in the onset of a depressive episode.

Onset of depression

The following general propositions guide our conceptualization of the onset of depression

1. *Stressful events and circumstances are the trigger for most depressive reactions.* Most people do not become depressed, other than temporarily, even when truly dire events occur. As we argued earlier, vulnerable individuals' tendency to interpret the events in particular, negative, ways is essential for the onset of clinically significant depression.

2. *Cognitive vulnerability leads to the interpretation of the events or*

circumstances in depressive ways. As indicated previously, cognitive vulnerability to depression consists of negative schemas about the self that lead to the interpretation of the event as depleting one's worth and representing an inability to attain important sources of gratification. Note that this proposition distinguishes what is unique about a depressive reaction to a stressor, given ample evidence that stressors can also lead to anxiety, can trigger other psychopathology in relevantly-vulnerable individuals, or can cause or exacerbate medical conditions. The specificity for depression is hypothesized to reside in interpretations of personal worthlessness without means of obtaining needed sources of validation of self-worth.

3. *For many individuals, the cognitive vulnerability is specifically interpersonal, based on dependency needs and goals.* While any kind of event that is interpreted to mean depletion of self-worth and efficacy may lead to depression, interpersonal events may be especially "loaded" for individuals who have experienced adverse early childhood relations with significant others.

4. *While "fateful" events that are beyond the control of an individual may trigger depression in a cognitively vulnerable person, the role of the person in contributing to the environment and interpersonal context of their lives should not be overlooked as a source of negative events.* While the generation of stressors may be especially relevant to recurring or chronic depression, it is important to accord attention to "vulnerable environments."

5. *Many depressive histories begin in childhood; many others begin in adolescence or early adulthood.* Certain kinds of developmental transitions may be viewed as potentially challenging, especially to depression-vulnerable young people. These transitions are likely to include relationship losses, separation from parents, and perceived failures to attain such age-related goals as peer acceptance, intimate relationships, and work or academic achievement. Such considerations may contribute to our understanding of certain apparently high-risk groups, such as youth and females.

Our proposed framework for understanding the onset of depression is, therefore, a stress-diathesis approach. Moreover, we must distinguish between a "normal" depressive reaction and a clinically significant episode of depression. We propose that what is covered in this section is a depressive reaction of sufficient magnitude to meet clinical criteria, in contrast to a mild response to stressful conditions. However, the real test of clinical significance is duration; therefore, we will distinguish between mere onset of symptoms, and maintenance of symptoms over a sufficient period of time to result in a diagnosis of major depression (or, possibly, dysthymia). We discuss maintenance factors more extensively in the subsequent section.

The first stage in the onset of depression is the occurrence of an event or stressor that is construed by the individual as a depletion of personal worth (Box C in Figure 10.1). This event can be episodic (having a definite onset and ending), or can be an ongoing chronic condition, a minor hassle, or even an intrapsychic event, such as a memory or an anticipation or belief about particular circumstances. For many depressed persons, the event is objectively stressful, although its meaning and implications may be distorted according to preexisting schemas. For others, there may be actual distortion in perception of a minor event that is nonetheless accorded considerable personal significance. The crucial characteristic of the event is how it is interpreted (Box E in Figure 10.1). Depression is thought to be a response to beliefs about self-worth and the inability to obtain self-worth validation. Individuals with preexisting dependency goals or dysfunctional self- and other-representations may be especially susceptible to interpersonal negative events: they may view them as depleting of personal value, and believe that the particular event cannot be repaired and that no alternative source of personal worth validation is available. Note that although this is a form of perceived uncontrollability or hopelessness, it is specific to the repair or gratification of self-worth goals.

According to Beck (1967), events that involve themes of loss or rejection, years later, are postulated to reactivate schemata that developed during childhood, resulting in the negative affect and behavior characteristic of depression. As we noted in Chapter 6, this formulation of a "matching" of event to schema has received fairly consistent empirical support, especially for interpersonal vulnerability (or sociotropy). Because of the nature of the individuals' early negative experiences and their increased dependency, it is likely (but not imperative) that it will be interpersonally-oriented events that are perceived as depleting and without the possibility of resolution or of obtaining alternative self-worth validation, that prove to be most stressful. Thus, Paykel et al.'s (1969) finding that marital turmoil is the most frequently reported event preceding the onset of a depressive episode is consistent with this formulation, as is Paykel's (1979) observation that "social exit" events are especially depressing. Similarly, Brown, Bifulco, and Harris's (1987) report that many of the major events preceding depression in community samples were "loss" events, and Vaughn and Leff's (1976a) observation that depressed persons are particularly vulnerable to criticism from their spouses, are also consistent with the prominent role of interpersonal negative events in depression.

In the context of this formulation, and given our arguments in the previous section concerning the differential interpersonal vulnerability of males and females to developing episodes of depression, it is perhaps not surprising to find that the prevalence of depression among females is much higher than that of males. Onset of depression is a function of the interaction of perceived relevant stressors against a background of an elevated vulnerability to this disorder. The incidence of depression will be increased, therefore, to the extent that more stressors are perceived as relevant. Interestingly, data reported by Kessler and McLeod (1984) suggest that females may, in fact, be affected by a wider range of events than are males. That is, females appear to perceive more events as "relevant stressors" than do males. Specifically, Kessler and McLeod found that females are affected by life events that happen to others in their social environment (e.g. family members, neighbors), whereas males are typically affected only by events that happen directly to themselves (see also Whiffen & Gotlib, 1989b). Consequently, women have more opportunities for activation of schemas by relevant events and, therefore, for the onset of depression.

If the individual is unable to cope effectively with the relevant event, he or she may begin to exhibit depressive symptoms as the distress increases, and may also begin to display the dysfunctional interpersonal skills and schemas characteristics of depressed persons (Box F in Figure 10.1). Coping may be a function both of the nature of the instigating event and of the individual's coping skills, both cognitive and behavioral. To whatever extent the person lacks an immediately available coping response, however, he or she may increase the focus on the meaning and unsolvability of the problem. Indeed, Smith and Greenberg (1981), Lewinsohn et al. (1985) and Pyszczynski and Greenberg (1987) have recently proposed that an early symptom of depression is increased self-focus. This attentional style would exacerbate the depressive affect, both by interfering with effective problem-solving coping and by increasing rumination over the persistence of the stressor. In fact, several studies have reported that, compared with their nondepressed counterparts, depressed persons are characterized by less effective coping styles and behaviors. Specifically, depressed individuals have been found to engage in more emotion-focused coping (e.g. Billings & Moos, 1984; Folkman & Lazarus, 1986; Mitchell & Hodson, 1983; Nolen-Hoeksema, 1987). We would speculate, therefore, with Lazarus, that both primary (event-focused) and secondary (coping-focused) appraisal processes are critical in the initial distress response. Indeed, depression onset may be the specific response to the content of the appraisal processes.

In sum, therefore, one major pathway to depression involves the impact of stressful events impinging on individuals who, likely because of adverse early experiences and resultant attachment and personality difficulties, are exceptionally vulnerable to develop depression.

We should make some further comment here about the events and circumstances that trigger depressive reactions. As we argued earlier, stressful life events are not necessarily independent entities that "happen to" vulnerable persons. Rather, these individuals often play a major role in generating stressors in their lives. Women may marry dysfunctional men with whom intimate relationships are difficult, and the potential for loss is great, offering yet another explanation for the elevated prevalence of depression among women. Certain individuals may be excessively dependent on others, or overvalue others' regard for them so that they are susceptible to perceived slights. Interpersonally vulnerable individuals may have unrealistic expectations of others, thereby generating conflict. Moreover, they may lack adequate skills for resolving conflict with peers, family members, bosses, and other individuals. Regardless of whether the stress is internally or externally generated, however, our position is that it interacts with the cognitive style and personality characteristics of vulnerable individuals to lead to the onset of depressive symptoms. We turn our attention now to processes by which initial depressive symptoms in response to interpretations of events may be maintained or exacerbated.

Maintenance of depression

The following two propositions are associated with the maintenance of depression over sufficient time to attain clinical significance.

1. *Interpersonal processes play a critical role in the maintenance and exacerbation of depression.* Not only do depressive symptoms typically elicit negative reactions from others, but the depression-prone person may be especially sensitive to others' rejection. Moreover, cognitive representations of others' availability, as well as interpersonal skills in obtaining and maintaining supportive social relationships, may diminish the actual or perceived resources available to help support the depressed person.

2. *Cognitive processes, based on preexisting vulnerability, also play a role in intensifying and perpetuating depression.* In addition to depressive content described earlier, the organization of depressogenic schemas determines what happens after the initial emotional response to stressors. The likelihood of significant, persisting depression is affected by: (a) the extent to which depressive material is accessible in information networks; (b) the extent to which negative self- and other-representations are absolutistic, as would occur with developmentally early acquisition; and (c) the extent to which competing positive self-representations are unavailable.

Once depressive symptoms appear, two factors may converge to maintain and exacerbate the depression. The first factor is interpersonal, and involves both the expression of the individual's depression, in terms of symptoms and dysfunctional interpersonal schemas and social skills (Box F in Figure 10.1), and the responses of significant others to the depressive's symptomatic behavior (Box G). As the literature we reviewed earlier in this volume clearly indicates, depressed persons are less socially skillful than are their nondepressed counterparts: they use less eye contact in interaction, they talk less, they speak more softly and more monotonously, and they are slower to respond to others' verbalizations. In addition, perhaps because of their increased level of self-focus, the content of the conversational behavior of depressed persons is often negatively toned or overtly hostile, inappropriately self-disclosing, and centered around themes of self- devaluation, sadness, and helplessness. We have noted that depressed persons are characterized by elevated interpersonal dependency, which might manifest itself as "clinginess." We have also reviewed literature indicating that depressed individuals have poor conflict-resolution skills. Thus, when they create interpersonal difficulties through their depressive style and behaviors, they are unlikely to readily resolve these situations. Finally, given the interpersonal style of depressed persons, it is not surprising that the results of a number of investigations that we also reviewed earlier indicate that people are reluctant to interact with a depressed person; in fact, when they do interact they behave negatively toward the depressed individual. Considered collectively, the results of these studies suggest that depressives have an aversive interpersonal style to which others ultimately respond with negativity and rejection.

An additional interpersonal element that may hamper resolution of depression is the limited social resource network that the depression-prone person may experience. As we noted in Chapter 6, research suggests that both the size and quality of the social network may be diminished for depressed individuals, even when they are not depressed. There are numerous unresolved issues in this literature, one of which involves the characteristics of depression-prone persons that limit their interpersonal contacts. In keeping with our general framework, we speculate that the limited interpersonal contacts of depressed persons is a function both of skill deficits and of schema-driven negative representations and expectations of other people that might result in diminished efforts to seek out or maintain social relationships.

The second factor involved in the maintenance of depression, which interacts with these interpersonal processes, concerns the depressed individual's increased accessibility to negative constructs and his or her perceptions and interpretations of negative reactions of others (Box H in Figure 10.1). As we noted earlier, the results of recent investigations indicate that depressed persons are characterized by an elevated accessibility to negative constructs, a "readiness" to perceive or attend to negative aspects of themselves and their environment (e.g. Gotlib & McCann, 1984; Gotlib & Cane, 1987; Gotlib, MacLachlan, & Katz, 1988). Teasdale (1988), for example, contends that when they are in a depressed state, some individuals experience increased accessibility to negative constructs:

> ... if constructs related to a global negative view of the self, such as worthless, pathetic, or no good, or to a totally hopeless view of the future, or to interpretations of the world in terms of severe loss and deprivation become accessible, then experiences are much more likely to be interpreted as highly aversive and uncontrollable, and the vicious cycle is likely to become established. (p. 255)

Because of this increased accessibility to negative aspects of the self and environment, depressed persons will also have little difficulty noticing the negative responses emitted by others around them. Indeed, even if the responses of others are mixed or ambiguous, and include both positive and negative behaviors as Coyne (1976b) contends, the cognitive style of depressed individuals ensures that they will attend more readily and more strongly to the negative than to the positive behaviors (cf. Gotlib, 1983). Note that it is not necessary to postulate that depressed individuals manifest inaccurate or negatively distorted perceptions of their environment. Rather, we are suggesting simply that depressed persons exhibit increased accessibility and attention to the negative behaviors of significant others, responses engendered through the depressives' own symptomatic behaviors.

Thus, we now have a depressed individual who is acutely aware of the negative behavior and rejection demonstrated by those around him. Moreover, depressed persons are not only aware of negative aspects of the environment, but, as Lewinsohn, Lobitz, and Wilson (1973) demonstrated, they are particularly sensitive to, and aroused by, negative situations. Given the increased needs for dependency that characterize depressed persons, it is not difficult to understand that perceptions of rejection would be especially distressing. The negative affect and rejection expressed by others reactivates the depressed individual's schemas or memories of rejection, loss, or uncontrollability, and likely also heightens feelings of dependency. As a result, the depressed person becomes even more depressed, and more symptomatic. Coyne (1976b) argues that this renewed display of symptoms is intended to regain the support from others that was initially offered when the depressed individual first became symptomatic. Regardless of the purpose of this exacerbation of symptoms, the point remains that these depressive behaviors lead others to become even more negative or to withdraw further. Because the depressed individual has little difficulty perceiving and focusing on these negative behaviors, the cycle worsens. Thus, not only do depressed persons engender negative, or ambivalent responses from others in their social environment, but their tendency to focus on or attend to these negative behaviors only serves to compound the situation and increase their depression. In turn, the relationship between the depressed individuals and their friends and family is further degraded. Indeed, depressed persons may not even *have* friends or family, a confidant relationship, or alternative social resources. All of these factors contribute to the maintenance or escalation of the negative interactional sequences described earlier.

Again, it is instructive to consider the relevance of this formulation in accounting for the elevated prevalence of depression among women. We stressed the importance of the depressed individual's perceptions of the negative responses of others to their symptomatic behavior in maintaining or exacerbating a depressive episode. Given the likelihood of an anxious attachment style in depressed females, in addition to their increased dependency needs, it is likely that they will also be more vigilant and aware of negative responses of others, and will also be more sensitive to these negative responses, than will depressed males. Moreover, as Nolen-Hoeksema (1987) suggested, the introspective and ruminative coping style of depressed females would tend to maintain or prolong depressive episodes. In contrast, depressed males more likely have avoidant attachment styles and tend to use denial to a greater extent than do females, both of which would tend to shorten the length of their depressive episodes.

In sum, vulnerable individuals who are at risk for developing a depressive episode by virtue of negative early experiences are exposed to stressors and begin to exhibit symptoms of depression. These displays of depressive behavior elicit negative or ambivalent responses and signs of rejection from significant others. The depressed individuals perceive these negative responses and, perhaps because these responses activate schemata related to loss or feelings of dependency, find them particularly aversive. Furthermore, the increased self-focus of the depressed individuals makes it especially difficult for them to disattend from this negative environment and from their own negative cognitions and affect. Unfortunately, the resultant persistent depressive behaviors serve to further alienate others in the environment, which, in turn, exacerbates the depression. In keeping with our premise that different factors may come into play in different stages of the course of depression, we next consider processes involved in recovery and relapse.

Recovery from depressive episodes

There is relatively little research data to guide hypotheses concerning recovery from depression; consequently, the following ideas are particularly brief and speculative. One possibility is that depression is generally self-limiting unless specifically prolonged because of ongoing circumstances (Box I in Figure 10.1). By self-limiting, we suggest both a biological and a psychological basis for resolution. There is some suggestion from the results of research on pharmacotherapy of depression that most major depressions have a particular cycle, such that "premature" withdrawal of medication may result in relapse or recurrence (see brief review in Hammen, 1991a; Hollon, Shelton, & Loosen, 1991). It is possible to interpret this information, along with data on the typical course of depression, to suggest a time-limited course of depression, from which most people eventually return to their baseline state.

From a more active perspective, to the extent that many depressive reactions are responses to the interpretations of actual events, resolutions of events—both actually and cognitively—would be expected to reduce depressive symptoms (Box I). Generally speaking, the concept of "time heals" means that people's interpretations of the meaning and implications of events alter as time passes. This is presumably due both to cognitive and emotional distancing and habituation, as well as to actual changes in the person's environment. New sources of gratification may be obtained, or problematic situations may be resolved. For these same reasons, and given these same processes, we might speculate that continuing stressors, ongoing difficulties, and actual limitations on one's access to personally enhancing experiences would contribute to chronic depression (Box J in Figure 10.1). Clearly, however, much more research is required to examine factors involved in recovery from depression.

Depression relapse or recurrence

As noted in Chapter 1, most clinically significant depressions recur at some points in the person's lifetime. Against that background, we offer the following propositions

1. *To the extent that vulnerability conditions continue (cognitive, interpersonal, and environmental), the person will be susceptible to recurrences of major depression when meaningful negative events occur.* This is a straightforward prediction based on the assumption that many vulnerability factors are relatively stable. Under triggering conditions, the sequence would involve similar steps as we described earlier in onset and maintenance processes.

2. *Additionally, however, over a developmental course the vulnerable individual is likely to have increasing experiences that shape his or her environmental context in ways that promote increased likelihood of depression.* Particularly in the interpersonal domain, deficient self-esteem, negative representations of others, and dysfunctional social skills and problem-solving behaviors may contribute to a life context that contributes both to negative event occurrence and to inadequate resources for helping to resolve them.

3. *The depressive experiences themselves may alter the environmental context of the individual in negative ways.* We speculate that increasingly, prolonged or repeated depressions alter relations with other people. Marital relationships, relationships with children, the spouse's adjustment and the children's

adjustment that are affected by the depressed adult will also contribute to circumstances that are stressful. Moreover, prolonged or repeated depression that leads to difficulties in sustaining work, or that results in treatment-related expenses, may contribute to ongoing occupational and financial strains that themselves are stressful. Finally, repeated depression undoubtedly not only undermines individuals' self-esteem and belief in their ability to cope with stressors, but moreover, promotes fears and "depression about depression."

Research has identified relatively few factors that are empirically linked with depression relapse. One factor, however, stands out: as we discussed in Chapter 1, there is a strong body of data indicating that past depression predicts future depression (e.g. Belsher & Costello, 1988; Keller, 1988). Relatedly, double depression (i.e. major depressive episode superimposed on dysthymic disorder) is also associated with greater likelihood of relapse (reviewed in Keller, 1988). We speculate that this empirical relation embodies the propositions we listed above: continuation of stable vulnerability factors, increasing the context of potential negative events, and depression that alters personal and social resources available for effective coping. This empirical association reminds us that most people do not get depressed, and that many of our studies based on depressed populations are really about depression relapse.

Beyond past depression, few other predictors of relapse/recurrence have been consistently identified. There is some evidence that young women may be more susceptible to relapse (e.g. Lewinsohn, Hoberman, & Rosenbaum, 1988; Lewinsohn, Zeiss, & Duncan, 1989), although the data are not entirely consistent. For example, although Coryell, Endicott, and Keller (1991) did not find sex differences in relapse of depression, but did find that younger patients (i.e. under age 40) had more relapses than did their older counterparts. We speculate that the greater risk for relapse found in women and younger people may be due to their elevated vulnerability to marital and family stressors. For instance, a woman with a history of early adversity in childhood might be especially likely to find the tasks of being an intimate spouse and functional parent to be fraught with difficulties. Perhaps lacking appropriate skills to deal with these challenges, and yet having dependency needs and negative expectations of others' responsiveness and caring, the typical milestones of early adulthood might be especially problematic for depression-vulnerable individuals.

We also especially emphasize the process of stress-generation in persons vulnerable to depression. The extent to which maladaptive mate selection may occur, the tendency for depressed parents to have depressed and dysfunctional children, and other ways in which depressed or depression-prone people affect their life contexts, contribute to both episodic and chronic life stressors. These predictions are supported by research linking relapse to stressors (e.g. Lewinsohn, Hoberman, & Rosenbaum, 1988), and to dysfunctional family relationships (e.g. Hooley, Orley, & Teasdale, 1986; Swindle, Cronkite, & Moos, 1989).

CONCLUDING COMMENTS

Throughout this book we have reviewed the findings of investigations examining cognitive and interpersonal aspects of depression. It is clear from our reviews that depression involves deficits in both these areas of functioning. Moreover, in our discussions of this research, we identified outstanding issues in these areas of study, and offered directions for further investigation. In this chapter we have attempted to integrate the results of this research in presenting a conceptualization of depression that ascribes importance to interpersonal and to cognitive factors, both in the etiology and maintenance of this disorder, and in the processes of recovery and relapse.

We believe that the formulation we have presented in this chapter has important implications for approaches to depression assessment and intervention. We have implicated both cognitive and interpersonal factors in this disorder; consequently, it is critical that therapists be cognizant of both these aspects of depressive functioning. In particular, clinicians must be sensitive to the reactive and dynamic nature of depression. As we have noted, depressed individuals affect family members and significant others through their depressive symptomatology. In turn, these family members may, in any number of ways, inadvertently maintain or exacerbate the depression, by reinforcing the depressed individuals' schemas for loss, helplessness, or uncontrollability, or by exhibiting increased rejection. For example, family members may attempt to be helpful to the depressed person by relieving him of all household responsibilities. Paradoxically, this action may make the depressed individual feel useless, strengthening his schemata concerning helplessness and dependency, and leading to deeper depression. Alternatively, family members may give advice to the depressed person about how he should cope, and then feel frustrated or angry when their advice fails to have its intended effect. The depressed person, perceiving and being particularly sensitive to this negative affect, feels rejected and becomes more depressed, leading the family members themselves to feel like greater failures for being unable to help. This downward-spiralling cycle may continue until some intervention is activated, or until the depressed person recovers.

In the context of our conceptualization, it is clear that the clinician must attend to both the individual and the family if she or he is to deal comprehensively with the depression. In terms of the individual, for example, it is important to assess and deal with the content of the schemas, early memories, or "working models" that may increase the individual's vulnerability to the onset and persistence of the depression. In this context, such instruments as the Child Report of Parent Behavior Inventory (Schaefer, 1965) and the Parental Bonding Instrument (Parker, Tupling, & Brown, 1979) may be particularly useful in assessing depressed persons' perceptions of their parents during their childhoods. Measures developed by Hazan and Shaver (1987) and Collins and Read (1990) will also be useful in helping to assess the depressed individual's style of attachment to significant others.

Similarly, the therapist must also assess and attempt to alter the negative cognitive or information-processing style of the depressed person. As we noted in Chapters 5 and 8, there are a number of instruments available to assess the cognitive functioning of depressed patients. The Dysfunctional Attitude Scale, the Attributional Style Questionnaire, and the Automatic Thoughts Questionnaire are among the most frequently used self-report measures of cognitive functioning, assessing depressed patients' tendencies to maintain dysfunctional beliefs, to hold themselves responsible for negative events, and to perceive their environment as out of their control. In addition, it is imperative that the therapist consider the implications of this negative cognitive functioning for the depressive's interpersonal behavior. The therapist must focus on the interpersonal dynamics of the depressed individual, and must attempt to understand the depression within the context of the depressed person's social system. For example, the therapist must not only examine what the family members or other significant persons in the depressed individual's environment are doing that may be contributing to the maintenance or exacerbaton of the depression, but should also explore what these persons can do differently. In this regard, assessment instruments such as the Family Environment Scale and the Spouse Observation Checklist will be useful, as will the clinician's direct observations of the depressed person's interpersonal behavior. A husband's responses to his wife's depressive behavior, for example, can provide critical information about how the couple is attempting to deal with the depression, and can also identify potential targets for intervention.

Finally, the clinician must utilize the information obtained through this assessment to develop an appropriate treatment program designed to alter the depressed individual's dysfunctional cognitions and interpersonal behavior, as well as the responses of others in the depressed person's environment. A detailed discussion of intervention procedures for use with depressed patients is clearly beyond the scope of this presentation. We described in Chapter 8 procedures that are useful in altering dysfunctional cognitions and, in Chapter 9, techniques and programs that have been found to be helpful in initiating and maintaining more adaptive interpersonal functioning. Readers who are interested in a more comprehensive presentation of treatment principles and techniques derived from this perspective are referred to Gotlib and Colby (1987). In addition to these procedures, however, it is clear from the conceptualization we presented earlier in this chapter that vulnerability to depression involves long-standing cognitive, interpersonal, and personality characteristics. Consequently, if we are to make significant headway in reducing the probability of *relapse* of this debilitating disorder, it is likely that interventions will have to adopt a stronger focus on these more intractable factors.

References

Abraham, K. (1911/1985). Notes on the psychoanalytic investigation and treatment of manic-depressive insanity and allied conditions. In J.C. Coyne (Ed.), *Essential papers on depression*. New York: New York University Press.

Abrahams, M.J., & Whitlock, F.A. (1969). Childhood experience and depression. *British Journal of Psychiatry*, **115**, 883–888.

Abramson, L.Y., Alloy, L.B., & Metalsky, G.I. (1988). The cognitive diathesis stress theories of depression: Toward an adequate evaluation of the theories' validities. In L.B. Alloy (Ed.), *Cognitive processes in depression* (pp. 3–30). New York: Guilford.

Abramson, L.Y., & Martin, D. (1981). Depression and the causal inference process. In J. Harvey, W. Ickes, & R. Kidd (Eds), *New directions in attribution research* (pp. 117–168). Hillsdale, NJ: Erlbaum.

Abramson, L.Y., Metalsky, G.I., & Alloy, L.B. (1989). Hopelessness depression: A theory-based subtype of depression. *Psychological Review*, **96**, 358–372.

Abramson, L.Y., Seligman, M.E.P., & Teasdale, J. (1978). Learned helplessness in humans: Critique and reformulation. *Journal of Abnormal Psychology*, **87**, 49–74.

Achenbach, T.M., & Edelbrock, C.S. (1983). *Manual for the Child Behavior Checklist and Revised Child Behavior Profile*. Burlington, VT: Department of Psychiatry, University of Vermont.

Achenbach, T.M., McConaughy, S.H., & Howell, C.T. (1987). Child/adolescent behavioral and emotional problems: Implications of cross-informant correlations for situational specificity. *Psychological Bulletin*, **101**, 213–232.

Adrian, C., & Hammen, C. (in press). Children of depressed mothers: Stress exposure and responses to stressful life events. *Journal of Consulting and Clinical Psychology*.

Ainsworth, M.D.S. (1989). Attachment beyond infancy. *American Psychologist*, **44**, 709–716.

Ainsworth, M.D.S., Blehar, M.C., Waters, E., & Wall, S. (1978). *Patterns of attachment: A psychological study of the strange situation*. Hillsdale, NJ: Erlbaum.

Akiskal, H.S. (1982). Factors associated with incomplete recovery in primary depressive illness. *Journal of Clinical Psychiatry*, **43**, 266–271.

Akiskal, H.S. (1983). Dysthymic disorder: Psychopathology of proposed chronic depressive subtypes. *American Journal of Psychiatry*, **140**, 11–20.

Akiskal, H.S., Bitar, A.H., Puzantian, V.R., Rosenthal, T.L., & Walker, P.W. (1978). The nonsological status of neurotic depression: A prospective three- to four-year follow-up examination in light of the primary-secondary and unipolar-bipolar dichotomies. *Archives of General Psychiatry*, **35**, 756–766.

Akiskal, H.S., Hirschfeld, R.M.A., & Yerevanian, B.I. (1983). The relationship of personality disorders to affective disorders: A critical review. *Archives of General Psychiatry*, **40**, 801–810.

Albert, N., & Beck, A.T. (1975). Incidence of depression in early adolescence: A preliminary study. *Journal of Youth and Adolescence,* **4**, 301–307.

Allgood-Merten, B., Lewinsohn, P.M., & Hops, H. (1990). Sex differences and adolescent depression. *Journal of Abnormal Psychology,* **99**, 55–63.

Alloy, L.B., & Abramson, L.Y. (1979). Judgment of contingency in depressed and nondepressed students: Sadder but wiser? *Journal of Experimental Psychology: General,* **108**, 441–485.

Alloy, L.B., & Abramson, L.Y. (1988). Depressive realism: Four theoretical perspectives. In L.B. Alloy (Ed.), *Cognitive processes in depression* (pp. 223–265). New York: Guilford Press.

Alloy, L.B., Kelly, K.A., Mineka, S., & Clements, C.M. (1990). Comorbidity in anxiety and depressive disorders: A helplessness/hopelessness perspective. In J.D. Maser & C.R. Cloninger (Eds), *Comorbidity in anxiety and mood disorders* (pp. 499–543). Washington, DC: American Psychiatric Press.

Altmann, E.O., & Gotlib, I.H. (1988). The social behavior of depressed children: An observational study. *Journal of Abnormal Child Psychology,* **16**, 29–44.

Amenson, C.S., & Lewinsohn, P.M. (1981). An investigation of the observed sex difference in prevalence of unipolar depression. *Journal of Abnormal Psychology,* **90**, 1–13.

Anderson, C.A., & Hammen, C. (1991a). *Disturbed and nondisturbed siblings in high risk families: Correlates of vulnerability.* Manuscript under review.

Anderson, C.A., & Hammen, C. (1991b). *Psychosocial functioning in children at risk for depression: Longitudinal follow-up.* Manuscript under review.

Anderson, J.C., Williams, S., McGee, R., & Silva, P.A. (1987). DSM-III disorders in preadolescent children. *Archives of General Psychiatry,* **44**, 69–76.

Andreason, N.C., Scheftner, W., Reich, T., Hirschfeld, R.M.A., Endicott, J., & Keller, M.B. (1986). The validation of the concept of endogenous depression. *Archives of General Psychiatry,* **43**, 246–251.

Andrews, B., & Brown, G.W. (1988). Social support, onset of depression and personality: An exploratory analysis. *Social Psychiatry and Psychiatric Epidemiology,* **23**, 99–108.

Angold, A., Costello, E.J., Pickles, A., et al. (1987). The development of a questionnaire for use in epidemiological studies of depression in children and adolescents. Unpublished manuscript, London University.

Angst, J. (1984, April). *A prospective study on the course of affective disorders.* Paper presented at the National Institute of Mental Health Consensus Development Conference, Washington, DC.

Angst, J., Baastrup, P.C., Grof, P., Hippius, H., Poeldinger, W., & Weiss, P. (1973). The course of monopolar depression and bipolar psychoses. *Psychiatrie, Neurologie et Neurochirurgie,* **76**, 246–254.

Anthony, E.J. (1983). An overview of the effects of maternal depression on the infant and child. In H.L. Morrison (Ed.), *Children of depressed parents* (pp. 1–6). New York: Grune & Stratton.

Anthony, J.C., Folstein, M., Romanoski, A.J., Von Korff, M.R., Nestadt, G.R., Chahal, R., Merchant, A., Brown, C.H., Shapiro, S., Kramer, M., & Gruenberg, E.M. (1985). Comparison of the Lay Diagnostic Interview Schedule and a standardized psychiatric diagnosis. *Archives of General Psychology,* **42**, 667–675.

Antonuccio, D.O., Ward, C.H., & Tearnan, B.H. (1989). The behavioral treatment of unipolar depression in adult outpatients. In M. Hersen, R.M. Eisler, & P.M. Miller (Eds), *Progress in Behavior Modification,* Vol. 24 (pp. 152–191). New York: Sage.

Arieti, S., & Bemporad, J. (1978). *Severe and mild depression: The psychotherapeutic approach.* New York: Basic Books.

Arieti, S., & Bemporad, J. (1980). The psychological organization of depression. *American Journal of Psychiatry*, **137**, 1360–1365.

Arkowitz, H., Holliday, S., & Hutter, M. (1982, November). *Depressed women and their husbands: A study of marital interaction and adjustment.* Paper presented at the Annual Meeting of the Association for the Advancement of Behavior Therapy, Los Angeles.

Armsden, G., McCauley, E., Greenberg, M., Burke, P., & Mitchell, J. (1990). Parent and peer attachment in early adolescent depression. *Journal of Abnormal Child Psychology*, **18**, 683–697.

Arthur, J.A., Hops, H., & Biglan, A. (1982). *LIFE (Living in familial environments) coding system.* Unpublished manuscript, Oregon Research Institute, Eugene.

Asarnow, J.R. (1988). Peer status and social competence in child psychiatric inpatients: A comparison of children with depressive, externalizing, and concurrent depressive and externalizing disorders. *Journal of Abnormal Child Psychology*, **16**, 151–162.

Asarnow, J.R., & Bates, S. (1988). Depression in child psychiatric inpatients: Cognitive and attributional patterns. *Journal of Abnormal Child Psychology*, **16**, 601–615.

Asarnow, J.R., & Carlson, G.A. (1986). Depression self-rating scale: Utility with child psychiatric inpatients. *Journal of Consulting and Clinical Psychology*, **53**, 491–499.

Asarnow, J.R., Carlson, G.A., & Guthrie, D. (1987). Coping strategies, self-perceptions, hopelessness, and perceived family environments in depressed and suicidal children. *Journal of Consulting and Clinical Psychology*, **55**, 361–366.

Asarnow, J.R., Goldstein, M.J., Carlson, G.A., Perdue, S., Bates, S., & Keller, J. (1988). Childhood-onset depressive disorders: A follow-up study of rates of rehospitalization and out-of-home placement among child psychiatric inpatients. *Journal of Affective Disorders*, **15**, 245–253.

Bachrach, L.L. (1975). *Marital status and mental disorder: An analytical review.* National Institute of Mental Health DHEW Publication No. (ADM) 75-217. Washington, DC: US Government Printing Office.

Barber, J.P., & DeRubeis, R.J. (1989). On second thought: Where the action is in cognitive therapy for depression. *Cognitive Therapy and Research*, **13**, 441–457.

Bargh, J.A. (1982). Attention and automaticity in the processing of self-relevant information. *Journal of Personality and Social Psychology*, **43**, 425–436.

Barlow, D.H. (1988). *Anxiety and its disorders: The nature and treatment of anxiety and panic.* New York: Guilford Press.

Barnes, G.E., & Prosen, H. (1985). Parental death and depression. *Journal of Abnormal Psychology*, **94**, 64–69.

Barnett, P.A., & Gotlib, I.H. (1988a). Dysfunctional attitudes and psychosocial stress: The differential prediction of subsequent depression and general psychological distress. *Motivation and Emotion*, **12**, 251–270.

Barnett, P.A., & Gotlib, I.H. (1988b). Psychosocial functioning and depression: Distinguishing among antecedents, concomitants, and consequences. *Psychological Bulletin*, **104**, 97–126.

Barnett, P.A., & Gotlib, I.H. (1990). Cognitive vulnerability to depressive symptoms among men and women. *Cognitive Therapy and Research*, **14**, 47–61.

Barrett, J.E., Barrett, J.A., Oxman, T.E., & Gerber, P.D. (1988). The prevalence of psychiatric disorders in primary care practice. *Archives of General Psychiatry*, **45**, 1100–1106.

Barthe, D., & Hammen, C. (1981). A naturalistic extension of the attributional model of depression. *Personality and Social Psychology Bulletin*, **7**, 53–58.

Bartholomew, K. (1990). Avoidance of intimacy: An attachment perspective. *Journal of Social and Personal Relationships*, **7**, 147–178.

Bartholomew, K., & Horowitz, L.M. (1991). Attachment styles among young adults: A test of a four-category model. *Journal of Personality and Social Psychology*, **61**, 226–244.

Bartlett, F.C. (1932). *Remembering: A study in experimental and social psychology*. Cambridge: Cambridge University Press.

Beach, S.R.H., & O'Leary, D.K. (1986). The treatment of depression occurring in the context of marital discord. *Behaviour Therapy*, **17**, 43–50.

Beach, S.R.H., Sandeen, E.E., & O'Leary, K.D. (1990). *Depression in marriage*. New York: Guilford Press.

Bebbington, P. (1987). Marital status and depression: A study of English national admission statistics. *Acta Psychiatrica Scandanavica*, **75**, 640–650.

Beck, A.T. (1964). Thinking and depression: 2. Theory and therapy. *Archives of General Psychiatry*, **10**, 561–571.

Beck, A.T. (1967). *Depression: Clinical, experimental, and theoretical aspects*. New York: Harper & Row.

Beck, A.T. (1976). *Cognitive therapy and the emotional disorders*. New York: International Universities Press.

Beck, A.T. (1983). Cognitive therapy of depression: New perspectives. In P.J. Clayton & J.E. Barrett (Eds), *Treatment of depression: Old controversies and new approaches*. New York: Raven Press.

Beck, A.T., Brown, G., Steer, R.A., Eidelson, J.I., & Riskind, J.H. (1987). Differentiating anxiety and depression: A test of the cognitive content-specificity hypothesis. *Journal of Abnormal Psychology*, **96**, 179–183.

Beck, A.T., & Freeman, A. (1990). *Cognitive therapy of personality disorders*. New York: Guilford Press.

Beck, A.T., Rush, A.J., Shaw, B.F., & Emery, G. (1979). *Cognitive therapy of depression*. New York: Guilford Press.

Beck, A.T., Steer, R.A., & Garbin, M.G. (1988). Psychometric properties of the Beck Depression Inventory: Twenty-five years of evaluation. *Clinical Psychology Review*, **8**, 77–100.

Beck, A.T., Steer, R.A., Kovacs, M., & Garrison, B.E. (1985). Hopelessness and eventual suicidal: A ten-year prospective study of patients hospitalized for suicidal ideation. *American Journal of Psychiatry*, **142**, 559–563.

Beck, A.T., Ward, C.H., Mendelsohn, M., Mock, J., & Erbaugh, J. (1961). An inventory for measuring depression. *Archives of General Psychiatry*, **4**, 561–571.

Becker, R.E., & Heimberg, R.G. (1985). Social skills training approaches. In M. Hersen & A.S. Bellack (Eds), *Handbook of clinical behavior therapy with adults* (pp. 201–226). New York: Plenum Press.

Becker, R.E., Heimberg, R.G., & Bellack, A.S. (1987). *Social skills training treatment for depression*. New York, Pergamon Press.

Beckham, E.E., & Leber, W.R. (1985). *Handbook of depression: Treatment, assessment, and research*. Homewood, IL: Dorsey.

Bellack, A.S., Hersen, M., & Himmelhoch, J. (1981). Social skills training compared with pharmacotherapy and psychotherapy in the treatment of unipolar depression. *American Journal of Psychiatry*, **138**, 1562–1567.

Bellack, A.S., Hersen, M., & Himmelhoch, J. (1983). A comparison of social skills training, pharmacotherapy, and psychotherapy for depression. *Behavior Research and Therapy*, **21**, 101–107.

Belsher, G., & Costello, C.G. (1988). Relapse after recovery from unipolar depression:

A critical review. *Psychological Bulletin*, **104**, 84–96.

Benfield, C.Y., Palmer, D.J., Pfefferbaum, B., & Stowe, M.L. (1988). A comparison of depressed and nondepressed disturbed children on measures of attributional style, hopelessness, life stress, and temperament. *Journal of Abnormal Child Psychology*, **16**, 397–410.

Ben-Porath, Y.S., & Tellegen, A. (1990). A place for traits in stress research. *Psychological Inquiry*, **1**, 14–40.

Berti Ceroni, G., Neri, C., & Pezzoli, A. (1984). Chronicity in major depression: A naturalistic prospective study. *Journal of Affective Disorders*, **7**, 123–132.

Bettes, B. (1988). Maternal depression and motherese: Temporal and intonational features. *Child Development*, **59**, 1089–1096.

Beutler, L.E., Scogin, F., Kirkish, P., Schretlen, D., Corbishley, A., Hamblin, D., Meredith, K., Potter, R., Bamford, C.R., & Levenson, A.I. (1987). Group cognitive therapy and alprazolam in the treatment of depression in older adults. *Journal of Consulting and Clinical Psychology*, **55**, 550–556.

Bibring, E. (1953). The mechanism of depression. In P. Greenacre (Ed.), *Affective disorders* (pp. 14–47). New York: International Universities Press.

Bifulco, A.T., Brown, G.W., & Harris, T. (1987). Childhood loss of parent, lack of adequate parental care and adult depression: A replication. *Journal of Affective Disorders*, **12**, 115–128.

Biglan, A., Hops, H., Sherman, L., Friedman, L.S., Arthur, J., & Osteen, V. (1985). Problem-solving interactions of depressed women and their husbands. *Behavior Therapy*, **16**, 431–451.

Billings, A.G., Cronkite, R., & Moos, R. (1983). Social-environmental factors in unipolar depression: Comparisons of depressed patients and nondepressed controls. *Journal of Abnormal Psychology*, **93**, 119–133.

Billings, A.G., & Moos, R.H. (1982). Psychosocial theory and research on depression: An integrative framework and review. *Clinical Psychology Review*, **2**, 213–237.

Billings, A.G., & Moos, R.H. (1983). Comparisons of children of depressed and nondepressed parents: A social-environmental perspective. *Journal of Abnormal Child Psychology*, **11**, 463–485.

Billings, A.G., & Moos, R.H. (1984). Coping, stress, and social resources among adults with unipolar depression. *Journal of Personality and Social Psychology*, **46**, 877–891.

Billings, A.G., & Moos, R.H. (1985a). Life stressors and social resources affect posttreatment outcomes among depressed patients. *Journal of Abnormal Psychology*, **94**, 140–153.

Billings, A.G., & Moos, R.H. (1985b). Psychosocial processes of remission in unipolar depression: Comparing depressed patients with matched community controls. *Journal of Consulting and Clinical Psychology*, **53**, 314–325.

Billings, A.G., & Moos, R.H. (1986). Children of parents with unipolar depression: A controlled one-year follow-up. *Journal of Abnormal Child Psychology*, **14**, 149–166.

Birleson, P. (1981). The validity of depressive disorder in childhood and the development of a self-rating scale. *Journal of Child Psychiatry*, **22**, 73–88.

Birleson, P., Hudson, I., Buchanan, D.G., & Wolff, S. (1987). Clinical evaluation of a self-rating scale for depressive disorder in childhood (Depression Self-Rating Scale). *Journal of Child Psychology and Psychiatry*, **28**, 43–60.

Blackburn, I.M., Jones, S., & Lewin, R.J.P. (1987). Cognitive style in depression. *British Journal of Clinical Psychology*, **25**, 241–251.

Blackburn, I.M., & Smyth, P. (1985). A test of cognitive vulnerability in individuals prone to depression. *British Journal of Clinical Psychology*, **24**, 61–62.

Bland, R.C., Newman, S.C., & Orn, H. (1986). Recurrent and nonrecurrent depression: A family study. *Archives of General Psychiatry, 43*, 1085–1089.

Blaney, P.H. (1986). Affect and memory: A review. *Psychological Bulletin, 99*, 229–246.

Blaney, P.H., Behar, V., & Head, R. (1980). Two measures of depressive cognitions: Their association with depression and with each other. *Journal of Abnormal Psychology, 89*, 678–682.

Blatt, S.J. (1974). Level of object representation in anaclitic and introjective depression. *Psychoanalytic Study of the Child, 29*, 107–157.

Blatt, S.J., D'Affliti, P., & Quinlan, D.M. (1976). Experiences of depression in normal young adults. *Journal of Abnormal Psychology, 85*, 383–389.

Blatt, S.J., & Homann, E. (1992). Parent-child interaction in the etiology of dependent and self-critical depression. *Clinical Psychology Review, 12*, 47–91.

Blatt, S.J., Quinlan, D., Chevron, E., McDonald, C., & Zuroff, D. (1982). Dependency and self-criticism: Psychological dimensions of depression. *Journal of Consulting and Clinical Psychology, 50*, 113–124.

Blatt, S.J., Wein, S.J., Chevron, E., & Quinlan, D.M. (1979). Parental representations and depression in normal young adults. *Journal of Abnormal Psychology, 88*, 388–397.

Blazer, D., Swartz, M., Woodbury, M., Manton, K.G., Hughes, D., & George, L.K. (1988). Depressive symptoms and depressive diagnoses in a community population. *Archives of General Psychiatry, 45*, 1078–1084.

Blechman, E.A., McEnroe, M.J., Carella, E.T., & Audette, D.P. (1986). Childhood competence and depression. *Journal of Abnormal Psychology, 95*, 223–227.

Blehar, M.C., & Rosenthal, N.E. (1989). Seasonal affective disorders and phototherapy. *Archives of General Psychiatry, 46*, 469–474.

Blehar, M.C., Weissman, M.M., Gershon, E.S., & Hirschfeld, R.M.A. (1988). Family and genetic studies of affective disorders. *Archives of General Psychiatry, 45*, 289–292.

Block, J., Gjerde, P.F., & Block, J.H. (1991). Personality antecedents of depressive tendencies in 18-year-olds: A prospective study. *Journal of Personality and Social Psychology, 60*, 726–738.

Blumberg, S.H., & Izard, C.E. (1985). Affective and cognitive characteristics of depression in 10- and 11-year-old children. *Journal of Personality and Social Psychology, 49*, 194–202.

Blumberg, S.R., & Hokanson, J.E. (1983). The effects of another person's response style on interpersonal behavior in depression. *Journal of Abnormal Psychology, 92*, 196–209.

Blumenthal, M.D. (1967). Mental health among the divorced: A field study of divorced and never divorced persons. *Archives of General Psychiatry, 16*, 603–608.

Blumenthal, M.D. (1975). Measuring depressive symptomatology in a general population. *Archives of General Psychiatry, 32*, 971–978.

Boswell, P.C., & Murray, E.J. (1981). Depression, schizophrenia, and social attraction. *Journal of Consulting and Clinical Psychology, 49*, 641–647.

Bothwell, S., & Weissman, M.M. (1977). Social impairments four years after an acute depressive episode. *American Journal of Orthopsychiatry, 47*, 231–237.

Bower, G.H. (1981). Mood and memory. *American Psychologist, 36*, 129–148.

Bower, G.H., Gilligan, S.G., & Monteiro, K.P. (1981). Selectivity of learning caused by affective states. *Journal of Experimental Psychology: General, 110*, 451–473.

Bowlby, J. (1969). *Attachment and loss. Vol. 1. Attachment.* New York: Basic Books.

Bowlby, J. (1978). *Attachment and loss, Vol. 2: Separation: Anxiety and anger.* Harmondsworth, Middx.: Penguin.

Bowlby, J. (1981). *Attachment and loss, Vol. 3: Loss: Sadness and depression.* Harmondsworth, Middx.: Penguin.

Bowlby, J. (1988). Developmental psychiatry comes of age. *American Journal of Psychiatry,* **145,** 1–10.

Boyd, J.H., & Weissman, M.M. (1981). Epidemiology of affective disorders. *Archives of General Psychiatry,* **38,** 1039–1046.

Boyd, J.H., Weissman, M.M., Thompson, W.D., & Myers, J.K. (1982). Screening for depression in a community sample. *Archives of General Psychiatry,* **39,** 1195–1200.

Breier, A., Charney, D.S., & Heninger, G.R. (1985). The diagnostic validity of anxiety disorders and their relationship to depressive illness. *American Journal of Psychiatry,* **142,** 787–797.

Breier, A., Kelsoe, J.R. Jr., Kirwin, P.D., Beller, S.A., Wolkowitz, O.M., & Pickar, D. (1988). Early parental loss and development of adult psychopathology. *Archives of General Psychiatry,* **45,** 987–993.

Brent, D.A., Kupfer, D.J., Bromet, E.J., & Dew, M.A. (1988). The assessment and treatment of patients at risk for suicide. In A.J. Frances & R.E. Hales (Eds), *Review of psychiatry* (pp. 353–385). Washington, DC: American Psychiatric Press.

Bretherton, I., & Waters, E. (Eds). (1985). *Growing points of attachment theory and research. Monographs of the Society for Research in Child Development,* **50,** (1-2, Serial No. 209).

Brewin, C.R. (1985). Depression and causal attributions: What is their relation? *Psychological Bulletin,* **98,** 297–309.

Brewin, C.R., Andrews, B., & Gotlib, I.H. (in press). Psychopathology and early experience: A reappraisal of retrospective reports. *Psychological Bulletin.*

Breznitz, Z., & Sherman, T. (1987). Speech patterning of natural discourse of well and depressed mothers and their young children. *Child Development,* **58,** 395–400.

Brim, J.A., Witcoff, C., & Wetzel, R.D. (1982). Social network characteristics of hospitalized depressed patients. *Psychological Reports,* **50,** 423–433.

Brown, F. (1961). Depression and childhood bereavement. *Journal of Mental Science,* **107,** 754–777.

Brown, G.W. (1990). What about the real world? Hassles and Richard Lazarus. *Psychological Inquiry,* **1,** 19–22.

Brown, G.W., Andrews, B., Harris, T., Adler, Z., & Bridge, L. (1986). Social support, self-esteem and depression. *Psychological Medicine,* **16,** 813–831.

Brown, G.W., Bifulco, A., & Harris, T. (1987). Life events, vulnerability and onset of depression: Some refinements. *British Journal of Psychiatry,* **150,** 30–42.

Brown, G.W., Birley, J.L.T., & Wing, J.K. (1972). Influence of family life on the course of schizophrenic disorders: A replication. *British Journal of Psychiatry,* **121,** 241–258.

Brown, G.W., & Harris, T. (1978). *Social origins of depression.* London: Free Press.

Brown, G.W., Harris, T., & Bifulco, A. (1986). Long-term effects of early loss of parent. In M. Rutter, C.E. Izard, & P.B. Read (Eds), *Depression in young people: Clinical and developmental perspectives* (pp. 251–296). New York: Guilford Press.

Brown, R.A., & Lewinsohn, P.M. (1984). A psychoeductional approach to the treatment of depression: Comparison of group, individual, and minimal contact procedures. *Journal of Consulting and Clinical Psychology,* **52,** 774–783.

Brugha, T., Conroy, R., Walsh, N., Delaney, W., O'Hanlon, J., Dondero, E., Daly, L., Hickey, N., & Bourke, G. (1982). Social networks, attachments and support in minor affective disorders: A replication. *British Journal of Psychiatry,* **141,** 249–255.

Buchwald, A.M. (1977). Depressive mood and estimates of reinforcement frequency. *Journal of Abnormal Psychology,* **83,** 443–446.

Buhrmester, D. (1990). Intimacy of friendship, interpersonal competence, and adjustment during preadolescence and adolescence. *Child Development*, **61**, 1101–1111.

Burbach, D.J., & Borduin, C.M. (1986). Parent-child relations and the etiology of depression: A review of methods and findings. *Clinical Psychology Review*, **6**, 133–153.

Burbach, D.J., Kashani, J.H., & Rosenberg, T.K. (1989). Parental bonding and depressive disorders in adolescents. *Journal of Child Psychology and Psychiatry*, **30**, 417–429.

Burchill, S.A.L., & Stiles, W.B. (1988). Interactions of depressed college students with their roommates: Not necessarily negative. *Journal of Personality and Social Psychology*, **55**, 410–419.

Burge, D., & Hammen, C. (1991). Maternal communication: Predictors of outcome at follow-up in a sample of children at high and low risk for depression. *Journal of Abnormal Psychology*, **100**, 174–180.

Burke, K.C., Burke, J.D., Regier, D.A., & Rae, D.S. (1990). Age at onset of selected mental disorders in five community populations. *Archives of General Psychiatry*, **47**, 511–518.

Burnam, M.A., Wells, K.B., & Hays, R.D. (1990, August). *Depressive symptoms and disorder in general medical and mental health outpatient practices.* Paper prepared for the American Psychological Assocation meetings, Boston, MA.

Burns, D.D. (1980). *Feeling good: The new mood therapy.* New York: William Morrow.

Burns, D.D., & Nolen-Hoeksema, S. (1991). Coping styles, homework compliance, and the effectiveness of cognitive-behavioral therapy. *Journal of Consulting and Clinical Psychology*, **59**, 305–311.

Campbell-Goymer, N.R., & Allgood, W.C. (1984, March). *Cognitive correlates of childhood depression.* Paper presented at the annual conference of the Southeastern Psychological Association, New Orleans, LA.

Cane, D.B., & Gotlib, I.H. (1985). Implicit conceptualizations of depression: Implications for an interactional perspective. *Social Cognition*, **3**, 341–368.

Cane, D.B., Olinger, L.J., Gotlib, I.H., & Kuiper, N.A. (1986). Factor structure of the Dysfunctional Attitude Scale in a student population. *Journal of Clinical Psychology*, **42**, 307–309.

Caple, M.A., & Blechman, E.A. (1976, December). *Problem-solving and self-approval training with a depressed single mother: Case study.* Paper presented at the meeting of the Association for the Advancement of Behavior Therapy, New York.

Carey, M.P., Faulstich, M.E., Gresham, F.M., Ruggiero, L., & Enyart, P. (1987). Children's Depression Inventory: Construct and discriminant validity across clinical and nonreferred (control) populations. *Journal of Consulting and Clinical Psychology*, **55**, 755–761.

Carlson, G.A. (1983). Bipolar disorders in children and adolescents. In D.P. Cantwell & G.A. Carlson (Eds), *Affective disorders in childhood and adolescence: An update* (pp. 60–83). New York: Spectrum.

Carlson, G.A., & Cantwell, D.P. (1980). Unmasking masked depression in children and adolescents. *American Journal of Psychiatry*, **137**, 445–449.

Carlson, V., Cicchetti, D., Barnett, D., & Braunwald, K. (1989). Disorganized/disoriented attachment relationships in maltreated infants. *Developmental Psychology*, **25**, 525–531.

Carlson, G.A., & Kashani, J.H. (1988). Phenomenology of major depression from childhood through adulthood: Analysis of three studies. *American Journal of Psychiatry*, **145**, 1222–1225.

Carlson, G.A., & Strober, M. (1983). Affective disorders in adolescence. In D.P.

Cantwell & G.A. Carlson (Eds), *Affective disorders in childhood and adolescence: An update* (pp. 85–96). New York: Spectrum.

Carroll, B.J., Feinberg, M., Greden, J.F., Haskett, R.F., James, N., Steiner, M., & Tarika, J. (1980). Diagnosis of endogenous depression: Comparison of clinical, research and neuroendocrine criteria. *Journal of Affective Disorders*, **2**, 177–194.

Carroll, B.J., Feinberg, M., Smouse, P.E., Rawson, S.G., & Greden, J.F. (1981). The Carroll Rating Scale for Depression I. Development, reliability, and validation. *British Journal of Psychiatry*, **138**, 194–200.

Carroll, B., Fielding, J.M., & Blashki, T.G. (1973). Depression rating scales: A critical review. *Archives of General Psychiatry*, **28**, 361–366.

Carver, C.S., & Scheier, M.F. (1981). *Attention and self-regulation: A control theory approach to human behavior.* New York: Springer-Verlag.

Cassem, E.H. (1988). Depression secondary to medical illness. In A.J. Frances & R.E. Hales (Eds), *Review of psychiatry* (pp. 356–373). Washington, DC: American Psychiatric Press.

Chambers, W.J., Puig-Antich, J., Hirsch, M., Paez, P., Ambrosini, P.J., Tabrizi, M.A., & Davies, M. (1985). The assessment of affective disorders in children and adolescents by semistructures interview: Test-retest reliability. *Archives of General Psychiatry*, **42**, 696–702.

Chambers, W.J., Puig-Antich, J., Tabrizi, M.A., & Davies, M. (1982). Psychotic symptoms in prepubertal major depressive disorder. *Archives of General Psychiatry*, **39**, 921–927.

Chodoff, P. (1972). The depressive personality. *Archives of General Psychiatry*, **27**, 666–677.

Cicchetti, D., & Schneider-Rosen, K. (1986). An organizational approach to childhood depression. In M. Rutter, C.E. Izard, & P.E. Read (Eds), *Depression in young people* (pp. 71–134). New York: Guilford Press.

Clark, D.A., Beck, A.T., & Stewart, B. (1990). Cognitive specificity and positive–negative affectivity: Complementary or contradictory views on anxiety and depression? *Journal of Abnormal Psychology*, **99**, 148–155.

Clark, D.M., & Teasdale, J.D. (1982). Diurnal variation in clinical depression and accessibility of memories of positive and negative experiences. *Journal of Abnormal Psychology*, **91**, 87–95.

Clark, L.A., & Watson, D. (1991). Tripartite model of anxiety and depression: Psychometric evidence and taxonomic implications. *Journal of Abnormal Psychology*, **100**, 316–336.

Clarkin, J.F., & Haas, G.L. (1988). Assessment of affective disorders and their interpersonal contexts. In J.F. Clarkin, G.L. Haas, & I.D. Glick (Eds), *Affective disorders and the family: Assessment and treatment* (pp. 29–50). New York: Guilford Press.

Clarkin, J.F., Haas, G.L., & Glick, I.D. (Eds). (1988). *Affective disorders and the family: Assessment and Treatment.* New York: Guilford Press.

Clausen, J., & Yarrow, M. (1955). Introduction: Mental illness and the family. *Journal of Social Issues*, **11**, 3–5.

Clayton, P.J. (1984, April). *Overview of recurrent mood disorders: Definitions and natural course.* Paper presented at the National Institute of Mental Health Consensus Development Conference, Washington, DC.

Cleary, P.D., & Mechanic, D. (1983). Sex differences in psychological distress among married people. *Journal of Health and Social Behavior*, **24**, 111–121

Coates, D., & Wortman, C.B. (1980). Depression maintenance and interpersonal control. In A. Baum & J.E. Singer (Eds), *Advances in environmental psychology*, Vol.

2, *Applications of personal control* (pp. 149–182). Hillsdale, NJ: Erlbaum.

Cochran, S., & Hammen, C. (1985). Perceptions of stressful life events and depression: A test of attributional models. *Journal of Personality and Social Psychology, 48,* 1562–1571.

Cohler, B.J., Grunebaum, H.U., Weiss, J.L., Hartman, C.R., & Gallant, D.H. (1977). Child care attitudes and adaptation to the maternal role among mentally ill and well mothers. *American Journal of Orthopsychiatry, 46,* 123–133.

Cohn, J.F., Campbell, S.B., Matias, R., & Hopkins, J. (1990). Face-to-face interactions of postpartum depressed and nondepressed mother-infant pairs at 2 months. *Developmental Psychology, 23,* 583–592.

Cohn, J.F., Matias, R., Tronick, E., Connell, D., & Lyons-Ruth, K. (1986). Face-to-face interactions of depressed mothers and their infants. In E. Tronick & T. Field (Eds), *Maternal depression and infant disturbance.* (New Directions for Child Development, No. 34, pp. 31–46). San Francisco: Jossey-Bass.

Cohn, J.F., & Tronick, E.Z. (1983). Three-month-old infants' reaction to simulated maternal depression. *Child Development, 54,* 185–193.

Cole, D.A. (1990). The relation of social and academic competence to depressive symptoms in childhood. *Journal of Abnormal Psychology, 99,* 422–429.

Cole, D.A. (1991). Preliminary support for a competency-based model of depression in children. *Journal of Abnormal Psychology, 100,* 181–190.

Cole, D.A., & Carpentieri, S. (1990). Social status and the comorbidity of child depression and conduct disorder. *Journal of Consulting and Clinical Psychology, 58,* 748–757.

Cole, D.A., & Rehm, L.P. (1986). Family interaction patterns and childhood depression. *Journal of Abnormal Child Psychology, 14,* 297–314.

Coleman, R.E., & Miller, A.G. (1975). The relationship between depression and marital maladjustment in a clinic population: A multi-trial, multi-method study. *Journal of Consulting and Clinical Psychology, 43,* 647.

Collins, N., & Read, S. (1990). Adult attachment, working models, and relationship quality in dating couples. *Journal of Personality and Social Psychology, 58,* 644–663.

Compas, B.E., Howell, D.C., Phares, V., Williams, R.A., & Giunta, C.T. (1989a). Risk factors for emotional/behavioral problems in young adolescents: A prospective analysis of adolescent and parental stress and symptoms. *Journal of Consulting and Clinical Psychology, 57,* 732–740.

Compas, B.E., Howell, D.C., Phares, V., Williams, R.A., & Ledoux, N. (1989b). Parent and child stress and symptoms: An integrative analysis. *Developmental Psychology, 25*(4), 550–559.

Compas, B.E., Wagner, B., Slavin, L., & Vannatta, K. (1986). A prospective study of life events, social support, and psychological symptomatology during the transition from high school to college. *American Journal of Community Psychology, 14,* 241–257.

Comrey, A.L. (1957). A factor analysis of items on the MMPI Depression scale. *Educational and Psychological Measurement, 18,* 578–585.

Conrad, M., & Hammen, C. (1989). Role of maternal depression in perceptions of child maladjustment. *Journal of Consulting and Clinical Psychology, 57,* 663–667.

Cook, W., Asarnow, J., Goldstein, M., Marshall, V., & Weber, E. (1990). Mother-child dynamics in early-onset depression and childhood schizophrenia spectrum disorders. *Development and Psychopathology, 2,* 71–84.

Coryell, W., Endicott, J., & Keller, M. (1990). Outcome of patients with chronic affective disorder: A five-year follow-up. *American Journal of Psychiatry, 147,* 1627–1633.

Coryell, W., Endicott, J., & Keller, M. (1991). Predictors of relapse into major depressive disorder in a nonclinical population. *American Journal of Psychiatry*, **148**, 1353–1358.

Costello, A.J. (1987). Structured interviewing for the assessment of child psychopathology. In J.D. Noshpitz (Ed.), *Basic handbook of child psychiatry* (pp. 143–152). New York: Basic Books.

Costello, A.J. (1988). Scales to assess child and adolescent depression: Checklists, screens, and nets. *Journal of the American Academy of Child and Adolescent Psychiatry*, **27**, 726–737.

Costello, C.G. (1972). Depression: Loss of reinforcers or loss of reinforcer effectiveness? *Behavior Therapy*, **3**, 240–247.

Costello, C.G. (1982). Social factors associated with depression: A retrospective community study. *Psychological Medicine*, **12**, 329–339.

Costello, C.G., & Comrey, A.L. (1967). Scales for measuring depression and anxiety. *Journal of Psychology*, **66**, 303–313.

Costello, E.J., & Angold, A. (1988). Scales to assess childhood and adolescent depression: Checklists, screens and nets. *Journal of the American Academy of Childhood and Adolescent Psychiatry*, **27**, 726–737.

Costello, E.J., Costello, A.J., Edelbrock, C., Burns, B.J., Dulcan, M.K., Brent, D., & Janiszewski, S. (1988). Psychiatric disorders in pediatric primary care: Prevalence and risk factors. *Archives of General Psychiatry*, **45**, 1107–1116.

Costello, E.J., Edelbrock, C.A., & Costello, A.J. (1985). Validity of the NIMH Diagnostic Interview Schedule for Children: A comparison between psychiatric and pediatric referrals. *Journal of Abnormal Child Psychology*, **13**, 579–595.

Coyne, J.C. (1976a). Depression and the response of others. *Journal of Abnormal Psychology*, **85**, 186–193.

Coyne, J.C. (1976b). Toward an interactional description of depression. *Psychiatry*, **39**, 28–40.

Coyne, J.C., & Bolger, N. (1990). Doing without social support as an explanatory concept. *Journal of Social and Clinical Psychology*, **9**, 148–158.

Coyne, J.C., & Gotlib, I.H. (1983). The role of cognition in depression: A critical appraisal. *Psychological Bulletin*, **94**, 472–505.

Coyne, J.C., & Gotlib, I.H. (1986). Studying the role of cognition in depression: Well-trodden paths and cul-de-sacs. *Cognitive Therapy and Research*, **10**, 695–705.

Coyne, J.C., Kessler, R.C., Tal, M., Turnbull, J., Wortman, C.B., Greden, J.F. (1987). Living with a depressed person. *Journal of Consulting and Clinical Psychology*, **55**, 347–352.

Craighead, W.E., Hickey, K.S., & DeMonbreun, B.G. (1979). Distortion of perception and recall of neutral feedback in depression. *Cognitive Therapy and Research*, **3**, 291–298.

Crook, T., & Eliot, J. (1980). Parental death during childhood and adult depression. *Psychological Bulletin*, **87**, 252–259.

Crook, T., Raskin, A., & Eliot, J. (1981). Parent-child relationships and adult depression. *Child Development*, **52**, 950–957.

Crowther, J.H. (1985). The relationship between depression and marital maladjustment: A descriptive study. *Journal of Nervous and Mental Disease*, **173**, 227–231.

Cummings, E.M. (1990). Classification of attachment on a continuum of felt security: Illustrations from the study of children of depressed parents. In M.T. Greenberg, D. Cicchetti, & E.M. Cummings (Eds), *Attachment during the preschool years*. Chicago: University of Chicago Press.

Cummings, E.M., & Cicchetti, D. (1990). Attachment, depression, and the transmission of depression. In M.T. Greenberg, D. Cicchetti, & E.M. Cummings (Eds), *Attachment during the preschool years*. Chicago: University of Chicago Press.

Curry, J.F., & Craighead, W.E. (1990). Attributional style in clinically depressed and conduct disordered adolescents. *Journal of Consulting and Clinical Psychology*, **58**, 109–115.

Cutrona, C.E. (1983). Causal attributions and perinatal depression. *Journal of Abnormal Psychology*, **92**, 161–172.

Cutrona, C.E. (1984). Social support and stress in the transition to parenthood. *Journal of Abnormal Psychology*, **93**, 378–390.

Cutrona, C.E. (1989). Ratings of social support by adolescents and adult informants: Degree of correspondence and prediction of depressive symptoms. *Journal of Personality and Social Psychology*, **57**, 723–730.

Cutrona, C.E., Russell, D., & Jones, R. (1984). Cross-situational consistency in causal attributions: Does "attributional style" exist? *Journal of Personality and Social Psychology*, **47**, 1043–1058.

Cutrona, C.E., & Troutman, B.R. (1986). Social support, infant temperament, and parenting self-efficacy: A mediational model of postpartum depression. *Child Development*, **57**, 1507–1518.

Cytryn, L., McKnew, D.H., & Bunney, W.E. (1980). Diagnosis of depression in children: A reassessment. *American Journal of Psychiatry*, **137**, 22–25.

Dattilio, F.M., & Padesky, C.A. (1990). *Cognitive therapy with couples*. Sarasota, FL: Professional Resource Exchange.

Davenport, Y.B., Ebert, M.H., Adland, M.L., & Goodwin, F.K. (1977). Couples group therapy as an adjunct to lithium maintenance of the manic patient. *American Journal of Orthopsychiatry*, **47**, 495–502.

Davenport, Y.B., Zahn-Waxler, C., Adland, M.L., & Mayfield, A. (1984). Early child-rearing practices in families with a manic-depressive parent. *American Journal of Psychiatry*, **141**, 230–235.

Dean, A., & Ensel, W.M. (1982). Modelling social support, life events, competence and depression in the context of age and sex. *Journal of Community Psychology*, **10**, 392–408.

DeMonbreun, B.G., & Craighead, W.E. (1977). Distortion of perception and recall of positive and neutral feedback in depression. *Cognitive Therapy and Research*, **1**, 311–329.

Dempsey, P.A. (1964). Unidimensional depression scale for the MMPI. *Journal of Consulting Psychology*, **28**, 364–370.

Dennard, D.O., & Hokanson, J.E. (1986). Performance on two cognitive tasks by dysphoric and nondysphoric students. *Cognitive Therapy and Research*, **10**, 377–386.

Depue, R.A., Krauss, S., Spoont, M.R., Arbisi, P. (1989). General Behavior Inventory identification of unipolar and bipolar affective conditions in a nonclinical university population. *Journal of Abnormal Psychology*, **98**, 117–126.

Depue, R.A., & Monroe, S.M. (1986). Conceptualization and measurement of human disorder and life stress research: The problem of chronic disturbance. *Psychological Bulletin*, **99**, 36–51.

Depue, R.A., Slater, J., Wolfstetter-Kausch, H., Klein, D., Gopelrud, E., & Farr, D. (1981). A behavioral paradigm for identifying persons at risk for bipolar depressive disorder: A conceptual framework and five validation studies. *Journal of Abnormal Psychology*, **90**, 381–439.

Derogatis, L.R., Lipman, R.S., & Covy, L. (1973). The SCL-90: An outpatient psychiatric rating scale. *Psychopharmacology Bulletin*, **9**, 13–28.

Derry, P., & Kuiper, N.A. (1981). Schematic processing and self-reference in clinical depression. *Journal of Abnormal Psychology*, **90**, 286–297.

DeRubeis, R.J., Evans, M.D., Hollon, S.D., Garvey, M.J., Grove, W.M., & Tuason, V.B. (1990). How does cognitive therapy work? Cognitive change and symptom change in cognitive therapy and pharmacotherapy for depression. *Journal of Consulting and Clinical Psychology*, **58**, 862–869.

DeRubeis, R.J., & Feeley, M. (1990). Determinants of change in cognitive therapy for depression. *Cognitive Therapy and Research*, **14**, 469–482.

Devins, G.M., Binik, Y.M., Hollomby, D.J., Barre, P.E., & Guttmann, R.D. (1981). Helplessness and depression in end-stage renal disease. *Journal of Abnormal Psychology*, **90**, 531–545.

Digdon, N., & Gotlib, I.H. (1985). Developmental considerations in the study of childhood depression. *Developmental Review*, **5**, 162–199.

DiMascio, A., Weissman, M.M., Prusoff, B.A., Neu, C., Zwilling, M., & Klerman, G.L. (1979). Differential symptom reduction by drugs and psychotherapy in acute depression. *Archives of General Psychiatry*, **36**, 1450–1456.

Dobson, K. (1989). A meta-analysis of the efficacy of cognitive therapy for depression. *Journal of Consulting and Clinical Psychology*, **57**, 414– 419.

Dobson, K.S., & Breiter, H.J. (1983). Cognitive assessment of depression: Reliability and validity of three measures. *Journal of Abnormal Psychology*, **92**, 107–109.

Dobson, K.S., & Shaw, B.F. (1987). Specificity and stability of self-referent encoding in clinical depression. *Journal of Abnormal Psychology*, **96**, 34–40.

Doerfler, L.A., Felner, R.D., Rowlison, R.T., Raley, P.A., & Evans, E. (1988). Depression in children and adolescents: A comparative analysis of the utility and construct validity of two assessment measures. *Journal of Consulting and Clinical Psychology*, **56**, 769–772.

Dohrenwend, B.P., & Shrout, P.E. (1985). "Hassles" in the conceptualization and measurement of life stress variables. *American Psychologist*, **40**, 780–785.

Dohrenwend, B.P., Shrout, P.E., Egri, G., & Mendelsohn, P.S. (1980). Measures of nonspecific psychological distress and other dimensions of psychopathology in the general population. *Archives of General Psychiatry*, **37**, 1229–1236.

Dohrenwend, B.P., Shrout, P.E., Link, B., Martin, J., & Skodol, A. (1986). Overview and initial results from a risk-factor study of depression and schizophrenia. In J.E. Barrett (Ed.), *Mental disorder in the community: Progress and challenges.* New York: Guilford Press.

Downey, G., & Coyne, J.C. (1990). Children of depressed parents: An integrative review. *Psychological Bulletin*, **108**, 50–76.

Dykman, B.M., Abramson, L.Y., Alloy, L.B., & Hartlage, S. (1989). Processing of ambiguous and unambiguous feedback by depressed and nondepressed college students: Schematic biases and their implications for depressive realism. *Journal of Personality and Social Psychology*, **56**, 431–445.

Dykman, B.M., Horowitz, L.M., Abramson, L.Y., & Usher, M. (1991). Schematic and situational determinants of depressed and nondepressed sutdents' interpretation of feedback. *Journal of Abnormal Psychology*, **100**, 45–55.

Eaves, G., & Rush, A.J. (1984). Cognitive patterns in symptomatic and remitted unipolar major depression. *Journal of Abnormal Psychology*, **93**, 31–40.

Egeland, B., & Farber, E.A. (1984). Infant-mother attachment: Factors related to its development and changes over time. *Child Development*, **55**, 753–771.

Egeland, B., & Sroufe, L.A. (1981). Developmental sequelae of maltreatment in infancy. *New Directions for Child Development*, **11**, 77–92.

Eisler, R., Hersen, M., Miller, P., & Blanchard, E. (1975). Situational determinants of assertive behavior. *Journal of Consulting and Clinical Psychology*, **43**, 330–340.

Elkin, I., Parloff, M.B., Hadley, S.W., & Autry, J.H. (1985). NIMH treatment of depression collaborative research program. *Archives of General Psychiatry*, **42**, 305–316.

Elkin, I., Shea, T., Watkins, J.T., Imber, S.D., Sotsky, S.M., Collins, J. F., Glass, D.R., Pilkonis, P.A., Leber, W.R., Docherty, J.P., Fiester, S.J., & Parloff, M.B. (1989). National Institute of Mental Health treatment of depression collaborative research program. *Archives of General Psychiatry*, **46**, 971–982.

Emslie, G.J., Rush, A.J., Weinberg, W.A., Rintelmann, J.W., & Roffwarg, H.P. (1990). Children with major depression show reduced rapid eye movement latencies. *Archives of General Psychiatry*, **47**, 119–124.

Endicott, J., Cohen, J., Nee, J., Fleiss, J., & Sarantakos, S. (1981). Hamilton Depression Rating Scale, extrated from regular and change versions of the Schedule for Affective Disorders and Schizophrenia. *Archives of General Psychiatry*, **38**, 98–103.

Endicott, J., & Spitzer, R.L. (1978). A diagnostic interview: The Schedule for Affective Disorders and Schizophrenia. *Archives of General Psychiatry*, **35**, 837–844.

Ensel, W.M. (1986). Sex, marital status, and depression: The role of life events and social support. In N. Lin, A. Dean, & W.M. Ensel (Eds), *Social support, life events, and depression* (pp. 231–247). Montreal: Academic Press.

Erickson, M.F., Sroufe, L.A., & Egeland, B. (1985). The relationship between quality of attachment and behavior problems in preschool in a high-risk sample. *Monographs of the Society for Research in Child Development*, **50**, 147–166.

Farmer, R., & Nelson-Gray, R.O. (1990). Personality disorders and depression: Hypothetical relations, empirical findings, and methodological considerations. *Clinical Psychology Review*, **10**, 453–476.

Feather, N.T., & Barber, J. (1983). Depressive reactions and unemployment. *Journal of Abnormal Psychology*, **92**, 185–195.

Feather, N.T., & Davenport, P.R. (1981). Unemployment and depressive affect: A motivational and attributional analysis. *Journal of Personality and Social Psychology*, **41**, 422–436.

Fendrich, M., Weissman, M.M., & Warner, V. (in press). Screening for depressive disorder in children and adolescents: Validating the CES-DC. *American Journal of Epidemiology*.

Fennell, M.J.V., & Campbell, E.A. (1984). The Cognitions Questionnaire: Specific thinking errors in depression. *British Journal of Clinical Psychology*, **23**, 81–92.

Ferster, C.B. (1973). A functional analysis of depression. *American Psychologist*, **28**, 857–870.

Field, T. (1984). Early interactions between infants and their postpartum depressed mothers. *Infant Behavior and Development*, **7**, 517–522.

Field, T., Healy, B., Goldstein, S., & Guthertz, M. (1990). Behavior-state matching and synchrony in mother-infant interactions of nondepressed versus depressed dyads. *Developmental Psychology*, **26**, 7–14.

Field, T., Healy, B., Goldstein, S., Perry, S., Bendell, D., Schanberg, S., Zimmerman, E. A., & Kuhn, C. (1988). Infants of depressed mothers show "depressed" behavior even with nondepressed adults. *Child Development*, **59**, 1569–1579.

Field, T., Sandberg, D., Garcia, R., Vega-Lahr, N., Goldstein, S., & Guy, L. (1985). Pregnancy problems, postpartum depression and early mother-infant interactions. *Developmental Psychology*, **21**, 1152–1156.

Finch, A.J., Jr., Saylor, C.F., & Edwards, G.L. (1985). Children's Depression Inventory: Sex and grade norms for normal children. *Journal of Consulting and Clinical Psychology*, **53**, 424–425.

Finlay-Jones, R., & Brown, G.W. (1981). Types of stressful life event and the onset of anxiety and depressive disorders. *Psychological Medicine*, **11**, 803–815.

Fiske, S., & Linville, P. (1980). What does the schema process buy us? *Personality and Social Psychology Bulletin*, **6**, 543–557.

Fleming, A., Ruble, D., Flett, G., & Shaul, D. (1988). Postpartum adjustment in first-time mothers: Relations between mood, maternal attitudes, and mother-infant interactions. *Developmental Psychology*, **24**, 71–81.

Foley, S.H., Rounsaville, B.J., Weissman, M.M., Sholomskas, D., & Chevron, E. (1989). Individual versus conjoint interpersonal psychotherapy for depressed patients with marital disputes. *International Journal of Family Psychiatry*, **10**, 29–42.

Folkman, S., & Lazarus, R.S. (1986). Stress process and depressive symptomatology. *Journal of Abnormal Psychology*, **95**, 107–113.

Forehand, R., Brody, G.H., Long, N., & Fauber, R. (1988). The interactive influence of adolescent and maternal depression on adolescent social and cognitive functioning. *Cognitive Therapy and Research*, **12**, 341–350.

Forehand, R., Lautenschlager, G.J., & Graziano, W.G. (1986). Parents' perceptions and parent-child interactions in clinic-referred children: A preliminary investigation of the effects of maternal depressive moods. *Behaviour Research and Therapy*, **24**, 73–75.

Forehand, R., Wells, K., McMahon, R., Griest, D., & Rogers, T. (1982). Maternal perception of maladjustment in the clinic-referred children: An extension of earlier research. *Journal of Behavioral Assesssment*, **4**, 145–151.

Frank, E., Kupfer, D.J., & Perel, J.M. (1989). Early recurrence in unipolar depression. *Archives of General Psychiatry*, **46**, 397–400.

Freden, L. (1982). *Psychosocial aspects of depression*. Chichester, England: John Wiley.

Freud, S. (1917/1961). Mourning and melancholia. In J. Strachey (Ed. and Trans.), *The standard edition of the complete psychological works of Sigmund Freud* (Vol. 14). London: Hogarth Press.

Friedman, A.S. (1964). Minimal effects of severe depression on cognitive functioning. *Journal of Abnormal and Social Psychology*, **69**, 237–243.

Friedman, A.S. (1975). Interaction of drug therapy with marital therapy in depressive patients. *Archives of General Psychiatry*, **32**, 619–637.

Friedman, R.C., Hurt, S.W., Clarkin, J.F., Corn, R., & Aronoff, M.S. (1983). Symptoms of depression among adolescents and young adults. *Journal of Affective Disorders*, **5**, 37–43.

Frommer, E.A., & O'Shea, G. (1973). Antenatal identification of women liable to have problems in managing their infants. *British Journal of Psychiatry*, **123**, 149–156.

Fuchs, C.Z., & Rehm, L.P. (1977). A self-control behavior therapy program for depression. *Journal of Consulting and Clinical Psychology*, **45**, 206–215.

Gallagher, D.E., & Thompson, L.W. (1982). Treatment of major depressive disorder in older adult outpatients with brief psychotherapies. *Psychotherapy: Theory, Research, and Practice*, **19**, 482–490.

Garber, J., Kriss, M.R., Koch, M., & Lindholm, L. (1988). Recurrent depression in adolescents: A follow-up study. *Journal of the American Academy of Child and Adolescent Psychiatry*, **27**, 49–54.

Garrison, C.Z., Jackson, K.L., Marsteller, F., McKeown, R., & Addy, C. (1990). A longitudinal study of depressive symptomatology in young adolescents. *Journal of the American Academy of Child and Adolescent Psychiatry*, **29**, 581–585.

Gelfand, D.M., & Teti, D.M. (1990). The effects of maternal depression on children. *Clinical Psychology Review*, **10**, 320–354.

Gerlsma, C., Emmelkamp, P.M.G., & Arrindell, W.A. (1990). Anxiety, depression, and perception of early parenting: A meta-analysis. *Clinical Psychology Review*, 10, 251–277.

Gershon, E.S., Hamovit, J.H., Guroff, J.J., & Nurnberger, J.I. (1987). Birth-cohort changes in manic and depressive disorders in relatives of bipolar and schizoaffective patients. *Archives of General Psychiatry*, 44, 314–319.

Giambra, L.M. (1977). Independent dimensions of depression: Factor analysis of three self-report depression measures. *Journal of Clinical Psychology*, 33, 928–935.

Glazer, H.I., Clarkin, J.F., & Hunt, H.F. (1981). Assessment of depression. In J.F. Clarkin & H.I. Glazer (Eds), Depression: Behavioral and directive intervention strategies (pp. 3–30). New York: Garland STPM Press.

Glick, I.D., Clarkin, J.F., Spencer, J.H., Haas, G.L., Lewis, A.B., Peyser, J., DeMane, N., Good-Ellis, M., Harris, E., & Lestelle, V. (1985). A controlled evaluation of inpatient family intervention: I. Preliminary results of the six-month follow-up. *Archives of General Psychiatry*, 42, 882–886.

Goetz, R.R., Puig-Antich, J., Ryan, N., Rabinovich, H., Ambrosini, P.J., Nelson, B., & Krawiec, V. (1987). Electroencephalographic sleep of adolescents with major depression and normal controls. *Archives of General Psychiatry*, 44, 61–68.

Goldberg, J.O., Shaw, B.F., & Segal, Z.V. (1987). Concurrent validity of the Millon Clinical Multiaxial Inventory Depression scales. *Journal of Consulting and Clinical Psychology*, 55, 785–787.

Goldin, L. R., & Gershon, E. S. (1988). The genetic epidemiology of major depressive illness. In A. J. Frances & R. E. Hales (Eds), *Review of psychiatry* (Vol. 7, pp. 149–167). Washington, DC: American Psychiatric Press.

Golding, J.M. (1988). Gender differences in depressive symptoms: Statistical considerations. *Psychology of Women Quarterly*, 12, 61–74.

Golding, J.M. (1989). Role occupancy and role-specific stress and social support as predictors of depression. *Basic and Applied Social Psychology*, 10, 173–195.

Golin, S., & Terrell, R. (1979). Motivational and associative aspects of mild depression in skill and chance tasks. *Journal of Abnormal Psychology*, 86, 389–401.

Golin, S., Terrell, F., Weitz, J., & Drost, P.L. (1979). The illusion of control among depressed patients. *Journal of Abnormal Psychology*, 88, 454–457.

Gong-Guy, E., & Hammen, C. (1980). Causal perceptions of stressful life events in depressed and nondepressed clinic outpatients. *Journal of Abnormal Psychology*, 89, 662–669.

Goodman, S.H. (1992). Understanding the effects of depressed mothers on their children. In E.F. Walker, B.A. Cornblatt, & R.H. Dworkin (Eds), *Progress in experimental personality and psychopathology research*, Vol. 15. (p.p. 47–109). New York: Springer Publishing Company.

Goodman, S.H., & Brumley, H.E. (1990). Schizophrenic and depressed mothers: Relational deficits in parenting. *Developmental Psychology*, 26, 31–39.

Gopelrud, E., & Depue, R.A. (1985). Behavioral response to naturally occurring stress in cyclothymia and dysthymia. *Journal of Abnormal Psychology*, 94, 128–139.

Gordon, D., Burge, D., Hammen, C., Adrian, C., Jaenicke, C., & Hiroto, D. (1989). Observations of interactions of depressed women with their children. *American Journal of Psychiatry*, 146, 50–55.

Gotlib, I.H. (1981). Self-reinforcement and recall: Differential deficits in depressed and nondepressed psychiatric patients. *Journal of Abnormal Psychology*, 90, 521–530.

Gotlib, I.H. (1982). Self-reinforcement and depression in interpersonal interaction: The role of performance level. *Journal of Abnormal Psychology*, 91, 3–13.

Gotlib, I.H. (1983). Perception and recall of interpersonal feedback: Negative bias in depression. *Cognitive Therapy and Research*, 7, 399–412.

Gotlib, I.H. (1984). Depression and general psychopathology in university students. *Journal of Abnormal Psychology*, **93**, 19–30.

Gotlib, I.H. (1991). Explanatory style: A question of balance. *Psychological Inquiry*, **2**, 27–30. (Invited Commentary).

Gotlib, I.H., & Asarnow, R.F. (1979). Interpersonal and impersonal problem-solving skills in mildly and clinically depressed university students. *Journal of Consulting and Clinical Psychology*, **47**, 86–95.

Gotlib, I.H., & Beatty, M.E. (1985). Negative responses to depression: The role of attributional style. *Cognitive Therapy of Research*, **9**, 91–103.

Gotlib, I.H., & Cane, D.B. (1987). Construct accessibility and clinical depression: A longitudinal approach. *Journal of Abnormal Psychology*, **96**, 199–204.

Gotlib, I.H., & Cane, D.B. (1989). Self-report assessment of depression and anxiety. In P.C. Kendall & D. Watson (Eds), *Anxiety and depression: Distinctive and overlapping features* (pp. 131–169). Orlando, FL: Academic Press.

Gotlib, I.H., & Colby, C.A. (1987). *Treatment of depression: An interpersonal systems approach*. New York: Pergamon Press.

Gotlib, I.H., & Hooley, J.M. (1988). Depression and marital distress: Current status and future directions. In S. Duck (Ed.), *Handbook of personal relationships* (pp. 543–570). Chichester, England: John Wiley.

Gotlib, I.H., & Lee, C.M. (1989). The social functioning of depressed patients: A longitudinal assessment. *Journal of Social and Clinical Psychology*, **8**, 223–237.

Gotlib, I.H., & Lee, C.M. (1990). Children of depressed mothers: A review and directions for future research. In C.D. McCann & N.S. Endler (Eds), *Depression: New directions in theory, research, and practice* (pp. 187–208). Toronto: Wall & Thompson.

Gotlib, I.H., Lewinsohn, P.M., Seeley, J.R., & Rohde, P. (1991, December). *Cognition in depression: A separation of pessimism and attributional style*. Paper presented at the Annual Meeting of the Society for Research in Psychopathology, Harvard University, Cambridge, MA.

Gotlib, I.H., & McCabe, S.B. (1990). Marriage and psychopathology: A critical examination. In F. Fincham & T. Bradbury (Eds), *The psychology of marriage: Conceptual, empirical, and applied perspectives* (pp. 226–257). New York: Guilford Press.

Gotlib, I.H., & McCabe, S.B. (1992). An information-processing approach to the study of cognitive functioning in depression. In E.F. Walker, B.A. Cornblatt, & R.H. Dworkin (Eds), *Progress in experimental personality and psychopathology research*, Vol. 15. (pp. 131–161). New York: Springer Publishing Company.

Gotlib, I.H., & McCann, C.D. (1984). Construct accessibility and depression: An examination of cognitive and affective factors. *Journal of Personality and Social Psychology*, **47**, 427–439.

Gotlib, I.H., MacLachlan, A.L., & Katz, A.N. (1988). Biases in visual attention in depressed and nondepressed individuals. *Cognition and Emotion*, **2**, 185–200.

Gotlib, I.H., & Meltzer, S.J. (1987). Depression and the perception of social skill in dyadic interaction. *Cognitive Therapy and Research*, **11**, 41–53.

Gotlib, I.H., & Meyer, J.P. (1986). Factor analysis of the Multiple Affect Adjective Check List: A separation of positive and negative affect. *Journal of Personality and Social Psychology*, **50**, 1161–1165.

Gotlib, I.H., Mount, J.H., Cordy, N.I., & Whiffen, V.E. (1988). Depressed mood and perceptions of early parenting: A longitudinal investigation. *British Journal of Psychiatry*, **152**, 24–27.

Gotlib, I.H., & Olson, J.M. (1983). Depression, psychopathology, and self-serving attributions. *British Journal of Clincal Psychology*, **22**, 309–310.

Gotlib, I.H., & Robinson, L.A. (1982). Responses to depressed individuals: Discrepancies between self-report and observer-rated behaviour. *Journal of Abnormal Psychology*, **91**, 231–240.

Gotlib, I.H., Wallace, P.M., & Colby, C.A. (1990). Marital and family therapy for depression. In B.B. Wolman & G. Stricker (Eds), *Depressive disorders: Facts, theories, and treatment methods* (pp. 396–424). New York: John Wiley.

Gotlib, I.H., & Whiffen, V.E. (1989a). Depression and marital functioning: An examination of specificity and gender differences. *Journal of Abnormal Psychology*, **98**, 23–30.

Gotlib, I.H., & Whiffen, V.E. (1989b). Stress, coping, and marital satisfaction in couples with a depressed wife. *Canadian Journal of Behavioral Science*, **21**, 401–418.

Gotlib, I.H., Whiffen, V.E., Mount, J.H., Milne, K., & Cordy, N.I. (1989). Prevalence rates and demographic characteristics associated with depression in pregnancy and the postpartum. *Journal of Consulting and Clinical Psychology*. **57**, 269–274.

Gotlib, I.H., Whiffen, V.E., Wallace, P.M., & Mount, J.H. (1991). A prospective investigation of postpartum depression: Factors involved in onset and recovery. *Journal of Abnormal Psychology*, **100**, 122–132.

Gove, W.R. (1972). The relationship between sex roles, marital status, and mental illness. *Social Forces*, **51**, 34–44.

Gove, W.R., & Tudor, J.F. (1973). Adult sex roles and mental illness. *American Journal of Sociology*, **78**, 812–835.

Greenberg, M., Cicchetti, D., & Cummings, E.M. (Eds). (1990). *Attachment beyond infancy*. Chicago: University of Chicago Press.

Greene, B.L., Lustig, N., & Lee, R.R. (1976). Marital therapy when one spouse has a primary affective disorder. *American Journal of Psychiatry*, **133**, 827–830.

Griest, D., Forehand, R., Wells, K., & McMahon, R. (1980). An examination of differences between nonclinic and behavior-problem clinic-referred children and their mothers. *Journal of Abnormal Psychology*, **89**, 497–500.

Griest, D., Wells, K.C., & Forehand, R. (1979). An examination of predictors of maternal perceptions of maladjustment in clinic-referred children. *Journal of Abnormal Psychology*, **88**, 277–281.

Guidano, V.F., & Liotti, G. (1983). *Cognitive processes and emotional disorders*. New York: Guilford Press.

Gurtman, M. (1986). Depression and the response of others: Reevaluating the reevaluation. *Journal of Abnormal Psychology*, **95**, 99–101.

Haaga, D.A.F., Dyck, M.J., & Ernst, D. (1991). Empirical status of cognitive therapy of depression. *Psychological Bulletin*, **110**, 215–236.

Haas, G.L., Glick, I.D., Clarkin, J.F., Spencer, J.H., Lewis, A.B., Peyser, J., DeMane, N., Good-Ellis, M., Harris, E., & Lestelle, V. (1988). Inpatient family intervention: A randomized clinical trial. II. Results at hospital discharge. *Archives of General Psychiatry*, **45**, 217–224.

Hahlweg, K., Reisner, L., Kohli, G., Vollmer, M., Schindler, L., & Revenstorf, D. (1984). Development and validity of a new system to analyze interpersonal communication: Kategoriensystem für partnerschaftliche interaction. In K. Hahlweg & N.S. Jacobson (Eds), *Marital interaction: Analysis and modification*. New York: Guilford Press.

Haley, G.M., Fine, S., Marriage, D., Moretti, M.M., & Freeman, R.J. (1985). Cognitive bias and depression in psychiatrically disturbed children and adolescents. *Journal of Consulting and Clinical Psychology*, **53**, 535–537.

Hamilton, E.W., & Abramson, L.Y. (1983). Cognitive patterns and major depressive disorder: A longitudinal study in a hospital setting. *Journal of Abnormal Psychology*, **92**, 173–184.

Hamilton, M. (1960). A rating scale for depression. *Journal of Neurology, Neurosurgery and Psychiatry*, **12**, 56–62.

Hammen, C.L. (1980). Depression in college students: Beyond the Beck Depression Inventory. *Journal of Consulting and Clinical Psychology*, **48**, 126–128.

Hammen, C.L. (1981). Assessment: A clinical and cognitive emphasis. In L.P. Rehm (Ed.), *Behavior therapy for depression: Present status and future directions* (pp. 255–277). New York: Academic Press.

Hammen, C. (1985). Predicting depression: A cognitive-behavioral perspective. In P.C. Kendall (Ed.), *Advances in cognitive-behavioral research and therapy*, Vol. 4 (pp. 30–74). New York: Academic Press.

Hammen, C. (1988). Self cognitions, stressful events, and the prediction of depression in children of depressed mothers. *Journal of Abnormal Child Psychology*, **16**, 347–360.

Hammen, C. (1990). Cognitive approaches to depression in children: Current findings and new directions. In B. Lahey and A. Kazdin (Eds), *Advances in Clinical Child Psychology*, Vol. 13 (pp. 139–173). New York: Plenum Press.

Hammen, C. (1991a). *Depression runs in families: The social context of risk and resilience in children of depressed mothers*. New York: Springer-Verlag.

Hammen, C. (1991b). The generation of stress in the course of unipolar depression. *Journal of Abnormal Psychology*, **100**, 555—561.

Hammen, C. (1991c). Mood disorders (Unipolar Depression). In M. Hersen & S. Turner (Eds), *Adult psychopathology and diagnosis*, Second Edition. New York: John Wiley.

Hammen, C., Adrian, C., Gordon, D., Burge, D., Jaenicke, C., & Hiroto, D. (1987). Children of depressed mothers: Maternal strain and symptom predictors of dysfunction. *Journal of Abnormal Psychology*, **96**, 190–198.

Hammen, C., Adrian, C., & Hiroto, D. (1988). A longitudinal test of the attributional vulnerability model in children at risk for depression. *British Journal of Clinical Psychology*, **27**, 37–46.

Hammen, C., Burge, D., & Adrian, C. (1991). Timing of mother and child depression in a longitudinal study of children at risk. *Journal of Consulting and Clinical Psychology*, **59**, 341–345.

Hammen, C., Burge, D., Brown, G., & Stansbury, K. (1991). *A three generation family context model of depression*. Manuscript under review.

Hammen, C., Burge, D., Burney, E., & Adrian, C. (1990a). Longitudinal study of diagnoses in children of women with unipolar and bipolar affective disorder. *Archives of General Psychiatry*, **47**, 1112–1117.

Hammen, C., Burge, D., & Stansbury, K. (1990b). Relationship of mother and child variables to child outcomes in a high risk sample: A causal modeling analysis. *Developmental Psychology*, **26**, pp. 24–30.

Hammen, C., & Cochran, S. (1981). Cognitive correlates of life stress and depression in college students. *Journal of Abnormal Psychology*, **90**, 23–27.

Hammen, C., Davila, J., Brown, G., Ellicott, A., & Gitlin, M. (1992). Psychiatric history and stress: Predictors of severity of unipolar depression. *Journal of Abnormal Psychology*, **101**, 45–52.

Hammen, C., Ellicott, A., & Gitlin, M. (in press). Stressors and Sociotropy/Autonomy: A longitudinal study of their relationship to the course of bipolar disorder. Manuscript under review/invited issue of *Cognitive Therapy and Research*.

Hammen, C., Ellicott, A., Gitlin, M., & Jamison, K.R. (1989). Sociotropy/autonomy and vulnerability to specific life events in unipolar and bipolar patients. *Journal of Abnormal Psychology*, **98**, 154–160.

Hammen, C.L., & Glass, D.R. (1975). Depression, activity, and evaluation of reinforcement. *Journal of Abnormal Psychology*, **84**, 718–721.

Hammen, C., & Goodman-Brown, T. (1990). Self-schemas and vulnerability to specific life stress in children at risk for depression. *Cognitive Therapy and Research*, **14**, 215–227.

Hammen, C., Gordon, D., Burge, D., Adrian, C., Jaenicke, C., & Hiroto, D. (1987). Maternal affective disorders, illness, and stress: Risk for children's psychopathology. *American Journal of Psychiatry*, **144**, 736–741.

Hammen, C., & Krantz, S.E. (1985). Measures of psychological processes in depression. In E.E. Beckham & W.R. Leber (Eds), *Handbook of depression: Treatment, assessment, and research* (pp. 408–444). Homewood, IL: Dorsey Press.

Hammen, C., Krantz, S., & Cochran, S. (1981). Relationships between depression and causal attributions about stressful life events. *Cognitive Therapy and Research*, **5** 351–358.

Hammen, C., Marks, T., deMayo, R., & Mayol, A. (1985a). Self-schemas and risks for depression: A prospective study. *Journal of Personality and Social Psychology*, **49**, 1147–1159.

Hammen, C., Marks, T., Mayol, A., and deMayo, R. (1985b). Depressive self-schemas, life stress, and vulnerability to depression. *Journal of Abnormal Psychology*, **94**, 308–319.

Hammen, C., Mayol, A., deMayo, R., & Marks, T. (1986). Initial symptom levels and the life event-depression relationship. *Journal of Abnormal Psychology*, **95**, 114–122.

Hammen, C.L., & Padesky, C.A. (1977). Sex differences in the expression of depressive responses on the Beck Depression Inventory. *Journal of Abnormal Psychology*, **86**, 609–614.

Hammen, C.L., & Peters, S.D. (1977). Differential responses to male and female depressive relations. *Journal of Consulting and Clinical Psychology*, **45**, 994–1001.

Hammen, C.L., & Peters, S.D. (1978). Interpersonal consequences of depression: Responses to men and women enacting a depressed role. *Journal of Abnormal Psychology*, **87**, 322–332.

Harrington, R., Fudge, H., Rutter, M., Pickles, A., & Hill, J. (1990). Adult outcomes of childhood and adolescent depression: Psychiatric status. *Archives of General Psychiatry*, **47**, 465–473.

Harris, T., Brown, G.W., & Bifulco, A. (1986). Loss of parent in childhood and adult psychiatric disorder: The role of lack of adequate parental care. *Psychological Medicine*, **16**, 641–659.

Harris, T., Brown, G.W., & Bifulco, A. (1987). Loss of parent in childhood and adult psychiatric disorder: The role of social class position and premarital pregnancy. *Psychological Medicine*, **17**. 163–183.

Hartup, W.W. (1989). Social relationships and their developmental significance. *American Psychologist*, **44**, 120–126.

Hathaway, S.R., & McKinley, J.C. (1951). *The Minnesota Multiphasic Personality Inventory Manual* (rev. edn). New York: Psychological Corporation.

Hautzinger, M., Linden, M., & Hoffman, N. (1982). Distressed couples with and without a depressed partner: An analysis of their verbal interaction. *Journal of Behaviour Therapy and Experimental Psychology*, **13**, 307–314.

Hazan, C., & Shaver, P. (1987). Romantic love conceptualized as an attachment process. *Journal of Personality and Social Psychology*, **52**, 511–524.

Helzer, J.E., Robins, L.N., McEvoy, L.T., Spitznagel, E.L., Stoltzman, R.K., Farmer, A., & Brockington, I.F. (1985). A comparison of clinical and diagnostic interview schedule diagnoses. *Archives of General Psychiatry*, **42**, 657–666.

Henderson, A.S., Byrne, D.G., & Duncan-Jones, P. (1981). *Neurosis and the social environment*. Sydney, Australia: Academic Press.

Herjanic, B., & Reich, W. (1982). Development of a structured psychiatric interview for children: Agreement between child and parent on individual symptoms. *Journal of Abnormal Child Psychology*, **10**, 307–324.

Hersen, M., Bellack, A.S., Himmelhoch, J.M., & Thase, M.E. (1984). Effects of social skills training, amitriptyline, and psychotherapy in unipolar depressed women. *Behavior Therapy*, **15**, 21–40.

Hinchliffe, M., Hooper, D., & Roberts, F.J. (1978). *The melancholy marriage*. New York: John Wiley.

Hiroto, D.S., & Seligman, M.E.P. (1975). Generality of learned helplessness in man. *Journal of Personality and Social Psychology*, **31**, 311–327.

Hirschfeld, R.M.A. (1981). Situational depression: Validity of the concept. *British Journal of Psychiatry*, **139**, 297–305.

Hirschfeld, R.M.A. (1984, April). *NIMH collaborative study on psychobiology of illness*. Paper presented at the National Institute of Mental Health Consensus Development Conference, Washington, DC.

Hirschfeld, R.M.A., & Cross, C.K. (1982). Epidemiology of affective disorders: Psychosocial risk factors. *Archives of General Psychology*, **39**, 35–46.

Hirschfeld, R.M.A., & Davidson, L. (1988). Risk factors for suicide. In A.J. Frances & R.E. Hales (Eds), *Review in psychiatry* (pp. 307–333). Washington, DC: American Psychiatric Press.

Hirschfeld, R.M.A., Klerman, G.L., Andreason, N.C., Clayton, P.J., & Keller, M.B. (1986). Psycho-social predictors of chronicity in depressed patients. *British Journal of Psychiatry*, **148**, 648–654.

Hirschfeld, R.M.A., Klerman, G.L., Chodoff, P., Korchin, S., & Barrett, J. (1976). Dependency–self-esteem–clinical depression. *Journal of the American Academy of Psychoanalysis*, **4**, 373–388.

Hirschfeld, R.M.A., Klerman, G.L., Clayton, P.J., & Keller, M.B. (1983). Personality and depression: Empirical findings. *Archives of General Psychiatry*, **40**, 993–998.

Hoberman, H.M. (1990). Behavioral treatments for unipolar depression. In B.B. Wolman & G. Stricker (Eds), *Depressive disorders: Facts, theories, and treatment methods* (pp. 310–342). New York: John Wiley.

Hoberman, H.M., & Lewinsohn, P.M. (1985). The behavioral treatment of depression. In E.E. Beckham & W.R. Leber (Eds), *Handbook of depression: Treatment, assessment, and research* (pp. 39–81). Homewood, IL: Dorsey Press.

Hoberman, H.M., Lewinsohn, P.M., & Tilson, M. (1988). Group treatment of depression: Individual predictors of outcome. *Journal of Consulting and Clinical Psychology*, **56**, 393–398.

Hodgens, J.B., & McCoy, J.F. (1989). Distinctions among rejected children on the basis of peer-nominated aggression. *Journal of Clinical Child Psychology*, **18**, 121–128.

Hodges, K. (1986). Assessing children with a clinical research interview: The Child Assessment Schedule (CAS). In R.J. Prinz (Ed.) *Advances in behavioral assessment of children and families*, Vol. 3 (pp. 203–233). Greenwich, CT: JAI Press.

Hodges, K. (1990). Depression and anxiety in children: A comparison of self-report questionnaires to clinical interview. *Psychological Assessment: A Journal of Consulting and Clinical Psychology*, **2**, 376–381.

Hodges, K., & Craighead, W.E. (1990). Relationship of Children's Depression Inventory factors to diagnosed depression. Psychological Assessment: A *Journal of Consulting and Clinical Psychology*, **2**, 489–492.

Hodges, K., Kline, J., Stern, L., Cytryn, L., & McKnew, D. (1982). The development of a child assessment interview for research and clinical use. *Journal of Abnormal Child Psychology*, **10**, 173–189.

Hodges, K., McKnew, D., Cytryn, L., Stern, L., & Kline, J. (1982). The Child Assessment Schedule (CAS) diagnostic interview: A report on reliability and validity. *Journal of the American Academy of Child Psychiatry*, **21**, 468–473.

Hoen-Hyde, D., Schlottmann, R.S., & Rush, A.J. (1982). Perceptions of social interactions in depressed psychiatric patients. *Journal of Consulting and Clinical Psychology*, **50**, 164–172.

Hokanson, J.E., Hummer, J.T., & Butler, A.C. (1991). Interpersonal perceptions by depressed college students. *Cognitive Therapy and Research*, **15**, 443–457.

Hokanson, J.E., Loewenstein, D.A., Hedeen, C., & Howes, M.J. (1986). Dysphoric college students and roomates: A study of social behaviors over a three-month period. *Personality and Social Psychology Bulletin*, **12**, 311–324.

Hokanson, J.E., Rubert, M.P., Welker, R.A., Hollander, G.R., & Hedeen, C. (1989). Interpersonal concomitants and antecedents of depression among college students. *Journal of Abnormal Psychology*, **98**, 209–217.

Hokanson, J.E., Sacco, W.P., Blumberg, S.R., & Landrum, G.C. (1980). Interpersonal behavior of depressive individuals in a mixed-motive game. *Journal of Abnormal Psychology*, **87**, 322–332.

Holahan, C.J., & Moos, R.H. (1991). Life stressors, personal and social resources, and depression: A 4 year structural model. *Journal of Abnormal Psychology*, **100**, 31–38.

Hollon, S.D., DeRubeis, R.J., & Evans, M.D. (1987). Causal mediation of change in treatment for depression: Discriminating between nonspecificity and noncausality. *Psychological Bulletin*, **102**, 139–149.

Hollon, S.D., Evans, M.D., & DeRubeis, R.J. (1988). Preventing relapse following treatment for depression: The cognitive pharmacotherapy project. In T.M. Field, P.M. McCabe, & N. Schneiderman (Eds), *Stress and coping across development*. New York: Erlbaum.

Hollon, S.D., & Kendall, P.C. (1980). Cognitive self-statements in depression: Development of an automatic thoughts questionnaire. *Cognitive Therapy and Research*, **4**, 383–395.

Hollon, S.D., Kendall, P.C., & Lumry, A. (1986). Specificity of depressotypic cognitions in clinical depression. *Journal of Abnormal Psychology*, **95**, 52–59.

Hollon, S.D., & Najavits, L. (1988). Review of empirical studies on cognitive therapy. In A. Tasman, R. Hales, & A. Frances (Eds), *Review of psychiatry*, Vol. 7 (pp. 643–666). Washington, DC: American Psychiatric Press.

Hollon, S.D., Shelton, R., & Loosen, P. (1991). Cognitive therapy and pharmacotherapy for depression. *Journal of Consulting and Clinical Psychology*, **59**, 88–99.

Holmes, S.J., & Robins, L.N. (1987). The influence of childhood disciplinary experience on the development of alcoholism and depression. *Journal of Child Psychology and Psychiatry*, **28**, 399–415.

Holmes, S.J., & Robins, L.N. (1988). The role of parental disciplinary practices in the development of depression and alcoholism. *Psychiatry*, **51**, 24–35.

Hooley, J.M. (1985). Expressed emotion: A review of the critical literature. *Clinical Psychology Review*, **5**, 119–139.

Hooley, J.M. (1986). Expressed emotion and depression: Interactions between patients and high versus low-expressed emotion spouses. *Journal of Abnormal Psychology*, **95**, 237–246.

Hooley, J.M., Orley, J., & Teasdale, J.D. (1986). Levels of expressed emotion and relapse in depressed patients. *British Journal of Psychiatry*, **148**, 642–647.

Hooley, J.M., & Teasdale, J.D. (1989). Predictors of relapse in unipolar depressives: Expressed emotion, marital distress, and perceived criticism. *Journal of Abnormal Psychology*, **98**, 229–237.

Hoover, C.F., & Fitzgerald, R.G. (1981). Marital conflict of manic-depressive patients. *Archives of General Psychiatry*, **38**, 65–67.

Hops, H., Biglan, A., Sherman, L., Arthur, J., Friedman, L., & Osteen, V. (1987). Home observations of family interactions of depressed women. *Journal of Consulting and Clinical Psychology*, **55**, 341–346.

Hops, H., Lewinsohn, P.M., Andrews, J.A., & Roberts, R.E. (1990). Psychosocial correlates of depressive symptomatology among high school students. *Journal of Clinical Child Psychology*, **19**, 211–220.

Hops, H., Wills, T., Patterson, G.R., & Weiss, R.L. (1972). *Marital interaction coding system (MICS)*. University of Oregon and Oregon Research Institute (NAPS Document #02077). Eugene, OR.

Howes, M.J., & Hokanson, J.E. (1979). Conversational and social responses to depressive interpersonal behavior. *Journal of Abnormal Psychology*, **88**, 625–634.

Howes, M.J., Hokanson, J.E., & Loewenstein, D.A. (1985). Induction of depressive affect after prolonged exposure to a mildly depressed individual. *Journal of Personality and Social Psychology*, **49**, 1110–1113.

Hussian, R.A., & Lawrence, P.S. (1981). Social reinforcement of activity and problem-solving training in the treatment of depressed institutionalized elderly patients. *Cognitive Therapy and Research*, **5**, 57–69.

Ilfeld, F.W. (1977). Current social stressors and symptoms of depression. *American Journal of Psychiatry*, **134**, 161–166.

Imber, S.D., Pilkonis, P.A., Sotsky, S.M., Elkin, I., Watkins, J.T., Collins, J.F., Shea, M.T., Leber, W.R., & Glass, D.R. (1990). Mode-specific effects among three treatments for depression. *Journal of Consulting and Clinical Psychology*, **58**, 352–359.

Ingram, R.E. (1984). Toward an information-processing analysis of depression. *Cognitive Therapy and Research*, **8**, 443–477.

Ingram, R.E. (1990). Self-focused attention in clinical disorders: Review and a conceptual model. *Psychological Bulletin*, **107**, 156–176.

Ingram, R.E., & Reed, M.R. (1986). Information encoding and retrieval processes in depression: Findings, issues, and future directions. In R.E. Ingram (Ed.), *Information processing approaches to clinical psychology* (pp. 131–150). New York: Academic Press.

Ivens, C., & Rehm, L.P. (1988). Assessment of childhood depression: Correspondence between reports by child, mother, and father. *Journal of the American Academy of Child and Adolescent Psychiatry*, **27**, 738–741.

Jacobsen, R.H., Lahey, B.B., & Strauss, C.C. (1983). Correlates of depressed mood in normal children. *Journal of Abnormal Child Psychology*, **11**, 29–40.

Jacobson, E. (1971). *Depression: Comparative studies of normal, neurotic, and psychotic conditions*. New York: International Universities Press.

Jacobson, N.S., & Anderson, E. (1982). Interpersonal skills deficits and depression in college students: A sequential analysis of the timing of self-disclosures. *Behavior Therapy*, **13**, 271–282.

Jacobson, N.S., Dobson, K., Fruzzeti, A.E., Schmaling, K.B., & Salusky, S. (1991). Marital therapy as a treatment for depression. *Journal of Consulting and Clinical Psychology*, **59**, 547–557.

Jacobson, N.S., & Margolin, G. (1979). *Marital therapy: Strategies based on social learning and behavior exchange principles*. New York: Brunner/Mazel.

Jacobson, S., Fasman, J., & DiMascio, A. (1975). Deprivation in the childhood of depressed women. *The Journal of Nervous and Mental Disease*, **160**, 5–3.

Jaenicke, C., Hammen, C., Zupan, B., Hiroto, D., Gordon, D., Adrian, C., & Burge, D. (1987). Cognitive vulnerability in children at risk for depression. *Journal of Abnormal Child Psychology*, **15**, 559–572.

Johnson, J.E., Petzel, T.P., Hartney, L.M., & Morgan, R.A. (1983). Recall of importance ratings of completed and uncompleted tasks as a function of depression. *Cognitive Therapy and Research*, **7**, 51–56.

Joyce, P.R., & Paykel, E.S. (1989). Predictors of drug response in depression. *Archives of General Psychiatry*, **46**, 89–99.

Kahn, J., Coyne, J.C., & Margolin, G. (1985). Depression and marital disagreement: The social construction of despair. *Journal of Social and Personal Relationships*, **2**, 447–461.

Kandel, D.B., & Davies, M. (1982). Epidemiology of depressive mood in adolescents. *Archives of General Psychiatry*, **39**, 1205–1212.

Kandel, D.B., & Davies, M. (1986). Adult sequelae of adolescent depressive symptoms. *Archives of General Psychiatry*, **43**, 255–262.

Kanfer, F.H. (1977). The many faces of self-control, or behavior modification changes its focus. In R.B. Stuart (Ed.), *Behavioral self-management*. New York: Brunner/Mazel.

Kanner, A.D., Coyne, J.C., Schaefer, C., & Lazarus, R.S. (1981). Comparison of two modes of stress measurement: Daily hassels and uplifts versus major life events. *Journal of Behavioural Medicine*, **4**, 1–39.

Karno, M., Hough, R.L., Burnam, A., Escobar, J.I., Timbers, D.M., Santana, F., & Boyd, J.H. (1987). Lifetime prevalence of specific psychiatric disorders among Mexican Americans and non-Hispanic whites in Los Angeles. *Archives of General Psychiatry*, **44**, 695–701.

Kashani, J.H., Cantwell, D.P., Shekim, W.O., & Reid, J.C. (1982). Major depressive disorder in children admitted to an inpatient community mental health center. *American Journal of Psychiatry*, **139**, 671–672.

Kashani, J.H., & Carlson, G.A. (1987). Seriously depressed preschoolers. *American Journal of Psychiatry*, **144**, 348–350.

Kashni, J.H., Carlson, G.A., Beck, N.C., Hoeper, E.W., Corcoran, C.M., McAllister, J.A., Fallahi, C., Rosenberg, T.K., & Reid, J.C. (1987). Depression, depressive symptoms, and depressed mood among a community sample of adolescents. *American Journal of Psychiatry*, **144**, 931–934.

Kashani, J.H., Holcomb, W.R., & Orvaschel, H. (1986). Depression and depressive symptoms in preschool children from the general population. *American Journal of Psychiatry*, **143**, 1138–1143.

Kashani, J.H., Husain, A., Shekim, W.O., Hodges, K.K., Cytryn, L., & McKnew, D.H. (1981). *American Journal of Psychiatry*, **138**, 143–153.

Kashani, J.H., Rosenberg, T.K., & Reid, J.C. (1989). Developmental perspectives in child and adolescent depressive symptoms in a community sample. *American Journal of Psychiatry*, **146**, 871–875.

Kashani, J., & Simonds, J.F. (1979). The incidence of depression in children. *American Journal of Psychiatry*, **136**, 1203–1205.

Kaslow, N. (1990). Development of depression. Paper presented at the W.T. Grant Consortium, November, 1990.

Kaslow, N.J., Racusin, G.R. (in press). Childhood depression: Current issues and future directions. In A.E. Kazdin, A.S. Bellack, & M. Hersen (Eds), *International handbook of behavior modification therapy and research*. New York: Plenum Press.

Kaslow, N.J., Rehm, L.P., Pollack, S.L., & Siegel, A.W. (1988). Attributional style and self-control behavior in depressed and nondepressed children and their parents. *Journal of Abnormal Child Psychology*, **16**, 163–175.

Kaslow, N.J., Rehm, L.P., & Siegel, A.W. (1984). Social-cognitive and cognitive correlates of depression in children. *Journal of Abnormal Child Psychology*, **12**, 605–620.

Katon, W., & Roy-Byrne, P.P. (1991). Mixed anxiety and depression. *Journal of Abnormal Psychology*, **100**, 337–345.

Kazdin, A.E. (1990). Childhood depression. *Journal of Child Psychology and Psychiatry*, **31**, 121–160.

Kazdin, A.E., French, N.H., Unis, A.S., & Esveldt-Dawson, K. (1983). Assessment of childhood depression: Correspondence of child and parent ratings. *Journal of the American Academy of Child Psychology*, **22**, 157–164.

Kazdin, A.E., Rodgers, A., & Colbus, D. (1986). The Hopelessness Scale for Children: Psychometric characteristics and concurrent validity. *Journal of Consulting and Clinical Psychology*, **54**, 241–245.

Keitner, G., & Miller, I. (1990). Family functioning and major depression: An overview. *American Journal of Psychiatry*, **147**, 1128–1137.

Keitner, G.I., Ryan, C.E., Miller, I.W., Kohn, R., & Epstein, N.B. (1991). 12-month outcome of patients with major depression and comorbid psychiatric or medical illness (compound depression). *American Journal of Psychiatry*, **148**, 345–350.

Keller, K.E. (1983). Dysfunctional attitudes and cognitive therapy for depression. *Cognitive Therapy and Research*, **7**, 437–444.

Keller, M.B. (1985). Chronic and recurrent affective disorders: Incidence, course, and influencing factors. In D. Kemali & G. Recagni (Eds), *Chronic treatments in neuropsychiatry*. New York: Raven Press.

Keller, M.B. (1988). Diagnostic issues and clinical course of unipolar illness. In A.J. Frances & R.E. Hales (Eds), *Review of psychiatry* (pp. 188–212). Washington, DC: American Psychiatric Press.

Keller, M.B., Beardslee, W., Lavori, P.W., Wunder, J., Dorer, D.L., & Samuelson, H. (1988). Course of major depression in non-referred adolescents: A retrospective study. *Journal of Affective Disorders*, **15**, 235–243.

Keller, M.B., Lavori, P.W., Endicott, J., Coryell, W., & Klerman, G.L. (1983). "Double depression": Two year follow-up. *American Journal of Psychiatry*, **140**, 689–694.

Keller, M.B., Lavori, P.W., Rice, J., Coryell, W., & Hirschfeld, R.M.A. (1986). The persistent risk of chronicity in recurrent episodes of nonbipolar major depressive disorder: A prospective follow-up. *American Journal of Psychiatry*, **143**, 24–28.

Keller, M.B., Shapiro, R.W., Lavori, P.W., & Wolfe, N. (1982). Recovery in major depressive disorder: Analysis with the life table and regression models. *Archives of General Psychiatry*, **39**, 905–910.

Kendall, P.C., Cantwell, D.P., & Kazdin, A.E. (1989). Depression in children and adolescents: Assessment issues and recommendations. *Cognitive Therapy and Research*, **13**, 109–146.

Kendall, P.C., Hollon, S., Beck, A.T., Hammen, C., & Ingram, R. (1987). Issues and recommendations regarding use of the Beck Depression Inventory. *Cognitive Therapy and Research*, **11**, 289–300.

Kennedy, E., Spence, S.H., & Hensley, R. (1989). An examination of the relationship between childhood depression and social competence amongst primary school children. *Journal of Child Psychology and Psychiatry*, **30**, 561–573.

Kessler, R.C., & McLeod, J.D. (1984). Sex differences in vulnerability to undesirable life events. *American Sociological Review*, **49**, 620–631.

Kiecolt-Glaser, J.K., Dyer, C.S., & Shuttleworth, E.C. (1988). Upsetting social interactions and distress among Alzheimer's disease family care-givers: A replication and extension. *American Journal of Community Psychology*, **16**, 825–837.

Kiesler, D.J. (1984). *Research manual for the Impact Message Inventory*. Richmond, Virginia: Virginia Commonwealth University.

King, D.A., & Heller, K. (1984). Depression and the response of others: A reevaluation. *Journal of Abnormal Psychology*, **93**, 477–480.

Klein, D.N. (1990). Symptom criteria and family history in major depression. *American Journal of Psychiatry*, **147**, 850–854.

Klein, D.N., & Depue, R.A. (1984). Continued impairment in persons at risk for bipolar affective disorder: Results of a 19-month follow-up study. *Journal of Abnormal Psychology*, **93**, 345–347.

Klein, D.N., Taylor, E.B., Dickstein, S., & Harding, K. (1988). Primary early-onset dysthymia: Comparison with primary nonbipolar nonchronic major depression on demographic, clinical, familial, personality, and socioenvironmental characteristics and short-term outcome. *Journal of Abnormal Psychology*, **97**, 387–398.

Klein, M. (1934). A contribution to the psychogenesis of manic-depressive states. In *Contributions to psycho-analysis, 1921–1945* (pp. 282–310). London: Hogarth Press.

Klerman, G.L., Lavori, P.W., Rice, J., Reich, T., Endicott, J., Andreason, N.C., Keller, M.C., & Hirschfeld, R.M.A. (1985). Birth-cohort trends in rates of major depressive disorder among relatives of patients with affective disorder. *Archives of General Psychiatry*, **42**, 689–695.

Klerman, G.L., & Weissman, M.M. (1989). Increasing rates of depression. *Journal of the American Medical Association*, **261**, 2229–2235.

Klerman, G.L., Weissman, M.M., Rounsaville, B.J., & Chevron, E. (1984). *Interpersonal psychotherapy of depression*. New York: Basic Books.

Kobak, R., & Sceery, A. (1988). Attachment in late adolescence: Working models, affect regulation, and representations of self and others. *Child Development*, **59**, 135–146.

Kochanska, G., Kuczynski, L., Radke-Yarrow, M., & Welsh, J.D. (1987). Resolutions of control episodes between well and affectively ill mothers and their young children. *Journal of Abnormal Child Psychology*, **15**, 441–456.

Koegel, P., Burnam, A., & Farr, R.K. (1988). The prevalence of specific psychiatric disorders among homeless individuals in the inner city of Los Angeles. *Archives of General Psychiatry*, **45**, 1085–1092.

Kovacs, M. (1978). *Interview schedule for children* (ISC) (10th revision). Pittsburgh, PA: University of Pittsburgh School of Medicine.

Kovacs, M. (1983, October 12–15). *DSM-III: The diagnosis of depressive disorders in children: An interim appraisal*. Paper presented at the American Psychiatric Association Invitaitonal Workshop, DSM-III: An Interim Appraisal, Washington, DC.

Kovacs, M. (1989). Affective disorders in children and adolescents. *American Psychologist*, **44**, 209–215.

Kovacs, M., & Beck, A.T. (1978). Maladaptive cognitive structures in depression. *American Journal of Psychiatry*, **135**, 525–533.

Kovacs, M., Feinberg, T.L., Crouse-Novak, M.A., Paulauskas, S.L., & Finkelstein, R. (1984a). Depressive disorders in childhood: I. A longitudinal prospective study of characteristics and recovery. *Archives of General Psychiatry*, **41**, 229–237.

Kovacs, M., Feinberg, T.L., Crouse-Novak, M., Paulauskas, S.L., Pollock, M., & Finkelstein, R. (1984b). Depressive disorders in childhood: II. A longitudinal study of the risk for a subsequent major depression. *Archives of General Psychiatry*, **41**, 643–649.

Kovacs, M., Gatsonis, C., Paulauskas, S.L., & Richards, C. (1989). Depressive disorders in childhood: IV. A longitudinal study of comorbidity with and risk for anxiety disorders. *Archives of General Psychiatry*, **46**, 776–782.

Kowalik, D.L., & Gotlib, I.H. (1987). Depression and marital interaction: Concordance between intent and perception of communication. *Journal of Abnormal Psychology*, **96**, 127–134.

Krantz, S., & Hammen, C.L. (1979). Assessment of cognitive bias in depression. *Journal of Abnormal Psychology*, **88**, 611–619.

Krantz, S.E., & Moos, R.H. (1987). Functioning and life context among spouses of remitted and nonremitted depressed patients. *Journal of Consulting and Clinical Psychology*, **55**, 353–360.

Kuiper, N.A. (1978). Depression and causal attributions for success and failure. *Journal of Personality and Social Psychology*, **36**, 236–246.

Kuiper, N.A., Olinger, L.J., & Martin, R.A. (1990). Are cognitive approaches to depression useful? In C.D. McCann and N.S. Endler (Eds), *Depression: New directions in theory, research and practice* (pp. 53–75). Toronto: Wall & Emerson.

Kutcher, S.P., & Marton, P. (1989). Parameters of adolescent depression: A review. *Psychiatric Clinics of North America*, **12**, 895–932.

Larson, R.W., Raffaelli, M., Richards, M.H., Ham, M., & Jewell, L. (1990). Ecology of depression in late childhood and early adolescence: A profile of daily states and activities. *Journal of Abnormal Psychology*, **99**, 92–102.

Lasher, B.J., & Lynn, S.J. (1981, August). *Depressed versus nondepressed college students' responses to evaluative personal feedback*. Paper presented at the meeting of the American Psychological Association, Los Angeles.

Lavik, N.J. (1982). Marital status in psychiatric patients. *Acta Psychiatrica Scandanavica*, **65**, 15–28.

Lazarus, R.S. (1990). Theory-based stress measurement. *Psychological Inquiry*, **1**, 3–13.

Lazarus, R.S., & Folkman, S. (1984). *Stress, appraisal, and coping*. New York: Springer Verlag.

Lazarus, R.S., & Folkman, S. (1987). Transactional theory and research on emotions and coping. *European Journal of Personality*, **1**, 141–169.

Leber, W.R., Beckham, E.E., & Danker-Brown, P. (1985). Diagnostic criteria for depression. In E.E. Beckham, & W.R. Leber (Eds), *Handbook of depression: Treatment, assessment, and research* (pp. 343–371). Homewood, IL: Dorsey Press.

Lee, C.M., & Gotlib, I.H. (1989a). Clinical status and emotional adjustment of children of depressed mothers. *American Journal of Psychiatry*, **146**, 478–483.

Lee, C.M., & Gotlib, I.H. (1989b). Maternal depression and child adjustment: A longitudinal analysis. *Journal of Abnormal Psychology*, **98**, 78–85.

Lee, C.M., & Gotlib, I.H. (1991a). Adjustment of children of depressed mothers: A ten-month follow-up. *Journal of Abnormal Psychology*, **100**, 473–477.

Lee, C.M., & Gotlib, I.H. (1991b). Family disruption, parental availability, and child adjustment: An integrative review. In R.J. Prinz (Ed.), *Advances in the behavioral assessment of children and families*, Vol. 5 (pp. 166–199). London: Jessica Kingsley Publishers.

Lefkowitz, M.M., & Burton, N. (1978). Childhood depression: A critique of the concept. *Psychological Bulletin, 85,* 716–726.

Lefkowitz, M.M., & Tesiny, E.P. (1980). Assessment of childhood depression. *Journal of Consulting and Clinical Psychology, 48,* 43–50.

Lefkowitz, M.M., & Tesiny, E.P. (1985). Depression in children: Parent, teacher, and child perspectives. *Journal of Abnormal Child Psychology, 8,* 221–235.

Lefkowitz, M.M., Tesiny, E.P., & Solodow, W. (1989). A rating scale for assessing dysphoria in youth. *Journal of Abnormal Child Psychology, 17,* 337–347.

Leitenberg, H., Yost, L.W., & Carroll-Wilson, M. (1986). Negative cognitive errors in children: Questionnaire development, normative data, and comparisons between children with and without self-reported symptoms of depression, low self-esteem, and evaluation anxiety. *Journal of Consulting and Clinical Psychology, 54,* 528–536.

Leon, G.R., Kendall, P.C., & Garber, J. (1980). Depression in children: Parent, teacher, and child perspectives. *Journal of Abnormal Child Psychology, 8,* 221–235.

Levitt, E.E., & Lubin, B. (1975). *Depression: Concepts, controversies, and some new facts.* New York: Springer Verlag.

Lewinsohn, P.M. (1974). A behavioral approach to depression. In R.J. Friedman & M.M. Katz (Eds), *The psychology of depression: Contemporary theory and research* (pp. 157–185). New York: John Wiley.

Lewinsohn, P.M., Antonuccio, D.O., Breckenridge, J., & Teri, L. (1987). *The coping with depression course: A psychoeducational intervention for unipolar depression.* Eugene, OR: Castalia.

Lewinsohn, P.M., & Atwood, G.E. (1969). Depression: A clinical research approach. *Psychotherapy: Theory, Research, and Practice, 6,* 166–171.

Lewinsohn, P.M., Biglan, A., & Zeiss, A.M. (1976). Behavioral treatment of depression. In P.O. Davidson (Ed.), *The behavioral management of anxiety, depression and pain* (pp. 91–146). New York: Brunner/Mazel.

Lewinsohn, P.M., Clark, G.N., Hops, H., & Andrews, J. (1990). Cognitive-behavioral treatment for depressed adolescents. *Behavior Therapy, 21,* 385–401.

Lewinsohn, P.M., Duncan, E.M., Stanton, A.K., & Hautzinger, M. (1986). Age at first onset for nonbipolar depression. *Journal of Abnormal Psychology, 95,* 378–383.

Lewinsohn, P.M., Fenn, D.S., Stanton, A.K., & Franklin, J. (1986). Relation of age at onset to duration of episode in unipolar depression. *Journal of Psychology and Aging, 1,* 63–68.

Lewinsohn, P.M., Hoberman, H.M., & Rosenbaum, M. (1988). A prospective study of risk factors for unipolar depression. *Journal of Abnormal Psychology, 97,* 251–264.

Lewinsohn, P.M., Hoberman, H., Teri, L., & Hautzinger, M. (1985). An integrative theory of depression. In S. Reiss & R. Bootzin (Eds), *Theoretical issues in behavior therapy* (pp. 331–359). New York: Academic Press.

Lewinsohn, P.M., Hops, H., Roberts, R., & Seeley, J.R. (1988, November). *Adolescent depression: Prevalence and psychosocial aspects.* Paper presented at the American Public Health Association's Annual Meeting, Boston, MA.

Lewinsohn, P.M., Lobitz, W.C., & Wilson, S. (1973). "Sensitivity" of depressed individuals to aversive stimuli. *Journal of Abnormal Psychology, 81,* 259–263.

Lewinsohn, P.M., Mischel, W., Chaplin, C., & Barton, R. (1980). Social competence and depression: The role of illusory self-perceptions. *Journal of Abnormal Psychology, 89,* 203–217.

Lewinsohn, P.M., Rohde, P., Seeley, J.R., & Hops, H. (1991). Comorbidity of unipolar depression: I. Major depression with dysthymia. *Journal of Abnormal Psychology*, **100**, 205–213.

Lewinsohn, P.M., & Rosenbaum, M. (1987). Recall of parental behavior by acute depressives, remitted depressives, and non-depressives. *Journal of Personality and Social Psychology*, **52**, 611–619.

Lewinsohn, P.M., & Schaffer, M. (1971). The use of home observations as an integral part of the treatment of depression: Preliminary report of case studies. *Journal of Consulting and Clinical Psychology*, **37**, 87–94.

Lewinsohn, P.M., Steinmetz, J.L., Larson, D.W., & Franklin, J. (1981). Depression related cognitions: Antecedent or consequence? *Journal of Abnormal Psychology*, **91**, 213–219.

Lewinsohn, P.M., Sullivan, J.M., & Grosscup, S.J. (1980). Changing reinforcing events: An approach to the treatment of depression. *Psychotherapy: Theory, Research, and Practice*, **47**, 322–334.

Lewinsohn, P.M., & Teri, L. (1982). Selection of depressed and nondepressed subjects on the basis of self-report data. *Journal of Consulting and Clinical Psychology*, **50**, 590–591.

Lewinsohn, P.M., Youngren, M.A., & Grosscup, S.J. (1979). Reinforcement and depression. In R.A. Depue (Ed.), *The psychobiology of the depressive disorders: Implications for the effects of stress* (pp. 291–315). New York: Academic Press.

Lewinsohn, P.M., Zeiss, A.M., & Duncan, E.M. (1989). Probability of relapse after recovery from an episode of depression. *Journal of Abnormal Psychology*, **98**, 107–116.

Lewis, L., Mercatoris, M., Cole, C.S., & Leonard, A. (1980, November). *The self-control process in episodic depression*. Paper presented at the meeting of the Association for the Advancement of Behavior Therapy. New York.

Libet, J., & Lewinsohn, P.M. (1973). The concept of social skill with special reference to the behavior of depressed persons. *Journal of Consulting and Clinical Psychology*, **40**, 304–312.

Lin, N., Dean, A., & Ensel, W.M. (Eds). (1986). *Social support, life events, and depression*. Montreal: Academic Press.

Livingood, A.B., Daen, P., & Smith, B.D. (1983). The depressed mother as a source of stimulation for her infant. *Journal of Clinical Psychology*, **39**, 369–375.

Lloyd, C. (1980a). Life events and depressive disorder reviewed. I. Events as predisposing factors. *Archives of General Psychiatry*, **37**, 529–535.

Lloyd, C. (1980b). Life events and depressive disorders reviewed: II. Events as precipitating factors. *Archives of General Psychiatry*, **37**, 541–548.

Lloyd, G.G., & Lishman, W.A. (1975). Effects of depression on the speed of recall of pleasant and unpleasant experiences. *Psychological Medicine*, **5**, 173–180.

Lubin, B. (1965). Adjective check lists for measurement of depression. *Archives of General Psychiatry*, **12**, 57–62.

Lubin, B. (1967/1981). *Manual for depression adjective check lists.* San Diego: Educational and Industrial Testing Service.

Lyons-Ruth, K., Zoll, D., Connell, D., & Grunebaum, H.U. (1986). The depressed mother and her one-year-old infant: Environment, interaction, attachment, and infant development. In E. Tronick & T. Field (Eds), *Maternal depression and infant disturbance* (New Directions for Child Development), No. **34**, pp. 31–46). San Francisco: Jossey-Bass.

MacLeod, C., & Mathews, A.M. (1991). Cognitive-experimental approaches to the emotional disorders. In R. Martin (Ed.), *Handbook of behavior therapy and psychological science* (pp. 116–150). New York: Pergamon Press.

MacLeod, C., Mathews, A., & Tata, P. (1986). Attentional biases in emotional disorders. *Journal of Abnormal Psychology*, **95**, 15–20.

MacPhillamy, D.J., & Lewinsohn, P.M. (1971). *The Pleasant Events Schedule*. Unpublished manuscript, University of Oregon, Eugene.

Mahoney, M.J. (1974). *Cognition and behavior modification*. Cambridge, MA: Ballinger.

Main, M., Kaplan, N., & Cassidy, J.C. (1985). Security in infancy, childhood and adulthood: A move to the level of representation. In I. Bretherton & E. Waters (Eds), Growing points of attachment theory and research (pp. 66–104). *Monographs of the Society for Research in Child Development*, **5**, (1–2, Serial No. 209).

Manly, P.C., McMahon, R.J., Badley, C.F., & Davidson, P.O. (1982). Depressive attributional style and depression following childbirth. *Journal of Abnormal Psychology*, **91**, 245–254.

Marks, T., & Hammen, C.L. (1982). Interpersonal mood induction: Situational and individual determinants. *Motivation and Emotion*, **6**, 387–399.

Maser, J.D., & Cloninger, C.R. (Eds). (1990). *Comorbidity in anxiety and mood disorders*. Washington, DC: American Psychiatric Press.

Mathews, A., & Bradley, B. (1983). Mood and the self-reference bias in recall. *Behaviour Research and Therapy*, **21**, 233–240.

Mattison, R.E., Handford, H.A., Kales, H.C., Goodman, A.L., & McLaughlin, R.E. (1990). Four-year predictive value of the Children's Depression Inventory. *Psychological Assessment: A Journal of Consulting and Clinical Psychology*, **2**, 169–174.

Mayer, J.M. (1977). Assessment of depression. In P. McReynolds (Ed.), *Advances in psychological assessment*, Vol. 4 (pp. 358–425). San Francisco: Jossey-Bass.

McCabe, S.B., & Gotlib, I.H. (1991a). *Attentional processing in clinically depressed Subjects: A longitudinal investigation*. Manuscript under editorial review.

McCabe, S.B., & Gotlib I.H. (1991b). *Interactions of couples with and without a depressed spouse: Self-report and observations of problem-solving situations*. Manuscript under editorial review.

McCauley, E., Mitchell, J.R., Burke, P., & Moss, S. (1988). Cognitive attributes of depression in children and adolescents. *Journal of Consulting and Clinical Psychology*, **56**, 903–908.

McDowall, J. (1984). Recall of pleasant and unpleasant words in depressed subjects. *Journal of Abnormal Psychology*, **93**, 401–407.

McKnew, D.H., Cytryn, L., Efron, A.M., Gershon, E.S., & Bunney, W.E., Jr. (1979). Offspring of manic-depressive patients. *British Journal of Psychiatry*, **134**, 148.

McLean, P. (1976). Therapeutic decision-making in the behavioral treatment of depression. In P.O. Davidson (Ed.), *The behavioral management of anxiety, depression, and pain* (pp. 54–89). New York: Brunner/Mazel.

McLean, P. (1981). Remediation of skills and performance deficits in depression: Clinical steps and research findings. In J. Clarkin & H. Glazer (Eds), *Behavioral and directive strategies* (pp. 172–204). New York: Garland Publishing.

McLean, P.D., & Hakstian, A.R. (1979). Clinical depression: Comparative efficacy of outpatient treatments. *Journal of Consulting and Clinical Psychology*, **47**, 818–836.

McLean, P.D., & Hakstian, A.R. (1990). Relative endurance of unipolar depression treatment efects: A longitudinal follow-up. *Journal of Consulting and Clinical Psychology*, **58**, 482–488.

McLean, P.D., Ogston, L., & Grauer, L. (1973). Behavioral approach to the treatment of depression. *Journal of Behaviour Therapy and Experimental Psychiatry*, **4**, 323–330.

McNair, D.M. (1974). Self-evaluations of antidepressants. *Psychopharmacologia*, **37**, 281–302.

McNair, D.M., Lorr, M., & Droppleman, L.F. (1971). *Profile of mood states*. San Diego: EdiTS/Educational and Industrial Testing Service.

McNiel, D.E., Arkowitz, H.S., & Pritchard, B.E. (1987). The response of others to face-to-face interaction with depressed patients. *Journal of Abnormal Psychology*, **96**, 341–344.

Mendels, J., Weinstein, N., & Cochrane, C. (1972). The relationship between depression and anxiety. *Archives of General Psychiatry*, **27**, 649–653.

Merikangas, K.R. (1982). Assortative mating for psychiatric disorders and psychological traits. *Archives of General Psychiatry*, **39**, 1173–1180.

Merikangas, K.R. (1984). Divorce and assortative mating among depressed patients. *American Journal of Psychiatry*, **141**, 74–76.

Merikangas, K., Prusoff, B., & Weissman, M. (1988). Parental concordance for affective disorders: Psychopathology in offspring. *Journal of Affective Disorders*, **15**, 279–290.

Merikangas, K., Weissman, M., Prusoff, B., & John, K. (1988). Assortative mating and affective disorders: Psychopathology in offspring. *Psychiatry*, **51**, 48–57.

Merluzzi, T.V., & Boltwood, M.D. (1989). Cognitive assessment. In A. Freeman, K.M. Simon, L.E. Beutler, & H. Arkowitz (Eds), *Comprehensive handbook of cognitive therapy* (pp. 249–266). New York: Plenum Press.

Metalsky, G.I., Abramson, L.Y., Seligman, M.E.P., Semmel, A., & Peterson, C. (1982). Attributional styles and life events in the classroom: Vulnerability and invulnerability to depressive mood reactions. *Journal of Personality and Social Psychology*, **43**, 612–617.

Metalsky, G.I., Halberstadt, L.J., & Abramson, L.Y. (1987). Vulnerability and invulnerability to depressive mood reactions: Toward a more powerful test of the diathesis-stress and causal mediation components of the reformulated theory of depression. *Journal of Personality and Social Psychology*, **52**, 386–393.

Miller, I.W., Epstein, N.B., Bishop, D.S., & Keitner, G.I. (1985). The McMaster Family Assessment Device: Reliability and validity. *Journal of Marital and Family Therapy*, **22**, 345–356.

Miller, I.W., Klee, S.H., & Norman, W.H. (1982). Depressed and nondepressed inpatients' cognitions of hypothetical events, experimental tasks, and stressful life events. *Journal of Abnormal Psychology*, **91**, 78–81.

Miller, I.W., & Norman, W.H. (1979). Learned helplessness in humans: A review and attribution-theory model. *Psychological Bulletin*, **86**, 93–118.

Miller, I.W., Norman, W.H., & Keitner, G.I. (1989). Cognitive- behavioral treatment of depressed inpatients: Six- and twelve-month follow-up. *American Journal of Psychiatry*, **146**, 1274–1279.

Miller, P.M., & Ingham, J.G. (1976). Friends, confidants and symptoms. *Social Psychiatry*, **11**, 51–58.

Miller, W.R., & Seligman, M.E.P. (1975). Depression and learned helplessness in man. *Journal of Abnormal Psychology*, **84**, 228–238.

Millon, T. (1983). *Millon clinical multiaxial inventory manual* (3rd edn). Minneapolis: Interpretive Scoring Systems.

Mills, M., Puckering, C., Pound, A., & Cox, A. (1985). What is it about depressed mothers that influences their children's functioning? In J.E. Stevenson (Ed.), *Recent research in developmental psychopathology* (pp. 11–17). Oxford, England: Pergamon Press.

Miranda, J., & Persons, J.B. (1988). Dysfunctional attitudes are mood state dependent. *Journal of Abnormal Psychology*, **97**, 251–264.

Miranda, J., Persons, J.B., & Byers, C.N. (1990). Endorsement of dysfunctional beliefs depends on current mood state. *Journal of Abnormal Psychology*, **97**, 251–264.

Mitchell, R.E., Cronkite, R.C., & Moos, R.H. (1983). Stress, coping and depression among married couples. *Journal of Abnormal Psychology*, **92**, 443–448.

Mitchell, R.E., & Hodson, C.A. (1983). Coping with domestic violence—social support and psychological health among battered women. *American Journal of Community Psychology*, **11**(6), 629–645.

Monroe, S.M., Bromet, E.J., Connell, M.M., & Steiner, S.C. (1986). Social support, life events, and depressive symptoms: A 1-year prospective study. *Journal of Consulting and Clinical Psychology*, **54**, 424–431.

Monroe, S.M., Imhoff, D.F., Wise, B.D., & Harris, J.E. (1983). Prediction of psychological symptoms under high risk psychosocial circumstances: Life events, social support and symptom specificity. *Journal of Abnormal Psychology*, **92**, 338–350.

Monroe, S.M., & Simons, A.D. (1991). Diathesis-stress theories in the context of life stress research: Implications for the depressive disorders. *Psychological Bulletin*, **110**, 406–425.

Moos, R.H., Cronkite, R.C., Billings, A.G., & Finney, J.W. (1983). *The Health and Daily Living Form manual*. Stanford: Social Ecology Laboratory.

Moos, R., & Moos, B. (1981). *Family Environment Scale Manual*. Palo Alto, Calif.: Consulting Psychologists Press.

Moos, R.H., & Swindle, R.W. (1990). Person-environment transactions and the stressor-appraisal-coping process. *Psychological Inquiry*, **1**, 30–32.

Moran, P.W., & Lambert, M.J. (1983). A review of current assessment tools for monitoring changes in depression. In M.J. Lambert, E.R. Christensen, & S.S. DeJulio (Eds), *The assessment of psychotherapy outcome* (pp. 304–355). New York: John Wiley.

Moretti, M., Fine, S., Haley, G., & Marriage, K. (1985). Childhood and adolescent depression. *Journal of the American Academy of Child Psychiatry*, **24**, 298–302.

Mueller, D.P. (1980). Social networks: A promising direction for research on the relationship of the social environment to psychiatric disorder. *Social Science Medicine*, **14**, 147–161.

Mullins, L.L., Siegel, L.J., & Hodges, K. (1985). Cognitive problem-solving and life event correlates of depressive symptoms in children. *Journal of Abnormal Child Psychology*, **13**, 305–314.

Munro, A. (1966). Parental deprivation in depressive patients. *British Journal of Psychiatry*, **112**, 443–457.

Murphy, G.E., Simons, A.D., Wetzel, R.D., et al. (1984). Cognitive therapy and pharmacotherapy: Singly and together in the treatment of depression. *Archives of General Psychiatry*, **41**, 33–41.

Murphy, J.M., Monson, R.R., Olivier, D.C., Sobol, A.M., & Leighton, A.H. (1987). Affective disorders and mortality. *Archives of General Psychiatry*, **44**, 473–480.

Myers, J.K., & Weissman, M.M. (1980). Use of a self-report symptom scale to detect depression in a community sample. *American Journal of Psychiatry*, **137**, 1081–1084.

Myers, J.K., Weissman, M.M., Tischler, G.L., Holzer III, C.E., Leaf, P.J., Orvaschel, H., Anthony, J.C., Boyd, J.H., Burke, J.D., Kramer, M., & Stoltzman, R. (1984). Six-month prevalence of psychiatric disorders in three communities: 1980–1982. *Archives of General Psychiatry*, **41**, 959–967.

Nelson, G. (1982). Parental death during childhood and adult depression: Some additional data. *Social Psychiatry*, **17**, 37–42.

Nelson, G.M., & Beach, S.R.H. (1990). Sequential interaction in depression: Effects of depressive behavior on spousal aggression. *Behavior Therapy*, **21**, 167–182.

Nelson, L.D. (1987). Measuring depression in a clinical population using the MMPI. *Journal of Consulting and Clinical Psychology*, **55**, 788–790.

Nelson, R.E. (1977). Irrational beliefs in depression. *Journal of Consulting and Clinical Psychology*, **45**, 1190–1191.

Nelson, III, W.M., & Politano, P.M. (1990). Children's Depression Inventory: Stability over repeated administrations in psychiatric inpatient children. *Journal of Clinical Child Psychology*, **19**, 254–256.

Nezu, A.M. (1986). Efficacy of a social problem-solving therapy approach for unipolar depression. *Journal of Consulting and Clinical Psychology*, **54**, 196–202.

Nezu, A.M. (1987). A problem-solving formulation of depression: A literature review and proposal of a pluralistic model. *Clinical Psychology Review*, **7**, 121–144.

Nezu, A.M., Nezu, C.M., & Perri, M.G. (1989). *Problem-solving therapy for depression: Theory, research, and clinical guidelines*. New York: John Wiley.

Nezu, A.M., & Perri, M.G. (1989). Social problem-solving therapy for unipolar depression: An initial dismantling investigation. *Journal of Consulting and Clinical Psychology*, **57**, 408–413.

Nezu, A.M., & Ronan, G.F. (1985). Life stress, current problems, problem solving, and depressive symptoms: An integrative model. *Journal of Consulting and Clinical Psychology*, **53**, 693–697.

Nietzel, M.T., & Harris, M.J. (1990). Relationship of dependency and achievement/autonomy to depression. *Clinical Psychology Review*, **10**, 279–297.

Nietzel, M., Russell, R., Hemmings, K., & Gretter, M. (1987). Clinical significance of psychotherapy for unipolar depression: A meta-analytic approach to social comparison. *Journal of Consulting and Clinical Psychology*, **55**, 156–161.

NIMH/NIH Consensus Development Conference Statement. (1985). *American Journal of Psychiatry*, **142**, 469–476.

Nisbett, R.E., & Wilson, T.D. (1977). Telling more than we can know: Verbal reports on mental processes. *Psychological Review*, **84**, 231–259.

Noh, S., & Avison, W.R. (1988). Spouses of discharged psychiatric patients: Factors associated with their experience of burden. *Journal of Marriage and the Family*, **50**, 377–389.

Noh, S., & Turner, R.J. (1987). Living with psychiatric patients: Implications for the mental health of family members. *Social Science and Medicine*, **25**, 263–271.

Nolen-Hoeksema, S. (1987). Sex differences in unipolar depression: Evidence and theory. *Psychological Bulletin*, **101**, 259–282.

Nolen-Hoeksema, S. (1990). *Sex differences in depression*. Stanford, CA: Stanford University Press.

Nolen-Hoeksema, S., Girgus, J.S., & Seligman, M.E.P. (1986). Learned helplessness in children: A longitudinal study of depression, achievement, and explanatory style. *Journal of Personality and Social Psychology*, **51**, 435–442.

Nuckolls, K.B., Cassel, J., & Kaplan, B.H. (1972). Psychosocial assets, life crisis, and the prognosis of pregnancy. *American Journal of Epidemiology*, **95**, 431–441.

O'Hara, M.W., Neunaber, D.J., & Zekoski, E.M. (1984). Prospective study of postpartum depression: Prevalence, course, and predictive factors. *Journal of Abnormal Psychology*, **93**, 158–171.

O'Hara, M.W., Rehm, L.P., & Campbell, S.B. (1982). Predicting depressive symptomatology: Cognitive-behavioural models and postpartum depression. *Journal of Abnormal Psychology*, **91**, 457–461.

O'Leary K.D., & Beach, S.R.H. (1990). Marital therapy: A viable treatment for depression. *American Journal of Psychiatry*, **147**, 183–186.

O'Leary, K.D., Riso, L.P., & Beach, S.R.H. (1990). Attributions about the marital discord/depression link and therapy outcome. *Behavior Therapy*, **21**, 413–422.

Oatley, K., & Bolton, W. (1985). A social-cognitive theory of depression in reaction to life events. *Psychologica Review*, **92**, 372–388.

Odegaard, O. (1946). Marriage and mental disease: A study in social psychopathology. *Journal of Mental Science*, **92**, 35–59.

Olinger, L.J., Kuiper, N.A., & Shaw, B.F. (1987). Dysfunctional attitudes and stressful life events: An interactive model of depression. *Cognitive Therapy and Research*, **11**, 25–40.

Oliver, J., Handal, P., Finn, T., & Herdy, S. (1987). Depressed and nondepressed students and their siblings in frequent contact with their families: Depression and perceptions of the family. *Cognitive Therapy and Research*, **11**, 501–515.

Olson, D.H., Portner, J., & Bell, R. (1982). *FACES II. Family Adaptability and Cohesion Evaluation Scales*. Family Social Science, University of Minnesota, St. Paul, MN.

Orvaschel, H., Puig-Antich, J., Chambers, W., Tabrizi, M.A., & Johnson, R. (1982). Retrospective assessment of prepubertal major depression with the Kiddie-SADS-E. *Journal of the American Academy of Child Psychiatry*, **21**, 392–397.

Orvaschel, H., Walsh-Allis, G., & Ye, W. (1988). Psychopathology in children of parents with recurrent depression. *Journal of Abnormal Child Psychology*, **16**, 17–28.

Pagel, M.D., Erdly, W.W., & Becker, J. (1987). Social networks: We get by with (and in spite of) a little help from our friends. *Journal of Personality and Social Psychology*, **53**, 793–804.

Paley, B. (1990). *Depression in adolescence*. University of California, Los Angeles, Department of Psychology. Unpublished paper.

Panaccione, V.F., & Wahler, R.G. (1986). Child behavior, maternal depression, and social coercion as factors in the quality of child care. *Journal of Abnormal Child Psychology*, **14**, 263–278.

Parker, G. (1981). Parental reports of depressives: An investigation of several explanations. *Journal of Affective Disorders*, **3**, 131–140.

Parker, G. (1986). Validating an experiential measure of parental style: The use of a twin sample. *Acta Psychiatrica Scandinavica*, **73**, 22–27.

Parker, G., Tupling, H., & Brown, L.B. (1979). A parental bonding instrument. *British Journal of Medical Psychology*, **52**, 1–10.

Parker, J.G., & Asher, S.R. (1987). Peer relations and later personal adjustment: Are low-accepted children at risk? *Psychological Bulletin*, **102**, 357–389.

Pattison, E.M., de Francisco, D., Wood, P., Frazier, H., & Crowder, J. (1975). A psychosocial kinship model for family therapy. *American Journal of Psychiatry*, **132**, 1246–1251.

Paykel, E.S. (1979). Recent life events in the development of the depressive disorders: Implications for the effects of stress. In R.A. Depue (Ed.), *The psychobiology of the depressive disorders* (pp. 245–262). New York: Academic Press.

Paykel, E.S., Myers, J.K., Dienelt, M.N., Klerman, G.L., Lindenthal, J.J., & Pepper, M.P. (1969). Life events and depression: A controlled study. *Archives of General Psychiatry*, **21**, 753–760.

Pearlin, L.I., & Johnson, J.S. (1977). Marital status, life-strains, and depression. *American Sociological Review*, **42**, 704–715.

Perris, C., Holmgren, S., Von Knorring, L., & Perris, H. (1986). Parental loss by death in the early childhood of depressed patients and of their healthy siblings. *British Journal of Psychiatry*, **148**, 165–169.

Persons, J.B., & Burns, D.D. (1985). Mechanisms of action of cognitive therapy: The relative contributions of technical and interpersonal interventions. *Cognitive Therapy and Research*, **9**, 539–551.

Persons, J.B. (1989). *Cognitive therapy in practice: A case formulatin approach.* New York: W.W. Norton.

Persons, J.B., & Rao, P.A. (1985). Longitudinal study of cognitions, life events, and depression in psychiatric inpatients. *Journal of Abnormal Psychology,* **94,** 51–63.

Petersen, A.C., Sarigiani, P.A., & Kennedy, R.E. (1991). Adolescent depression: Why more girls? *Journal of Youth and Adolescence,* **20,** 247–271.

Peterson, C. (1991). The meaning and measurement of explanatory style. *Psychological Inquiry,* **2,** 1–10.

Peterson, C., Rosenbaum, A.C., & Conn, M.K. (1985). Depressive mood reactions to breaking up: Testing the learned helplessness model of depression. *Journal of Social and Clinical Psychology,* **3** 161–169.

Peterson, C., Schwartz, S.M., & Seligman, M.E.P. (1981). Self-blame and depressive symptoms. *Journal of Personality and Social Psychology,* **41,** 253–259.

Peterson, C., & Seligman, M.E.P. (1984). Causal explanations as a risk factor for depression: Theory and evidence. *Psychological Review,* **91,** 347–374.

Peterson, C., Semmel, A., von Baeyer, C., Abramson, L.Y., Metalsky, G.I., & Seligman, M.E.P. (1982). The Attributional Style Questionnaire. *Cognitive Therapy and Research,* **6,** 287–300.

Peterson, L., Mullins, L.L., & Ridley-Johnson, R. (1985). Childhood depression: Peer reactions to depression and life stress. *Journal of Abnormal Child Psychology,* **13,** 597–609.

Pfohl, B., Stangl, D., & Tsuang, M.T. (1983). The association between early parental loss and diagnosis in the Iowa 500. *Archives of General Psychiatry,* **40,** 965–967.

Phillips, K.A., Gunderson, J.G., Hirschfeld, R.M.A., & Smith, L.E. (1990). A review of the depressive personality. *American Journal of Psychiatry,* **147,** 830–837.

Plantes, M.M., Prusoff, B.A., Brennan, J., & Parker, G. (1988). Parental representations of depressed outpatients from a U.S.A. sample. *Journal of Affective Disorders,* **15,** 149–155.

Power, M. (1988). Cognitive failures dysfunctional attitudes and symptomatology: A longitudinal study. *Cognition and Emotion,* **2,** 133–143.

Poznanski, E.O., Cook, S.C., & Carroll, B.J. (1979). A depression rating scale for children. *Pediatrics,* **64,** 442–450.

Puig-Antich, J. (1982). Major depression and conducte disorder in prepuberty. *Journal of the American Academy of Child Psychiatry,* **21,** 118–128.

Puig-Antich, J., Chambers, W., & Tabrizi, M.A. (1983). The clinical assessment of current depressive episodes in children and adolescents: Interview with parents and children. In B.P. Cantwell & G.A. Carlson (Eds), *Affective disorders in childhood and adolescence* (pp. 157–180). New York: SP Medical and Scientific Books.

Puig-Antich, J., Dahl, R., Ryan, N., Novacenko, H., Goetz, D., Goetz, R., Twomey, J., & Klepper, T. (1989). Cortisol secretion in prepubertal children with Major Depressive Disorder. *Archives of General Psychiatry,* **46,** 801–809.

Puig-Antich, J., Lukens, E., Davies, M., Goetz, D., Brennan-Quattrock, J., & Todak, G. (1985a). Psychosocial functioning in prepubertal major depressive disorders: I. Interpersonal relationships during the depressive episode. *Archives of General Psychiatry,* **42,** 500–507.

Puig-Antich, J., Lukens, E., Davies, M., Goetz, D., Brennan-Quattrock, J., & Todak, G. (1985b). Psychosocial functioning in prepubertal major depressive disorders: II. Interpersonal relationships after sustained recovery from affective episode. *Archives of General Psychiatry,* **42,** 511–517.

Pyszczynski T., & Greenberg, J. (1987). Self-regulatory perseveration and the depressive self-focusing style: A self-awareness theory of reactive depression. *Psychological Bulletin*, **102**, 122–138.

Pyszczynski T., Greenberg, J., Hamilton, J., & Nix, G. (1991). On the relationship between self-focused attention and psychological disorder: A critical reappraisal. *Psychological Bulletin*, **110**, 538–543.

Radke-Yarrow, M., Cummings, E.M., Kuczynski, L., & Chapman, M. (1985). Patterns of attachment in two- and three-year olds in normal families and families with parental depression. *Child Development*, **56**, 884–893.

Radloff, L. (1975). Sex differences in depression: The effects of occupation and marital status. *Sex Roles*, **1**, 249–265.

Radloff, L.S. (1977). The CES-D Scale: A new self-report depression scale for research in the general population. *Applied Psychological Measurment*, **1**, 385–401.

Rado, S. (1928). The problem of melancholia. *International Journal of Psychoanalysis*, **9**, 420–438.

Raps, C.S., Peterson, C., Reinhard, K.E., Abramson, L.Y., & Seligman, M.E.P. (1982). Attributional style among depressed patients. *Journal of Abnormal Psychology*, **91**, 102–108.

Raskin, A., Boothe, H.H., Reatig, N.A., Schulterbrandt, J.G., & Odle, D. (1971). Factor analyses of normal and depressed patients' memories of parental behavior. *Psychological Reports*, **29**, 871–879.

Reda, M.A., Carpiniello, B., Secchiaroli, L., & Blanco, S. (1985). Thinking, depression, and antidepressants: Modified and unmodified beliefs during treatment with amitryptiline. *Cognitive Therapy and Research*, **9**, 135–143.

Rehm, L.P. (1976). Assessment of depression. In M. Hersen & A.S. Bellack (Eds), *Behavioral assessment: A practical handbook* (pp. 246–295). New York: Pergamon Press.

Rehm, L.P. (1977). A self-control model of depression. *Behavior Therapy*, **8**, 787–804.

Rehm, L.P. (1990). Cognitive and behavioral theories. In B.B. Wolman & G. Stricker (Eds), *Depressive disorders: Facts, theories, and treatment methods* (pp. 64–91). New York: John Wiley.

Rehm, L.P. (in press). Psychotherapies for depression. In B. Bloom and K. Schlesinger (Eds), *Boulder Symposium on Clinical Psychology: Depression*. Hillsdale, NJ: Lawrence Erlbaum Associates.

Rehm, L.P., Fuchs, C.Z., Roth, D.M., Kornblith, S.J., & Romano, J.M. (1979). A comparison of self-control and assertion skills treatments of depression. *Behavior Therapy*, **10**, 429–442.

Reich, J., Noyes, R., Hirschfeld, R., Coryell, W., & O'Gorman, T. (1987). State and personality in depressed and panic patients. *American Journal of Psychiatry*, **144**, 181–187.

Reiss, D., Plomin, R., & Hetherington, E.M. (1991). Genetics and psychiatry: An unheralded window on the environment. The *American Journal of Psychiatry*, **148**, 283–291.

Renne, K.S. (1971). Health and marital experience in an urban population. *Journal of Marriage and the Family*, **33**, 338–350.

Reynolds, W.M., Anderson, G., & Bartell, N. (1985). Measuring depression in children. *Journal of Abnormal Child Psychology*, **13**, 513–526.

Reynolds, W.M., & Coats, K.I. (1986). A comparison of cognitive behavioral-therapy and relaxation training for the treatment of depression in adolescents. *Journal of Consulting and Clinical Psychology*, **54**, 653–660.

Richters, J.E. (in press). Depressed mothers as informants about their children: A review of the evidence for distortion. *Psychological Bulletin*.

Riskind, J.H., Beck, A.T., Berchick, R.J., Brown, G., & Steer, R.A. (1987). Reliability of DSM-III diagnoses for major depression and generalized anxiety disorder using the Structured Clincial Interview for DSM-III. *Archives of General Psychiatry*, **44**, 817–820.

Riskind, J.H., & Rholes, W.S. (1984). Cognitive accessibility and the capacity of cognitions to predict future depression: A theoretical note. *Cognitive Therapy and Research*, **8**, 1–12.

Riskind, J.H., Rholes, W.S., & Eggers, J. (1982). The Velten mood induction procedure: Effects on mood and memory. *Journal of Consulting and Clinical Psychology*, **50**, 146–147.

Roberts, R.E. (1980). Reliability of the CES-D in different ethnic contexts. *Psychiatry Research*, **2**, 125–134.

Roberts, R.E., Andrews, J.A., Lewinsohn, P.M., & Hops, H. (1990). Assessment of depression in adolescents using the Center for Epidemiologic Studies Depression Scale. *Psychological Assessment: A Journal of Consulting and Clinical Psychology*, **2**, 122–128.

Roberts, R.E., Lewinsohn, P.M., & Seeley, J.R. (1991). Screening for adolescent depression: A comparison of depression scales. *Journal of the American Academy of Child and Adolescent Psychiatry*, **30**, 58–66.

Roberts, R.E., & O'Keefe, S.J. (1981). Sex differences in depression reexamined. *Journal of Health and Social Behavior*, **22**, 394–400.

Roberts, R.E., & Vernon, S.W. (1983). The Center for Epidemiologic Studies Depression Scale: Its use in a community sample. *American Journal of Psychiatry*, **140**, 41–46.

Robins, C.J. (1988). Depression and attributions: Why is the literature so inconsistent? *Journal of Personality and Social Psychology*, **54**, 880–889.

Robins, C.J. (1990). Congruence of personality and life events in depression. *Journal of Abnormal Psychology*, **99**, 393–397.

Robins, C.J., & Block, P. (1988). Personal vulnerability, life events, and depressive symptoms: A test of a specific interational model. *Journal of Personality and Social Psychology*, **54**, 847–852.

Robins, C.J., Block, P., & Peselow, E.D. (1989). Relations of sociotropic and autonomous personality characteristics to specific symptoms in depressed patients. *Journal of Abnormal Psychology*, **98**, 86–88.

Robins, C.J., & Hinkley, K. (1989). Social-cognitive processing and depressive symptoms in children: A comparison of measures. *Journal of Abnormal Child Psychology*, **17**, 29–36.

Robins, C.J., & Luten, A.G. (1991). Sociotropy and autonomy: Differential patterns of clinical presentation in unipolar depression. *Journal of Abnormal Psychology*, **100**, 74–77.

Robins, E., & Guze, S.B. (1972). Classification of affective disorders: The primary-secondary, the endogenous, and the neurotic-psychotic concepts. In T.A. Williams, M.M. Katz, & J.A. Shield (Eds), *Recent advances in the psychobiology of depressive illness*. Washington, DC: Department of Health, Education & Welfare.

Robins, L.N., Helzer, J.E., Croughan, J., & Ratcliff, K.S. (1981). National Institute of Mental Health Diagnostic Interview Schedule: Its history, characteristics, and validity. *Archives of General Psychiatry*, **38**, 381–389.

Robins, L.N., Helzer, J.E., Weissman, M.M., Orvaschel, H., Gruenberg, E., Burke, J.D., & Regier, D.A. (1984). Lifetime prevalence of specific psychiatric disorders in three sites. *Archives of General Psychiatry*, **41**, 949–958.

Robinson, L., Berman, J., & Neimeyer, R. (1990). Psychotherapy for the treatment of depression: A comprehensive review of controlled outcome research. *Psychological Bulletin*, **108**, 30–49.

Rohde, P., Lewinsohn, P., & Seeley, J.R. (1990). Are people changed by the experience of having an episode of depression? A further test of the scar hypothesis. *Journal of Abnormal Psychology*, **99**, 264–271.

Rohde, P., Lewinsohn, P., & Seeley, J. (1991). Comorbidity of unipolar depression: II. Comorbidity with other mental disorders in adolescents and adults. *Journal of Abnormal Psychology*, **100**, 214–222.

Romano, B.A., & Nelson, R.O. (1988). Discriminant and concurrent validity of measures of children's depression. *Journal of Clinical Child Psychology*, **17**, 255–259.

Rosenblatt, A., & Greenberg, J. (1991). Depression and interpersonal attraction: The role of perceived similarity. *Journal of Personality and Social Psychology*, **55**, 112–119.

Roth, D., Bielski, R., Jones, J., Parker, W., & Osborn, G. (1982). A comparison of self-control therapy and combined self-control therapy and antidepressant medication in the treatment of depression. *Behavior Therapy*, **13**, 133–144.

Rothman, D., Sorrells, J., & Heldman, P. (1976). *A Global Assessment Scale for children*. Oakland, CA: Alameda County Child and Family Mental Health Services.

Rounsaville, B.J., Weissman, M.M., Prusoff, B.G., & Herceg-Baron, R.L. (1979). Marital disputes and treatment outcome in depressed women. *Comprehensive Psychiatry*, **20**, 483–489.

Roy, A. (1981). Role of past loss in depression. *Archives of General Psychiatry*, **38**, 301–302.

Ruscher, S.M., & Gotlib, I.H. (1988). Marital interaction patterns of couples with and without a depressed partner. *Behavior Therapy*, **19**, 455–470.

Rush, A.J., Beck, A.T., Kovacs, M., Weissenburger, J., & Hollon, S.D. (1982). Comparison of the effects of cognitive therapy and pharmacotherapy on hopelessness and self-concept. *American Journal of Psychiatry*, **139**, 862–866.

Rush, A.J., Shaw, B.F., & Khatami, M. (1980). Cognitive therapy for depression: Utilizing the couples system. *Cognitive Therapy and Research*, **4**, 103–113.

Rush, A.J., Weissenburger, J., & Eaves, G. (1986). Do thinking patterns predict depressive symptoms? *Cognitive Therapy and Research*, **10**, 225–236.

Rushing, W. (1979). Marital status and mental disorder: Evidence in favor of a behavioral model. *Social Forces*, **58**, 540–556.

Rutter, M. (1986). The developmental psychopathology of depression: Issues and perspectives. In M. Rutter, C.E. Izard, & P.B. Read (Eds), *Depression in young people* (pp. 3–30). New York: Guilford Press.

Rutter, M. (1989). Isle of Wight revisited: Twenty-five years of child psychiatric epidemiology. *American Academy of Child and Adolescent Psychiatry*, **28**, 633–653.

Rutter, M., & Quinton, P. (1984). Parental psychiatric disorder: Effects on children. *Psychological Medicine*, **14**, 853–880.

Ryan, N.D., Puig-Antich, J., Ambrosini, P., Rabinovich, H., Robinson, D., Nelson, B., Iyengar, S., & Twomey, J. (1987). The clinical picture of major depression in children and adolescents. *Archives of General Psychiatry*, **44**, 854–861.

Sacco, W.P., & Beck, A.T. (1985). Cognitive therapy of depression. In E.E. Beckham and W.R. Leber (Eds), *Handbook of depression: Treatment, assessment, and research* (pp. 3–38). Homewood, IL: Dorsey Press.

Sacco, W.P., & Graves, D.J. (1984). Childhood depression, interpersonal problem-solving, and self-ratings of performance. *Journal of Clinical Child Psychology*, **13**, 10–15.

Safran, J.D. (1990a). Towards a refinement of cognitive therapy in light of interpersonal theory: I. Theory. *Clinical Psychology Review*, **10**, 87–105.

Safran, J.D. (1990b). Towards a refinement of cognitive therapy in light of interpersonal theory: II. Practice. *Clinical Psychology Review*, **10**, 107–121.

Safran, J.D., & Segal, Z.V. (1990). *Interpersonal process in cognitive therapy*. New York: Basic Books.

Sameroff, A.J., Seifer, R., & Zax, M. (1982). Early development of children at risk for emotional disorder. *Monographs of the Society for Research in Child Development*, **47** (7, Serial No. 199).

Sanderson, W.C., Beck, A.T., & Beck, J. (1990). Syndrome comorbidity in patients with major depression or dysthymia: Prevalence and temporal relationships. *American Journal of Psychiatry*, **147**, 1025–1028.

Sarason, I.G., Levine, H.M., Basham, R.B., & Sarason, B.R. (1983). Assessing social support: The Social Support Questionnaire. *Journal of Personality and Social Psychology*, **44**, 127–139.

Sargeant, J.K., Bruce, M.L., Florio, L.P., & Weissman, M.M. (1990). Factors associated with 1-year outcome of major depression in the community. *Archives of General Psychiatry*, **47**, 519–526.

Saylor, C.F., Finch, A.J., Baskin, C.H., Furey, W., & Kelly, M.M. (1984). Construct validity for measures of childhood depression: Application of multitrait-multimethod methodology. *Journal of Consulting and Clinical Psychology*, **52**, 977–985.

Saylor, C.F., Finch, A.J., Spirito, A., & Bennett, B. (1984). The Children's Depression Inventory: A systematic evaluation of psychometric properties. *Journal of Consulting and Clinical Psychology*, **52**, 955–967.

Schaefer, A., Brown, J., Watson, C.G., Plemel, D., DeMotts, J., Howard, M.T., Petrik, N., & Balleweg, B.J. (1985). Comparison of the validities of the Beck, Zung, and MMPI depression scales. *Journal of Consulting and Clinical Psychology*, **53**, 415–418.

Schaefer, E.S. (1965). Children's reports of parental behaviour: An inventory. *Child Development*, **36**, 413–424.

Schleifer, S.J., Keller, S.E., Bond, R.N., Cohen, J., & Stein, M. (1989). Major depressive disorder and immunity. *Archives of General Psychiatry*, **46**, 81–87.

Schless, A.P., Schwartz, L., Goetz, C., & Mendels, J. (1974). How depressives view the significance of life events. *British Journal of Psychiatry*, **125**, 406–410.

Schmaling, K.B., & Jacobson, N.S. (1990). Marital interaction and depression. *Journal of Abnormal Psychology*, **99**, 229–236.

Schulberg, H.C., McClelland, M., & Burns, B.J. (1987). Depression and physical illness: The prevalence, causation and diagnosis of comorbidity. *Clinical Psychology Review*, **7**, 145–167.

Segal, Z.V., & Shaw, B.F. (1986). Cognition in depression: A reappraisal of Coyne and Gotlib's critique. *Cognitive Therapy and Research*, **10**, 779–793.

Segal, Z.V., Shaw, B.F., Vella, D.D., & Katz, R. (1992). Cognitive and life stress predictors of relapse in remitted unipolar depressed patients: A test of the congruency hypothesis. *Journal of Abnormal Psychology*, **101**, 26–36.

Seligman, M.E.P. (1975). *Helplessness: On depression, development, and death*. San Francisco, W.H. Freeman.

Seligman, M.E.P., Abramson, L.Y., Semmel, A., & von Baeyer, C. (1979). Depressive attributional style. *Journal of Abnormal Psychology*, **88**, 242–247.

Seligman, M.E.P., & Maier, S.F. (1967). Failure to escape traumatic shock. *Journal of Experimental Psychology*, **74**, 1–9.

Seligman, M.E.P., Peterson, C., Kaslow, N.J., Tenenbaum, R.L., Alloy, L.B., & Abramson, L.Y. (1984). Attributional style and depressive symptoms among children. *Journal of Abnormal Psychology*, **93**, 235–241.

Selmi, P.M., Klein, M.H., Greist, J.H., Sorrell, S.P., & Erdman, H.P. (1990). Computer-administered cognitive-behavioral therapy for depression. *American Journal of Psychiatry*, **147**, 51–56.

Shain, B.N., Naylor, M., & Alessi, N. (1990). Comparison of self-rated and clinician-rated measures of depression in adolescents. *American Journal of Psychiatry*, **147**, 793–795.

Shaw, B.F., Vallis, T.M., & McCabe, S.B. (1985). The assessment of the severity and symptom patterns in depression. In E.E. Beckham & W.R. Leber (Eds), *Handbook of depression: Treatment, assessment, and research* (pp. 372–409). Homewood, IL: Dorsey.

Shea, M.T., Pilkonis, P.A., Beckham, E., Collins, J.F., Elkin, I., Sotsky, S.M., & Docherty, J.P. (1990). Personality disorders and treatment outcome in the NIMH Treatment of Depression Collaborative Research Program. *American Journal of Psychiatry*, **98**, 468–477.

Shipley, C.R., & Fazio, A.F. (1973). Pilot study of a treatment for psychological depression. *Journal of Abnormal Psychology*, **82**, 372–376.

Shrout, P.E., Link, B. G., Dohrenwend, B. P., Skodol, A. E., Stueve, A., & Mirttznik, J. (1989). Characterizing life events as risk factors for depression: The role of fateful loss events. *Journal of Abnormal Psychology*, **98**, 460–467.

Siegel, J.M., & Brown, J.D. (1988). A prospective study of stressful circumstances, illness symptoms, and depressed mood among adolescents. *Developmental Psychology*, **24**, 715–721.

Silverman, J.S., Silverman, J.A., & Eardley, D.A. (1984). Do maladaptive attitudes cause depression? *Archives of General Psychiatry*, **41**, 28–30.

Simons, A.D., Garfield, S.L., & Murphy, G.E. (1984). The process of change in cognitive therapy and pharmacotherapy: Changes in mood and cognitions. *Archives of General Psychiatry*, **41**, 45–51.

Simons, A. D., Lustman, P.J., Wetzel, R.D., & Murphy. G.E. (1985). Predicting responses to cognitive therapy of depression: The role of learned resourcefulness. *Cognitive Therapy and Research*, **9**, 79–89.

Simons, A.D., Murphy, G.E., & Levine, J.C. (1984). *Relapse after treatment with cognitive therapy and/or pharmacotherapy: Results after one year*. Paper presented at the 15th annual meeting of the Society for Psychotherapy Research, Lake Louise, Alberta, Canada.

Simons, A.D., Murphy, G.E., Levine, J.L., et al. (1986). Cognitive therapy and pharmacotherapy for depression: Sustained improvement over one year. *Archives of General Psychiatry*, **43**, 43–48.

Sims, A. (1977). Prognosis in the neurosis. *American Journal of Psychoanalysis*, **37**, 155–161.

Singer, J.A., & Salovey, P. (1988). Mood and memory: Evaluating the network theory of affect. *Clinical Psychology Review*, **8**, 211–251.

Skinner, B.F. (1953). *Science and human behavior*. New York: Free Press.

Slife, B.D., Miura, S., Thompson, L.W., Shapiro, J.L., & Gallagher, D. (1984). Differential recall as a function of mood disorder in clinically depressed patients: Between- and within-subject differences. *Journal of Abnormal Psychology*, **93**, 391–400.

Small, S.A., & Robins, C.J. (1988). The influence of induced depressed mood on visual recognition thresholds: Predictive ambiguity of associative network models of mood and cognition. *Cognitive Therapy and Research*, **12**, 295–304.

Smith, T.W., & Greenberg, J. (1981). Depression and self-focused attention. *Motivation and Emotion*, **5**, 323–331.

Smucker, M.R., Craighead, W.E., Craighead, L.W., & Green, B.J. (1986). Normative and reliability data for the Children's Depression Inventory. *Journal of Abnormal Child Psychology*, **14**, 25–39.

Snaith, R.P., Ahmed, S.N., Mehta, S., & Hamilton, M. (1971). Assessment of the severity of primary depressive illness: Wakefield Self-Assessment Depression Inventory. *Psychological Medicine*, **1**, 143–149.

Sorenson, S.B., Rutter, C.M., & Aneshensel, C.S. (1991). Depression in the community: An investigation into age of onset. *Journal of Consulting Clinical Psychology*, **59**, 541–546.

Sotsky, S.M., Glass, D.R., Shea, T., Pilkonis, P.A., Collins, J.J., Elkin, I., Watkins, J.T., Imber, S.D., Leber, W.R., Moyer, J., & Oliveri, M.E. (1991). Patient predictors of response to psychotherapy and pharmacotherapy: Findings in the NIMH treatment of depression collaborative research program. *American Journal of Psychiatry*, **148**, 997–1008.

Spanier, G.B. (1976). Measuring dyadic adjustment: New scales for assessing the quality of marriage and similar dyads. *Journal of Marriage and the Family*, **38**, 15–28.

Spencer, J.H., Glick, I.D., Haas, G.L., Clarkin, J.F., Lewis, A.B., Peyser, J., DeMane, N., Good-Ellis, M., Harris, E., & Lestelle, V. (1988). A randomized clinical trial of Inpatient Family Intervention, III: Effects at 6-month and 18-month follow-ups. *American Journal of Psychiatry*, **145**, 1115–1121.

Spieker, S.J., & Booth, C. (1988). Family risk typologies and patterns of insecure attachment. In J. Belsky & T. Nezworski (Eds), *Clinical implications of attachment* (pp. 95–135). Hillsdale, NJ: Erlbaum.

Spielman, L.A., & Bargh, J.A. (1990). Does the depressive self-schema really exist? In C.D. McCann & N.S. Endler (Eds), *Depression: New directions in theory, research, and practice* (pp. 111–126). Toronto: Wall & Emerson.

Spitz, R. (1946). Anaclitic depression. *Psychoanalytic Study of the Child*, **2**, 313–342.

Spitzer, R.L., Williams, J.B.W., Gibbon, M., & First, M.B. (1990). *User's guide for the Structured Clinical Interview for DSM-III-R*. Washington, DC: American Psychiatric Press.

Sroufe, L.A. (1979). Socioemotional development. In J. Osofsky (Ed.), *Handbook of infant development* (1st edn) (pp. 462–516). New York: John Wiley.

Steer, R.A., Beck, A.T., Riskind, J.H., & Brown, G. (1986). Differentiation of generalized anxiety and depression disorders by the Beck Depression Inventory. *Journal of Clinical Psychology*, **42**, 475–478.

Steinmetz, J.L., Lewinsohn, P.M., & Antonuccio, D.O. (1983). Prediction of individual outcome in a group intervention for depression. *Journal of Consulting and Clinical Psychology*, **51**, 331–337.

Stern, S.L., & Mendels, J. (1980). Affective disorders. In A.E. Kazdin, A.S. Bellack, & M. Hersen (Eds), *New perspectives in abnormal psychology* (pp. 204–226). New York: Oxford University Press.

Steuer, J., Mintz, J., Hammen, C., Hill, M., Jarvik, L., McCarley, T., Motoike, P., & Rosen, R. (1984). Cognitive-behavioral and psychodynamic group psychotherapy in treatment of geriatric depression. *Journal of Consulting and Clinical Psychology*, **52**, 180–189.

Strack, S., & Coyne, J.C. (1983). Social confirmation of dysphoria: Shared and private reactions to depression. *Journal of Personality and Social Psychology*, **44**, 798–806.

Strauss, C.C., Forehand, R., Smith, K., & Frame, C.L. (1986). The association between social withdrawal and internalizing problems of children. *Journal of Abnormal Child Psychology*, **14**, 525–535.

Strober, M., Green, J., & Carlson, G.A. (1981). The reliability of psychiatric diagnosis in hospitalized adolescents. *Archives of General Psychiatry*, **38**, 141–145.

Strober, M., Lampert, C., Schmidt, S., & Morrell, W. (in press). The course of major depressive disorder in adolescents: I. Recovery and risk of manic switching in a 24-month prospective, naturalistic follow-up of psychotic and nonpsychotic subtypes. *Journal of the American Academy of Child and Adolescent Psychiatry*.

Stroop, J.R. (1935). Studies of interference in serial verbal reactions. *Journal of Experimental Psychology*, **18**, 643–662.

Stuart, R. (1980). *Helping couples change*. New York: Guilford Press.

Sweeney, P.D., Anderson, K., & Bailey, S. (1986). Attributional style in depression: A meta-analytic review. *Journal of Personality and Social Psychology*, **50**, 974–991.

Swindle, R.W., Cronkite, R.C., & Moos, R.H. (1989). Life stressors, social resources, coping and the 4 year course of unipolar depression. *Journal of Abnormal Psychology*, **98**, 468–477.

Tanaka-Matsumi, J., & Kameoka, V.A. (1986). Reliabilities and concurrent validities of popular self-report measures of depression, anxiety, and social desirability. *Journal of Consulting and Clinical Psychology*, **54**, 328–333.

Targum, S.D., Dibble, E.D., Davenport, Y.B., & Gershon, E.S. (1981). Family attitudes questionnaire: Patients and spouses view bipolar illness. *Archives of General Psychiatry*, **38**, 562–568.

Teasdale, J.D. (1983). Negative thinking in depression: Cause, effect, or reciprocal relationship? *Advances in Behaviour Research and Therapy*, **5**, 3–25.

Teasdale, J.D. (1985). Psychological treatments for depression: How do they work? *Behaviour Research and Therapy*, **23**, 157–165.

Teasdale, J.D. (1988). Cognitive vulnerability to persistent depression. *Cognition and Emotion*, **2**, 247–274.

Teasdale, J.D., & Dent, J. (1987). Cognitive vulnerability to depression: An investigation of two hypotheses. *British Journal of Clinical Psychology*, **26**, 113–126.

Teasdale, J.D., & Fennell, M.J.V. (1982). Immediate effects on depression of cognitve therapy interventions. *Cognitive Therapy and Research*, **6**, 343–352.

Teasdale, J.D., & Fogarty, S.J. (1979). Differential effects of induced mood on retrieval of pleasant and unpleasant events from episodic memory. *Journal of Abnormal Psychology*, **88**, 248–257.

Teasdale, J.D., & Russell, M.L. (1983). Differential effects of induced mood on the recall of positive, negative and neutral words. *British Journal of Clinical Psychology*, **33**, 163–172.

Tennant, C., Bebbington, P., & Hurry, J. (1980). Parental death in childhood and risk of adult depressive disorder: A review. *Psychological Medicine*, **10**, 289–299.

Tesiny, E.P., & Lefkowitz, M.M. (1982). Childhood depression: A six-month follow-up study. *Journal of Consulting and Clinical Psychology*, **50**, 778–780.

Thase, M., Simons, A., Cahalane, J., McGeary, J., & Harden, T. (1991). Severity of depression and response to cognitive behavior therapy. *American Journal of Psychiatry*, **148**, 784–789.

Thoits, P.A. (1983a). Dimensions of life events that influence psychological distress: An evaluation and synthesis of the literature. In H.B. Kaplan (Ed.), *Psychosocial stress: Trends in theory and research* (pp. 33–103). New York: Academic Press.

Thoits, P.A. (1983b). Multiple identities and psychological well-being: A reformulation and test of the social isolation hypothesis. *American Sociological Reviews*, **48**, 174–187.

Tisher, M., & Lang, M. (1983). The Children's Depression Scale. In D.P. Cantwell

& G.A. Carlson (Eds), *Affective disorders in childhood and adolescence* (pp. 181–203). New York: S.P. Medical & Scientific Books.

Troutman, B.R., & Cutrona, C.E. (1990). Nonpsychotic postpartum depression among adolescent mothers. *Journal of Abnormal Psychology*, **99**, 69–78.

Tsuang, M.T., & Simpson, J.C. (1985). Mortality studies in psychiatry: Should they stop or proceed? *Archives of General Psychiatry*, **42**, 98–103.

Turner, R.W., Ward, M.F., & Turner, D.J. (1979). Behavioral treatment for depression: An evaluation of therapeutic components. *Journal of Clinical Psychology*, **35**, 166–175.

Ulrich-Jakubowski, D., Russell, D.W., & O'Hara, M.W. (1988). Marital adjustment difficulties: Cause or consequence of depressive symptomatology? *Journal of Social and Clinical Psychology*, **7**, 312–318.

Vaughn, C.E., & Leff, J.P. (1976a). The influence of family and social factors on the course of psychiatric illness: A comparison of schizophrenic and depressed neurotic patients. *British Journal of Psychiatry*, **129**, 125–137.

Vaughn, C.E., & Leff, J.P. (1976b). The measurement of expressed emotion in the families of psychiatric patients. *British Journal of Social and Clinical Psychology*, **15**, 157–165.

Vestre, N.D., & Caulfield, B.P. (1986). Perception of neutral personality descriptions by depressed and nondepressed subjects. *Cognitive Therapy and Research*, **10**, 31–36.

von Bertalanffy, L. (1968). *General systems theory.* New York: Braziller.

Walker, E., Downey, G., & Nightingale, N. (1989). The nonorthogonal nature of risk factors: Implications for research on the causes of maladjustment. *Journal of Primary Prevention*, **9**, 143–163.

Waring, E.M., Chamberlaine, C.H., McCrank, E.W., Stalker, C.A., Carver, C., Fry, R., & Barnes, S. (1988). Dysthymia: A randomized study of cognitive marital therapy and antidepressants. *Canadian Journal of Psychiatry*, **33**, 96–99.

Warner, V., Weissman, M.M., Fendrich, M., Wickramaratne, P., & Moreau, D. (1991). *The course of major depression in the offspring of depressed parents: Incidence, recurrence, recovery.* Manuscript under review.

Warren, R.E. (1972). Stimulus encoding and memory. *Journal of Experimental Psychology*, **94**, 90–100.

Waters, E., Vaughn, B., & Egeland, B. (1980). Individual differences in mother-infant relationships at age one: Antecedents in neonatal behavior in an urban, economically disadvantaged sample. *Child Development*, **51**, 208–216.

Watson, D., & Clark, L.A. (1984). Negative affectivity: The disposition to experience aversive emotional states. *Psychological Bulletin*, **96**, 465–490.

Watson, D.A., Clark, L.A., & Carey, G. (1988). Positive and negative affectivity and their relation to anxiety and depressive disorders. *Journal of Abnormal Psychology*, **97**, 346–353.

Watson, D., & Tellegen, A. (1985). Toward a consensual structure of mood. *Psychological Bulletin*, **98**, 219–235.

Webster-Stratton, C., & Hammond, M. (1988). Maternal depression and its relationship to life stress, perceptions of child behavior problems, parenting behaviors, and child conduct problems. *Journal of Abnormal Child Psychology*, **16**(3), 299–315.

Weiner, B., Frieze, I., Kukla, A., Reed, L., Rest, S., & Rosenbaum, R.M. (1971). *Perceiving the causes of success and failure.* Morristown, NJ: General Learning Press.

Weinstein, S.R., Noam, G.G., Grimes, K., Stone, K., & Schwab-Stone, M. (1990). Convergence of DSM-III diagnoses and self-reported symptoms in child and adolescent inpatients. *Journal of the American Academy of Child and Adolescent Psychiatry*, **29**, 627–634.

Weintraub, S. (1987). Risk factors in schizophrenia: The Stony Brook high-risk project. *Schizophrenia Bulletin*, **13**, 439–450.

Weiss, B., & Weisz, J.R. (1988). Factor structure of self-reported depression: Clinic-referred children versus adolescents. *Journal of Abnormal Psychology*, **97**, 492–495.

Weiss, B., Weisz, J.R., Politano, M., Carey, M., Nelson, W.M., & Finch, A.J. (1991). Developmental differences in the factor structrue of the children's depression inventory. *Psychological Assessment: A Journal of Consulting and Clinical Psychology*, **3**, 38–45.

Weiss, R.L., Hops, H., & Patterson, G.R. (1973). A framework for conceptualizing marital conflict, technology for altering it, and some data for evaluating it. In L.A. Hamerlynck, L.C. Handy, & E.J. Mash (Eds), *Behavior change: Methodology, concepts, and practice*. Champaign, IL: Research Press.

Weissman, A.N. (1978). *Development and validation of the Dysfunctional Attitudes Scale*. Paper presented at the annual meeting of the Association for the Advancement of Behavior Therapy, Chicago.

Weissman, A.N., & Beck, A.T. (1978). *Development and validation of the Dysfunctional Attitude Scale: A preliminary investigation*. Paper presented at the annual meeting of the American Educational Research Association, Toronto, Ontario, Canada.

Weissman, M.M. (1987). Advances in psychiatric epidemiology: Rates and risks for depression. *American Journal of Public Health*, **77**, 445–451.

Weissman, M.M. (1988). Psychopathology in the children of depressed parents: Direct interview studies. In D.L. Dunner and E.S. Gershon (Eds), *Relatives at risk for mental disorders* (pp.143–159). New York: Raven Press.

Weissman, M.M., & Boyd, J.H. (1983). The epidemiology of affective disorders: Rates and risk factors. In L. Grinspoon (Ed.), *Psychiatry update*, Vol. II. Washington, DC: American Psychiatric Press.

Weissman, M.M., Gammon, G.D., John, K., Merikangas, K.R., Warner, V., Prusoff, B.A., & Sholomskas, D. (1987). Children of depressed parents: Increased psychopathology and early onset of major depression. *Archives of General Psychology*, **44**, 847–853.

Weissman, M.M., & Klerman, G.L. (1977). Sex differences in the epidemiology of depression. *Archives of General Psychiatry*, **34**, 98–111.

Weissman, M.M., & Klerman, G.L. (1990). Interpersonal psychotherapy for depression. In B.B. Wolman & G. Stricker (Eds), *Depressive disorders: Facts, theories, and treatment methods* (pp. 379–395). New York: John Wiley.

Weissman, M.M., Klerman, G.L., Prusoff, B.A., Sholomskas, D., & Padian, N. (1981). Depressed outpatients: Results one year after treatment with drugs and/or interpersonal psychotherapy. *Archives of General Psychiatry*, **38**, 51–55.

Weissman, M.M., Leckman, J.F., Merikangas, K.R., Gammon, G.D., & Prusoff, B.A. (1984). Depression and anxiety disorders in parents and children: Results from the Yale family study. *Archives of General Psychiatry*, **41**, 845–852.

Weissman, M.M., Merikangas, K.R., Wickramaratne, P., Kidd, K.K., Prusoff, B.A., Leckman, J.F., & Pauls, D.L. (1986). Understanding the clinical heterogeneity of major depression using family data. *Archives of General Psychiatry*, **43**, 430–434.

Weissman, M.M., Orvaschel, H., & Padian, N. (1980). Children's symptoms and social functioning self report scales. *Journal of Nervous Mental Disorders*, **168**, 736–740.

Weissman, M.M., & Paykel, E.S. (1974). *The depressed woman: A study of social relationships*. Chicago: University of Chicago Press.

Weissman, M.M., Paykel, E.S., & Klerman, G.L. (1972). The depressed woman as a mother. *Social Psychiatry*, **7**, 98–108.

Weissman, M.M., Prusoff, B.A., DiMascio, A., Neu, C., Goklaney, M., & Klerman, G.L. (1979). The efficacy of drugs and psychotherapy in the treatment of acute depressive episodes. *American Journal of Psychiatry*, **136**, 555–558.

Weissman, M.M., Sholomskas, D., Pottenger, M., Prusoff, B.A., & Locke, B.Z. (1977). Assessing depressive symptoms in five psychiatric populations: A validation study. *American Journal of Epidemiology*, **106**, 203–214.

Weissman, M.M., Wickramaratne, P., Warner, V., John, K., Prusoff, B.A., Merikangas, K.R., & Gammon, G.D. (1987). Assessing psychiatric disorders in children: Discrepancies between mothers' and children's reports. *Archives of General Psychiatry*, **44**, 747–753.

Weisz, J.R., Stevens, J.S., Curry, J.F., Cohen, R., Craighead, W.E., Burlingame, W.V., Smith, A., Weiss, B., & Parmelee, D.X. (1989). Control-related cognitions and depression among inpatient children and adolescents. *Journal of the American Academy of Child and Adolescent Psychiatry*, **28**, 358–363.

Weisz, J.R., Weiss, B., Wasserman, A.A., & Rintoul, B. (1987). Control-related beliefs and depression among clinic-referred children and adolescents. *Journal of Abnormal Psychology*, **96**, 149–158.

Wells, K.B., Stewart, A., Hays, R.D., Burnam, M.A., Rogers, W., Daniels, M., Berry, S., Greenfield, S., & Ware, J. (1989). The functioning and well being of depressed patients: Results from the medical outcome study. *Journal of the American Medical Association*, **262**, 914–919.

Wenzlaff, R.M., & Berman, J.S. (1985). *Judgemental accuracy in depression*. Paper presented at the meeting of the American Psychological Association, Los Angeles.

Whiffen, V.E., & Gotlib, I.H. (1989a). Infants of postpartum depressed mothers: Temperament and cognitive status. *Journal of Abnormal Psychology*, **98**, 274–279.

Whiffen, V.E., & Gotlib, I.H. (1989b). Stress and coping in maritally satisfied and dissatisfied couples. *Journal of Social and Personal Relationships*, **6**, 327–344.

Whisman, M.A., Miller, I.W., Norman, W.H., & Keitner, G.I. (1991). Cognitive therapy with depressed inpatients: Specific effects on dysfunctional cognitions. *Journal of Consulting and Clinical Psychology*, **59**, 282–288.

Whitaker, A., Johnson, J., Shaffer, D., Rapoport, J.L., Kalikow, K., Walsh, B.T., Davies, M., Braiman, S., & Dolinsky, A. (1990). Uncommon troubles in young people: Prevalence estimates of selected psychiatric disorders in a nonreferred adolescent population. *Archives of General Psychiatry*, **47**, 487–496.

Widiger, T.A., & Frances, A.J. (1989). Epidemiology, diagnosis, and comorbidity of borderline personality disorder. In A. Tasman, R.E. Hales, & A.J. Frances (Eds), *Review of psychiatry* (pp. 8–24). Washington, DC: American Psychiatric Press.

Wierzbicki, M., & McCabe, M. (1988). Social skills and subsequent depressive symptomatology in children. *Journal of Clinical Child Psychology*, **17**, 203–208.

Williams, J.G., Barlow, D.H., & Agras, W.S. (1972). Behavioral measurement of severe depression. *Archives of General Psychiatry*, **27**, 330–333.

Williams, J.M.G. (1985). Attributional formulation of depression as a diathesis-stress model: Metalsky et al. reconsidered. *Journal of Personality and Social Psychology*, **48**, 1572–1575.

Williams, J.M.G., & Nulty, D.D. (1986). Construct accessibility, depression and the emotional stroop task: Transient mood or stable structure? *Personality and Individual Differences*, **7**, 485–491.

Williams, J.M.G., Watts, F.N., MacLeod, C., & Mathews, A. (1988). *Cognitive psychology and emotional disorders*. Chichester, England: John Wiley.

Winer, D.L., Bonner, T.O., Blaney, P.H., and Murray, E.J. (1981). Depression and social attraction. *Motivation and Emotion*, 5, 153–166.

Winokur, G. (1979). Unipolar depression: Is it divisible into autonomous subtypes? *Archives of General Psychiatry*, 24, 135–144.

Wise, E.H., & Barnes, D.R. (1986). The relationship among life events, dysfunctional attitudes, and depression. *Cognitive Therapy and Research*, 10, 257–266.

Wolfe, V.V., Finch, A.J., Saylor, C.F., Blount, R.L., Pallmeyer, T.P., & Carek, D.J. (1987). Negative affectivity in children: A multitrait-multimethod investigation. *Journal of Consulting and Clinical Psychology*, 55, 245–250.

Wright, J.H., & Salmon, P.G. (1990). Learning and memory in depression. In C.D. McCann & N.S. Endler (Eds), *Depression: New directions in theory, research, and practice* (pp. 211–236). Toronto: Wall & Thompson.

Yarkin, K., Harvey, J.L., & Bloxom, B.M. (1982). Cognitive sets, attribution, and social interaction. *Journal of Personality and Social Psychology*, 41, 243–252.

Young, L.D., Moore, S.D., & Nelson, R.E. (1981, November). *Effects of depression on acceptance of personality feedback*. Paper presented at the meeting of the Association for the Advancement of Behavior Therapy, Toronto, Canada.

Youngren, M.A., & Lewinsohn, P.M. (1980). The functional relationship between depression and problematic behavior. *Journal of Abnormal Psychology*, 89, 333–341.

Zahn-Waxler, C., Cummings, E.M., Iannotti, R.J., & Radke-Yarrow, M. (1984). Young children of depressed parents: A population at risk for affective problems. In D. Cicchetti (Ed.), *Childhood depression*. (New directions for child development, no. 26, pp. 81–105). San Francisco: Jossey-Bass.

Zeiss, A.M., Lewinsohn, P.M., & Munoz, R.F. (1979). Nonspecific improvement effects in depression using interpersonal, cognitive, and pleasant events focused treatments. *Journal of Consulting and Clinical Psychology*, 47, 427–439.

Zimmerman, M., Black, D.W., & Coryell, W. (1989). Diagnostic criteria for melancholia: The comparative validity of DSM-III and DSM-III-R. *Archives of General Psychiatry*, 46, 361–368.

Zimmerman, M., & Coryell, W. (1987). The Inventory to Diagnose Depression (IDD): A self-report scale to diagnose major depressive disorder. *Journal of Consulting and Clinical Psychology*, 55, 55–59.

Zimmerman, M., & Coryell, W. (1988). The validity of a self-report questionnaire for diagnosing major depressive disorder. *Archives of General Psychiatry*, 45, 738–740.

Zimmerman, M., Coryell, W., Corenthal, C., & Wilson, S. (1986). A self-report scale to diagnose major depressive disorder. *Archives of General Psychiatry*, 43, 1076–1081.

Zimmerman, M., Coryell, W., & Pfohl, B. (1986). Validity of familial subtypes of primary unipolar depression. *Archives of General Psychiatry*, 43, 1090–1096.

Zimmerman, M., Coryell, W., Stangl, D., & Pfohl, B. (1987). Validity of an operational definition for neurotic unipolar major depression. *Journal of Affective Disorders*, 12, 29–40.

Zimmerman, M., Pfohl, B., Coryell, W., Stangle, D., & Corenthal, C. (1988). Diagnosing personality disorder in depressed patients. *Archives of General Psychiatry*, 45, 733–737.

Zimmerman, M., & Spitzer, R.L. (1989). Melancholia: From DSM-III to DSM-III-R. *The American Journal of Psychiatry*, 146, 20–28.

Zis, A.P., & Goodwin, F.K. (1979). Major affective disorder as a recurrent illness: A clinical review. *Archives of General Psychiatry*, 36, 835–839.

Zung, W.W.K. (1965). A self-rating depression scale. *Archives of General Psychiatry*, 13, 508–516.

Zung, W.W.K. (1971). A rating instrument for anxiety disorders. *Psychosomatics*, **12**, 371–379.

Zuroff, D.C. (1981). Depression and attribution: Some new data and a review of old data. *Cognitive Therapy and Research*, **5**, 273–281.

Zuroff, D.C., Colussy, S.A., & Wielgus, M.S. (1983). Selective memory and depression: A cautionary note concerning response bias. *Cognitive Therapy and Research*, **7**, 223–232.

Zuroff, D. C., & Mongrain, M. (1987). Dependency and self-criticism: Vulnerability factors for depressive affective states. *Journal of Abnormal Psychology*, **96**, 14–22.

Index

Page numbers in *italics* refer to figures and tables.

abuse, parental, 57, 179
academic achievement
  adolescent depression, 47
  childhood depression, 46–7
accommodation model of cognitive
    therapy, 207
achievement events, 150–1
adaptive behavior, 71
  changes, 194
adolescent depression
  academic achievement, 47
  anxiety, 45–6
  closeness with parents, 60
  comorbidity, 44–6
  course of disorder, 46–50
  CWD course, 219
  duration of episodes, 48, 48–9
  features, 39–41
  gender differences, 39, 40–1, 43
  incidence, 37, 39, 39–46, 40
  interpersonal functioning, 61
  medication, 44
  psychosocial factors, 147
  rates of, 20
  relationship success, 56
  self-reported, 39–40, 41
  sex differences, 60
  stability of symptoms, 47–8
  stressors, 59
  substance abuse, 45
  suicidal behavior, 47
  symptoms, 42
  work history, 47
adverse childhood experiences,
    253

adverse early environment, 178–80
adverse interpersonal environment
    reports, 181
affect
  depressed, 95
  positive, 95
affection in marriages, 169
affectionless control, 180
age
  effects on depression incidence, 18,
    19
  and recurrence of depression, 28
age of onset
  adult depression, 50–1
  childhood depression, 49–50
  demographic trends, 35
  unipolar depression, 24–5
alcoholism, 175
  familial, 10
  parental effects, 179
alternatives, generation of, 83
ambivalence in relationships, 68
amitriptyline, 231
anaclitic depression, 37
antecedent effects, moderation of
    impact, 84–5
antidepressant medication
  in children and adolescents, 44
  see also pharmacological therapy
antisocial personality disorder, 175
anxiety, 14, 15–17
  comorbidity with depression, 46,
    134
  in depressed children and
    adolescents, 45–6

anxiety (*cont.*)
   disorder attentional functioning,
      134
   with major depression, 15
   separation, 45
anxiety-depression syndrome, mixed,
   16
anxious attachment style, 262
appetite loss, 68
appraisal
   coping-focused, 258
   as determinant of impact of
      stressors, 143
   event-focused, 258
arbitrary inference, 75
Areas of Change Questionnaire
   (AOC), 227
assertion
   negative, 221
   positive, 221
assessment
   contextual threat method, 146
   of coping, 143
assortative mating, 175, 191
assumptions, silent, 196
attachment
   anxious style, 262
   bonds, 70, 249
   insecure, 187, 250–1, 252
   pattern prediction, 250
   theory, 211, 214
attachment difficulties, 249–52
   negative schema, 250
attachment quality
   measurement, 250
   and vulnerability to depression,
      251–2
attachment-based characteristics of
      intimate relationships, 251
attentional bias
   by nondepressed subjects, 134
   to negative information, 137
   to negative stimuli, 127, 129
attentional processing, 130–6
attitudes
   dysfunctional, 206
   negative, 76
attributional style, 82
   in children, 63–4
   depressotypic, 122
   in learned helplessness, 119

   negative, 126, 137
   negative and problem-solving, 83
   postmorbid, 125
   postpartum depression, 123, 124
   prediction value, 123
   stability, 125
   and stressful events, 123–4
   temporal relation of depression
      with, 122–7
Attributional Style Questionnaire
   (ASQ), 120–1, 197–8, 266
attributional tendencies, 79–80
attributions
   of depressed individuals, 120–2
   global, 120, 121, 122
   stable, 120, 121
   stressful life events, 121–2
   of uncontrollability, 79–80
automatic responding, 76
Automatic Thoughts Questionnaire
   (ATQ), 197, 266
autonomous individuals, 77
autonomy
   and self-worth, 254
   see also sociotropy-autonomy
aversive event management, 218–19

Beck Depression Inventory (BDI),
   93–5, 234
   adolescent depression, 40
   clinical significance of change, *238*
behavior
   expectations of, 162
   measures of observation, 112
   school, 189
behavior of depressed persons
   aversive, 161, 165
   induction of negative affect, 161,
      162, 165
behavioral activation, 194, 195
Behavioral Assertiveness Test, 216
behavioral assessment of depression,
   216–18
behavioral marital therapy, 230–1,
   236–7
behavioral theories of depression,
   71–4
   Costello's, 71–2
   Cotes and Wortman's, 73–4
   Coyne's, 73

Ferster's, 71
Lewinsohn's, 72–3
Skinner's, 71
behavioral therapy, 216–17
  problem-solving therapy, 224–5
  self-control therapy, 223–4
  social skills, 220
behavioral treatment of depression,
  218–25
  increasing pleasant activities,
    218–19
Bellevue Index of Depression, 111
bereavement, 149
  childhood, 143
biological factors in depression, 246
bipolar affective disorder, couples
  therapy, 232–3
bipolar depression
  differential diagnosis, 13
  spouse reaction, 170
birth cohort effects, 20
bonds, see attachment, bonds

Camberwell Family Interview (CFI),
  229
care-eliciting behavior, 70
caregiver, 249
  see also mother
Carroll Rating Scale for Depression,
  92
causal model of depression, 253
causality hypothesis, 143
causation hypothesis in marital status,
  167
Centre for Epidemiological Studies
  Depression Scale (CES-D), 93,
  95–6
  for adults and children, 105–6
chaining, 71–2
Child Assessment Schedule (CAS), 42,
  110, 183
Child Report of Parent Behavior
  Inventory, 266
childhood
  aversive, 178
  of depressed patient, 176–81
  loss, 146
  negative experiences, 76
  problematic object-relationships, 68
  rates of depression, 20

retropsective reports, 180–1
childhood depression
  abuse, 57
  academic achievement, 46–7
  age of onset, 49–50
  anxiety, 45–6
  biological markers, 43–4
  cognitive correlates, 62–5
  cognitive markers, 43–4
  comorbidity, 44–6, 66
  conduct disorders, 44
  continuity to adulthood, 50–2
  course of disorder, 46–50
  daily hassles as stressors, 59
  demographic trends, 35
  depressive subtypes, 43
  developmental effects, 66
  diagnosis, 36, 37
  difference of processes from adult,
    124–5
  duration of episodes, 48–9
  friendliness, 53, 54
  incidence, 37–46
  interpersonal functioning, 52–6, 61
  manifestation, 36
  medication, 44
  middle years, 38–9
  mother buffering stress effects, 60,
    61
  neglect, 57
  parent–child interactions, 57
  parental effects, 176
  peer relationships, 52–6
  predictors, 51–2
  preschool children, 37–8
  with psychiatric disorders, 45
  recurrence, 49, 50
  relapse, 49, 51
  REM latency, 44
  sex differences, 52
  social behavior, 54–5
  social functioning, 55–6
  and social status, 52
  stability of symptoms, 47–8
  stressful life events, 58–61
  suicidal behavior, 47
  time spent alone, 53
  traumatic circumstances, 60
  unique features, 65
  vulnerability, 60–1, 64
  vulnerability predictors, 66

children
    adjustment and adverse family
        functioning, 186
    adverse early environment, 178–80,
        253
    assessment of parents, 266
    behavior problems, 190
    of depressed mothers, 186–8
    depressed mother's perception, 190
    discrepancies in reports of
        depression with informants,
        107–8
    genetic contribution to risk of
        depression, 184–5
    insecure attachment to depressed
        mothers, 187
    intimate relations, 226
    IQ and maternal responsiveness,
        188
    maternal rejection, 249
    negative interactions of depressed
        mother, 188
    outcome with depressed parents,
        182–3
    psychosocial difficulties, 191
    reciprocal influences with
        depressed mothers, 190
    risk with depressed parents, 183
    risk for disorder, 175–6
    and unipolar depressed mothers,
        189
Children's Affective Rating Scale, 111
Children's Depression Inventory
    (CDI), 103–5
Children's Depression Rating Scale
    (CDRS), 111
Children's Report of Parental
    Behavior Inventory (CRPBI),
    178–9
chronic depression, subtypes, 12
chronicity of symptoms, 29–31
circadian rhythms, disruption, 11
co-occurring disorders, 13–17
cognition
    assessment, 197–8
    in coping, 245
    dysfunctional, 116–19, 137
    effect on environmental events,
        87–8
    functional relationship with
        depression, 113

and interpersonal environment,
    140
measures of depressive, 112
negative, 88
and social behavior, 140
cognitive change, 205–7
cognitive dysfunction, stability, 137
cognitive factors, 84
cognitive functioning
    of depressed individuals, 114–17
    formerly depressed patients, 137
    impairment, 113
    in interpersonal marital therapy,
        241
    negative by currently depressed
        individuals, 137
    negative schema effects, 135
    normalization following recovery,
        136
cognitive mediation, 245
cognitive model of depression, 114–19
    cognitive functioning of depressed
        individuals, 114–17
    temporal relation with
        dysfunctional cognitions,
        117–19
cognitive processes in maintenance of
    depression, 259
cognitive restructuring assignments,
    195–6
cognitive theories of depression,
    74–87
    differential activation hypothesis,
        85–7
    hopelessness theory, 80–1
    learned helplessness model, 78–80
    problem-solving theory, 83–4
    self-control theory, 81–3
    self-focus theories, 84–5
cognitive therapy, 193
    accommodation model, 207
    acute treatment, 213
    alternative approaches, 210
    assessment of cognitions, 197–8
    change in negative thoughts, 205
    cognitive change, 205–7
    comparative efficacy, 203
    computer administration, 202
    constructivist, 211
    developments in, 204–9
    evaluation of effectiveness, 198–204

experience of therapists, 202
group, 202
imipramine comparison, 206
individual, 202
integration into interpersonal
    intervention, 243, 244
interpersonal schemas in, 211–13
mechanisms of change in, 204–8
methods, 194–8
models of change, 207
mood change, 205
new developments, 209–13
patients doing best in, 208
for personality disorders, 210
predictors of outcome, 208
prevention of relapse, 201
psychodynamically orientated
    therapy, 209
range of applications, 202–3
relapse prevention, 213
relapse/recurrence, 200
in severe depression, 204
specific techniques, 204
with tricyclic antidepressants, 199
cognitive triad, 75, 114
cognitive vulnerability, 137, 255–6
mediating effects, 149–50
and stressful life events, 148
theories, 138
cognitive-behavioral therapy, 194–6
efficacy, 198–9
color-naming response latency, 130–3,
    135, 136
chronicity, 133
communication
maladaptive, 230
marital, 230
in marriages, 169
patterns of depressed couples, 171
skills enhancement, 220
comorbid disorders, 13, 14
comorbidity, childhood depression,
    44–6
compensatory change models of
    cognitive therapy, 207
compensatory skills model of
    cognitive therapy, 207
compound depression, 13
concentration difficulties of depressed
    persons, 113
conduct disorders in children, 44

conflict avoidance, 189
confrontation avoidance, 187
congruency process, 152
construct accessibility, negative, 135
context of depression, 245–6
contextual threat, 144, 146
continuity between mild and severe
    depression, 6–7
conversational skills, 221
coping
    assessment of, 143
    cognition in, 245
    contingency plans for, 222
    emotion-focused, 147
    marriage effects, 168
    and personal and social resources,
        146–7
    problem-solving, 147
    resources, 86
    response lack, 258
    responses, 34
    skills training, 222
Coping with Depression (CWD)
    course, 219
coping strategies
    in cognitive therapy, 208
    personality disorders, 210
coping-focused appraisal, 258
cortisol, 178
Costello–Comrey Anxiety and
    Depression Scales, 98–9
cultural aspects of depression, 1, 2
cultural background to depression, 19

daily event log, 217
daily hassles, 59, 144
debility cycle, 23
demographic differences in
    depression incidence, 18–20
demographic trends in depression, 35
dependency
    and depression vulnerability, 152
    emotional, 254
    interpersonal, 260
    needs and goals, 256
    and self-esteem, 254
dependent behavior, reinforcement,
    163
Depression Adjective Checklist
    (DACL), 98, 231

depression node activation, 127
depression spectrum disease, 10
depression-coping responses, 34
depression-stress cycle, 10–11
depressive attribution style in
    children, 63–4
depressive episodes, 7
Depressive Experiences
    Questionnaire, 150, 152
depressive neurosis, *see* dysthymia
depressive processes, heterogeneity,
    246
depressogenic attributional style, 80,
    81
depressogenic conditions, children's,
    62
depressogenic process, triggers, 84
depressotypic attributional style, 122
development of depression, 246–65
    maintenance, 259–63
    onset, 255–9
developmental effects, childhood
    depression, 66
developmental psychopathology
    theory of depression, 252
deviation-amplifying process, 73
dexamethasone suppression test
    (DST), 9
diagnosis, interview measures, 90–2
diagnostic criteria, 4–6
Diagnostic Interview for Children and
    Adolescents (DICA), 110
Diagnostic Interview Schedule for
    Children (DISC), 110–11
Diagnostic Interview Schedule (DIS),
    91–2
diathesis
    for depression, 77
    and stress, 77
diathesis-stress theories of depression,
    81
differential activation hypothesis,
    85–7, 119
disease subtypes, 7
disorder subtypes, 7
distractor conditions, 133, 135–6
distress, 17
domain-specific attributional
    tendencies, 87
dominant goal, 254
dominant other, 254

double depression, 28–9
    in children, 48, 49
doxepin, 233
dreams, adolescent, 42
DSM-III-R
    classification of melancholia, 8
    cognitive function impairment, 13
    criteria for childhood depression,
        37, 41
    structured clinical interview for, 91
    syndromes, 4–6
duration of symptoms, 33
Dyadic Adjustment Scale, 227, 234
dysfunctional attitudes, 116
    maintenance, 136
Dysfunctional Attitudes Scale (DAS),
    116, 150, 151, 197, 198, 266
    cognitive change, 205
dysfunctional cognition, 116–17
    causal role in depression, 117
    measurement sensitivity, 138
    prediction of depression, 118
    priming by dysphoric mood, 119
    temporal relation of depression
        with, 117–19
dysfunctional mate selection, 175
dysphoria
    childhood, 65
    marital effects, 171
    priming of dysfunctional cognition,
        119
    sustained in children, 64
    in women, 51
dysthymia, 6, 7, 9
    in children and adolescents, 37
    co-occurrence with major
        depression, 14
    early-onset, 25, 30
    primary early-onset, 12

education, 19
empiricism, collaborative, 194
endogenous depression, 8
endorphins, 178
environment
    adverse early, 178–80
    distorted perception, 125
    dysfunctional transactions with,
        155
    negative recall, 136

perception and interpretation, 115
positive distortion, 116
Epidemiological Catchment Area
(ECA) studies, 91
epidemiology of depressive disorders, 17–21
episodic depression, 11
ethnicity, 19
event-focused appraisal, 258
expectations of behavior, 162
experience, heightened attention to negative aspects, 127
expressed emotion (EE), 174, 229
extinction schedule, 71

familial pure depressive disease, 10
family
adverse environment, 248
affective disorder history, 30
assessment, 226–30
assessment of functioning, 112
assessment of interactions with, 228
attitudes of members towards depressed patient, 229
child's functioning in, 47
dysfunctional, 65, 176
dysfunctional interactions, 189
effects of depressed person, 1, 3, 265
functioning assessment, 228
interactions after depression, 158
interactions with marital therapy, 230
negative relations in functioning, 181
quality of relationships as factor in depression, 185–6
social environment, 73
Family Adaptability and Cohesion Evaluation Scales (FACES), 228
Family Environment Scale (FES), 228, 266
family functioning
adverse and child adjustment, 186
with depressed youngsters, 58
quality, 215
Family Role Task and Activity Scale, 232
fateful loss events, 149

feedback, evaluative, 115
friendliness, childhood depression, 53, 54
friends, of depressed people, 164, 165
functioning, impaired of depressed persons, 2, 21–3

General Behavior Inventory (GBI), 101–2
General Systems Theory (GST), 241–2
genetic contribution to risk of depression in children, 184–5
Global Assessment Scale for Children, 183
Global Improvement Clinical Scale, 232
goal attainment, self-control therapy, 223
group cohesiveness, positive perception, 219
guilt feelings, 68

Hamilton rating scale for depression (HRSD), 92
helplessness, development, 79
high-risk groups, 256
homelessness, 23
hopelessness, 31, 149
childhood depression, 62
theory, 80–1
Hopelessness Scale, 42
hostile feelings, 68

imipramine, 206
immunities, 85
Impact Message Inventory (IMI), 227–8
incidence of depression, 1
independence, encouragement to, 180
infants
behavior, 70
response to depressed mothers, 187
information processing, 127–36
attentional processing, 130–6
faulty, 75
inhibition, excessive, 83
Inpatient Family Intervention (IFI), 239–40

interactions with depressed people,
    162
intergenerational transmission of
    depression, 253
internality, depressed elderly patients,
    121
interpersonal approaches to marital
    therapy, 237–42
    assessment, 240–1
    efficacy, 243
    treatment, 241
interpersonal behavior, inadequate,
    220
interpersonal communication,
    maladaptive, 230
interpersonal dependency, 253, 260
Interpersonal Dependency Inventory,
    152
interpersonal dysfunction, 212
interpersonal environment
    and cognition, 140
    perceived loss of control over, 222
interpersonal events, negative, 192
interpersonal factors, vulnerability, 88
interpersonal functioning
    childhood depression, 52–6, 61
    of depressed people, 164–5
    improvement, 241–2
    problematic, 215
interpersonal life events, 149–53
interpersonal processes in
    maintenance of depression, 259
Interpersonal Psychotherapy (IPT),
    237–9
    efficacy in treatment of major
        depression, 238–9
interpersonal relationships, 215
    difficulties in close, 171
    disruption by depression, 191
    emotional supportiveness, 156
    impaired, 70
    improving, 215–16
    marital satisfaction, 172–3
    positive, 77–8
    stressful, 159
interpersonal schema, 211–13
    maladaptive, 213
interpersonal skill acquisition, 248
interpersonal style
    aversive, of depressed people, 163
    negative, 161

interpersonal systems approach to
    treatment of depression, 242
interpersonal therapy, 202
interpersonal-oriented therapy, 243
Interview Schedule for Children (ISC),
    110
Inventory of Psychic and Somatic
    Complaints, 232
Inventory to Diagnose Depression
    (IDD), 102
Iowa classification system of neurotic
    depression, 10–11

K-SADS, see Schedule for Affective
    Disorders for School-Age
    Children
Kategoriensystem für
    Partnerschaftliche Interaction
    (KPI), 228

learned helplessness model of
    depression, 78–80, 119–27
    attributions of depressed
        individuals, 120–2
    causal attributions, 79
    reformulated, 137
    temporal relation with attributional
        style, 122–7
learned resourcefulness, 208
life circumstances of patient, 27
Life Event and Difficulty Schedule,
    145
life events, 141
    interpersonal, 149–53
    meaningful, 145
    measurement, 138
    negative, 80
    social support in moderation of
        relationship with depression,
        158–9
    vulnerability and sociotropy-
        autonomy, 149–52
    see also stressful life events
listening task, dichotic, 132–3, 135–6
lithium, 233
Living in Familial Environments
    Coding System (LIFE), 229
loss
    childhood, 146

internality of attributions, 85
internalization of feelings, 69
  parental, 176–8
  of personal relationship, 149
  and self-worth, 85, 149
  value to self-concept, 149
loss in childhood, 68
loss events, fateful, 142–3

McMaster Family Assessment Device, 228
magnification, 75
maintenance of depression, 259–63
  accessibility to negative constructs, 260–2
  dependency, 260
  recovery from episodes, 262–3
  social network, 260
major depression, 4–5
  co-occurrence of dysthymia, 14
  cognitive function impairment, 113
  duration, 26
  early-onset, 25
  efficacy of interpersonal psychotherapy, 238–9
  social functioning of children, 55
  young-adult homeless, 23
major depressive episodes, 2–4, 4–5
  recurrence, 27–9
  relapse, 27–9
  symptom incidence, 12
maladaptive beliefs, 194
management strategies, contingent, 223
marital assessment, 226–30
marital discord, 243
  model of depression, 233–7
marital distress, 168–76
  adverse early interpersonal relations, 175
  characterological disorders, 175
  depressive episodes leading to, 170–3, 175–6
  leading to depressive episodes, 173–6
  preceding depression, 173
  psychiatric outcome, 174
marital functioning, 227
  quality, 215
Marital Interaction Coding System (MICS), 228

Marital Relations Inventory, 232
marital relationship
  dissatisfaction with, 169
  negative interactions, 171–2
  quality, 168, 191
  recovery from depression, 173
marital satisfaction
  interpersonal relationships, 172–3
  and marital therapy, 235, 237
marital status, 19–20
  and depression, 166–76
marital therapy, 226–42
  behaviorally-orientated conjoint, 230
  change in marital adjustment, 236
  effectiveness in depression treatment, 231–3
  interpersonal approaches, 237–42
  interpersonal behavior feedback, 230
  involvement of spouses and relatives, 242
  on marital discord model of depression, 233–7
  and marital satisfaction, 235, 237
marriage
  of depressed individuals, 191
  gender interactions, 168
  negative interactions, 215
  protective function, 168
  women to dysfunctional men, 259
maternal interaction quality, 189
measures of depression, adult, 90–102
  Costello–Comrey Anxiety and Depression Scales, 98–9
  Depression Adjective Check Lists, 98
  General Behavior Inventory, 101–2
  interview measures for diagnoses and symptoms, 90–2
  Inventory to Diagnose Depression (IDD), 102
  Millon Clinical Multiaxial Inventory (MCMI), 99–100
  MMPI-D Scale, 96–7
  Profile of Mood States, 100–1
  self-report measures, 92–8
  Symptom Checklist-90, 100
  Zung Self-rating Depression Scale (SDS), 97–8

measures of depression, children and
    adolescents, 103–12
  CES-D scale, 105–6
  Children's Depression Inventory,
    103–5
  discrepancies in reports, 107–8
  interview assessment, 109–11
  interviews for symptom severity,
    111
  self-report, 103–9
medical conditions causing depressive
    symptoms, 13–14
melancholia, 5, 8
  symptom severity, 8–9
melancholic depression, 8–9
memory
  and clinical improvement, 129
  depression-associated patterns, 129
  negative, 128
  retrieval times, 128
  valenced, 128
Millon Clinical Multiaxial Inventory
    (MCMI), 99–100
minimization, 75
Minnesota Multiphasic Personality
    Inventory (MMPI-D), 96–7
  D–30, 97
mood
  change in cognitive therapy, 205
  duration of depression, 4
  state, 2
  symptoms, 3
mood-congruent encoding of
    information, 129
mood-induction studies, 129
mortality, 31, 32
mother
  attachment bond to child, 249
  buffering stress effects of child, 60,
    61
  loss of, 69
  rejection of child, 179, 249
mother–child relationship, 69–70
mother–infant attachment process, 211
mothers, depressed, 215
  accuracy of perception of children,
    190
  and children with behavior
    problems, 190
  context, 191
  and difficult children, 190

insecure attachment of children,
    187, 250–1, 252
  interpersonal dysfunction, 185
  marital relationship, 191
  maternal responsiveness, 188
  negative interactions with child,
    188
  negativity towards infants, 187
  observations on, 186–8
  parenting tasks, 192
  reciprocal influences with children,
    190
  relationships with infants, 186–7
  and school-age children, 188–90
  and well-functioning children, 190
  see also postpartum depression

Negative Affectivity (NA), 17
negative attributional style, 126
negative cognitive bias in children,
    62–3
negative constructs, 260–2
negative events, contribution to
    occurrence, 155
negative feelings, 2, 3
negative self-schema, 76, 77
negative statement endorsement,
    126–7
negative thoughts of depressants, 75
neuroendocrine dysfunction, 88–9
neurotic depression, 9
  criteria, 9
  Iowa classification system, 10–11
  see also dysthymia
NIMH Treatment of Depression
    Collaborative Research
    Program, 201, 203

object-relations
  perspective of depression, 70
  theories, 209
obsessive compulsive disorder, 45
occasion setters, 80
onset of depression, 255–9
  duration, 256–7
  prediction, 33
  self-worth validation in, 257
  stressors, 256–7, 258
overprotection, parental, 180

paradigms, assessment of information
    processing, 127
parent–child attachment, 88
parent–child interactions in childhood
    depression, 57
parent–child relationships, 176–90
    negative, 181
parental affection, 179
Parental Bonding Instrument (PBI),
    179–80, 266
parental care
    poor, 146
    quality following parent loss, 177
    versus indifference, 180
parental discord, 179
parental functioning
    impairment in depressed women,
        184–90
    and indirect reports of depressed,
        185–6
parental loss
    of depressed patient, 176–8
    quality of care following, 177
parenting
    dysfunctional, 10, 155
    quality, 179, 181–2
    self-concept and stress, 252–3
parents
    assessment by children, 266
    effects of childhood depression,
        176
    emotional unavailability, 249
    interpersonal dysfunction, 185
    offspring of depressed, 182–3
    with psychopathology and effect of
        children, 155
    separation from, 249
    underreporting of children's
        depression, 108
parents, depressed
    age of onset of depression in
        children, 50
    children of, 45
    psychosocial functioning of
        children, 191
patient–therapist relationship, 205
peers
    functioning with, 47
    measures of interactions, 112
    relationships in childhood
        depression, 52–6

perceptions of self, 3–4
persistence rates, 31
person–environment transaction, 144
personality
    disturbance in neurotic depression,
        10
    predictors of childhood depression,
        51–2
    types, 138
personality characteristics
    autonomous, 87
    sociotropic, 87
    susceptibility to depression, 249
    trait-like individual differences, 143
    vulnerability to depression, 253–5
personality disorders
    coexistence with depression, 14–15
    cognitive therapy for, 210
    resistance, 210
pharmacological therapy, 200, 201,
    203
    cognitions, 206
    see also antidepressant medication
phenomenology of depression, 2–4
    age differences, 41–4
phobia, 45
phototherapy, 11
pleasant events and improvement in
    depression, 218–19
Pleasant Events Schedule (PES), 217
postpartum depression, 59
    attributional style, 123, 124
    early parenting, 179–80
    response to infants, 186
preadolescent children, 38–9, 40
    social relations of depressed, 55
prediction of depression, 116, 118
    Brown's work, 145
    major life events, 147
    onset, 26–7, 28, 33
prediction value of attributional style,
    123
pregnancy
    attributional style, 123
    teenage, 59
preschool children, 37–8, 41
    abuse and neglect, 57
    symptoms of depression, 42
primary depression, 11
problem-solving
    behavioral therapy, 221

problem-solving (*cont.*)
  component processes, 225
  maladaptive behavior, 230
  skills, 10, 83–4, 224, 225
  theory, 83–4
  therapy, 224–5
Profile of Mood States (POMS),
  100–1
prolonged depression, 1
protest-despair-detachment pattern,
  37
psychiatric comorbidity, 14–15
psychiatric conditions, overlap with
  depression, 34–5
Psychiatric Epidemiology Research
  Instrument (PERI), 142
Psychiatric Rating Scale, 232
psychoanalytic theories of depression,
  67–71
  Abraham's, 68
  Bowlby's, 70
  Freud's, 68–9
  Jacobson's, 70
  Klein's, 69–70
  Rado's, 69
  vulnerability factors, 68
psychodynamically oriented therapy,
  209
psychometric assessment, 6
psychoneuroimmunology, 32
psychosocial factors
  in adolescent depression, 147
  in risk of depression, 185
psychosocial models of depression,
  147
psychotherapy, marital and family-
  orientated, 231–2
psychotic depression, course of, 9

race and depression incidence, 19
rates of depression, 20–1
reactive depression, 8
  self-regulatory preservation theory,
    85
recall
  bias and recovery from depressive
    episode, 129–30
  pattern of depressed individuals,
    128
  of stimuli, 129

recovery from depression, 27, 262–3
  complete, 9
recurrence of depression, 3–4, 7, 263–5
  childhood, 49, 50
reinforcement
  effectiveness, 72, 74
  positive, 72
  rate, 72, 74
  social, 72
reinforcers, 71–2
rejection
  awareness of depressed individual,
    261
  of depressed persons, 162, 163
  parental, 179, 249
relapse, 27, 263–5
  childhood depression, 49, 51
  chronicity, 29–30
  contributing factors, 28
  incidence, 264
  prevention, 267
  risk period, 28
  stressful conditions in, 30
relationships
  attachment-based characteristics of
    intimate, 251
  difficulties in adolescent
    depression, 56
REM latency, 44
resources, personal and social, 146–7
response interference, 130
responses to depressed individuals,
  161
risk factors, 31, 35
  adverse family environment, 249
  for nonremission, 158
  psychosocial, 185
role functioning, 21, 22
  difficulties of children and
    adolescents, 46
role occupancy, 19
role-play tests, 216, 220
roommates, depressed, 163–4, 165

satisfaction, effect of childhood
  experiences, 248
scar hypothesis, 32, 33
Schedule for Affective Disorders and
  Schizophrenia (SADS), 90–1

Schedule for Affective Disorders for
  School-Age Children (K-SADS),
  109
schema, 76–7
  acquisition by developing child,
    248
  activation, 138
  and childhood experiences, 255
  in depression prediction, 118
  dysfunctional, 212
  effects on subsequent action and
    cognition, 211
  enduring, 133
  enduring negative, 116
  interpersonal, 212
  interpersonal in cognitive therapy,
    211–13
  measurement, 127, 138
  negative with attachment
    difficulties, 250
  negative in depressed persons, 134,
    135
  priming, 138
  self-report measures, 116
  superordinate, 138
  vulnerability factors, 134
school performance measures, 112
seasonal affective disorder (SAD), 11
secondary depression, 11
selection hypothesis in marital status,
  167
selective abstraction, 75
self-blame, 121
self-concept
  negative, 62, 64, 115
  parenting and stress, 252–3
self-condemnation, 70
self-control, 1, 2
  behavior deficits, 82
  model, 62
  therapy, 223–4
Self-Control Schedule, 208
self-denigration, 68
self-esteem
  interpersonal loss, 69
  labile, 253–4
  loss, 68
self-evaluation, 226
  deficit, 82, 223
  negative, 115, 136
  negative by children, 62

self-focus
  increased, 258
  theories, 84–5
self-image, negative, 85
self-monitoring, 226
  deficits, 223
self-punishment, 82–3
self-regulation model, 81–2
self-regulatory preservation theory of
    reactive depression, 85
self-reinforcement, 82–3, 223, 226
  deficits, 223
self-report
  data, 126
  measures, 92–8
self-reproach, 70
self-reward, 83
self-worth
  and autonomy, 254
  effect of childhood experiences,
    248
  inability to obtain validation, 257
  loss, 149
  validation, 257
sex differences, 18, 20
  adolescent depression, 39, 40–1, 43
  childhood depression, 52
  demographic trends, 35
  onset age of unipolar depression,
    24–5
  persistent depression rate, 31
sexual functioning in marriages, 169
situational factors, 84
social behavior, 160–5
  childhood depression, 54–5
  of children and maternal
    responsiveness, 188
  and cognition, 140
social dysfunction
  of depressed people, 158
  relationship with depression, 158–9
social environment, 73–4
  relationship of depressed patient
    with, 217–18
social exit, 149
  events, 257
social functioning, 21
  childhood depression, 53, 55–6
  of depressed individuals, 157–8
social isolation, childhood depression,
  53

social networks, 155–60
  negative interactions, 156, 160
  perceptions of, 157
  size, 156
social problem-solving skills, 224
social relationships
  depression effects, 88
  negative features, 159
social resource network, 260
social skills, 72–3, 226
  assessment, 216
  deficits, 160
  of depressed individuals, 88, 260
  improvement, 215–16
  therapy, 219–23
  training program, 220–1, 222, 223
social status, and childhood
    depression, 52
social support, 86, 155–60
  moderation of relationship
      between life events and
      depression, 158–9
socioeconomic status, 19
sociotropic individuals, 77
sociotropy, 254
sociotropy-autonomy, and
    vulnerability to depression,
    149–52
Sociotropy-Autonomy Scale, 150, 152
somatic/retarded activities, 95
sporadic depressive disease, 10
spouse
  assessment of interactions with,
    228
  of depressed person, 170
  disorders and depressed spouse,
    175
  intimate relations, 226
  in marital therapy, 232
  prior to depressive episodes,
    174
Spouse Observation Checklist (SOC),
    228, 266
stability
  attributional style, 125
  dysfunctional, 116
  vulnerability factors, 130
'Strange Situation', 250
stress
  assessment in context, 144
  chronic, 25

and diathesis, 77
in dysfunctional cognition, 118
life events, 88
model of depression, 143
and personal and social resources,
    146–7
in relapse, 30
self-concept and parenting, 252–3
in unipolar women, 153–4
stress generation, 23, 61, 153–5
  families of origin, 154–5
  in people vulnerable to depression,
    264–5
stress-symptom occurrence,
    transactional process, 59
stressful life events, 10, 22, 23, 141–9
  and attributional style, 123–4
  attributions, 121–2, 137
  Brown's work, 144–6
  and cognitive vulnerability, 148
  Dohrenwends' work, 142–3
  generation, 11
  Lazarus' work, 143–4
  Lewinsohn and Moos' work, 146–7
  predictive in children, 60
  and social support, 158–9
  trigger for depressive reactions,
    255
  vulnerability to, 152
stressors
  appraisal as determinant of impact,
    143
  association with depression, 148
  in childhood depression, 61
  in children, 58–9
  complexity, 138
  daily hassles, 59, 144
  in depressed people, 88
  differential vulnerability to, 64
  disruption of behavior patterns, 84
  relevant, 258
  response to, 8
Stroop color-naming task, 130–3, 135
structured clinical interview for DSM-
    III-R (SCID), 91
substance use disorders, 14
suicidal behavior, childhood
    depression, 47
suicide, 31
  ideation, 42
Symptom Checklist–90 (SCL–90), 100

symptoms of depression, 3
   chronic, 27
   chronicity, 29–31
   duration, 4, 33
   epidemiology, 17–21
   impact on functioning, 21
   intermittent, 27
   measure of severity in children,
      111
   and negative attribution style in
      children, 63–4
   stability in children, 47–8

task assignments, graded, 195
temporal relation of depression with
      dysfunctional cognitions, 117–19
therapist
   allegiance to particular therapy,
      199
   characteristics, 196
therapist–client relationship, 194, 195
thinking
   automatic negative, 195–6, 204
   depression as disorder of, 193
   difficulties of depressed persons,
      113
   maladaptive, 208–9
   negative, 75, 205
Third Force, 194
thought-catching, 194, 195–6
transactions in depression, 246
treatment
   inadequate, 30
   response to, 9
treatment-resistant depression, 209–10,
      214
tricyclic antidepressant therapy, 199,
      200
triggering events for depression, 246

uncontrollability attributes, 79–80
unemployment, 121–2
unipolar depressed women, 153–4
   children of, 154
   interactions with children, 189
   stressful life events, 155
unipolar depression
   age of onset, 24–5
   in children, 43

course of disorder, 23–33
   early onset, 25
   Iowa classification system, 10
   offspring of mothers, 49
   rediagnosis, 13
   subtypes, 7–12
   typical course, 24
   women and stress generation, 61
unmarried individuals, 167
utilization hypothesis in marital
      status, 167

Velten Mood Induction statements,
      128
verbal behavior, in marital
      relationships, 172
vulnerability factors, 77
   cognitive, 147
   complexity, 138
   interpersonal, 88
   loss in childhood, 68
   negative schemas, 134
   stable, 130
vulnerability to depression, 26, 27, 85,
      247–55
   adverse parent–child experiences,
      248
   attachment difficulties, 249–52
   and attachment quality, 251–2
   biological factors, 246
   childhood experiences, 248
   children of depressed parents, 183
   cognitive, 88, 147
   continuation of, 263
   and dependency, 152
   for depressive episodes, 138
   domain-specific, 81
   dysfunctional parenting, 248
   early parent–child relationships,
      176
   environmental context of
      experiences, 263–4
   as function of environment, 246
   increased likelihood, 263
   interpersonal, 88, 150, 153
   and links between parenting self-
      concept and stress, 252–3
   major life events, 145
   marriage-related stress, 173
   and negative events, 86

vulnerability to depression (*cont.*)
  negative interpersonal events,
    192
  neuroendocrine dysfunction, 88
  parental care quality, 177
  personality characteristics, 253–5
  refinement of measures, 139
  and relapse in clinical patients,
    151
  relapse or recurrence, 263–5
  and sociotropy-autonomy, 149–52
  stable cognitive, 137
  stress generation, 264–5

stressful life events, 152
vulnerability to interpersonal life
  events, 149–53

women
  impaired functioning with
    depression, 22–3
  see also mother; mothers, depressed

Zung Self-rating Depression Scale
  (SDS), 97–8

Index compiled by Jill Halliday